TALKING BACK

Toward a Latin American Feminist Literary Criticism

Debra A. Castillo

Cornell University Press

ITHACA AND LONDON

THIS BOOK HAS BEEN PUBLISHED WITH THE AID OF A GRANT FROM
THE HULL MEMORIAL PUBLICATION FUND OF CORNELL UNIVERSITY.

First published 1992 by Cornell University Press.
First printing, Cornell Paperbacks, 1992.
Second printing 1995.

International Standard Book Number 0-8014-2608-1 (cloth)
International Standard Book Number 0-8014-9912-7 (paper)
Library of Congress Catalog Card Number 91-27789

Printed in the United States of America

*Librarians: Library of Congress cataloging information appears
on the last page of the book.*

⊗ The paper in this book meets the minimum requirements of the
American National Standard for Information Sciences—Permanence of
Paper for Printed Library Materials, ANSI Z39.48-1984.

*This book is for my children,
Carlos and Melissa,
and for my mother*

Contents

Recetario

Pero, señora, ¿qué podemos saber las mujeres sino filosofías de cocina?

Sor Juana Inés de la Cruz

Lo importante es aplicar esa lección fundamental que aprendimos de nuestras madres, las primeras, después de todo, en enseñarnos a bregar con el fuego: el secreto de la escritura, como el de la buena cocina, no tiene absolutamente nada que ver con el sexo, sino con la sabiduría con que se combinan los ingredientes.

Rosario Ferré

¿Qué me aconseja usted para la comida de hoy, experimentada ama de casa, inspiración de las madres ausentes y presentes, voz de la tradición, secreto a voces de los supermercados? Abro un libro al azar y leo: "La cena de don Quijote." Muy literario pero muy insatisfactorio. Porque don Quijote no tenía fama de gourmet sino de despistado. Aunque un análisis más a fondo del texto nos revela, etc., etc., etc. "Pajaritos de centro de cara." Esotérico. ¿La cara de quién? . . . "Bigos a la rumana." Pero ¿a quién se supone usted que se está dirigiendo? Si yo supiera lo que es estragón y ananá no estaría consultando este libro porque sabré muchas otras cosas.

Rosario Castellanos

Afanosamente se dió a la tarea de leer la lista de ingredientes de suculentas salsas y fue como pescar en un río revuelto de millares de palabras de todas tallas y colores, exóticas especias que se deslizaban igual que anguilas entre el ir y venir de sus dedos afanosos, fragrantes yerbas que le recordaban, no sabía por qué, extrañas botánicas costeras, sensuales condimentos a cuyo sólo nombre se excitaban califas y marajás soñolientos. Y ante aquel lujurioso derroche de nombres—tarragonsalsifiperfoliadazafranperejil—que apretadamente luchaban por asirse a su memoria, se sintió cohibida, con la terrible sensación de poquedad tantas veces experimentada a lo largo de sus treinta y seis años.

Carmen Lugo Filippi

La mirada de Pedro la había hecho recuperar la confianza en el amor que éste la profesaba. Había pasado meses envenenada con la idea de que, o Pedro le había mentido el día de la boda al declararle su amor sólo por hacerla sufrir, o que con el tiempo Pedro realmente se había enamorado de Rosaura. Esta inseguridad había nacido cuando él, inexplicablemente, había dejado de festejarle sus platillos. Tita se esmeraba con angustia en cocinar cada día mejor. Desesperada, por las noches, obviamente después de tejer un buen tramo de su colcha, inventaba una nueva receta con la intención de recuperar la relación que entre ella y Pedro había surgido a través de la comida. De esta época de sufrimiento nacieron sus mejores recetas.

Y así como un poeta juega con las palabras, así ella jugaba a su antojo con los ingredientes y con las cantidades, obteniendo resultados fenomenales.

Laura Esquivel

This is the way I pictured it:

His wife in the kitchen wearing a freshly ironed apron, stirring a pot of soup, whistling a whistle-while-you-work tune, and preparing frosting for some cupcakes so that when he drove home from work, tired and sweaty, he would enter his castle to find his cherub baby in a pink day suit with newly starched ribbons crawling to him and his wife looking at him with pleasing eyes and offering him a cupcake.

It was a good image I wanted him to have and everyday I almost expected him to stop, put down his lunch pail and cry at the whole scene. If it wasn't for the burnt cupcakes, my damn varicose veins, and Marge blubbering all over her daysuit, it would have made a perfect snapshot.

Helena Maria Viramontes

Dejaron un pan en la mesa,
mitad quemado, mitad blanco,

. . . . .

Huele a mi madre cuando dió su leche,
huele a tres valles por donde he pasado:
a Aconcagua, a Pátzcuaro, a Elqui,
y a mis entrañas cuando yo canto.

Gabriela Mistral

Su preparación resultaba ser una cosa muy complicada y tomaba tiempo. Primero los colocaba en un cajón con pasto y les daban una hierba rara que ellos comían, al parecer con mucho agrado, y que les servía de purgante. Allí pasaban un día. Al siguiente los bañaban cuidadosamente para no lastimarlos, los secaban y los metían en la olla llena de agua fría, hierbas de olor y especias, vinagre y sal.

Cuando el agua se iba calentando empezaban a chillar, a chillar, a chillar. . . . Chillaban a veces como niños recién nacidos, como ratones aplastados, como murciélagos, como gatos estrangulados, como mujeres histéricas.

Amparo Dávila

Nadie puede consumir una mujer entera.

Juan José Arreola

Here. Take this gingerbread lady
and put her in your oven.
. . . . .
we must all eat sacrifices.
We must all eat beautiful women.

Anne Sexton

El hijo comió cazuelas de corazón con patatas, que le guisó su madre
con el corazón traspasado por cuatro llagas . . . : cuatro llagas abiertas
por cuatro espadas bañadas en aceite del huerto de los Olivos y li-
mones del sur caliente y trágico para aderezar una amarga ensalada—
madre e hijo en el Gólgota de la más lívida tristura—, bañada con
gotas de vinagre también, que eran lágrimas, que eran sangre.

Carmen Gómez Ojea

Diríamos que a medida cortábamos la cebolla, llorábamos; pero al
pelar las capas artificialmente superpuestas sobre nuestra identidad
como mujer latinoamericana, encontrábamos un centro. Orale, a
tomar la sartén por el mango y a guisar.

Patricia Elena González

Furtivement, tu vérifies dans la glace que tu existes encore, et tu
retournes à ta cuisine. . . . Avec ton lait, ma mère, tu m'as donné la
glace.

Luce Irigaray

Preface

Conversations between my mother-in-law and me often seem based on an exchange of recipes: hers for *carnitas,* mine for muffins, hers for *chiles en nogada,* mine for *enchiladas suizas.* We compare our methods for making *mole poblano,* and reminisce about particular successes and failures with fresh fish. She applauds my handiness at desserts and deplores my appalling inability to make rice well. We discuss issues of taste and problems of availability of ingredients (by the way, for all readers isolated far from Mexican groceries, *epazote* is a common weed known up north as "lamb's quarters") and worry about the effects on tried and true methods of cookery when they are transferred to Mexico City's higher altitude and less efficient stoves. Inevitably, we struggle to convey our stories about cooking in words the other will understand, with some failures. I think in cups and pounds; she thinks in liters and kilos. *Sazonar* is a verb with an infinity of slippery meanings in my mother-in-law's vocabulary; "yeast" and "kneading" need explanation rather than direct translation, for my mother-in-law has never made bread. Other, less predictable factors also intervene. A recipe is not a blueprint, and any experienced cook will concur that it is almost impossible to stick to the script, even the first time through. It is less a formula than a general model; less an axiom of unchanging law and more a theory of possibilities; more a springboard than a restricting cage. We each have our own unformulated theory of how foodstuffs fit together, and we endlessly tinker with ingredients and proportions. For both of us, to some degree, the kitchen is the "room of our own" Virginia Woolf recommends as essential to women's spiritual advancement, the place where we write—or more often speak—our cooking secrets and our lives.

This book is something like a recipe, that is, an act of implied reciprocity. As Susan J. Leonardi has written, "even the root of *recipe*—the Latin *recipere*—implies an exchange, a giver and a receiver. Like a story, a recipe needs a recommendation, a context, a point, a reason to be" (340). Leonardi examines the embeddedness of the recipe's discourse as akin to "the literality of human reproducibility" (344), a model precisely and exactly handed down, but allowing for infinite variation, an archetype and a metaphorical description of a gendered discourse. Furthermore, a good recipe book, she says, "reproduces the social context of recipe sharing—a loose community of women that crosses the social barriers of class, race, and generation" (342). Leonardi's compelling use of the recipe as a model for a certain kind of feminine discourse that works through the manipulation of homey metaphors drawn from the domestic sphere is convincing partly because we so badly want to be convinced: at last, we dream, a common ground for positing a community of women. Yet the nostalgia and the utopia both she and I have evoked in different terms obscure the historical problem of the limitation of women's exchange to certain levels—recipes, cosmetics—and its exclusion from others.

The "Recetario" to this book suggests the common language, but also demonstrates that recipe sharing has a sinister as well as a celebratory side. The recipe serves as an index of female creative power; it also describes a giving of the self to appease another's hunger, leaving the cook weakened, starving. To have access to speech, to recipe sharing, she must feed others, often from her most intimate self, whether as a poetically distanced presence in Gabriela Mistral's equation bread = mother's milk, or through a more baldly defined cannibalism in Sexton's "We must all eat beautiful women." Her own work and her hunger, both physical and textual, go too often unrecognized. As Argentine novelist Silvina Bullrich wryly observes, men who believe in the dignity of men and the importance of their intellectual enterprise do not always transfer that belief to the dignity of women or their work:

> Suele causarme gracia que cuando alguien me llama y me pregunta si estoy ocupada, contesto:
> "—Estaba escribiendo."
> Ah, en ese caso, piensa mi interlocutor, puedo seguir hablando. Es mucho más fuerte como argumento decir:

"—Se me están quemando las tostadas . . . He puesto algo al horno y
tengo que sacarlo . . ."
La inmediatez ineludible del trabajo manual justifica las tareas fe-
meninas. Su trabajo intelectual la vuelve sospechosa. (107–8)

It generally amuses me that when someone calls and asks if I am busy, I
answer, "I was writing."
In that case, my caller thinks, I can keep talking. It is a much stronger
argument to say, "The toast is burning . . . I put something in the oven
and have to take it out . . ."
The unavoidable immediacy of manual labor justifies feminine tasks.
Her intellectual work makes her suspect.

Sharing recipes in the august pages of respected journals like *PMLA* is
one way of talking back to Bullrich's inopportune caller. Uncovering
the sinister undercurrents in the rituals of eating and being fed is
another. Dissimulation of intellectual as manual labor, yet a third. And
if this book is to offer a selection of such modes of talking to and talking
back in a community of women, in a larger human community, it
clearly cannot do so as a unified, step-by-step single-argument recipe.
Neither, of course, can it do so without establishing the basic contours
of a provisional list of ingredients. For Latin American feminists, the
list almost inevitably includes such names as Virginia Woolf and Simone de Beauvoir along with Sor Juana Inés de la Cruz, Gabriela
Mistral, and Flora Tristán. Significantly, the continental names are
evoked not necessarily as models to emulate but rather as points of
triangulation to mediate their own discourses, to help delimit boundaries, and to provide a common ground for discussion.
    This is clearly the case in Victoria Ocampo's letter to Virginia Woolf,
in which she talks back to the British writer and critic. Ocampo cele-
brates the room Virginia Woolf has been able to discover and unlock
but recognizes that Woolf's key does not necessarily fit a Latin American keyhole; that key Ocampo has to discover herself. Meanwhile, she
reads of Woolf's hunger as she looks through the keyhole into Woolf's
room, and her own hunger increases. She sees Woolf describe herself
as a devourer of books—"Like most uneducated Englishwomen, I like
reading . . . books in the bulk. Lately my diet has become a trifle
monotonous" (Woolf 112)—and wishes she had such riches to devour,
such "uneducation" to bolster her abilities. She listens to Woolf describe Brontë and Austen in terms of starvation, and writes, "In a

social context similar to that which weighed on Charlotte Brontë and Jane Austen more than a hundred years ago, I began to write and to live; similar, but worse, Virginia" (*Testimonios* 1:13). She reminds her English counterpart that there are many battles being fought that Woolf neglected to take into consideration, or that Woolf mistakenly believed already won.

Early in *A Room of One's Own*, Woolf contrasts the spiritual and physical repletion attained at two very different meals, a luncheon at a famous men's college and a dinner at the corresponding women's college. Wit and intelligence, she finds, have a direct correlation to the quality and quantity of foodstuffs. It is worth quoting at length:

> The lunch on this occasion began with soles, sunk in a deep dish, over which the college cook had spread a counterpane of the whitest cream, save that it was branded here and there with brown spots like the spots on the flanks of a doe. After that came the partridges . . . with all their retinue of sauces and salads, the sharp and the sweet, each in its order; their potatoes, thin as coins but not so hard; their sprouts, foliated as rosebuds but more succulent. And no sooner had the roast and retinue been done with than the silent serving man, the Beadle himself perhaps in a milder manifestation, set before us, wreathed in napkins, a confection which rose all sugar from the waves. To call it a pudding and so relate it to rice and tapioca would be an insult. Meanwhile the wineglasses had flushed yellow and flushed crimson; had been emptied; had been filled. And thus by degrees was lit, halfway down the spine, which is the seat of the soul, . . . the more profound, subtle, and subterranean glow, which is the rich yellow flame of rational intercourse. (10–11)

Dinner at the women's college could not offer a greater contrast. The soup is thin, the plates unattractive, the main course plain, the dessert—prunes and custard—"uncharitable . . . as a miser's heart." Conversation, she observes, is equally stringy, homely, dry, and uncharitable, since "a good dinner is of great importance to good talk. One cannot think well, love well, sleep well, if one has not dined well. The lamp in the spine does not light on beef and prunes" (18). Ocampo has no banquet to describe, no lush luncheons or impoverished dinners to share with her British mentor, only her insistently repeated emphasis on her poverty and her intense hunger, hunger such that beef and prunes would constitute a banquet, wine and partridges an impossible dream. Still, Ocampo's hunger, however real, has this in common with that of her English counterpart: for both, despite the difference in intensity, their hunger is a spiritual thing. What would Virginia Woolf say to those whose hunger is spiritual but also entirely physical? For example, the Bolivian mine worker's wife Domitila Barrios de Chungara, when she writes of a "receta para industrializar el hambre" (Acebey 262) 'recipe to industrialize hunger' or provides her list of "ingredientes para una huelga de hambre" (19) 'ingredients for a hunger strike,' is giving a recipe for revolution that derives from her own experience of a woman's double and despairing hunger, for decent food and for justice.

Woolf's book, an essential book, does not foresee the diversity of women writers who would take it up with a spiritual hunger similar to, or different from, hers, looking in Woolf's pages for a key to the pantry/room she so tantalizingly describes. Neither does Woolf take into account the valences of class, race, age, religion, nor does she concern herself with varieties of cultural experience. Ocampo's response to the British writer reminds us of the obvious fact that we too often forget or ignore: there is, as Elaine Showalter says, "a critic-position as well as a subject-position" ("Criticism" 368). And Catharine Stimpson recalls for us some of the specifics of that position as they apply in the particular case of Virginia Woolf: "Before publication, [Woolf's] anxiety about being read as a writer was inseparable from anxiety about being read as a lesbian. After publication, relief at being read as a successful writer was inseparable from relief at being a successful woman, that is, married" (130). Ultimately, then, Ocampo, herself a privileged woman, hints that it would be a grave mistake to appropriate Woolf (and implicitly, we might add, de Beauvoir or Julia Kristeva or Hélène Cixous or Showalter or any other theorist) uncritically for a Latin American critical practice, for her theories and her conclusions derive from specific conditions that may not be duplicated in Latin America, where circumstances of race, gender, class, and cultural relationships exist which may not obtain in the Anglo-French sphere. By extension, we can conclude that all hermeneutic systems inevitably set up such boundaries and that the drawing of these boundary lines is, in the broad sense, a political and cultural act.[1]

---

[1] I would agree with Diana Fuss that this necessary construction of boundaries only "becomes a problem when the central category of difference under consideration blinds us to other modes of difference and implicitly delegitimates them" (116). Fuss quite

Compare, for example, the conditions of Woolf's subject position with that Rosario Castellanos bitterly, angrily ascribes to herself in her drama *The Eternal Feminine*: "The person responsible for this monstrosity isn't, as logic decrees, an author, a man. No. It's . . . let me put it this way so as not to sin against Christian charity . . . it's a woman. If this term can be applied to someone lacking in decorum and scruples and who rejects the mission which nature has given her, to be the dove for the nest" (Ahern 351). The critic in the text specifies her reasons for this condemnation in terms that strongly recall Woolf, but with a difference: "Rosario Castellanos doesn't even have the excuse of being single. It's worse: divorced, which, by my way of thinking, doesn't justify her in any way, but does explain her cynicism, her shamelessness, and her aggressiveness. Her marital failure, for which, no doubt, she's the only one to blame, encourages her to slap the cheek of a society to which she is no longer worthy of belonging" (Ahern 351–52). Woolf, according to Stimpson, feared being considered too "shrill" or "feminine" (129) and finds comfort in her successful marriage; she still can count on that support, on both a personal and a social level, and can think back through foremothers such as Austen, the Brontës, and George Eliot, to help her imagine the conditions of possibility for a hypothetical sister of Shakespeare. But Castellanos has no such mechanism to fall back on, no husband to give her validity, not even a tradition of women writers to support her efforts.

Victoria Ocampo defines one boundary condition, Domitila Barrios de Chungara another, Rosario Castellanos yet a third. These conditions are real, and examination of the specificity of historical and social problems concerning Latin American women of different races and classes not only gives us a more nuanced understanding of the particular conditions under which a feminist practice is undertaken in these countries but helps refine distinctions between first- and third-world feminist theories. Let me, nevertheless, and by way of setting boundaries, quickly distance myself from three theoretical/strategic positions still given great currency in debates around Latin American feminist criticisms.

One is the idealization of any product of a woman's voice or pen as beautiful and true. This sentimentalization takes many forms, from

---

rightly sees this delegitimating tactic as an ideological tool for reducing difference to irrelevance and either authorizing or deauthorizing individuals on the basis of spurious constructions of identities.

ignoring harsh, character-damaging behavior on the part of women, to composing meaningless panegyrics to an abstract womanhood of the sort I recently read in a preface to a new book on Mexican women short story writers: "Woman is everything: breath, dignity, love; she is the best of us, and the best that can happen to us" (Monsreal 9–10). Augustín Monsreal seems to intend this praise to be romantic and invigorating; instead, his celebratory variation on supply-side aesthetics is so uncritical as to suggest its own collapse, either into an inverse sexist essentialism that replaces the image of Man with a hypostatized figure of Woman or, conversely, into a neocolonialist reappropriation of the sign of the Feminine for a reconstructed courtly love aesthetic.

The second position from which I must distance myself is the other extreme of seeing women's literature as inherently limited when held up to a "universal" standard. I use Mexican critic Sara Sefchovich here as a convenient shorthand for this stand, but I could name many others who make similar statements. Sefchovich finds that, because of women's historical lack of access to high culture, their unsophisticated use of the expressive capabilities of language reflects their belatedness in sitting down to the cultural banquet table: "Women's writing has common characteristics precisely because of their lack of appropriation of the world: little complexity, less problematization, a flat and even linear structure, a less-rich language, less formal innovation, less experimentation, and less metaphor" (1.17). This perception of the innate inferiority of women's writing, she insists, reflects not a value judgment on her part but pure (if understandable, given the historical suppression of women) fact; it is, in her words, "realidad comprobable." Sefchovich regrets her need to be harsh but comments, "In analysis, as in the pleasure of reading, there is no masculine or feminine, no black or white, only good literature" (19). What Sefchovich fails to recognize is the degree to which the terms that structure her "analysis," "fact," or "reality" are themselves vexed and historically conditioned. Wlad Godzich's refutation of this stand is incisive: "One needs to ask oneself, though, what is the wisdom, if not the validity, of a selection that seeks to fit women writers within a canon previously defined on the basis of masculinist traits?" (21). And Showalter argues that while reflecting a serious ongoing concern in feminist criticism, the type of androgynist poetics espoused by such critics as Sefchovich "can be an unexamined misogyny that demands a spurious 'universality' from women's writing, as integrationist poetics did from black writers, as well as a form of feminine self-hatred" ("Criticism" 360). Ethel Krauze, a young writer and critic from Mexico, talks back to those who uncritically adopt these sorts of variations on masculinist assumptions when she sensibly argues that the historical positioning of the gendered self applies to all the products of the imagination:

> Sentía que lo femenino, como se ha interpretado durante toda la historia, me acercaba más a la zoología que a la humanidad, me incrustaba más en una provisionalidad permanente donde nunca dejaría de ser mujer, nunca podría hacer verdadera literatura: la que hacen los hombres. Pero ganó mi terquedad. Me eché a escribir y punto, por la sola gana de contar cosas: la literatura no tiene sexo. Y salieron estas páginas donde rondan las mujeres acaso más de lo que yo me hubiera propuesto. Y leyéndolas advertí . . . pues, que es el mundo de siempre, con sus pantanos y sus ardores, sólo que visto, o mejor, sentido desde el perfil de la mujer. La literatura masculina ha dado lo suyo: describir al hombre e inventar a la mujer, probablemente la literatura femenina cubra la otra mitad, ahí donde la mujer sea de veras ella misma, y el hombre comience a mirarse, para su propia perplejidad, desde los ojos de ella. (Quoted in Robles 328)

> I felt that the feminine, as it has been interpreted throughout history, approximated me to zoology more than to humanity, inserted me more into a permanent provisionality where I would never stop being a woman, where I would never be able to create true literature: the literature men make. But my stubbornness won out. I started to write, period, with the sole desire of telling things: literature has no sex. And out came these pages where women dominate perhaps more than I might have proposed. And reading them over, I realized, then, that it is the same world, with its swamps and its heat, only that it is seen, or better, felt, from a woman's profile. Masculine literature has made its contribution: to describe men and invent women; probably feminine literature covers the other half, there where woman is really herself, and man begins to look at himself, in his own perplexity, out of her eyes.

What Krauze proposes is not the successive approximation of writing by women to a supposedly sexless but inherently masculinist model of "good" writing but rather the development of male writing's complementary other side. Krauze, furthermore, signals the impossibility of doing anything else, for she is both a woman and a writer, not a transvestite man. Her work will of necessity be inflected by this historical, social, and sexual positioning, and it is, moreover, to her advantage to recognize the usefulness of exploring the potentialities in writing from a woman's point of view. In so doing, the female writers will instigate what Silvia Molloy calls "a new praxis of writing, subverting the authoritarian language that puts them 'in their place,' displacing themselves" (García Pinto 147). And from this other place, women authors can complete an image of the world that has, inevitably, been only half drawn.

Third, I distance myself from those writers and critics who condemn all writing not concerned with immediate social and political action as bourgeois, elitist, decadent, and so on. Work in the social and political arena is urgently required and vitally important; it is not, however, the charge of this particular piece of writing, nor is it the sole mode of activism. I recognize, and share, the anguish and self-doubt of academics whose crises of consciousness lead us to periodic bouts of self-condemnation on the grounds that our work has no concrete, practical application, but I also worry that activists who make demagogic generalizations about the futility of academic discourse border on a dangerous antiintellectualism. The academic world is also part of the real world, if only a small part, and I believe that its effect on the interlocking relationships that make up our world is significant in shaping both perceptions and actions in other social spheres. In 1843 Marx wrote in a letter, "Until now, philosophers kept the solution of all mysteries inside their desks, and the stupid uneducated world merely had to open its mouth and the fried dove of absolute knowledge would fly in. . . . It is not our task to construct the future and to deal with everything once and for all, but it is clear what we have to do at present—I am thinking of the *merciless criticism of everything that exists*" (quoted in White, epigraph). It is our task as academics to speak critically, to keep our mouths shut against the fried doves (of nests, of knowledge), whether we cook them ourselves or have them served up to us by others. It is our job to complicate truth claims and representations of absolute knowledge. It is a form of activism to talk back to those who would restrict possibilities to a narrow set of formulas, rigidly applied. This task is also, broadly speaking, a political one, and it is not negligible.

If these are the attitudes I keep out, what remains is the description of those elements I include; a stew is not a cake, after all, though both may, on occasion, contain flour, and carrots. Some of the ingredients:

(1) Latin American feminisms are developing in multiple directions, not always compatible with directions taken by Anglo-European feminisms and frequently in discord with one another. It would be premature to try to invent an overarching theory to account for these developments; rather, I hope to offer a continually self-questioning theorizing, anchored in specific texts.

(2) At its best Latin American feminist writing is antihegemonic and challenges a monumentalizing or totalizing view of literature. It is, therefore, multiply voiced and tends to operate within a field of sinuous and shifting positionalities rather than from a single, fixed position. I am, accordingly, less interested in theorizing about the game of literary position than in understanding the strategic moves involved in a sequence of impermanent positionalities, and I would argue for complication of possibilities even at the expense of a perceived lack of rigor. The focus on specific strategies seems to me to offer the most productive mode of reading texts without reductionism or oversimplification to fit the exigencies of a single, overspecific theoretical model.

(3) I make no rigid distinction between fictional and critical writings, although the degree to which a work can be mined for theoretical/ strategic insights varies greatly. Such a refusal to make rigid discriminations is in keeping with a general tendency in Latin America, where the relationship between the writer and the critic tends to come unstuck, and so many of the best writers are also the best critics and theoreticians.

(4) I am well aware that this book, written in English and bearing the imprint of a U.S. academic publisher, has inserted itself into an ongoing discussion about feminisms at a very particular level. Thus, to facilitate the dialogue with non–Latin Americanist feminists, all quotations from works in languages other than English have been translated in the body of the book. Where official translations exist, I have quoted from those editions, with occasional modifications. Too often, however, I have been forced to use my own translations. Quotations in the original languages appear throughout the text when we need to savor the particularities of a specific voice.

(5) I recognize, too, that this book talks to and with Latin America itself only in a very peculiar, mediated fashion.

Chapter 1 provides background and defines some of the general conditions of possibility for at least one type of Latin American feminist criticism. It provides, if you will, the list of ingredients in the recipe that will be elaborated and developed in Chapters 2 through 7, with reference to specific strategic interventions in fictional texts. The Conclusion comes back to the question of the role of the Latin Americanist as feminist critic in this postmodern, postcolonial scene. Finally, the bookends—"Recetario" and "Uñas y Huesos"—sandwich the whole, with a chorus of voices in the original languages, without translation or mediation by commentary.[2] These voices complement, comment on, and sometimes contradict each other and the pages they enclose. Here the writers, though fragmented and reassembled by conscious intent, appear in their own words, without the film of translation. They remind me, and in the ongoing reciprocity of the recipe, the reader as well, whom we are talking to and who is talking back to us, and in what terms.

This, like all books, owes vast debts to a great many people, many of whom I have never met: people like Doris Sommer and Jean Franco, whose work has helped create the conditions of possibility of my own. Of those I know well, I particularly need to recognize the generous continuing support of those who first introduced me to the nature of the intellectual enterprise, although they may be surprised by the direction that enterprise has since taken, especially Peter Komanecky, Melvin Friedman, and Herbert Blau. Among those who participated in and helped give direction to my thinking are the members of my Hispanic Feminisms seminar, especially Gerard Aching, Yaw Agawu-Kakraba, Carlos Cañuelas, Catherine Den Tandt, Sandra Dunn, Laura García Moreno, Cecelia Lawless, Luiza Moreira, Kavita Panjabi, and Mayra Santos Febres. My ideas were shaped by contact with theirs, and theirs have certainly found their way into this book. I thank them for their enthusiasm and apologize for oversimplifications and distortions. I am grateful also for the much needed support of my colleagues at Cornell: Mary Gaylord, John Kronik, and José Piedra in particular have been unstinting of time and energy. Special thanks go to Celeste Schenck and the two anonymous readers for Cornell University Press, who provided marvelously detailed and helpful readings of the whole manuscript. They caught so many infelicities of thought and expression that the ones remaining must be charged to my account rather than their good will. My husband, Carlos, already knows that *all* my work, and not just this, for good or ill, rests on the strong basis of his encouragement.

---

[2]For translations, see the Appendix.

I also thank the following authors and publishers for permission to reprint illustrations:

Denise Chávez. *The Last of the Menu Girls*. Houston: Arte Público, 1986.

Jacques Ehrmann. "Les structures de l'échange dans *Cinna*." *Les Temps Modernes* 246 (Nov. 1966): 931.

Carlos Fuentes. *Christopher Unborn*. Trans. Alfred J. MacAdam and the author. New York: Farrar, Straus and Giroux, 1989.

Octavio Paz. *El signo y el garabato*. Mexico: Joaquín Mortiz, 1973.

Antoine Saint-Exupéry. Illustrations from *Le Petit Prince* written and drawn by Antoine de Saint-Exupéry, copyright 1943 by Harcourt Brace Jovanovich and renewed in 1971 by Consuelo de Saint-Exupéry.

And I express my particular gratitude to Mayra Santos Febres for permission to quote from her unpublished poetry.

DEBRA A. CASTILLO

Ithaca, New York

Talking Back

1

Toward a Latin American
Feminist Literary Practice

Elaine Showalter's well-known essay "Feminist Criticism in the Wilderness" contains an enormously attractive schematic summary of several major trends in recent feminist criticism: "English feminist criticism, essentially Marxist, stresses oppression; French feminist criticism, essentially psychoanalytic, stresses repression; American feminist criticism, essentially textual, stresses expression" (186). The temptation to try to complement this formula with one strikingly pertinent to Latin America is almost overwhelming: Latin American feminist criticism, essentially fragmentary, stresses compression. Latin American feminist criticism, essentially communal, stresses concession. Latin American feminist criticism, essentially aesthetic, stresses impression(ism). Latin American feminist criticism, essentially maternalistic, stresses consumption. (No, that doesn't sound quite right.) But unfortunately for those of us who would like to imagine a new, neatly distinctive category, although many works of a Latin American feminist bent have appeared in the United States and in the various countries of Latin America in recent years, no particularized, clearly innovative theory has as yet emerged. Perhaps we might conclude that Latin American feminist criticism, essentially underdeveloped, incites depression. Such studies as have appeared in academic publications often seem too easily categorizable as either (a) largely impressionistic, content-based analyses of the representations of women in traditional texts or (b) efforts to recuperate works by women for the Latin American literary canon with theoretical tools borrowed mostly from the

1

Anglo-American or French varieties of feminist thought.[1] Says Hernán Vidal, summarizing the conclusions of various colleagues: "In the experience and judgment of our consultants, a great deal of material is circulating whose assumption of feminism or whose analytic and interpretative criteria, reduce themselves to a mere instrumental application of already-canonized theories from French and Anglo-Saxon criticism to a specific work, without revealing the cultural norms that motivated the scholar to select the chosen text or examining the possible contribution of this exercise to the feminist cause" (8). We may or may not agree with the specific terms and implicit call to social action of Vidal's critique; nevertheless, he quite concisely captures the essence of the most nagging question surrounding Latin American feminist critical activity.

The intent of this book is, first of all, to explore the theoretical issues involved in the hypothetical construction of a (various) specifically Hispanic feminism(s); second, to discuss some of the strategies of a feminist literary practice in the Latin American context and to offer sample applications of these strategies to readings of specific texts; and finally, to suggest some of the difficulties inherent in the analysis of "a different writing" by what we might call, with a willfully reversed transvaluation of Julio Cortázar's derisive term, el lector hembra (the female reader). This first chapter provides an overview of some of the conditions that inflect the evolving infrastructure of Latin American feminist theory and also proposes a set of sample strategies that I have found useful in focusing critical practice. I borrow advisedly from both first-world and Latin American(ist) criticism what is pertinent and insightful, while trying to avoid the pitfalls of adhering too closely to the unsatisfactory recipe of combining Anglo-American and French theory in equal parts and seasoning with a dash of Latin American fiction.

To appropriate theories foreign to Latin America for a Latin American feminist practice is not in and of itself a negative act; too often, nevertheless, the indiscriminate or weakly motivated application of

---

[1]Examples of the representation of women in traditional texts include Sharon Magnarelli's 1985 book, *The Lost Rib: Female Characters in the Spanish-American Novel*, or any number of recent anthologies of essays on women writers. Sandra Cypress's magnificent discourse analyses of Rosario Castellanos's novels offer one variety of the second type of appropriative strategy; Margo Glantz's Barthes-influenced explorations of peculiarly Latin American mythologies and literary styles provide another.

French or American or British theory can continue the kind of destructive stereotype described by Jean Franco: " 'British intellectuals: Latin American revolutionaries' was the wording of an ad I once saw in the *New Statesman* in England. It summed up nicely the separation of intellectual and manual labor along the axis of metropolis and periphery, as well as suggesting the flow of revolutionary action into areas where people know no better than to fight. The conclusion is that the Third World is not much of a place for theory" ("Beyond" 503). In response to this perceived lack of theory, metropolitan intellectuals have frequently attempted to fill the perceived vacuum with more or less critically and historically informed ventriloquism. Franco continues: "Metropolitan discourses on the Third World have generally adopted one of three devices: (1) *exclusion*—the Third World is irrelevant to theory; (2) *discrimination*—the Third World is irrational and thus its knowledge is subordinate to the rational knowledge produced by the metropolis; and (3) *recognition*—the Third World is only seen as the place of the instinctual" (504). Strikingly, in this era of gender and race consciousness, the first world continues to subject the third to analyses that relegate its cultural production to that group of activities traditionally associated with the implicitly inferior feminine realm. Even more strikingly, prominent third-world and third-worldist writers seem to participate *uncritically* in this subordination.

Such activities on the part of metropolitan critics (and I exclude neither Franco nor myself from this adjuration) require the greatest vigilance. They cannot be dismissed as aberrations unilaterally deriving from a politically untenable assumed relation to the traditionally male preserves of theoretical activity but must also be guarded against in respect to the varieties of feminist thought. We can assume, as Gayatri Spivak reminds us, that "varieties of feminist theory and practice must reckon with the possibility that, like any other discursive practice, they are marked and constituted by, even as they constitute, the field of their production" ("Imperialism" 319). It is important for the Latin Americanist to resist the categorical work of reason that follows from the special a priori assumptions deriving from insufficiently considered appropriations of metropolitan theories of feminism carried over into analyses of Latin American literature. It is absolutely essential for the critic to take into account both the vast differences in the field of production and the distinctive qualities of the object of study that may very well, if ignored, lead to either blindness

to or erroneous evaluation of cultural products. It is crucial, furthermore, to attend not only to matters of content and context but also to
what we may call, following Alice Jardine, considerations of "enunciation."[2] In other words, there may be considerable overlap between, for
example, Roland Barthes's theories and Margo Glantz's novels, but
there are also serious disjunctions. The careful critic will take from
Barthes only what is useful and pertinent and stir that material together with other critical/theoretical approaches that complement it.
In such a confection, the French flavoring will add richness and consis-
tency to the broth without overwhelming or denaturing the soup.

Furthermore, the destructiveness of the stereotype of Latin America
as the land of emotion and practice rather than critical thought is
not limited to its widespread acceptance in the first world, where it
is given various patronizing forms by such publications as the *New
Statesman*. More destructive yet is the internalization of the stereotype
in a kind of pan-Latin inferiority complex, most destructive when most
subtlely masked. I am struck, for example, that even so acute a critic
and original a thinker as Octavio Paz falls victim to this tendency.
Difference and originality continue to elude the Mexicans and, by
extension, other Latin Americans, he suggests, to this day: "The contradiction of New Spain is recorded in Sor Juana's silence. It is not
difficult to decipher its meaning. The impossibility of creating a new
poetic language was but one aspect of a greater impossibility: that of
creating . . . a new thought." We can leave aside the debatability of
Paz's critique of Sor Juana; the issue here is the unquestioned acceptance of a posited cultural inferiority complex that aggravates an already overdetermined weight of pessimism. If we follow the lines of
Paz's critique, we are forced to conclude that Latin America is a pale
copy of the West, unable to think for itself or to create anything new
not only because criticism of existing structures is unfamiliar and
unpalatable; the entire philosophical infrastructure of society is based
on the prohibition of criticism. To carve out an access to criticism
would, according to this argument, free the nations of Latin America

---

[2]"I discovered that the differences between male-written and female-written texts of
modernity were not, after all, in their so-called 'content,' but in their enunciation: in
their modes of discourse ('sentimental,' ironic, scientific, etc.); in their twisting of female
obligatory connotations, of inherited genealogies of the feminine, in their haste or
refusal to use the pronouns 'I' or 'we'; in their degree of willingness to gender those
pronouns as female" (119).

from this impasse but would also change their natures so radically that they would lose their essential identity. Paz concludes sweepingly, in a much cited phrase: "We Hispanic peoples have never become truly modern because, by contrast with other Western peoples, we never knew an age of criticism" (*Quetzalcóatl* xiv–xv). Almost every term of this grand overgeneralization is highly contestable, but it is important to signal that the perceived lack of criticism has a way of turning into an actual paucity, and one too easily explained by way of an appeal to the nature of the "Hispanic" as opposed to "other Western peoples." In this respect, as in others, Latin America requires a rewriting of its history.

Clearly, one of the major difficulties confronting the Latin Americanist is the ingrained belief that feminist theory in Latin America, like other aesthetic and political theories, currently lags behind feminist practice or can be characterized as subordinate to the more highly developed metropolitan discourses. Speech and action sweep ahead of theoretical guidance; scattered bits of formalization are only beginning to see and conceive and reconstruct themselves after the fact of specific social and political activity, and they do so in the tentative theories that, paradoxically and frustratingly, may at times seem more reactionary than the revolution that produced them, may seem to be marked by an unconscious refusal to attend to the implications of their own discourses. We can read thusly the curious wavering in Marta Traba's simultaneous recognition and rejection of the "universals" of narrative discourse. The resulting "situation of inferiority" depends on an unquestioning validation of the assumptions encoded in the "universal" qualities of good literature; undecidably, the situation has been superseded either because women's literature now more closely approximates the masculinist model of values or because that model itself has been rejected. Traba quite rightly points to the pervasive misreading of women's texts, misreadings derived from applying a specific set of inappropriate cultural, ideologic, and aesthetic assumptions to a different group of texts as if they were universal values. Several questions remain, however. If women writers of Latin America do not, in general, subscribe to the values encoded in the phrase "of universal reach," why not? Is there in these works a conscious attempt to undermine the masculinist definitions of universality? If women do not write works that, according to these traditional values, are recognizably innovative, what are they doing instead? Is there another set of strategies that can more accurately understand the kinds of underrecognized innovations in these texts by women? Under what conditions and with what limitations can the discerning reader identify and evaluate such discursive practices?

So too might one explore the implicit assumptions behind one of the best-known and most frequently cited essays in the Latin American feminist corpus. Sara Castro-Klarén's "Crítica literaria femenista y la escritora en América latina" (Feminist literary criticism and the Latin American woman writer) seems to point almost too neatly to a binary division of labor similar to that already recognized by Franco: literary critics on the one hand (or the one side of the ocean), the Latin American woman writer on the other. Indeed, Castro-Klarén's paper highlights a call to action in which she recognizes, "We now have a goodly number of texts written by Latin American women, but we still have not elaborated theoretical positions derived from the reading of *those* texts" (43). In a more recent essay, Castro-Klarén specifically takes up the discussion begun in her "Teoría de la crítica literaria . . ." ("In a way, what I would like to do here is to continue the essay written five years ago" [Vidal 95]), in which she updates the debate between Anglo-American and French varieties of criticism through an evocation of the stylized dance of antagonistic partners, contrasting Showalter's "gynocriticism" (cultural and historical in orientation) to Jardine's "gynesis" (writing as a woman). She ends this essay, like her earlier one, with an imperative call to action: "The study of Latin American literature is ripe for a re-writing of its history. The figure of Women and the subsequent problematics implied by its presence should cause a profound re-thinking of the possible history of Latin America and its symbolic systems" (Vidal 105). That is, Latin American literature and history and the history of literature require immediate and profound reexamination. Such necessary reexamination, with the concomitant reconstruction of a literary genealogy that moves women from the footnotes to the main text, that fills in the temporal and topographical gaps between Sor Juana Inés de la Cruz, who lived in the seventeenth century, and Luisa Valenzuela, who lives in the twentieth, represents, indeed a transgenerational biographical (or, radically, autobiographical) act. It is also a politic and political strategic move.

Castro-Klarén clarifies the need to take into account the special circumstances of "la loca criolla en el ático" 'the criolla madwoman in the attic.' Yet, "la loca criolla en el ático" carries with her a heavy load of potential misrecognitions and wayward double meanings. "The madwoman in the attic" refers specifically to Sandra Gilbert and Susan Gubar's classic text and to Castro-Klarén's call for critical work of parallel importance in Latin American letters; it refers, in Gilbert and Gubar's work, to Bertha, Rochester's mad first wife in Charlotte Brontë's *Jane Eyre*, a role recreated from Bertha's point of view in Jean Rhys's brilliant 1966 novel *Wide Sargasso Sea*. Bertha, of course, is both mad and criolla; in both books her heritage is West Indian rather than British. Brontë, the nineteenth-century novelist, is archetypically British, the daughter of a relatively poor but respectable family. Rhys, the twentieth-century writer who takes a more sympathetic view of the madwoman, is, like her character, a creole, born in Dominica, one of the British colonies in the West Indies, of a creole mother and a Welsh father. The first word we must unpack, then, is the word *loca*. Clearly, the madwoman bears quite different ideological meanings in *Jane Eyre* and in *Wide Sargasso Sea*, distinctions that might well be explored in terms of a colonizer versus a colonized point of view. But in Latin (as opposed to British) America, *loca* has a range of significations quite different from those obtaining in either of the English-language books, as the juxtaposition "loca en el ático"/"loca de la Plaza de Mayo" immediately underlines. Her madness, and her sanity, are differently coded and valued.

Second, analysis of "la loca criolla en el ático" would have to take into account specific race and class issues. It will be necessary to complement the study of "la loca *criolla*" (that is, an American-born white woman of Spanish descent) with studies of other women, perhaps less literate, less proficient as writers, or at least less published, but altogether dominant in sheer numbers: *la mestiza, la indígena, la negra, la mulata*. They too are mad, in both English senses of the word, and perhaps in both the English and the Spanish senses as well. But given the predominance of the criolla voice, who speaks when speaking of them? Who are they? Who is the subject, and who is the object of discourse? Who the writer, and who the critic?

Finally, study of "la loca criolla en el ático" does not occur in a vacuum but takes its stand in a specific place. Bertha's attic is a forerunner of Woolf's room and also has its analogous representations in those other rooms where women have been confined by custom and tradition: the kitchen, the bedroom. Furthermore, I find a strange propriety and unholy delight in the Spanish definition of *ático*. Its first meaning is adjectival; it refers to something Attic (from Athens) and therefore signifies "elegant." My dictionary gives the example of "Attic taste." A woman of Attic taste would, I suppose, have a facility for both physical and linguistic elegancies; she would also (the criolla again) have to possess the economic security to allow her to develop these tastes. The second meaning of *attic* in Spanish is the familiar noun referring to the room under the roof of one's house, that room in middle- and upper-class Latin American households all too easily given over to the maid. It is hard to imagine an Attic attic; more common would be the Attic front room and the cluttered storage space under the eaves. In Latin American women's writing, one way these two rooms intersect is in the vexed and exploitative relationships between mistress and servants, in the sexually charged contacts between master and servant. In other works, the woman's Attic surface is a subterfuge for the attic where the secret self takes refuge. I cannot hope to deconstruct all the ramifications of "la loca (cuerda) criolla-mestiza-mulata-indígena-negra (¿ática?) en el ático–sala de estar–cuarto propio–cocina (de la casa, de la escritura)" in a single book and must content myself with a more limited agenda.

Woman's Place is in the Home, with a Broken Foot

Let us begin with a simple definition. In "Self-Sacrifice Is a Mad Virtue," Mexican poet, novelist, and diplomat Rosario Castellanos offered a detailed, if embittered, description of the typical criolla, whose value system Castellanos exposes as quite mad. When we look at Mexican women, she tells us, our first impression is of irreducible diversity: the Indian girl tending sheep in Chiapas seems not to belong to the same species as the university science student; the provincial girl swathed in clothing from head to toe doesn't seem to live in the same century as the bikini-clad water-skier in Acapulco; the servant girl who has just discovered the blender doesn't have much in common with the airline hostess, bored from so many international flights. Cultural, economic, and temporal strata militate against any attempt to lump these women together. Yet, Castellanos finds much that links them:

In Mexico, when we utter the word *woman*, we refer to a creature who is dependent upon male authority: be it her father's, her brother's, her husband's, or her priest's. She is subject to alien decisions that dictate her personal appearance, her marital status, the career she is going to study, or the field of work she is going to enter. . . . The Mexican woman does not consider herself—nor do others consider her—to be a woman who has reached fulfillment if she has not produced children. . . .

Love for one's child supplants or substitutes for all other kinds of love, which qualify as less perfect because they presuppose reciprocity. . . . Self-sacrifice is the Mexican woman's most famous virtue. (Ahern 260–61)

In this formulation, women cannot do without a man to mediate for them in any social realm, and from this enforced dependency grows an unhealthy (mad) imprisonment in convention. Tradition, law, custom, the educational institutions—all militate against a woman's rebellion; there is in this projection no institutional framework to support such a movement. To say that February 1971 (when Castellanos first published this essay) is not now and that Mexico is not all Latin America is only too obviously true. Yet her point stands, just as the comparison between the stone-age Chiapaneca and the cosmopolitan woman stands. I let one example, from an Argentinian women's magazine, August 1, 1988, take the place of further argument. In a published report on the presidential campaign, the wife of one of the candidates was quoted as saying, "Mi marido es muy machista y yo también. Creo que a los hombres hay que dejarlos ir adelante. Total, desde atrás nosotras siempre hacemos lo que queremos. Hay que ser inteligentes, porque casi siempre las que manejamos todo somos nosotras, las mujeres" (Para Tí) 'My husband is very *machista* and so am I. I believe that men have to go first. After all, behind the scenes we always do whatever we want. We have to be intelligent, because the ones who really run the show are us, the women.' Perhaps this wife is thinking of the unlovely manipulations of the famous Eva Perón or of her less-apt successor in power, Isabel. In any case, the reference to the supposed, and very feminine, power that women exercise from behind the throne cannot fail to appear both manipulative ("we really run the show") and distastefully sly (we pretend to go along, give them lip service, and then "do whatever we want"). It begs the question so pointedly addressed by Castellanos which asks if what women want in this context is what men in positions of authority over them allow them to want.

In 1970 Castellanos published her important essay "La participación de la mujer mexicana en la educación formal" (Mexican women's participation in formal education), in which she details the manner in which theoretical equality between the sexes as coded in the legal right to a formal education is dissipated in the informal "education" of custom and traditional usage, which dictates matrimony and maternity as the only proper roles for women. Salaried employment is, says Castellanos, still conceived of as a temporary measure for single women who have not yet been so lucky as to catch a man and as an unfortunate necessity for those women whose men are not able to support the family comfortably. It is, she concludes, considered unnatural for a woman to *want* a career outside the home. For this reason, the relation of woman to work is seriously compromised: "And it is precisely the manner of taking employment which prevents women who work and receive a salary from developing, which prevents them from acquiring a certain degree of independence, which, although real, is lived as ficticious" (*Mujer* 29). Although the conditions in the workplace have changed enormously since 1970 and the idea of women who might wish to have a professional career is gaining greater acceptance, Castellanos's statement still resonates as generally correct, still carries a charge of wider applicability outside the strictly defined scene of salaried labor. In the workplace, in the privacy—or nonprivacy—of her home, in the public and political arenas, in the publishing houses, the Latin American woman is still largely a shadow construct. The independent existence of women, though real, is still perceived as a fiction, as an imaginary, incomplete derivative of the self-duplication—the derivative of Adam's rib, the Freudian castrate, the Jungian anima—of an overwhelmingly male ideological frame. To assume otherwise, to allow for a woman's independence or self-possession, would require the complete recalculation of an entire economic and philosophical system.

In relation to the particularities of Latin American women's lives Latin Americanists need to explore concrete questions of their opposition to or complicity in the established orders and their relationships to specific social, historical, political, and legal structures in their respective countries, how the problem of a continuing colonialism in some realms intersects with postcolonial structures in others. Moreover, the particular relationships between women and development in develop-*ing* countries demands closer examination. Such questions need to be further explored in relation to the unwritten codes of a philosophical tradition that creates the figure of a fictional woman as "truth-in-law," thus immensely complicating the relationships of women to the quotidian realities of their lives, blurring the imperative steps for the assumption of agency and effective subjectivity. The refusal to abide by old discursive traditions is, as Castellanos intuits and Spivak more directly states, both poetic and political, involving the careful critique of conventions that are both literary/rhetorical and ideological.

Racial issues are also adumbrated differently in the different countries of Latin America from their adumbration in the United States and Europe; they represent another layer of practical criticism that needs close attention. The issue of the *criolla* in the attic signaled by Castro-Klarén represents only one important area of investigation; careful theoretical examinations of *la mestiza* remain to be undertaken, and studies of *la indígena* that go beyond neoanthropological information retrieval are extraordinarily scarce. Jean Franco has hinted at some directions these studies may take in her important essay "Beyond Ethnocentrism: Gender, Power, and the Third-World Intelligentsia," where she makes the point that the historic confinement of mothers and daughters of good family is not only related to the systems of economic exchange common to most European societies but carries as well particular racist inflections. She offers a simple diagram:

mother	virgin
phallus	
not virgin	mother
not mother	virgin
(whore)	(Mary)

and notes in her commentary on this schema "the privatized and inward-looking Hispanic house and the fact that the virtual confinement of married women to the home had not only been required by the Church but was also intended to insure the purity of blood that Spanish society had imposed after the wars against the Moors" ("Beyond" 507). Women of good family who escape are madwomen by definition; another ethic rules women from other class or racial backgrounds. Implicitly, women who were not so restricted, who had access to the streets and to the beds of more than one man, were not only spiritually but also racially impure. Inasmuch as one sort of impurity implies the other, certain unacceptable practices—the rape/

seduction and then discarding of poor Indian or mestiza women for the convenience of upper-class white men—are commonly considered lesser infractions than the violation of a woman of the upper class.

Franco's study needs to be complemented by one developing the implications of her spatial diagram through the addition of a temporal axis that recognizes the progression virgin → mother → crone, by work on the anomalous but pervasive figure of the Indian mother-who-is-not-a-mother (girls and women who work as nanas for their more-advantaged employers' "pure-blood" children), and by other studies that take into account the very different organizations of female roles in indigenous societies.

Also needed are more profound studies of the multiply vexed relation between the two housewife figures—wife and servant. In a provocative study Cynthia Steele suggests several important avenues of investigation. She notes that the anachronistic employment of maids continues to flourish in middle-class working families and posits, among other factors, that for the married woman of middle- or upper-class status, the maid may "defer the need to confront her husband regarding the sexual division of household labor and childcare" (299). The maid buffers and displaces institutional critique, while well-to-do women retain a vested interest in conserving the class distinctions for the very purpose of ensuring themselves the advantages of a fragile feminist rhetorical position within and outside the home. There is no need for discussion or rebellion in the professional class; men do not do the housework or care for the children on a regular basis, but neither do their wives, who can pretend that their careers exempt them from such traditional female tasks. A gender issue is swiftly transformed into a nonproblem, resolved in intellectual castes or social class distinctions. Castellanos wryly notes, "When the last maid disappears, the cushion on which our conformity now rests, then our first furious rebel will appear" (Ahern 50). Implicitly, unpleasant household duties are no longer, in this modern age more aware of the theoretical intellectual equality of men's and women's minds, assigned according to a male/female axis; instead, they are distributed on the basis of superior/inferior human types. Manual labor is appropriate for those mentally unequipped to take on rigorous intellectual work. This conclusion further supports the twisted maternalism of the power dynamics that obtain in such situations. The mistress, says Steele, "rationalizes that she is doing her servant a favor by 'giving' her work, that in so doing she is protecting and sponsoring the less fortunate" (301).

From one side of the power axis, Rosario Castellanos writes, "Up to this time, I have had two long servanthoods, and I use that word with the full consideration of its ambivalence" (Ahern 167). Exploitation of the women who serve her also keeps the mistress bound up in an unhealthy relationship of dependence, keeps her from remembering that by displacing housekeeping tasks onto the maid the upper-class woman ensures the preservation of a noxious class-gender system, even if she deploys the rhetoric of feminism. Even worse: the use of the rhetoric of liberation sounds like bad faith coming from a woman who only uses it to her own advantage and who averts her eyes from the exploitation going on in her own home. It is not surprising, then, that from the other side of the power axis the maids and factory workers suspect feminism of being yet another imperialist weapon.[3] One of the responses to this oppression is a violent rejection of all that privileged women are and all they represent. Thus, for example, the Bolivian mine worker's wife Domitila Barrios de Chungara, in a famous altercation, confronts the chair of the Mexican delegation to a Tribuna del Año Internacional de la Mujer (Steering Committee of the International Year of the Woman):

> Señora, hace una semana que yo la conozco a usted. Cada mañana llega usted con un traje diferente; y sin embargo, yo no. Cada día llega usted pintada y peinada como quien tiene tiempo de pasar en una peluquería bien elegante y puede gastar buena plata en eso; y, sin embargo, yo no. Yo veo que usted tiene cada tarde un chofer en un carro esperándola a la puerta de este local para recogerla a su casa; y, sin embargo, yo no. Y para presentarse aquí como se presenta, estoy segura de que usted vive en una vivienda bien elegante, en un barrio también elegante, ¿no? Y, sin embargo, nosotras las mujeres de los mineros, tenemos solamente una pequeña vivienda prestada y cuando se muere nuestro esposo o se enferma o lo retiran de la empresa, tenemos noventa días para abandonar la viviendo y estamos en la calle.
>
> Ahora, señora, dígame: ¿tiene usted algo semejante a mi situación? ¿Tengo yo algo semejante a su situación de usted? Entonces, ¿de qué

---

[3]See, for example, Domitila Barrios de Chungara: "Yo considero que el machismo es también un arma del imperialismo, como lo es el femenismo" (Viezzer 8) 'I believe that machismo is also an imperialist weapon, as is feminism.'

igualdad vamos a hablar entre nosotras? ¿Si usted y yo no nos parecemos, si usted y yo somos tan diferentes? Nosotras no podemos, en este momento, ser iguales, aun como mujeres. (Viezzer 225)

Madam, I met you a week ago. Each morning you arrive with a different outfit; and nevertheless I do not. Each day you arrive made up and with your hair styled like someone who has time to go to a very expensive beauty salon and can afford to spend good money there; and nevertheless I do not. I see that you have a car with a driver waiting for you every afternoon to take you home; and nevertheless I do not. And in order to look the way you look, I am sure you live in a very elegant home in an area that is also elegant, right? And, nevertheless, we miners' wives have only a small, borrowed place to live, and when our husband dies, or when he is ill or retired from the company, we have ninety days to leave our home and we are in the street.

Now, tell me, Madam, do you have anything similar to my situation? Do I have anything similar to yours? Then what "equality" are we going to talk about between us? If we are not at all similar, if you and I are so different? Right now you and I cannot be equals, not even as women.

Domitila's rejection of the privileged woman derives from a long history of silencing and oppression, of being spoken about and spoken for, as if her needs were subsumed in the demands of the upper-class women who oppress women like her. Their differences, says the Bolivian mine worker's wife, are so salient as almost to constitute them as different species; even to say both are "women" is a grave misnomer.

Domitila is, of course, quite right to signal the bad faith and worse politics that allow a specific, shallow, privileged woman to suppose that she can speak to and for all women. Women are not a class. Yet, it has become fashionable in certain circles to sneer at *all* intellectualizing as somehow tainted because most of the women who write do tend to belong to a single class: the bourgeoisie. Since the stereotypical "rich girl" is so easy to mock—much easier to mock, in fact, than the stereotypical rich young man (the instant and overwhelming success of Guadalupe Loaeza's series of satirical articles on *las niñas bien* and *las reinas de Polanco* is a case in point)[4]—it is easy to lump all middle- and

---

[4]Loaeza's articles appeared in various Mexico City newspapers in the mid- to late eighties, and have been collected in various best-selling volumes including *Las niñas bien* (1987), which had the astronomical sales, for Latin America, of over fifty thousand copies the first year and nine reprintings by early 1990, and *Las reinas de Polanco* (1988).

upper-class women together under the same heading and discredit them by association. Thus we have the interesting phenomenon of the woman who writes in order to denigrate the value of writing, who theorizes that only the concrete activism of revolutionary politics stripped of romanticism can be valorized. Gioconda Belli's upper-class woman in the novel *La mujer habitada* so redeems herself: "Era lógico que le atrayera la idea de imaginarse 'compañera,' verse envuelta en conspiraciones, heroína romántica de alguna novela. . . . Pero nada tenía eso que ver con la realidad, con su realidad de niña rica, arquitecta de lujo con pretensiones de independencia y cuarto propio Virginia Woolf. Debía romper este interrogatorio constante, se dijo, este ir y venir de su yo racional a su otro yo" (105). " 'It was logical that the idea of imagining herself a "comrade" would attract her, to see herself involved in conspiracies, the romantic heroine of some novel. . . . But none of this had anything to do with her reality as a rich girl, as an architect of the rich with pretensions of independence and a Virginia Woolf–type room of her own. She ought to break out of this constant interrogation, she told herself, this to-and-fro between her rational "I" and her other "I." ' Belli's heroine, romantically, strips herself of romanticism and of her upper-class pretensions, to deliver herself body and soul to the revolution, to take the place of her (tragically) slain lover and die, also romantically, in the worthiest of causes: fighting for the freedom of her country at the side of the nobly inspired comrades from less privileged backgrounds.[5]

These culturally tagged icons, like those of the *niña bien*, the mother, the *muchacha*, and the nana, fraught as they are with the specifically Hispanic variations on considerations of blood, caste, and innate ability, need to be placed into serious studies that do not necessarily take the Eurocentric (French or Anglo-American) psychoanalytic or historical tradition as the crucial or unique point of departure. For example, Franco points to the importance of the immobility of the mother in view of the particular uncertainties of a postcolonial third world, the

---

[5]Carolyn Heilbrun marks a somewhat similar phenomenon in U.S. feminist circles: "Sneering at privileged women, whether or not they recognize their difference in experience from working-class women, has done nothing to aid the cause of feminism" (64). She finds that the complaints they have to make "are at the very heart of women's oppression: they include sexual abuse and the miseries of a hunger that is not physical and that can be felt by women of all races and classes" (63). Her observation remains generally valid for Latin America, although the connections linking issues of sex, race, and class are adumbrated somewhat differently.

insecurity about the potential for independent action in the larger social context: "The mother's body . . . offers the only unchanging territory in an uncertain world" ("Beyond" 508). Furthermore, "in a society scarred by the violence and death that inevitably accompanied imperialist penetration . . . it is not surprising to observe a certain 'feminization of values.'" It goes almost without saying that this "feminization of values" is ambiguously overdetermined in cultural practices that may, in compensation, overstress "macho" values while hiding the scars of an inbred inferiority complex that has, in actual historical practice, too frequently found its concrete referent in images of rape. In this manner the woman, as the primordial site for the metaphorical generation of discourse, must of necessity embody those unchanging, pristine values of permanence, privacy, immobility, and purity as the essential core of national identity. Franco again: "It is along this axis that social meanings accrue so that the *madre patria* in nationalist discourse is productive or sterile, prostituted or sacred" (508)—and, we might add, hermetically sealed or torn open.[6]

Streetwalking, even its innocent variants, is discouraged as an offense against this ingrained morality; it is appropriate only for racially and socially inferior women who are assumed to be promiscuously impure. Streetwalking as a political activity—the Madres de la Plaza de Mayo—is officially ignored as unintelligible madness, a displacement made possible by the tradition of seeing all deviance from the model of self-restricted, enclosed femininity as insane. *Una loca* represents the most common appellation for any woman who crosses the threshold of the home and who steps outside the traditional bounds of a proper, womanly *pudor* (decorum, but also modesty, humility, and purity) and *recato* (prudence, caution, shyness, also coyness). Penalties for departure from the norm vary from severe official reprisals (imprisonment of the leaders of the Madres, "the slamming of military boots into the body of a pregnant Domitila, or the murder of Rigoberta's family" [Mora 59]) to the apparently ridiculous: the disapproba-

---

[6]Jessica Benjamin would expand on this acute observation from the framework of an ideologically committed psychoanalytic practice. She writes, "I believe that this insistence on the division between public and private is sustained by the fear that anything public or 'outside' would merely intensify individual helplessness, that only the person we have not yet recognized as an outsider (mother and wife) can be trusted to provide us with care, that the only safe dependence is on someone who is not part of the struggle of all against all, and indeed, who is herself not independent" (202).

tion of "decent" society, exclusion from the "better" clubs, a perception of unfitness for the only natural work of women. Thus, says Margo Glantz, "the woman who symbolizes change is unworthy of any man" (*Lengua* 31). Transgression of the norm can be categorized and safely disposed of as unworthiness, even madness. By placing herself inappropriately in the public arena, the woman can also be subject to public humiliation. I offer only one small instance of the operation of the double standard as it polices transgression of sexual boundaries. Recently, the state-owned electric company (Companía de Luz) in Mexico required AIDS tests of all and *only* its female employees. The names of the two or three women who tested HIV positive were widely published, causing, as my (male) informant tells me, a good deal of harmless amusement to the majority, who began to speculate on the women's possible sexual partners, and some concealed concern to men hypothetically identified as the probable lovers (their bosses).

Even the ostentatiously chaste rebel suffers gravely for her sins against the established order, which prizes long-suffering motherhood as the only valid female virtue. Condemned by her infractions to remain single and lacking the excuse of duty to aging parents to justify her sacrifice of the joys of marriage and motherhood, *la solterona* slips from harmlessly eccentric into the odd single woman ostracized by her peers. She can be subject to further slippage from respectability in the transformation from the merely ostracized woman to the one who becomes by definition fair game for seduction attempts, since she cannot count on the backing of a man, any man, no matter how deficient as a husband, to provide her with the markers of acceptable social status.

Women active in oppositional political organizations tend to see the emancipation of women as an integral aspect, but only one aspect, of a general necessity for liberation of all human beings from oppression, including internal exploitation of working-class people by the well-to-do property owners, the politically motivated repression of basic human rights by government and social organizations, and the particularly charged issues of exploitation of developing societies by more developed nations. The emblematic example of a woman's organization based on social and political protest is that of the influential and much imitated Madres de la Plaza de Mayo in Argentina. In defiance of orders prohibiting public demonstrations, an ever-larger group of brave women began in the 1970s silently and publicly to protest the disappearance of their relatives abducted by the military regime, forcing the issue of the disappeared into the public eye. The focus of their protest was not violence against women per se but rather a violent and immoral system; that the protest was organized as the outrage of *mothers*, taking advantage of all the particular resonances of that word in Latin American societies and the culturally ingrained reverence surrounding the image of these traditionally silent and self-sacrificing women, lent their protest an added moral weight and emotional charge. The history of these women, and their foremothers, still needs to be written. Lucía Guerra-Cunningham writes:

> In Latin American history there are many examples of women who with obvious and still insufficiently analyzed political commitment have made strategic use of a feminine identity in order to carry out their activities. In the wars of independence, apart from espionage and the aid offered by patriotic women from their homes, the "mamitas" of Perú ought to be mentioned, women who traveled with the army to cook for the soldiers and frequently tricked the royalists by entering a city crying about the patriots' defeat. In the case of La Regalada, a countrywoman left her farmhouse nude so as to disconcert the royalist army by pretending to be insane to give the patriots time to prepare their assault. The activities of resistance against the Chilean and Argentine dictatorships have in the present day served as other manifestations of the strategic use of the feminine body in its traditional signification as mother. (Vidal 160)

These women represent what Sara Ruddick in her rigorous and pragmatic book *Maternal Thinking: Towards a Politics of Peace* considers an archetypal example of protective, nurturing components of "maternal thinking": forced by circumstances to move out of the home and take on an intensely assertive role in public and political affairs, they carry the lessons of child rearing with them into their new role. They stress restraint, adaptation, active nonviolence. In so doing, these "madwomen" have, as Franco puts it, "not only redefined public space by taking over the center of Buenos Aires . . . but have also interrupted military discourse (and now the silence of the new government)." Even more radically, "these women show that mothering is not simply tied to anatomy but is a position involving a struggle over meanings and the history of meanings" ("Beyond" 513–14).

Other factors also need to be taken into account to trace with any degree of accuracy the multiplicities of the Other Women's relations to feminism, including issues of class, a concept that needs to be considered and complicated far beyond the traditional outlines of a confrontational politics. Ofelia Schutte quite rightly points out the prevalent view that "a fundamental cause of human oppression lies in the disparity in privileges between rich and poor," but she demonstrates that under certain circumstances the ever-present complications of class and racial relations need to be complemented by an analysis that looks across class lines for the commonalities of repression of women ("Philosophy" 70). It is certainly true, of course, that in certain areas class oppression exercises priority over repression by sex; such is the case in relation to the specific structure of domestic work, in which middle- and upper-class women who can afford to free themselves from the pressures of the *doble jornada* of salaried job and housework continue to use servants to perform housekeeping and child-care chores. Jean Franco's warning in this respect is absolutely correct. Citing the much-repeated truism that the category "woman" represents an instance of oppression and can, therefore, stand for other class and racial struggles as well, Franco objects: "It is definitively NOT the same struggle" ("Apuntes" 35). Franco's point is well taken. The danger, however, is overgeneralization in applying the divisive considerations quite properly derived from recognition of exploitation across the board into areas of common concern. Schutte continues: "Moreover, at times feminism is erroneously viewed as a luxury associated with the lives of middle-class women. Important feminist programs such as the movement to legalize abortion are sometimes regarded suspiciously as expressions of bourgeois selfishness" (70).[7] In such cases, the failure to take into consideration the most basic questions of coercion, abuse, and violence against women, which cross class lines, while holding mental reservations about the importance of class distinctions, results in stagnation of an urgently required political agenda. Similarly, a confrontation on the question of class blurs other important considerations and is frequently blind to the sociosexual division of labor, including the allocation of salaried employment

---

[7]For example, Schutte cites a *Fem* study indicating that in Mexico, "where there is a limited abortion law, it is estimated that as much as twenty percent of female mortality may result from illegal abortions" (70), and that as many as one million illegal abortions (recall that the population of Mexico is about sixty million) are performed in that country each year.

along specific gender lines within and between the various class strat-
ifications.

We also need to account for generational factors. The situation of
women has changed in the past twenty or thirty years. As Doris Meyer
reminds us, whereas "women authors have remained outside many of
these literary-political debates until recent years," recently in both the
political and the literary spheres "the larger profile accorded women's
writing in Latin America has focused attention on another side of
human experience and has thereby called into question certain assumptions about societal values in a historical context. . . . Women
are writing about the problems of being female in Latin America, and
their words have a healthy, subversive resonance" (7–8). Women in
Latin America are consciously involved in a practice that has long been
recognized in their male counterparts. To play on a famous structural-
ist formulation, to write in Latin America is for them more than a verb,
transitive or intransitive—it is a revolutionary act.

Furthermore, there are now younger scholars, in academia and in
the public arena, whose attitudes have been at least partially shaped
by commitment to the developing debate about feminist issues in
Latin America and to the recognition that the discussion of women's
specific problems cannot be continually subordinated to and incor-
porated in the latest version of a masculinist theory of emancipation.
Ana Lydia Vega's fictional exchange in "La Gurúa Talía" humorously
points out the continuing problems attendant on the remnants of this
type of subordination in a contemporary setting when a modern Des-
demona writes to the advice column for help in dealing with the
rhetorical dominance of her creole Othello:

> [Desdémona the Long-Suffering]: When I shyly express my dissatisfac-
> tion with the confined urban status he has imposed on me, he gets
> hysterical and yells that "women's liberation is a North American capital-
> ist mythification to destroy the Puerto Rican revolutionary unity." Could
> he be right after all? . . .
> [Gurúa Talía]: This enlightened neomachismo is much more sophisti-
> cated and perverse than the traditional paleomachismo. It is endowed
> with "a good conscience" impermeable to critical bullets. Let me explain:
> Even if you cite Marx backward and forward that "woman is man's
> proletariat," he will always find a way to twist you up in his theoretical
> jungles. . . . His opportunistic rhetoric is infinitely chameleonic. (*Tramo*
> 266–67)

The infamous neomachista of this essay is yet another example of what Vega calls elsewhere, with striking concision, the "pobres-puertorriqueños-oprimidos-por-el-imperialismo-yanqui pero a la vez sinvergüenzas opresores de sus pobres-puertorriqueñas-oprimidas-por-el-imperialismo-yanqui mujeres" ("Bípeda" 45) 'poor-Puerto-Rican-men-oppressed-by-Yankee-imperialism but at the same time shameless oppressors of their poor-Puerto-Rican-oppressed-by-Yankee imperialism women.' Imperial imposition, Vega clearly indicates, is only one aspect of the politics of oppression, which have roots both deeper and more varied than the simplistic propaganda formulas used to deflect serious accusations of unequal treatment. The formulation of Antillean writer Maryse Condé offers a concise, general understanding of the issue that is as applicable to Spanish-speaking Latin America as it is to the French-speaking Caribbean: "The colonial problem was not that of the importation of a foreign culture and of its imposition onto a national reality which it slowly attempted to destroy—as is the case in most colonized countries. Rather, the problem lay in the difficulty inherent in the attempt to construct, from incongruous and dissimilar elements that coexist in such a general climate of aggression, harmonious cultural forms" (quoted in Lionnet 188–89). The result of this process of heterogeneous appropriation and adaptation is what Françoise Lionnet calls, in her striking metaphor, a "quilted state" (189). To consider the particularities of a Latin American feminist practice means to take into account the varying textures of the patches and the decorative stitchery of the quilt, to examine the implications of a heterogeneous culture, and to add to the analysis considerations of class and race. The critic must not forget the garment from which the patches were cut—or, to put it in another way, the pre-existing, if repressed or fading, ideological loadings—while appreciating the new pattern, with its inevitable misrecognitions and shifts in positionality.

To take only one instance, the lower-class woman—mulatta, mestiza, or Indian—is generally misconceived/misrecognized by the institutionalized culture under the image of an ignorant (uneducated, unused to metropolitan customs, clinging to quaint and inapplicable rural practices or superstitions) or stupid (uneducable) childbearer (generally as producer of many children), associated with food preparation and consumption (the overweight woman in braids perpetually patting out tortillas), primarily concerned with housework or, if in the

workplace, relegated to those jobs traditionally associated with domestic work (as servants, cleaning women, workers in clothing facto-
ries). The list of attributes sounds strikingly similar, with a slight shift
in modification to accommodate the overlay of a different value structure, to that associated with women from a more leisured class: ignorant (girls don't need schooling) or unintelligent (the better to massage
a man's ego), childbearer (the cult of the mother), primarily concerned
with the state of the house (supervising the servants) or handicrafts
associated with genteel domestic labors (fine embroidery, for example). Much work is required on the historical processes that resulted in
such inherited ideological loadings; there is an urgent need to study
the suturing of imaginary connotations and real conditions with an
eye both to the particular constellations of meaning structures in Latin
America and to the woefully misnamed "universals" of female solidarity. A much more nuanced awareness of the contingency of truth is
essential whenever we explore the interpellation (Louis Althusser's
word) of subjects-in-process in a socially committed reading.

Or to take another example, this one bearing on middle-class pre-
conceptions. Amy Kaminsky has incisively deconstructed the much-
abused phrase "No soy femenista, pero..." (I'm not a feminist, but...)
deployed as a protective mechanism by Latin American women critics
residing in Latin America (the situation, as she notes, is somewhat
different for Latinoamericanas who have lived abroad for a number of
years). Kaminsky was surprised to find that "feminist activity is much
more vital and diverse among political activists than among academics." Why? "One of the reasons that academic feminism . . . is so slow
to grow in Latin America and practically non-existent in its literary criticism and theory, is women scholars' fear of having their sexuality impugned." Bluntly speaking, they are nervous that "feminism" might
be used as a code word for "lesbian" (225). This misreading of feminist
activism as a specific preference for same-sex relations is, I submit,
only the first and least crucial of the critical misprisions. More important, the lesbian, or perceived lesbian, falls into the category of women
exempt from the respect mandated for decent women. For a woman
whose situation is already made precarious by her ambition for a
career, the threat inherent in a perceived rejection of the necessary,
and necessarily masculine, protective screen is vast and, understandably, gives pause. The question for the critic safely ensconced in her
U.S. institution is how to read these guarded admissions of support

and how to negotiate—as, for example, in the particular case of Sylvia Molloy, which Kaminsky examines—the disjunction between an entirely mainstream critical practice and a radically lesbian-feminist fictional production.

It would be impossible for me to explore the manifestations and implications of these social structures fully in the space of a single book. Such work, clearly, requires the participation of many scholars from many different fields: historians, ethnographers, anthropologists, sociologists, labor relations specialists, political scientists, and so on. My intention has merely been to underline some of the salient characteristics of these social constructions so as to provide a minimal understanding of how the social assumptions undergird and infect more strictly literary concerns, to offer a sketch of some of the forms of *la ¿loca? ¿criolla?* and to hint at the boundaries of her attic.

That women often participate in and actively promote their own victimization in this respect is commonly known and provides feminist activists and thinkers much puzzlement and embarrassment. Yet, feminist literary critics, too, have been caught in unwitting contradiction. Attentive to the theoretical implications of the subjugation of women, we may still be captured by the metaphor, now turned on its head, of woman as the embodiment of nature and may cite with approbation texts that are symptomatic of the historical repression of women. The idealization of the mother in traditional terms as the nurturing, desexualized woman whose only agency is found in abnegation, for example, is not the exclusive domain of reactionary thinkers and fictional writers. The "Boom" writers of the 1960s and 1970s, who deconstructed and resemanticized so many of the meaning systems of official mythology, seem to have been oblivious to the degree to which they reaffirmed the myth of the maternal body as equivalent to a state of nature and of maternal "nature" as an unproblematic concept. Terrifyingly enough, this institutionalization of the figure of the feminine as a natural, primordial, but containable and manageable element, is evident even in the works of the Latin American female writer who is best known internationally, the openly feminist Chilean novelist Isabel Allende, who has arrived belatedly on the "Boom" scene twenty years after its vogue but with the same assumptions intact. In all these works, the maternal body may be a utopian site, but the mother's lack of access to subjectivity is a nonnegotiable given. In literature as in life, in Jessica Benjamin's words, "the moment women take advantage of the logic of universality and rebel against their confinement to the domestic sphere, the advocates of autonomy trot out the hidden gender clause" (201).

Gayatri Spivak comes as close as anyone to defining this strange amorphousness of the postcolonial woman, this real/fictional existence even in the writing of our male feminist allies: "It is a bold and helpful thing to restore the female element when it is buried in gender-conventions. . . . It is excellent to posit this female element as the irreducible madness of truth-in-law, but we are daily reminded that a little more must be undertaken to budge the law's oppressive sanity." And she continues with specific reference to Jacques Derrida's formulations in his "Living On/*Border Lines*," the companion piece to his very gender-conscious "Law of Genre": "It is not really a question of the 'institution' being able to 'bear' our more 'apparently revolutionary ideological sorts of "content" ' [she quotes from "Living On"] because we do not threaten its institutionality. It is rather an awareness that even the strongest personal goodwill on Derrida's [or Donoso's or Gabriel García Márquez's or Carlos Fuentes's] part cannot turn him quite free of the massive enclosure of the male appropriation of woman's voice, with a variety of excuses: this one being, it is not *really* woman" ("Displacement" 190). Castellanos would agree. And here we are talking not about the simplistically conceived versions of the notions of truth and falsity or reality and fiction but about the significance of an impacted, overdetermined history in the assessment of the identity politics of a particular society at a particular moment.

Moreover, women writers are not exempt. As Castellanos writes self-critically in *El uso de la palabra* (The use of words), "The recurrent persistence of certain figures—the helpless child, the trapped adolescent, the defeated single woman, the cheated wife—constitutes the unity of those books. Is there no other option? Within those established limits, yes there are. Escape, madness, death. . . . If we consider it carefully, neither the first nor the second set of options are really ways of life; instead, they are forms of death" (229). Thus, even her own work has been unable to locate possibilities for women to fulfill themselves as human beings; instead, she finds herself falling into the stifling preestablished categories: forms of death, not ways of life. Her options are not Attic elegance or imaginative displacement but rather confinement to a single place—the attic or the kitchen—or escape into madness.

When we turn from the general socio-literary context to the more narrowly defined one of literary-historical conventions, the field of study is correspondingly open. Questions that might usefully be asked in relation to the underexamined texts produced by Latin American women authors may include a discussion of characteristic genres and the potential reasons for such genre choice (why, for example, the outpouring of lyric poetry and why the narrative emphasis on the autobiography or its near relative, the pseudomemoir?), as well as examination of the strategies employed in the construction of these texts, the nuances of their enunciative structures, the influence of ideological constraints in the construction of the typical narrative—fictional or nonfictional—of women's lives, the social function of these texts in the societies of Latin America, the reception of these texts by women readers, the role of the critic and theoretician.

Rosario Castellanos in an article on Simone de Beauvoir discusses in germ many of these issues. She divides women authors into three categories based on their reaction to a generalized ("universal") perception that women are emotional beings, capable of flashes of intuition but unable to maintain the sustained rational efforts of pellucid intelligence. Castellanos turns aside from such traditional expressions of the value of women's perceptions because of their presumed proximity to nature. For her, questions of the "natural" capabilities of women and men, in terms defined by traditional considerations of philosophical or intellectual adequacy as such, tend to short-circuit discussion. Philosophy, after all, is one of those "Attic" domains defined by the absence of women—mad or sane—or of "feminine" qualities. So too, the woman's room, the attic, is philosophically off limits, described from the outside as the absence of valorized, implicitly masculine qualities. "Lucidity," she writes, "is apparently a quality (or a disgrace?) awarded to women with great parsimony and extreme infrequency." Castellanos's marking of the word "apparently" and her humorous ambivalence about the value of lucidity—quality or disgrace—signal both her awareness of the operations of the system and her ability to resist the common tendency to be co-opted by the influential structures of power. Women may or may not be lucid; whether lucidity is bane or boon is left undecided. Instead, she continues, "they are conceded . . . the fugitive lightning bolt of intuitions that light up a phenomenon . . . as long as it doesn't require any previous discipline, any intelligent effort, any effort of attention, or any consistent will" (*Juicios* 19). Attention, will, and intelligence define the male-appropriated approach to an object of knowledge; to women are left the untutored "natural" responses: animal instinct and unexplained "lightning bolts" of intuition. Castellanos is unconvinced by either the traditional male value of lucidity (in its standard definition) or the traditional female value of intuition (as a second-rate substitute). Nevertheless, she recognizes the power of these clichés in determining a woman's relation to writing, her ability to frame self-concepts. The women who accept this theory follow the path of subordination and abnegation. They have been locked out of the Attic and into the attic by their own inherent disabilities and misperceptions.

To counter such perceptions, she defines the qualities of the strong writer, who is both lucid and visionary. It is, in fact, this quality of a socially committed, poetically tinged lucidity, rather than a strictly defined veracity or even verisimilitude, that is most outstanding in her own texts, both prose and poetry; she intentionally and seriously proposes a counterbalance and counterforce to confront the overdetermined murmurings of official history and the even more deadly substrata of impacted cultural usages. To uncover the hidden aspects of things and name them represent, for her, the primary use value of the fully realized feminine text as a recontextualization of specific reading and writing practices in terms of political strategies. Her position, and implicitly the position she stakes out for other strong Latin American woman writers as well, is one of alterity, of double-voicing, in an uncommon sense: not the commonplace denigration/apotheosis of woman as a vaguely defined and safely distanced Other but another woman, a mestiza/criolla parallel in another context to what Luce Irigaray provocatively calls the Other Woman, a creative woman for whom social commitment is an enabling condition of writing, the difficulties of which it would be naïve to underestimate.

Let me make this point somewhat more specifically with what is only a slightly hyperbolic statement: Latin American women do not write. From this statement depend other corollaries, other truisms of standard Latin American literary history. Latin American women certainly do not write narrative. What little they do write—poetry, mostly—deserves oblivion. What narrative they produce, straightforward neorealist domestic fiction, does not stand up to comparison with the work of the great male writers of the Boom and after and is mercifully relegated to a mere footnote. The occasional exceptions—

Western-trained and European-oriented women such as María Luisa
Bombal in Chile, Elvira Orphée, Victoria and Silvina Ocampo in
Argentina, the Puerto Ricans Rosario Ferré and Ana Lydia Vega,
the Brazilian Clarice Lispector, or the Mexicans Elena Garro, Margo
Glantz, Barbara Jacobs, and Elena Poniatowska (whose non-Hispanic-
sounding last names are almost too suggestive)—neatly demonstrate
the point, but they represent something of a conundrum in traditional
literary histories. Certainly these women refuse to subscribe to the
synthetic, neatly patterned style typical of the traditional, nineteenth-
century realism of male narrative or to the other, recognizably constructed, pseudodisconnected narratives of the Boom. Their works,
like their lives, are fragmented, other-directed, marginally fictional-
ized. Yet these women are the privileged minority in society and in
literary history. And even privileged women are discouraged from taking their work seriously; they write, as Castellanos would say, from a
fictional but very real state of dependence. Often the women writers of
Latin America are denigrated and safely categorized under the heading of the *poetisas* (the poetesses), whose supposedly delicate, "feminine" lyrics are the equivalent of their painstakingly beautiful, equally
ornamental, implicitly useless embroidery. Few are accorded the ac-
colades of strength, lucidity, intelligence; the virile virtues grudgingly
handed out to the extraordinary Sor Juana Inés de la Cruz.

Nevertheless, the vast majority of Latin American women, unless
they have the great good luck to have access to the advantages implicit
in names like Glantz or Poniatowska—the advantages of birth, education, and affluence—do not write at all. Period. Black, mestiza, and
Indian women tend to be poor and illiterate. The extraordinary cam-
pesina may, in extraordinary circumstances, dictate her testimonial to
a more privileged, politically compromised poet, anthropologist, or
novelist, but even in such cases the unlettered woman is stripped of
agency. Rosemary Geisdorfer Feal has made the striking observation
that the Spanish editions of Rigoberta Menchú's testimony are credited to Elizabeth Burgos, the ethnographer who took the Guatemalan
woman's testimony and edited it with her; in contrast, the English
edition lists Menchú as author and Burgos as editor, a telling shift. Feal
comments on the loss of agency implied in this co-optation of authorship and on the political significance of such power plays, which in
effect counter the testifiers' appeal to immediacy and authenticity by
screening their words with a veil of art. As Feal notes, "To call the

speakers subject or object denies the creative, autonomous act they perform when they recount their lives; to call them characters confines them to a fictive world" (101–2). Rigoberta Menchú's is not the only case of such often well-meaning appropriation; other examples include *Si me permiten hablar . . . Testimonio de Domitila, una mujer de las minas de Bolivia (Let me speak! Testimony of Domitila, a Woman of the Bolivian Mines)*, dictated to Moema Viezzer; *Me llamo Rigoberta Menchú y así me nació la conciencia (I, Rigoberta Menchú: An Indian Woman in Guatemala)*, dictated to Elizabeth Burgos; Leonor Cortina's *Lucía* (Mexico); Claribel Alegría and D. J. Flakoll's *No me agarran viva: La mujer salvadoreña en la lucha (They'll Never Take Me Alive)* (El Salvador); Patricia Verdugo and Claudio Orrego's *Detenidos-desaparecidos: Una herida abierta* (Detained-disappeared: An open wound) (Chile); or Elena Poniatowska's nonfiction novel, *Hasta no verte Jesús mío* (Until we meet again, my Jesus), recreating the life of a Mexico City laundress and former soldadera pseudonymously named Jesusa Palancares in (more or less) her own words. Despite these caveats and concerns, however, it is important to reiterate that all these works—testimonials, novels, poems, stories, and plays (and I do not exclude those of the misnamed *poetisas* and of the recognizably privileged Ocampos and Glantzes of Latin America)—demonstrate a signal "lucidity," all represent important contributions to the still-nascent emergence of women's voices into the public forum, with all the revisionary resonances implicit in the unstifling of radically different perspectives.

The general, if trite, conclusion usually drawn from such works as appear in adequate press runs from mainstream Latin American presses and make it to English translation is framed in Poniatowska's title "La literatura de mujeres es parte de la literatura de los oprimidos" (Women's literature is literature of the oppressed). It is a realization that has been made many times, in slightly different terms, by writers of the first world as well as the third. Regardless of the in-fighting and the rejection of similarities between classes and notwithstanding the real concerns raised, for example, in the problematical attribution of testimonial authorship, Poniatowska's statement is nonetheless true on a variety of levels and has specific implications for Latin America that are more than trite: (1) Literature by Latin American women can clearly *not* afford the luxurious impulses or the strange urges besetting middle-aged European men. The record that needs to be set straight is always a more than personal one; the threat, in countries where intellectuals regularly "disappear" is not existential angst or encroaching senility but government security forces. (2) For the critic, assertions about these texts must be accompanied by readings made cumbersome through the need to introduce, even to a knowledgeable audience, a group of works that barely circulate even (or especially) within their own countries. (3) The critic is condemned to feel an uneasy suspicion that she may be behaving in her own context like Spivak's description of Rudyard Kipling in India, as the unwitting, and therefore all the more culpable, participant in a questionable cultural translation from a colonial to metropolitan context which enacts a literary structure of rape.[8] Well-intentioned mistranslation and misapplication of theory, like the equally unintended misrepresentation or oversimplification of primary texts, are specters that loom large in the minds of dedicated cultural critics.

Nevertheless, having made these assertions, I am left with the bedrock commonsense conclusions that in traditional Latin American letters something (however defined) has been left out and that whatever the social or ideological interests involved in maintaining these absences or repressions, the result is impoverishment for the entire community. The recognition and reevaluation of the contributions of women writers will necessarily pose a healthy challenge to the dominant discourse. For many critics this is more than enough. The need to name is itself a driving force that not only allows for the reinscription and insertion of feminine voices in the canon but also provides a space for alteration of the terms of that discourse from a dynamic stance, simultaneously both inside and outside the canon. The tension, nevertheless, between a need for an established body of common texts as the foundation that makes theory possible and a very particularized fear of any intellectual or political totalization is not easy to resolve.

To take the further step and posit that the "Other Women" in Latin America are also and necessarily feminist by political or philosophical orientation or that they are primarily driven by an agenda that emphasizes women's rights would, however, be a grave error. The puzzling

---

[8]Spivak writes: "The incantation of the names, far from being a composition of place, is precisely that combination of effacement-of-specificity *and* appropriation that one might call violation" ("Imperialism," 329). And she continues with a more general lesson derived from her reading of Kipling: "Unless third-worldist feminist criticism develops a vigilance against such tendencies [e.g., the structure of translation-as-violation], it cannot help but participate in them" (331).

silence of female academics in Latin America, their pronounced and much-noted aversion to anything that might taint them as "feminist," has been variously interpreted (for example, see Kaminsky 225). The fact remains that professional work by female academics in Latin America, whether for fear that their sexual orientation will be impugned or out of concern about validation in a system that does not recognize women's studies as a legitimate area of academic inquiry, is notably, consistently, overwhelmingly mainstream in topic and approach. Few academics demonstrate the kind of radical commitment to the broad definition of feminist activity implicit in the words of playwright Griselda Gámbaro. Gámbaro begins: "As a rule, a work is considered to touch on the theme of feminism when its leading characters are women and are repressed or in rebellion." For Gámbaro, however, this narrow definition represents an unnatural restriction of the field of feminist activity: "As far as I'm concerned, a work is feminist insofar as it attempts to explain the mechanics of cruelty, oppression, and violence through a story that is developed in a world in which men and women exist" (18–19). The key words here are "and women"; Gámbaro's comprehensive feminism compels recognition of the existence of women—a step most academic women in Latin America, for whatever reason, have not yet been able to take.[9]

In this respect, the mothers who march silently with pictures of the missing children anticipate the voices of those who use print as a medium for struggle. Writing in Latin America is, for men as well as women, often carried out under dismal conditions either at home or in exile, under the pressure of long days spent in other work, against the instituted situations of subtle or overt censorship, sometimes at the risk of imprisonment, torture, disappearance. Critics and authors of fiction alike have recognized as one of their prime responsibilities the obligation to commit themselves to the "mad" struggle over the history of meanings, not only to reveal the ways in which rhetorical concerns discursively construct reality but also to intervene in and counter these processes of reality construction. As Reed Way Dasenbrock reminds us in a more general philosophical context, theory

[9]I do not mean to be inappropriately dismissive here; I applaud, for example, the efforts of Ana Rosa Domenella, Elena Urrutía, and other organizers and participants in the Colegio de México's "taller de literatura femenina mexicana" and the labors of that same country's "Centros de Documentación sobre la Mujer." To date, relatively few contributions have appeared in print, however.

politicized is not adequate political theory (*Redrawing* 23). A similar statement might be, and often is, made in reference to fictional works in Latin America, where Argentine poet and short story writer Jorge Luis Borges is frequently and legitimately criticized as elitist for eschewing political commitment in his works, and Mexican novelist Carlos Fuentes may be accused of obscurantism. Fiction politicized is often not enough; the reading public demands more concrete manifestations of commitment. The demands are met not only in the silent protest of the mothers but by vociferously and persistently speaking out against the abuse of human rights (as do Elena Poniatowska, Ernesto Sábato, and Manilo Argueta), by taking an active part in political processes (as do Mario Vargas Llosa and José Cárdenal), by offering the organs for the circulation of repressed, alternative histories to the official stories circulated by government officials (as do Gabriel García Márquez and Isabel Allende), and by opposing repressive regimes that make terror the only definition of injustice, by which tactic governments participate in blurring or evading demands for more equitable laws.

Men and women alert to these baroquely quilted constructions in Latin American post-colonial society in general and to their specific implications for a gender-conscious evaluation, may still bear the weight of a "prefeminist" past, but current discussions impinge on their consciousness, if only as an alluring alternative or a distant threat. Despite societal pressures, no longer are women uncritically telling themselves the same story men have told them, and told about them, for centuries; no longer is exploitation by colonial powers the sole measure of oppression. No longer are women wholeheartedly accepting the systems of value that denigrate or ridicule activities and language associated with the private sphere. The United Nations' sponsorship of an International Year of the Woman (1974) provided a tremendous impetus to feminist rethinkings of traditional gender relationships, an influence that is still being felt. As men and women from throughout the world met in conferences and symposia, they began the exchange of ideas and the exploration of issues of significance to women which are continuing today. The Mexican magazine *Fem* has been in circulation since 1977. In 1988 the Universidad Nacional Autónoma de México sponsored an "Encuentro Internacional de Filosofía y Femenismo," and conferences and publications from established presses throughout Latin America and the United States demonstrate an increasing interest in writing by Latin American women and a growing commitment to research in gender issues on the part of literary critics, philosophers, social scientists, anthropologists, and other scholars. The sign "woman" is remotivating itself.

For Castellanos, the renegotiation of the gap between reality and fiction in the perception of women and woman's work offers an opportunity for reinvention as well: "It is not enough to imitate models proposed to us, which offer solutions to circumstances different from our own. It is not even enough to discover who we are. We must invent ourselves" (*Eterno* 194). Implicitly, we have to "invent ourselves" through continual reelaboration, reworking the crazy quilt of custom.

Theory or Strategy: Tactical Considerations

In Latin America, the general bias toward a revolutionary rather than a theoretical mode is quite clear, and strategy has been given in application a clear advantage over abstraction. There are a number of reasons for this general preference, though the issue is vexed. Certainly in the history of Latin America revolutionary practice has consistently overrun revolutionary theory—the specific cases of the revolutions in Mexico, Cuba, and Nicaragua leap to mind immediately, as do the events surrounding the overthrow of the military junta in Argentina. The political theory of revolution is constructed hastily, in the midst of fighting, or in a more leisurely manner, a posteriori. Theory following from, rather than guiding, practice, it may be argued, is the only authentic Latin American way.

At present, the body of texts necessary to the elaboration of a theoretical stance is still being constructed; it would perhaps be premature and overly optimistic to insist on theoretical interventions when so much of the groundwork is yet to be done. Yet, theory, no matter how provisional, has a way of authenticating itself in academic discourse, and underdevelopment in theoretical work is not viewed with the same sympathy and understanding in philosophical circles as economic underdevelopment. Likewise, the need for considered and positioned theoretical stances particular to Latin America is urgent, not only in response to the specific conditions obtaining there but also to avoid the more general impasses of work in feminism which Jardine has noted in another context:

What I perceived was a series of impasses between theory and praxis: theories of women or the feminine and their insistence on the (always) potentially subversive power of the feminine in patriarchal culture had produced either no possibility for social and political praxis or had resulted in a praxis that I perceived as being reactionary for women. At the same time, those who had chosen to reject or ignore the major theorists . . . most often produced no theory at all, and, in any case—in their refusal to listen to their own discourse—their praxis was often more reactionary than that of their feminine-minded sisters. (260–61)

One of the most striking aspects of this theory/praxis double impasse is the debilitating effect of a theoretical deficit in preventing women from listening to the implications of their own discourse. One very obvious example is that of the prominent Mexican feminist who in a radio program urged women to respond to sexual harassment in the workplace by informing their employers that they have an active venereal disease—AIDS by preference.[10] As a method of dealing with oppression the recommendation is, at the very least, theoretically unconsidered.

Furthermore, as we have seen, in the perceived absence of indigenous theory, the Latin Americanist tends to conscript other theories to fill the gap, ironically, uncritically, and sometimes inappropriately utilizing the resources of a first-worldist approach in the service of the critique of imperialism, creating strange hybrids of dubious applicability and—in the context of the nations of Latin America—with unacceptable political ramifications. This is one of the major unresolved issues of postcolonial feminist theory. Because of the continuing fear of cultural imperialism in the postcolonial nations, critics as well as writers of fiction obsessively question authenticity and usability, both in theory and in practice. Thus, such qualities as honesty, inclusiveness, and wholeness of being are implicitly weighted as morally superior to, for example, aesthetic concerns, which are implicitly less honest, more selective, less useful or usable. The authentic has the generative and creative force of being able to cut through falsification and mere fantasy; it represents as well a counterforce to both disorder and to the totalitarian imposition of order by violence. Authenticity,

---

[10]The radio program was aired in the summer of 1988. I might add, also, that my companion, a female university professor, was enthusiastically supportive of this clever way of defusing unwanted sexual advances.

says Lionel Trilling in his classic definition, "implies the downward movement through all cultural superstructures to some place where all movement ends, and begins" (12). To be authentic is to have a certain weight and force; the implicit contrast is with experience that does not have this ontological weight and is, therefore, flighty, inauthentic.

I mention Trilling in this context, despite the fact that most postcolonial thinkers would reject him and all he represents out of hand, because his Arnoldian meditations on the nature of sincerity and authenticity in relation to the Victorian frame of mind strike me as extraordinarily pertinent to the postmodern postcolonial discussion. And because they are so strikingly pertinent, the whole discussion needs to be reframed and problematized, its underlying assumptions examined, including such basic problems as the nonuniversality of the concept of authenticity and the circumscribing of usability in relation to who is allowed access to a tradition and how it can be used. As is the case with Gioconda Belli's character who sees the logic and frightening attraction of the romance of the revolutionary "comrade" as a means of resolving the "constant interrogation . . . between her rational 'I' and her other 'I,'" so too other writers and thinkers are looking for a resolution that guarantees authenticity without having to have recourse to "a Virginia Woolf–type room of her own."

Theory or strategy? Both carry the first requirement of authenticity; "strategy," with its military connotations, also suggests an immediate, weighty, practical—if violent—usability rather than the more distanced, aestheticized usability of the flights of theory. In Latin America pure theory, like pure blood, has lost most of its metaphorical and rhetorical appeal as a political instrument. Additionally, in an officially mestizo continent, the threat of cultural miscegenation looms less large as a call for alarm. The widely known anthology of essays *La sartén por el mango: Encuentro de escritoras latinoamericanas* (The skillet by the handle: Encounter with Latin American women writers) not only provides a touchstone for gender-conscious analysis of Latin American women's texts but also implicitly positions itself in relation to the theory/strategy question. Patricia Elena González and Eliana Ortega group the essays into three sections highly resonant of the orientation of feminist thought in Latin America: first, "Strategies"; then, "Perspectives"; and finally, "Squid in their ink: Testimonials." It is worthwhile to repeat that the testimonial form—both the more or less traditional autobiography and the more recent poetic or anthropological reconstructions of oral history—so heavily emphasized in much third-world and third-worldist work on women, is clearly making its mark on the organization of feminist thought in the region. Already the recognition is widespread that, in Stephen Heath's words, "a woman reading is not the same as reading as a woman," and its logical corollary, "a man reading is never now not the same as reading as a man" ("Male Feminism" 26–27), is gaining currency. What it is to read as a woman in the Latin American context, however, is instructive. The concept relies, if we follow the implicit rhetoric of *Sartén*, on the traditional vocabulary of domesticity and the traditional role of the housewife exchanging information and housekeeping tips with her friends. "Skillet by the handle," "Squid in their ink," "The writing kitchen": such titles mark the public, philosophical call for legitimation of a space traditionally associated with and denigrated as female. Such titles also imply the imbrication of rhetorical modes in the production of meaning and demand a reading other than a traditional, literary, masculinist one.

The final essay of the "Strategies" section, Josefina Ludmer's "Tretas del débil" (Feints of the weak), presents a careful and attentive close reading of Sor Juana Inés de la Cruz's "Reply to Sor Filotea" which is clearly informed about but not determined by the various poststructuralist theories and implicitly engaged in the current feminist debates about representation, power, difference, and the ideological import of masculinist rhetorical and political conventions. Ludmer's "strategies" are never naïvely imagined, however, and they imply a specific "perspective" that both takes the woman writer out of a narrow repertoire of options for representability and at the same time reevaluates the importance for theory, and for a critique of imperialism itself, of a rhetoric derived from the private sphere:

> A fundamental datum is show there: that the regional spaces the dominant culture has extracted from the personal and the quotidian and has constituted as separate kingdoms (politics, science, philosophy) are constituted in the woman precisely at that point considered personal and are indissociable from it. And if the personal, private, and quotidian are included as a point of departure and perspective for other discourses and practices, they disappear as personal, private, and quotidian: that is one of the possible results of the feints of the weak. (54)

Ludmer brilliantly describes a reading practice that repoliticizes writing strategies without simply collapsing them into some reductionist version of use value, so as to effect a change in the conditions of representability which will assist in rescuing the past—recovering for the modern reader the genius of Sor Juana. She offers a repertoire of possible tactics useful in the present and with a continuing importance in the perspectives for the future.[11]

One of the most attractive features of Ludmer's essay is her deployment of the "tretas del débil" in a more theoretically generalizable framework. The weak (woman) strategically refers not only to Sor Juana and not only to the colonial nun but also to Ludmer, the postcolonial critic. In divining Sor Juana's tactics, Ludmer hints at her own: to take from tradition whatever is salvageable and useful, to borrow from other writers what is needful and helpful, to fill in the gaps with her own meditations. Likewise, I propose a parallel construction of a strategic practice for this book, as I try to build an applicable feminist strategy based on an infrastructure of evolved and evolving Latin American theory, while taking from first-world feminist theory that which seems pertinent and complementary. A pinch of this, and a smidgeon of that.

The sample strategies I shall outline offer general approximations that are tailored and made more specific to a particular author in the subsequent chapters. These outlines, shorter than essays, longer than definitions, provide some basic theoretical grounding for the strategies. Readers are advised to read in this section as in a recipe book: not beginning to end and top to bottom but picking and choosing at will or at random. I have one further note: the strategies are not mutually exclusive, even if the readings in chapters that follow may at times seem to give that impression. I could imagine, for example, taking an author and exploring the possibilities of a single brief text as

---

[11]I would also like to recognize the work of Lucía Guerra-Cunningham in the same direction, especially the passionate and provocative material included in "Estrategías discursivas de la mujer latinoamericana como subjeto/objeto de la escritura" (Discursive strategies of the Latin American woman as subject/object of writing), a section of her essay "Las sombras de la escritura." Guerra-Cunningham, like Ludmer and González and Ortega, uses the metaphor of discursive strategies to outline a potential feminist literary practice. Her list of suggestions includes "the aesthetic phenomena of silence and the void, the palimpsest, the diglossia of the feminine, mimicry with a transgressive value, and the feminization of other dominated groups, visible or blank margins that modify the assimilated intertextual space creating signifying fissures in the phallogocentric ideological system" (143). As this project was far advanced when Guerra-Cunningham's essay came to my attention, I welcome the partial overlap in our categories as independent validation of their significance.

it depicts an entire repertoire of strategic interventions. The current arrangement of the book seemed preferable, for it allowed for more variety in our literary diet.

Tactical Deployment

silence

One reaction to the pressures of the dominant social force is silence. Initially, however, silence is not a response but a condition imposed from outside: silencing, rather than silence freely chosen. Friedrich Nietzsche, whose ideas on women generally do not win him a place in the hearts of feminists, was nevertheless able to recognize the monstrous quality of an upper-class woman's "education" as a process of repression into silence. "They are supposed to have neither eyes nor ears, nor words, nor thoughts for this—their 'evil,'" he writes. As girls, they learn that they must not know too much, not even (or especially) about their own, originarily evil natures. Then, hurled into reality upon her marriage, the young woman is confronted with the "evil" her honor demands she not understand. Her response: "the same deep silence as before. Often a silence directed at herself, too. She closes her eyes to herself" (127–28). She is idealized/idolized in myth, in the fantasy constructions of culture, but the public show of respect forces the wife and mother into abjection. Constrained by the absolute requirement of ignorance as a condition of goodness and suitability for married life, she is unable to imagine a circumstance in which the silence may be broken. This silence is not always imposed from the outside; women have tended to accept the traditional role allotted them in exchange for the material comforts and social status accruing from a husband's name.

Octavio Paz sees a similar dynamic of reality construction in the specific case of the Mexican woman. In his 1959 classic, *The Labyrinth of Solitude*, he writes: "Woman is an incarnation of the life force, which is essentially impersonal. Thus it is impossible for her to have a personal, private life, for if she were to be herself—if she were to be mistress of her own desires, passions, or whims—she would be unfaithful to herself" (36–37). Like Nietzsche, by whom he is at least partially inspired, Paz sees the socially constructed figure of woman as a vessel (incarnating will but with no will of her own) as representing sexuality and desire but with no control over her own desire. By way of "compensation" for this repression, says Paz, "the myth of the 'long-suffering Mexican woman is created," internalizing and institutionalizing a socially approved iconic masochism. This idealized figure of the woman as nature's victim is hypostatized in the injunction "No one is allowed to be disrespectful to ladies," which officially recognizes and pays tribute to her suffering, while it further paralyzes the wife and mother behind a spurious mask of custom that insists upon seeing woman as a symbolic function. Paz continues: "This 'respect' is often a hypocritical way of subjecting her and preventing her from expressing herself. Perhaps she would usually prefer to be treated with less 'respect' (which, after all, is only granted to her in public) and with greater freedom and authenticity" (38). We have returned, once again, to the centrality of the concept of authenticity—this time, not as a personal quality but rather as a masculine social grace associated with the right to a public voice: "authentic" rather than "hypocritical" speech about women.

Paz's sympathetic reading of the plight of Mexican women may momentarily obscure the fact that even in the best of cases these women he describes have not yet been allowed to open their eyes and their mouths. Society does not allow women to express themselves, and neither does Paz; instead, he speaks for them. Paz's "perhaps" in his hypothetical creation of a woman's response sounds rather strikingly like Nietzsche's ventriloquism or Freud's famous question, "What do women want?" No woman's voice attests to the validity or inaccuracy of his suppositions. And even if women, as Paz supposes, do want to express themselves freely, authentically, Paz suggests that the entire fabric of society would be at risk and would naturally oppose them: "How can we agree to let her express herself when our whole way of life is a mask designed to hide our intimate feelings?" (38). The "our" here requires careful attention. It seems clear that the expansively inclusive phrase omits one-half of the species and suggests an applicability limited only to a community of men—"us (men)" versus "them (women)"—in which the function of women is not only to mask themselves in myth but also to provide a comfortable, silent, maleable mask for their men as well, so that their privacy can be protected. Men, in this model, have the choice of speech or silence, a choice contingent in either case upon the continued silence of women.

The revolutionary response to silencing is resemanticization: to use

silence as a weapon (to resort to silence) or to break silence with
hypocrisy. One scenario for a response of the repressed to the re-
presser may take form in the strong woman whose mode of resistance
consists in playing with the cherished myths of the dominant society
and secretly reversing their charge; for instance, here is a hoary tale,
much repeated, in Nietzsche's version: "When a man stands in the
midst of his own noise, in the midst of his own surf of plans and
projects, then he is apt also to see quiet, magical beings gliding past
him and to long for their happiness and seclusion: *women*. . . . Yet!
Yet! . . . The magic and the most powerful effect of women is, in
philosophical language, action at a distance *actio in distans:* but this
requires first and above all—distance" (124). It is worth pausing briefly
at this quotation, for the terms of Nietzsche's misogyny are archetypal.
In this little scene, the man, energetic, creative, full of plans and
projects and the stuff of philosophical discourse, looks on women as
the pure, silent, tranquil counterpoint to his own busy materiality and
nostalgically imagines the joys of her confinement, a confinement
that, he soon admits, is dictated not by the inexpressible wishes of the
women but by his own need for distance and silence to complement
his close-pressed world of noise. The woman is not, in Nietzsche's
scheme, the place of a powerful repressed otherness; rather, she is an
open space, a present/absent, voiceless aesthetic object. What is worse
is that women have been coerced into accepting this marginal, magical
role: it is, after all, the basis for Castellanos's critique of the first,
despised category of women writers, the mystic poets.

Derrida, in his comment on this passage, highlights the deconstruction of woman into an abstract figure of distancing: "As non-identity,
non-appearance, simulacrum, she is the *abyss of* distance, the distancing of distance, the thrust of spacing, distance itself—distance *as such,*
if one could still say that, which is no longer possible." I note without
comment Derrida's coy marking of the unsayable, "distance *as such,*"
the intermission of a Nietzschean philosophical language in the catalogue of negatives, and go on: "There is no essence of woman because
woman separates, and separates herself off from herself. From the
endless, bottomless depths, she submerges all essentiality, all identity,
all propriety, and every property. Blinded in such a way, philosophical
discourse flounders. . . . Woman is one name for this nontruth of
truth" ("Question" 179). In a single, lyrical evocation, truth and nontruth, madness, silence, blindness are all convulsively thrown to-

gether, along with more prosaic (weighty?) matters of propriety and property as the exclusive preserve of women. The rich stream of Nietzsche's prose, and of Derrida's exegesis, is sufficient to drown any individual woman. Silence and distance require no thinking subject, nothing approaching will or personality, only anonymity and representability. Says Rosario Castellanos: "Because personality is exactly what a woman has yet to achieve. Passively, she accepted being converted into a muse because it's necessary to remain at a distance and keep silent. And be beautiful" (*Mujer* 23).

A woman who is neither passive nor accepting may yet preserve the advantages of distance and silence for her own reasons, using distance to her advantage, using the mask of silence to slip away. Silence, once freed from the oppressive masculinist-defined context of aestheticized distance and truth and confinement and lack, can be reinscribed as a subversive feminine realm. Trinh T. Minh-ha briefly and suggestively sketches another scene: "On the one hand, we face the danger of inscribing femininity as absence, as lack and blank in rejecting the importance of the act of enunciation. On the other hand, we understand the necessity to place women on the side of negativity and work in undertones. . . . Silence is so commonly set in opposition to speech. Silence as a will to say or a will to unsay and as a language of its own has barely been explored" ("Not you" 73–74). Trinh's observation, which has clearly been influenced by her own work as a film maker, has enormous implications for a Latin American feminist practice, not only in film theory and in the study of films by Latin American women directors but also in the study of other works that choose not to create a spoken/written matrix of configurative meaning and only point mutely: Rosario Castellanos's novel *Balún-Canán*, for example, in which the pretextual silencing of the indigenous population of rural Chiapas is both signaled as the essential plot element and left essentially unbroken (it would be utopian and misleading to break that historical silence). Other fruitful areas of study would include close analyses of women's paintings, from the colonial period's intriguing *entelequias mudas* (mute entelechies), drawn at the behest of Catholic confessors, to the disturbing surrealistic self-portraits of Frida Kahlo and beyond.

Another scenario makes use of misleading speech to mask an essential silence. One such tactic, suggests Castellanos, is to use the myth of silence to create a free space for either intellectual activity or simple privacy: "Women have been accused of being hypocrites, and the accusation is not unfounded. But hypocrisy is the answer that the oppressed give to the oppressor, that the weak give to the strong, that the subordinates give to the master" (25); that is, she suggests, women give the oppressors the response they want to hear but maintain the mental reservations that permit a minimal independence of thought. "Sir," says Victoria Ocampo to one of the men charged with reforming Argentina's civil code in 1935, "slaves always try to deceive. Only free beings learn to despise lies" (*Testimonios* 10:44). She is referring, of course, to the accusation that women must be treated differently under the law because they are naturally mendacious, that they tell men one thing and then go out and do something quite different, that they practice subterfuge and covert manipulation.

Under old traditional codes, the woman—ambiguously the figure of truth or of untruth—remained silent and withdrawn. In the counterhegemonic response to this official silencing, she executes a dizzying dance of negativity, appropriating silence as a tactic neither for saying nor for unsaying but for concealing a coded speech between the lines of the said and the unsaid. In the felicitous phrase of Brazilian novelist Clarice Lispector, "since it is necessary to write, at least do not smudge the space between the lines with words" (*Legion* 114). This tactic of speaking between the lines and selectively, playfully, withholding speech is the essence of what Ludmer calls the transformatory machine of Sor Juana Inés de la Cruz's radical manipulation of her rhetoric:

La escritura de Sor Juana es una vasta máquina transformadora que trabaja con pocos elementos; en esta carta ["Respuesta a Sor Filotea"] la matriz tiene sólo tres, dos verbos y la negación: *saber, decir, no.* . . . Saber y decir, demuestra Juana, constituyen campos enfrentados para una mujer. . . . Decir que no se sabe, no saber decir, saber sobre el no decir: esta serie liga los sectores aparentemente diversos del texto (autobiografía, polémica, citas) y sirve de base a dos movimientos fundamentales que sostienen las tretas que examinaremos: en primer lugar, separación del saber del campo del decir; en segundo lugar, reorganización del campo del saber en función del no decir (callar). (48)

Sor Juana's writing is a vast transformatory mechanism that works with only a few elements: in this letter ["Reply to Sor Filotea"] the matrix has only three: two verbs and the negation: *to know, to say, not.* . . . To know and to say, Juana shows, constitute opposing camps for a woman. . . . To say that she does not know, not to know how to say, to know about not saying: this series links the apparently diverse sectors of the text (autobiography, polemic, quotation) and serves as the basis for two fundamental movements that sustain the tactics that we will examine: in the first place, the separation of knowledge from the field of speech; in the second place, the reorganization of the field of knowledge in function of not saying (keeping quiet).

I shall return to this quotation later to discuss how Sor Juana's manipulation of the code is based on an intimate understanding of the function of the negation which goes beyond the symbolic logic of "A"/"not-A"; that is, her intuition of a *no decir* that is quite different from *callar*, in which the traversal of speech by the negative allows for a trace of its passage, maintaining her essential self at a safe spatiotemporal distance that both permits her free play of thought and subtly establishes her own agency as the concealed subjectivity alone capable of bridging the gap of silence. At this point I merely wish to note that Sor Juana's letter, on the one hand, recognizes the injustice of the traditional imposition of silence on women; her argument against Saint Paul's statement—"Mulieres in Ecclesiis taceant, non enim permittitur eis loqui" 'Women are silent in church; they are not permitted to speak'—outlines an exegetical practice grounded in the scholastic tradition but clearly departing from it in a prototypical feminist reading. On the other hand, Sor Juana in her autobiographical revelations about the necessity to hide her knowledge also intimates that, in Ludmer's words, "silence constitutes a space of resistance before the power of the others" (50). For Sor Juana an obligatory early silence, which could be coded as untruth or as hypocrisy, is unmasked by her present breaking of silence (the confession or autobiography), in which her very frankness could well code other resistances, other silences.

As a political strategy, however, to embrace silence is clearly of limited value. Silence alone cannot provide an adequate basis for either a theory of literature or concrete political action. Eventually, the woman must break silence and write, negotiating the tricky domains of the said and the unsaid, the words written down, as Lispector would have it, smudging the page, and the words left, for whatever reason, between the lines. I am reminded of Eugen Gomringer's concrete poem, which raises the question of silence as a wall of silence and as the speaking/writing of the word "silence" in a disembodied command, a fact without a speaker, bricks in the wall:

silencio silencio silencio
silencio silencio silencio
silencio   silencio
silencio silencio silencio
silencio silencio silencio   (27)

Only in breaking silence—the chink in the wall—can the writer hope
to establish any form of critique, any potentially revolutionary opposition to the oppressive system.

By its very nature, however, any radical breaking of silence remains
a utopian exercise, always impaired by the system of discourse that
establishes silence as a norm and the transformatory mode as a revolutionary praxis. It is more reasonable in such circumstances to reflect
upon options for thwarting co-optation or recuperation of the feminine within established models through a practice of tactical resistance, of deliberately eschewing polished definition, deliberately
finessing issues of closure, deliberately unraveling the familiar, uncomfortable fabric of self and society. "I write," says Puerto Rican
Rosario Ferré, "because I am poorly adjusted to reality. . . . This destructive urge that moves me to write is tied to my need to hate, my
need for vengeance. I write so as to avenge myself against reality and
against myself; I write to give permanence to what hurts me and to
what tempts me" ("The Writer's Kitchen," 228). How to write of this
reality that both wounds and seduces is a recurrent problem; Ferré
cogently recognizes that her practice as a feminine, feminist writer is
inevitably bound up in her involvement with the relations of a dominantly masculinist power structure that seduces as it wounds her.
Ferré realistically, and painfully, reminds us that to write is for her to
write out of both hatred and love—not mere impossible rejection but
the effective resistance to co-optation inscribed in the bridging of
contradiction.

appropriation

In one of her autobiographical notes, Victoria Ocampo comments: "I
resisted reading in Spanish. . . . I was submerged in French and English literature, which is for us a little like our Greek and our Latin"
(*Testimonios* 10:15). Like her countryman Jorge Luis Borges, her early
education neatly suggested that Spanish was the oral language, En-

glish, French, and Italian, the languages of culture and intellectual activity. The mark of this early training is evident throughout Victoria Ocampo's writings. With the exception of the Chilean mestiza poet and Nobel Prize winner Gabriela Mistral, whom she greatly admired, Ocampo's most loving attention and most insistent references are to European authors—Virginia Woolf and Vita Sackville-West, George Eliot, Jane Austen, and the Brontës, Colette, the countess de Noailles, Claudel, Valéry, and Camus, Dante—many of whom she translated into Spanish for her fellow Argentinians. She dedicates the first volume of her *Testimonios* to Virginia Woolf, noting, "My only ambition is to be able to write one day, more or less well, more or less badly, but *like a woman*," and recognizing that all the essays in the volume were written under the particular sign of the spiritual hunger awoken in her by her conversations with and her reading the works of her English friend (8–9). But to live and write as a woman in the Argentina of 1935 was not as easy as in Virginia Woolf's England. Argentina, she explains in her letter to Woolf, is more like the England of the Brontës' time: "similar, but worse" (13).

Ocampo's consciousness of living in a infernal version of a Brontëan England rather than the more favorable climes of post-Victorian England, coupled with her desire to help create a more equitable situation for her fellow countrywomen, gives a particular messianic fervor to her prose, a particular urgency to her desire to share the fruits of her vast, polyglot reading with her compatriots. This same consciousness also sparks a recognition of the need to withhold herself from token, politically motivated praise. Thus, her acceptance speech for the Vaccaro Prize is carefully modulated to avoid the appearance of co-optation. The double entendres of her opening sentence are obvious even to the most complacent: "The Vaccaro Prize, awarded to me by the commission presided over by Doctor Bernardo Houssay (and that presidency says it all), recognizes excellences of the sort that . . . would justify in me an attitude similar to that of Sartre with the Nobel Prize" (*Testimonios* 7:231). Why then, after refusing so many prizes, does she accept this one? Her reasons are clearly, if ambiguously, political. She accepts for the other women, the ones who have not been granted the recognition they deserve. Her acceptance speech ends thus:

> When in 1953 a group of women were locked into the Buen Pastor prison, Mother Gertrudis asked us each to put an identifying sign on our aprons

so that we could be distinguished from each other. We got the idea it would be more worthwhile to write our entire names, and wear them on our breasts, where they could be easily seen. A prison mate, María Rosa González, embroidered my name in green thread on a strip of white ribbon. When I left jail . . . I unsewed my name and took it with me. It is one of my most precious souvenirs.

Gentlemen, friends: I will keep the Vaccaro Prize medal with that little white cloth ribbon. (240)

The whole scene is highly overdetermined. Ocampo reminds her audience of the marking of the prison apron—in itself the symbol of the housewife—with a rebellious sign, not the prison number that deindividualizes the inmates but, in a small revolutionary act, the entire name, embroidered (the womanly art) on a ribbon. Ocampo's identity is partly bound up in this ribbon, embroidered for her by another prisoner, a reminder both of solidarity within the prison walls and of the ineluctable walls themselves and the intolerance that puts all adult women into nameless aprons and encloses them behind the metaphorical walls of their home-prison. To preserve the Vaccaro medal, the almost-rejected award received from the hands of Bernardo Houssay, next to this humble product of a prisoner's making is an ambivalent gesture, reminding her (male) audience of her reasons—à la Sartre—for refusing the "honor," reminding her (female) audience of her ample reasons for accepting in their name. As she says earlier in the speech, referring to a line from Gabriela Mistral: "I see no valid reason for accepting this Vaccaro Prize from you, gentlemen friends, except that I too have chewed stones with my woman's gums" (239).

Ocampo would agree with Rosario Castellanos on the need for women to reinvent themselves, critically and creatively, and while repeatedly deploring her own inability to reinvent in the more traditionally creative genres—the novel, poetry—she puts her vast erudition to the task of a critical reelaboration in her voluminous essays and in her autobiography. The result of this indirect but careful critical attention to the situation of Latin American women through her readings of European women writers is a practice based on selective appropriation of whatever material may be available—A Room of One's Own, the poems of Valéry, the Vaccaro medal, a scrap of embroidered ribbon—for her cause. Through this means, Victoria Ocampo intends to invent the self through a judicious self-distancing, to observe the practices of her country meticulously by first sensitizing herself to its particular adumbrations of difference in her meditations on the works of others—of foreigners, men and women. From this perspective, it is useful to linger on the otherwise unmemorable final terms of Enrique Pezzoni's eulogy:

> The pages of Victoria Ocampo must be reread from this perspective [of tearing down myths]. Desire of approximation, heroic decision of distanciation. In 1929 Victoria wrote an article motivated by her reading of Henri Michaux's *Ecuador*. She tells Michaux: "Do you remember how much we admired certain ancient Chinese paintings where the void became sensual and significative through a branch or a bird drawn like a title on a corner of the cloth? The title of the void. In that empty space we recognized the protagonist, the principal intention of the artist . . . as that which sometimes issues forth from silence. Our pampa, our river remind me of those pictures. But in what strikes a chord with our soul, the brief drawing . . . is only sketched: the title is missing." Here, completely defined, is Victoria's adventure. . . . The true title is still missing. May we know how to find it. (150)

What is striking about this passage is not, as Pezzoni imagines, the lack of a proper name—in some sense the "true title" has long ago announced its existence in the embroidered ribbon—but the layering and revalorization of appropriation which create the composite image of the pampas according to Victoria Ocampo. Inspired by Michaux's *Ecuador*, she writes to share her definition of the pampas, which is, for both her and Michaux, mediated by her superimposition of Chinese painting: the Argentine landscape recreated through a bricolage of Chinese and French elements.

Compare this 1929 comment to her later evocation of the pampas, mediated now not by Michaux and Chinese painting (and, in my quotation, by Enrique Pezzoni) but by Emily Brontë, who never knew of the name her books were making for her; by Virginia Woolf, who was finally, posthumously, achieving the name her works deserved; and by Gabriela Mistral, the pen name of the Nobel-laureate poet whose given name, Lucila Godoy Alcayaga, is never mentioned:

> I feel as comforted by the success [of Virginia Woolf] as by that of Emily Brontë, lost in the Yorkshire moors. . . . I took Gabriela [Mistral] to several *estancias* near Mar de Plata during that summer, and together we looked at plants, stones, grasses. In Balcarce I showed her the *curro,* a

spiny bush covered in March with white flowers that smell like vanilla. The curro is considered a national plague; nevertheless I like it so much that when it flowers I always go to visit it. Gabriela later wrote to me: "I continue to live with the stones, the grasses, and the little animals from our America. . . . I see that geometry of thorns, that look and do not touch, that machine gun of silence. . . . You could be like that." (*Testimonios* 10:20–21)

The empty space defined nostalgically in her 1929 letter/essay to Michaux by a silence broken in the flap of a bird's painted wing has metamorphosed into something quite different in her recollections of Mistral's 1938 visit. The terms have changed, as has the nature of the appropriative gesture; it is now something less akin to the serenity of Chinese painting and more charged with the tensions of Emily Brontë's moors. And here, Ocampo frees herself from her private reluctance to give this affinity a name, the heritage of her training in the honorable shyness of a girl of good family. Through Mistral, she intimates her similarity to the curro, the "machine gun of silence," a common plague, a national symbol, a beautiful, ineradicable weed. In reconstructing the bits and pieces of her vast storehouse of knowledge to fit present needs, Ocampo not only gives herself over to the appropriative gestures of a transcultural bricolage but also struggles with the various forms and domains of cultural knowledge as they impinge upon, contradict, and clarify one another, outlining her own genealogy as a prickly, persistent weed, clearly sketching the configurations of her own region through a necessary attentiveness to the dual demands of an audience divided between the nativist and the Eurocentric.

cultivation of superficiality

In Julio Cortázar's 1963 novel *Rayuela* (*Hopscotch*) the disaffected thinker-as-potential-novelist Morelli expounds on his classification of readers—*lector alondra, lector hembra, lector cómplice* (lark reader, female reader, complicitous reader)—and vehemently argues against the perpetuation of the passive, superficial reader, *el lector hembra*, the reader who goes to books for (Heaven forbid!) pleasure. He demonstrates his determination to destroy the literature she/he reads as well as his/her reading of that literature: "What good is a writer if he can't destroy

literature? And us, we don't want to be female readers, what good are
we if we don't help as much as we can in that destruction" (451).
Cortázar's references to *el lector hembra* are tinged by ambiguity even as
to grammatical gender, making the apparently obvious English translation—"female reader"—an unacceptably straightforward variation
on the tension in Spanish between *el lector,* with its dominantly male,
implicitly "universal" gender marking, and *hembra,* the sign of the
female of the species. What is unambiguous is that Morelli appropriates the female-gendered composite as a symbol of negativity, of all
that is wrong with traditional texts and traditional readings of those
texts; at the same time, the nature of the obsession, paired to Morelli's
own inability ever to write the much-announced novel, suggests that
he needs the *lector hembra* more than he cares to admit. Loved and
hated, desired and despised, his/her superficiality permits *el lector
hembra* to escape from the commitment (or pose of commitment) to
serious prose typical of the highly touted *lector cómplice.* The female
reader's passivity allows him/her to be sucked into the text, but that
very passivity prevents the text from becoming his/her own.

It seems likely, ironically, that Morelli's *lector hembra*—despite what I
have said about its ambiguous gender marking in Spanish—is the
insufficiently thought-through appropriation of a hoary tradition designating the female reader (*la lectora*) as careless, superficial, "highly
emotional" (Traba 24), uninterested in and unable to grasp the deeper,
more complex meanings of abstract thought. Certainly the only person marked as a superficial thinker and a *lector hembra* in *Hopscotch* is a
woman, Maga, whose reading preferences include the works of the
nineteenth-century Spanish realist Benito Pérez Galdós, interspersed
with such magazines as *Elle* and *France soir.* "Oh Maga, how can you
swallow this stuff," Horacio comments interlinearly, as he watches
Maga read her realist novel; "your ignorance is of the kind that destroys all the little gardens now planted where once there had been
pleasure, poor girl" (202–3). Nevertheless, when the theoretician of
the exile group, Morelli, calls for the modern writer to break with the
conventions of narrative, "to provoke, assume a text that is out of line,
untied, incongruous, minutely antinovelistic," he is asking for the
creation of a text that will alienate, not educate, the *lector hembra,* "who
otherwise will not get beyond the first few pages, rudely lost and
scandalized, cursing at what he paid for the book" (406). Morelli
describes this hypothetical, unconventional text, the open text created

through the interaction of the author and the *lector cómplice*, in terms that remind us of *very* conventional gender arrangements. One is "to use the novel in that way, just as one uses a revolver to keep the peace. . . . To take from literature that part which is a living bridge from man to man" (406). The inability of *el lector hembra* to grasp this weapon reflects a subtle feminization of the reading process; when s/he tries to read an antinovel, "s/he will remain with something like a façade and we already know that there are very pretty ones" (408); that is, the *lector hembra* is capable of recognizing nothing but the makeup. And Morelli's own incoherent attraction to the style of the *lector hembra* is defined by an unidentified narrator as a yearning for "a crystallization in which nothing would remain subsumed, but where a lucid eye might peep into the kaleidoscope and understand the great polychromatic rose, understand it as a figure, an *imago mundi* that outside the kaleidoscope would be dissolved into a provincial living room, or a concert of aunts having tea and Bagley biscuits" (478).

In her seminal article "On the Superficiality of Women," Susan Noakes points out, through her readings of Rousseau, Sterne, Flaubert, and Dante, among others, that "it is Christianity that stresses that superficial reading (for 'adventure,' plot, to find out 'what happens') is not, as one might suppose today, merely stupid but, more importantly, morally wrong. . . . Readings that remain *on* the surface . . . engage the reader's desires rather than the reader's ideas" (347). Through the agency of desire, bad reading and carnal desires come to be associated; from there, says Noakes, it is only a small step to the effective conflation of terms: "Woman as seducer behaves like woman as reader; thus, woman reads in the same way she seduces" (344). Reading for enjoyment is reading as a woman, is reading in a morally deficient manner, is reading woman, woman reading: reading or seducing, she is the tempting, destructive figure of Eve. The horror of that notoriously damning eroticism is evident in Cortázar's text as well as Flaubert's; reading as a woman reads (that is, badly, superficially) is associated with moral depravity or mental derangement: on the one hand, Morelli's pedantic reminder that the new antinovel "debe ser de un *pudor* ejemplar" (454; my emphasis) 'must have an exemplary sense of decorum' (408) on the other, Horacio Oliviera's fall from the madhouse window at the end of the novel.

One response is to deny the superficiality. Thus, while Marta Traba acknowledges a system of judgment based on "degree of autonomy, its capacity to create a symbolic field through a new linguistic structure, and its universal reach" (23)—the traditional criteria for evaluating literary quality—she suggests that women's writing attends to a second, equally profound and valuable set of criteria. First, women's literature can serve a mediating function: "If the feminine text has been situated in proximity to . . . the culturally marginalized . . . it can, like all countercultures, mediate perfectly between the solitary producer and the untrusting receiver" (25). Second, says Traba, following upon the recognition of the woman writer's role as a representative of the margin and an intermediary with the center, the woman writer can learn to speak for herself (ironically, Traba, herself a woman writer, expresses this thought through Pierre Bourdieu): "To speak, instead of *being spoken*, could be one of the tasks of the counterculture" (26). Women reading/women writing provide, then, a viable, profound, and morally defensible alternative to the dominant cultural mode. Their work is different, surely, but not superficial; rather, it is complementary to the established norms of universality.

Rosario Castellanos's *lector(a) hembra* has another value. Implicitly recognizing and taking into account once again a tradition that marks women readers as superficial and morally deficient, she realigns the terms to right the misappropriation of the reading woman as immoral, while reversing the negative charge on the accusation of superficiality. Openly marked as a celebration of the unexplored potentiality of the female reader and the female novelist, her essay on María Luisa Bombal provides a counterpoint to Cortázar's meditations on moral and intellectual deficiency and Traba's call for a strategic appropriation of marginality and offers other possibilities for appropriation of texts, for establishment of rights of property and propriety. Hers is another program, another face, another place, another force, another interlocutor:

Cuando la mujer latinoamericana toma entre sus manos la literatura lo hace con el mismo gesto y con la misma intención con la que toma un espejo: para contemplar su imagen. Aparece primero el rostro. . . . Luego el cuerpo. . . . El cuerpo se viste de sedas y de terciopelos, que se adorna de metales y de piedras preciosas, que cambia sus apariencias como una víbora cambia su piel para expresar...¿qué?

Las novelistas latinoamericanas parecen haber descubierto mucho antes que Robbe-Grillet y los teóricos del *nouveau roman* que el universo es superficie. Y si es superficie pulámosla para que no oponga ninguna aspereza al tacto, ningún sobresalto a la mirada. Para que brille, para que resplandezca, para que nos haga olvidar ese deseo, esa necesidad, esa manía de buscar lo que está más allá, del otro lado del velo, detrás del telón.

Quedémonos, pues, con lo que se nos da: no el desarrollo de una estructura íntima, sino el desenvolvimiento de una sucesión de transformaciones. (*Mujer* 144–45)

When the Latin American woman takes a piece of literature between her hands she does it with the same gesture and the same intention as that with which she picks up a mirror: to contemplate her image. First the face appears . . . Then the body. . . . The body is dressed in silks and velvets, adorned with precious metals and jewels, which change her appearance as a snake changes its skin to express… What?

Latin American women novelists seem to have discovered long before Robbe-Grillet and the theoreticians of the *nouveau roman* that the universe is surface. And if it is surface, let us polish it, so that it leaves no roughnesses to the touch, no shock to the gaze. So that it shines, so that it sparkles, so that it makes us forget that desire, that need, that mania, for seeking out what is beyond, on the other side of the veil, behind the curtain.

Let us remain, therefore, with what has been given us: not the development of an intimate structure but the unenveloping of a series of transformations.

Castellanos here directly confronts the rhetorical tradition that defines good prose as clear, straightforward, masculine, and bad taste in prose as a fondness for the excessively ornamented and therefore effeminate. Thus, according to Jacqueline Lichtenstein, "when Cicero attempted to describe a simple style . . . he recommended leaving aside overly gaudy ornament and excessively bright colors, and taking as a model those beauties [the modest housewives] whose simplicity has no need for enhancement by pearls and makeup" (78). In her challenge to this ingrained metaphor Castellanos intuits the startling possibility of a feminine aesthetics as a radically different model for feminist politics. She rejects the meek, tidy housewife and evokes instead the unmistakable image of the bored upper-class woman, filing her nails (sharpening her claws?), slipping menacingly out of her Eve-snake skin, creating herself affirmatively in the appropriation of the polished, superficial, adjectival existence allotted her, making the fiction yet more impenetrably fictive until it glows as the revolutionary recognition of an amoral forgotten truth. Is excessive ornamentation belittled as the sign of an overly emotional femininity? Fine: she adopts wanton elegance as her rhetorical style and flaunts its seductiveness. The mirror is her talisman, is, like those flashing mirrors worn by the famous Knight of the Mirrors in *Don Quijote*, a weapon for dispelling, as it creates, illusion: aesthetics and politics brought home, as it were, from their travels, made homey, personal, private, quotidian.

In Castellanos's metaphorical history of language as an instrument for domination, she writes, "La propiedad quizá se entendió, en un principio, como corrección lingüística. . . . Hablar era una ocasión para exhibir los tesoros de los que se era propietario. . . . Pero se hablaba ¿a quién? ¿O con quién?" (*Mujer* 177). 'Propriety/property was perhaps understood, in the beginning, as a linguistic correction. . . . To speak was an occasion to exhibit the treasures of which one was proprietor. . . . But to whom did one speak? Or with whom?' To speak is to create a surface of propriety, of proprietary relationships that can be exploited in various directions. The works of these Latin American women novelists cited by Castellanos do not provide a model either to imitate or to appropriate, nor do they provide a mimetic reflection to contemplate, but rather a polished surface to triangulate desire in which the apexes of the triangle are (1) the adorned body of the text; (2) the implicitly male motivator and first recipient of this textual adornment; and (3) the female reader, a free space for self-invention. The cultivation of a polished superficiality suggests a willed, willful transvaluation of values which surpasses mere reversal. While leaving the surface of complacency available for the desiring eyes of those whom Alicia Partnoy, based on her bitter experience as a disappeared poet in the "little houses" of Argentine prisons, calls *el lector enemigo*, the woman writer produces a layered look for the discriminating eye of her *lectora hembra*, for whom the constructs of life as a staged aesthetic performance are not unfamiliar.

The literary correlative of making up, ostensibly for the other, covertly for the self, is the romance novel, *la novela rosa*, with its profoundly conservative ideological strategies and its severely limited social agenda. The *novela rosa* does not challenge the sorts of conventional assumptions about male-female relations which Castellanos outlines in "The Liberation of Love"; rather, it manipulates them in the service of a fantasy gratification that asserts the power of love to create a psychological space for a woman's victory over a man. It is a kind of cosmetic solution to a difficult and intricate problem of gender relationships. At the same time, however, love's victory is evanescent, limited to the single instant of the man's acknowledgment of the power of love; it can endure for the reader only in the formulaic repetition of this single paradigmatic moment of love declared and accepted. The narrative of the romance, then, is not about happiness achieved but about happiness frustrated or deferred, and it would not be an exaggeration to say, paradoxically, that romance narrative is premised on lack (of happiness, of love, of the right man). Once the woman receives acknowledgment of her man's love, the narrative ends with what we could call, playing on words, "the death of love." This inevitable conjunction of reciprocated love and the novel's conclusion may lead us to speculate on the proximity of death and marriage as the two traditional forms of narrative closure, but that would be another project.

Nevertheless, although the formula is restrictive, it at least allows space for a kind of resistance, a sort of control. Projecting beyond the end to the dream of middle-class life these novels sell, we can also imagine in them a paradigm for a woman's shrewd investment in the phallic stock market. Jan Cohn notes:

> Love was once suffered by *lovers*, by men entranced, enthralled, held in thrall by the eyes and mouths and hair of unobtainable mistresses. But men are now busy elsewhere, and they have left the field of love to women. Women have become the experts in love . . . ; as it turns out, though, women are considerably less futile as lovers than men. Love has an appropriate use and necessary consummation in marriage. So if love continues, in popular romance, to torment its victim, it is no vain enterprise; at least it pays off. (5)

The woman, once the idealized, dominant, but passive pole of the love relationship, has, through the romance novel, inverted the schema and, while appearing sweetly subordinate, has managed to accede to power and authority by the only route possible to her, through her emotional sway over a powerful man. Moreover, her values are revindicated as his values. As Tania Modleski reminds us, in novel after novel men recognize the importance of careful grooming and love of shopping: "The novels literally reverse the hierarchy pointed out by Virginia Woolf, for 'worship of fashion, the buying of clothes' are important—to both the woman and the man, who is usually even capable of identifying a material as 'tulle' " (17). Makeup revindicates itself in the land of make-believe.

The academic reader, trained to look beneath the surface, will recognize herself to be in the presence of such a militantly superficial text when her efforts to deploy the prevailing apparatus of knowledge seem to flounder or to render readings that are plausible but unsatisfying, readings that somehow fail to take into account the most arresting aspects of the work under consideration: the incongruities of its style, the twists of its plot, the elegant adornment of its form. In Rosario Ferré's story of the melding of upper-class white wife and lower-class black mistress, "When Women Love Men," discussed in greater detail in Chapter 4, such superficial elegancies provide the motor force of the plot, for example, in these complementary descriptions of the twinned protagonists: Isabel the Black, "the one who danced with the children to the rhythm of their cry Hersheybarskissesmilkyways" (178), and Isabel the White, at the end the very symbiosis itself of the two women, "swaying myself now back and forth on my red heels, through which come down, slow and silent like a tide, that blood that was rising from the base of my fingernails from so long ago, my blood soaked with Cherries Jubilee" (185). A feminist discussion of the humiliation of the two women, chained unhappily to the same man, a neo-Marxist study of the imbrication of race and class issues, a postcolonial political analysis of cultural infection in the highlighting of consumer products cited in English, a semiotic or hermeneutic dissection of the symbolism of the phrases—all are possible, enlightening, and finally insufficient, for they fail to take into account the sheer sensual delight, the colors and the tastes, the richness of the chocolate, the smoothness of the nail polish sliding through the veins, the pleasures, moral or immoral, of superficiality.

negation

Here I want to reiterate my admiration for Josefina Ludmer's superb commentary on Sor Juana Inés de la Cruz, "Tretas del débil," in which she delicately deconstructs the minimalist transformatory mechanism of Sor Juana's "Reply." Let us recall that in this letter to the bishop of Puebla Ludmer identifies but "three elements, two verbs and the negation: *to know, to say, not*" (48). Ludmer's analysis of the successive displacements of the verbs is brilliant; she places less emphasis, however, on the negation. I would like to return to the particularly "full" quality of the negation for Sor Juana which, in the particular instance cited by Ludmer, makes *no decir* (not speaking) and *callar* (remaining silent) actions of a different order. The negation, it seems to me, is not a transformatory mechanism at all in the sense defined by Ludmer. Rather, the insistent "no" of Sor Juana stands out in her text as the concrete, fully realized correlative of something like that which Pascal called the silence of infinite spaces, except that for Sor Juana, the silence evokes not fear but a sense of homecoming: a life-affirming negation that fills the emptiest zero-degree of her self-portrait with meaning. The "no" defines Sor Juana: not legitimate, not (unfortunately) a student, not quite a scholar, not a dilettante (though she has been accused of it), not a wife, not a typical religious woman, not a mystic certainly, not openly rebellious either.

Although her discussion of Sor Juana does not develop the implications of the insight, Ludmer hints at the possibility for another type of resistance in which negation does not serve only as an oppressor's means of establishing difference but is recuperated for other reasons by the oppressed: "The tactic . . . consists in that, for the assigned and accepted place, one changes not only the sense of that place but also the very sense of what is installed in it" (53). This tactic also implies a methodology for retaining a fertile spatial and temporal distance that allows the action of thought to occur, while suggesting the potential for a creative reappropriation of the negated elements, a transvaluation of values that permits bridging the gap of difference *on her own terms*. The logic of such reappropriation is neither symbolic nor political, but poetic, and based on the affirmative and constitutive power of the metaphor. Sor Juana Inés's "no" offers her both a mode of concealment and a method for discretely opening a passage to self-realization. Negation in the first, simple, merely oppositional sense neglects the possibilities for individual or communal agency in effecting the type of reciprocal adjustments suggested in Ludmer's reminder that what is changed is not only the meaning of place but also the meaning of what is included in that space. The double negation—refusal of subsumption in the dominant, refusal of alienation in the marginal—creates a disturbance in the fields of discourse, recalling the mutual dependence and reciprocal relations bridging the metaphorical gap between antagonistic ideologies. Or in Derrida's words, "There are always two *pas*'s, the one in the other, but without any possible inclusion, the one immediately affecting the other, but overstepping it by distancing itself from it. Always two *pas*'s, overstepping even their negation, according to the eternal return of the passive transgression and the repeated affirmation. . . . *Pas* is forgetting, *pas* of forgetting, doubly affirmed (yes, yes)" (quoted and translated by Fineman 140).

Sor Juana, as the wunderkind of her time, the cherished court poet who evolved into the misunderstood nun, forcibly silenced by jealous and bigoted churchmen, lived the hypostatization and the antagonism in her own body. Her "Reply to Sor Filotea" is its own testimentary ruin, studded with negatives. From the very first words of the letter, "no will of mine" (*Anthology* 205), to the final exhortation to "Sor Filotea" to change any aspect of the letter, "if the style . . . is not as it ought to be" (243), Sor Juana's letter is an insistent litany of negation: "there was nothing he could say" (205), "silence will say nothing, for that is precisely its function, *to say nothing*" (207), "he says he cannot tell it" (207), "and in truth I have never written except when pressured and forced to do so" (209), "my purpose in studying is not to write . . . but simply to see whether studying makes me less ignorant" (210), "I have studied many things, yet know nothing" (215), "for me, not learning (for I am not yet learned), merely wanting to learn has been so hard" (217), "still lacking mention are the outright difficulties which have worked directly to hinder and to prohibit my pursuit of learning" (218), and so on. Ludmer categorizes this minimalist dialectic in terms that recall the structuration of a musical piece: "*First: separation of knowledge from speech*," condensable into the formulation "not to say what she knows" (48–49); "*second movement: to know about not speaking.*" It is, significantly, this second movement that is accompanied by the annexation of other potential spaces for the free play of knowledge. Sor Juana writes:

> Pues ¿qué os pudiera contar, señora, de los secretos naturales que he descubierto estando guisando? Ver que un huevo se une y se fríe en la manteca o aceite y, por contrario, se despedaza en el almíbar; ver que para que el azúcar se conserve fluida basta echarle una muy mínima parte de agua en que haya estado membrillo u otra fruta agria. . . . Pero, señora, ¿qué podemos saber las mujeres, sino filosofías de cocina? ... Y yo suelo decir viendo estas cosillas: *Si Aristóteles hubiera guisado, mucho más hubiera escrito.* Y prosiguiendo en mi modo de cogitaciones, digo que esto es tan continuo en mí, que no necesito de libros. (*Obras* 4:460–61)

What could I not tell you, my Lady, of the secrets of nature I have discovered while cooking! That an egg holds together and fries in fat or oil, and that, on the contrary, it disintegrates in syrup. That, to keep sugar liquid, it suffices to add the tiniest bit of water in which a quince or some other tart fruit has soaked. . . . But, Madam, what is there for us women to know, if not bits of kitchen philosophy? . . . And I always say, when I see these details: If Aristotle had been a cook, he would have written much more. And continuing with my meditations, let me say that this line of thought is so constant with me that I have no need of books. (*Anthology* 225–26)

The interval between philosophy and books, cooking and Aristotle, is measured out like the discrete ingredients of a recipe, each in its proper time and space, each in its contribution to the whole, culminating in the surprising formulation, "I have no need of books," a statement that is, like much else in this subtly ironic essay, both clearly false and profoundly true. Popular mythology tells us that Sor Juana, deprived of her books and music, did not turn to the consolation of the cookstove; she died rapidly, miserably (folk myth, of course, has her dying considerably more rapidly and more miserably than biography). Still, the affirmation stands; the proper knowledge for women is limited to "kitchen philosophy." Yet as Sor Juana astutely recognizes, and her modern successors agree, the apparent limitation—women have no knowledge but knowledge of cooking—can be turned around: there is no knowledge that cannot be enriched by a knowledge of cooking, thus inspiring the image of an Aristotle among the eggs or those modern celebrations of a woman's traditional sphere recorded in *La sartén por el mango* (The skillet by the handle) or *Las mil y una calorías: Novela dietética* (A thousand and one calories: A dietetic novel) by Margo Glantz (1978), among other academic and literary concoctions we swallow with glee.

marginality

One of the more significant aspects of women's writing, says Marta Traba, is its marginality. Women naturally write from and of, if not necessarily to, the margins. Thus, the signal criterion of value in Traba's revised scheme of judgment is how well women perform this essential function of giving voice to the margin, both their own marginality and that of other marginalized groups: "The feminine text remains located in a space neighboring on . . . the cultural margins; in other words, if it operates, as it in fact does, from the perspective of marginalization, it can mediate perfectly well" (25). For this reason, the women writers of Latin America are in some sense privileged in their accessibility to the peripheries of culture, licensing them not only to speak of issues relating to private spaces but also to speak to and between and as intermediary for other marginalized groups: implicitly, the disadvantaged social groups, the Indians, the blacks.

Jean Franco would agree with this identification based on marginalization. She too categorizes women with blacks and indigenous peoples and finds that they share a common quality of archaism, a protective coating of anachronism that buffers them against a hostile system: "The belief systems of the indigenous, blacks, and women were *of necessity* archaic, for no other options were open to them. At the same time, this very anachronism provided them with 'regions of refuge' . . . that could be explosive when the state encroached on them" ("Beyond" 505–6). Ambiguously visible and invisible at the same time, negated and neglected by indifference, what Franco calls the "regions of refuge" of the marginalized could be turned into a political tool, could become central once the center turned its eye on them. Pragmatically then, one of the jobs of the woman writer is to probe delicately at the edges of this official indifference, to force the dominant culture to recognize these regions, to unleash their dormant power, to impinge upon official consciousness without inciting it to even harsher reprisals.

Accordingly, one of the springs of vitality in women's writing comes from its association with other marginalized groups: Cuban Lydia Cabrera's retellings of black folk tales, Mexican Rosario Castellanos's "indigenismo," which takes the form of passionate depictions of Yucatecan Indians for whom Spanish is a foreign tongue, Chilean Marjorie Agosín's militant giving of voice to her countrywomen's quilted handicrafts, the *arpilleras*. In this, as in much else, Sor Juana Inés de la Cruz is the forerunner. Recall, for example, the music of her villancico "Entre un negro y la música castellana" (Between a black man and Castilian music), which begins with her attempt to capture the rhythm of the spoken dialect:

—Acá tamo tolo
Zambio, lela, lela,

que tambié sabemo
cantaye las Leina. (*Obras* 2:26)[12]

In others of her villancicos, the linguistic salad—she calls these poems in mixed dialect *ensaladillas*—is even more highly spiced. In several of them she employs an exuberant and strikingly modern onomatopoeia that anticipates the more recent celebrations of oral poetry by such contemporary poets as Nicolás Guillén: "¡Ha, ha, ha! / ¡Monan vuchilá! / ¡He, he, he, / cambulé!" (*Obras* 2:72) Or here, where a song to San Pedro Nolasco called "Tocotín" is seasoned with the music of Nahuatl in a "Tocotín mestizo":

> Los Padres bendito
> tiene on Redentor;
> *amo nic neltoca*
> *quimati no Dios.*
> Sólo Dios *Piltzintli*
> del Cielo bajó,
> y nuestro *tlatlácol*
> nos lo perdonó.
> Pero esto *Teopixqui*
> dice en so sermón
> que este San Nolasco
> *mïechtin compró.*
>
> . . . . . .
> *Huel ni machicáhuac;*
> no soy hablador:
> *no teco qui mati.*
> que soy valentón. (*Obras* 2:41–42)[13]

Sor Juana's boundless interest in the music of the oral folk heritage leads her not only to these "mestizo" songs but also to record, in her famous "Villancico VIII," dedicated to the Virgin of Guadalupe, a nine-verse *tocotín* (a type of Aztec dance) entirely in Nahuatl (*Obras* 2:17).

[12]Literally translated: "Here we all are / zambio, lela, lela / we also know / how to sing to the queen."

[13]Spanish text, literally translated: "The Fathers have blessed / a Redeemer / *amo nic neltoca / quimati no Dios.* / Only God *Pilzintli* / came down from Heaven, / and our *tlatlácol* / forgave. / But this *Teopixqui* / says in his sermon / that this Saint Nolasco / *mïechtin compró* / . . . / *Huel ni machicáhuac;* / I am no gossip: / *no teco qui mati,* / I am brave."

Likewise, the poet Gabriela Mistral proudly wrote of her half-Indian heritage, and even that quintessential creole Victoria Ocampo discovered in her ancestry an Indian foremother whose presence she declared before the Academia Argentina de Letras in her ingression speech as a symbolic reintegration of two marginals—woman and Indian—into the literary mainstream:

> I learned then, that on my mother's side I descend from Irala, one of Mendoza's companions, and from a Guaraní Indian, Agueda. This Spaniard and this American had a daughter, whom the father recognized. . . . I pay no attention to either demagoguery or pedantry. But in my capacity as a woman, it is for me both a luxury and a compensation to be able to invite my Guaraní ancestress to this academy and to sit her between an Englishwoman [Virginia Woolf] and a Chilean [Gabriela Mistral] . . . because I in my turn *recognize* Agueda.
>   You might tell me that this all has nothing to do with literature. No. It has to do with immanent justice and perhaps with poetry. (*Testimonios* 10:22)

The particular weight of writing about marginals from a position of marginality, which creates an indissoluble bond of solidarity, is, perhaps, one of the twists Latin American women give to the more general recognition of the cultural and racial diversity of the continent common among Latin American writers and intellectuals.

Ocampo writes of her long-ago foremother, the Indian woman taken as a mistress by the white invader, known to her distant descendent only through the fortuitous circumstance of the invader's "recognition" of his illegitimate daughter. Ocampo heals that peremptory invader's recognition with one of her own. In her condition as woman she empathizes with her ancestor; she recognizes her and places her next to Woolf and Mistral, next to the theorist and the poet, with Ocampo on this dais of enshrined respectability in the world of letters. In recognizing her, Ocampo symbolically gives her back her name and place in history and in literature and forces her own listening public, her future colleagues of the academy, to recognize her as well, with all the implications their recognition implies. In inviting Ocampo to that body, they are opening the door to other ruptures of traditional restrictions. Thus, insofar as Ocampo, albeit distantly, breaks custom in her quality as mestiza as in her condition as the first woman to be invited to membership in that body, she also signals an act of retribution: the official recognition and validation of the voices of its marginalized citizens.

One might object that Ocampo's evacuation and reconstruction of her pedigree in her recognition of Agueda is only a poetic flourish, a rhetorical trope, mere superficiality. But the fiction of America as a mestizo continent is also a rhetorical construction, an unexamined official trope that forecloses any real knowledge and sanctions both ignorance and abuse. Official benevolence, as Ocampo reminds us, is no assurance of legitimacy, does not even guarantee recognition of the Indians' essential humanity.

What remains to be issued is a warning on the seductions of marginality. The Ghanaian philosopher Kwame Anthony Appiah recently published a position paper on African literature and criticism that is as applicable to Latin America as it is to the other side of the Atlantic, where he finds his principal focus. "We need to transcend the banalities of nativism," he writes. "On the one hand, we find theorists who emphasize the processes of demonization and subjection, the ways in which the margin is produced by the cultural dominant; . . . on the other (Other?) hand, talk about the production of marginality by the culturally dominant is wholly inadequate by itself." He concludes, "The point to be borne in mind here is not that ideologies, like cultures, exist antagonistically, but that they *only* exist antagonistically" (175). Appiah's acute observation reminds me of the multifarious ways in which the production of difference becomes a self-generating mechanism fueled partly by a legitimate need to assert autonomy, to maintain those "regions of refuge," and partly by demands understood to be emanating from the center, by what Barbara Johnson calls "the public's *in*difference to finding out that there *is* no difference," that, so to speak, "difference is a misreading of sameness, but it must be represented in order to be erased" (284). Marginality is a tool for both marking and masking very real differences, as well as for creating false differences out of the cultural, economic, philosophical, and ideological exigencies of an antagonistic politics. Double-talk, talking back, if unattended, can fall into the double crossing of that resistance.

the subjunctive mood

It is an operation of resistance similar to what Spivak calls "the structure of certification that we cannot not want to inhabit" ("Post-

Coloniality," author's notes from a film presentation and discussion at Cornell) which makes the tactical, textual resistances of deconstructive practice so attractive to many feminist theorists, offering, as it does, a powerful mode of double-voicing a text, of demonstrating a complex relationship to an oppressive system which allows for both the seductiveness and the hatred involved in the relationship to, for example, Ocampo's academy. It allows affection without the risk of recuperation and also creates a space for opposition without alienation and, thereby, a simple reversion into the field of acceptable, if inscrutable, otherness, a trap that even so acute a critic as Rosario Ferré cannot avoid because she cannot not want to inhabit that particular myth:

> Our literature very often finds itself determined by an immediate relationship to our bodies. . . . This biological fate curtails our mobility and creates very serious problems for us as we attempt to reconcile our emotional needs with our professional needs. . . . That is why women's literature has, so much more so than men's literature, concerned itself with interior experiences, experiences which have little to do with the historical, the social, and the political. Women's literature is also more subversive than men's because it often delves into forbidden zones— areas bordering on the irrational, madness, love, and death. ("The Writer's Kitchen" 242)

In her efforts to carve out a valid space for women's writing between the twin demands of professional and emotional life, Ferré falls back into the association of women's writing with a specific thematic content—love, death, madness—already reified as emblematic of women's writing by dominant discourse. It is only a small step from such celebration of women's typical themes to the patronizing enforcement of difference experienced by Victoria Ocampo when, enthusiastically committed to writing on Dante's *Divine Comedy,* she is advised by her mentor that "she ought to write on a topic more within reach, more personal" (*Testimonios* 10:17). Leslie Rabine has expressed her awareness of this risk very well at the end of her excellent *Signs* article on Maxine Hong Kingston: "Such is our present sociosymbolic order that feminine difference has to be expressed in a way acceptable to these institutions in order to even be recognized as feminine difference" (492). It is a chilling reminder in the context of gender studies as a whole and, unfortunately, an absolutely correct one. There is a degree of sanctioned illegitimacy, of authenticable, and therefore licit, license, in which the conflictual violence between difference and the same is resolved and reconciled in the mocking surface of reflection, a game of continually changing positional references, of changes that end up as always and only the same thing.

What Philip Lewis says about deconstruction is equally applicable to feminist practice and indirectly offers Rosario Ferré both warning and consolation: "Insofar as it exposes such instances of recuperation as structurally determined, it shows the folly of any attempt to overcome or escape them once and for all" (13). How then, if not thematically, is one to account for the often-expressed conviction that women's texts just "feel" different? One form of tactical resistance to such over-whelming pressures from the thematic conventions involves a practice of the deliberately conditional, what I would call, taking my example from Spanish grammar, a life lived in the subjunctive mood, attentive to nuance and capable of taking a cue from context without losing autonomy. It embodies "a metonymy of words," as Nicolas Abraham and Maria Torok would have it, representing the slippage as well as the continuity between the roles, an impassioned relationship to syntactical relations which reveals the covert markings of a cryptotype, a function without a concrete form. Its repertoire of techniques is varied, or alternatively, we could perhaps say that it is a unitary principle characterized by the multiple manifestations of a single theme.

I borrow others' words to circumscribe this practice (or practices) with helpful metaphors. Philip Lewis might say it involves "an impulse or pressure to cultivate artifice, affabulation—an infection, as it were, that pervades philosophic writing and promotes its resistance to the regimen of the *same*" (23). It is, therefore, like a benign virus that gives immunity to the onslaught of other diseases. Luce Irigaray sees not illness but war and childbirth and the murder of philosophy: "All that remains to be known is whether what they caught was not already dead: the poor present of an effigied copula. And whether in this fight they did anything but tear themselves apart. Making blood flow from their wounds, blood that still recalls a very ancient relationship with the mother. . . . Mimicking once again in that gesture what Plato was already writing, Socrates already telling. 'No question, they would put him to death.' It has long been inscribed—surely in the conditional tense of a myth—in their memories" (364).

Alice Jardine takes her metaphor from the description of "superficial" effects and marginal linguistic displacements: "I discovered that differences between male-written and female-written texts of modernity were not, after all, in their so-called 'contents,' but in their enunciation: in their modes of discourse ('sentimental,' ironic, scientific, etc.); in their twisting of female obligatory connotations, of inherited genealogies of the feminine; in their haste or refusal to use the pronouns 'I' or 'we'; in their degree of willingness to gender those pronouns as female; in their adherence to or dissidence from feminism as a movement; in the tension between their desire to remain radical and their desire to be taken seriously as theorists and writers in what remains a male intellectual community" (260–61). For Jardine, the cryptotype slips from function to function, from enunciation to modes of discourse to pronoun usage (always slippery), among other factors that help delimit its field without resolving into any simplistic form.

After all this, it is almost a relief to turn to the homier formulation of Luisa Valenzuela, who uses a simple, familiar, evocative scene to make her point. It is a scene, moreover, that echoes favorably with the elaborately framed appropriations of Victoria Ocampo, who talks about Argentina through a filter of French writers and Chinese art and Ecuadoran landscapes. Instead, Valenzuela makes use of a humble, native metaphor for her aesthetic practice:

> When I was a girl in the schools of my cattle-raising country, they used to make us write a composition about a predictable theme: The Cow. Today, trying to compose an essay about *body and writing,* I naturally think about the word (which is both body *and* writing) and naturally I think about the cow. . . .
>
> Cow-words like cow-women. Although the expression may appear to be an insult, it is simply the image of an interior cud-chewing, of digesting and understanding, which ultimately generates discourse.
>
> That's why I say that I believe in the existence of a feminine language, even though it may not yet have been completely defined and even though the boundary between it and other language . . . may be too subtle and ambiguous to be delineated. . . .
>
> What we women will do, and are now doing, is to effect a radical change in the electrical charge of words. ("Word" 96)

Resistance to the *same,* the slight but crucial differences of enunciation, the lyric evocation of the conditional tense of myth, the electrical charge of cow-words: these delicate distinctions and subtle displacements cipher a particular repertoire of linguistic practices that respond and correspond to the need of the Latin American woman writer to encode, in a more than trivial manner, her shifting set of mutually exclusive, equally valid, alternative roles. Since there is no syntax, no lexicon outside of language, women writers must refine such tools as they are given, transforming vocabularies and focusing attention on particular usages so as to achieve a greater working knowledge of the byways of cultural production. Commentary is intended not only to describe the ellipsis but also to recuperate, reintegrate, recodify the fragmented language of the female body, to construct, if such a thing is possible, a tentative dictionary of the unspoken.

The critical project in this respect bears a striking resemblance to the project of naming set Luisa Valenzuela's protagonist in the story "Other Weapons." For her, "the so-called Laura," all her past life is an ellipsis. Nouns are particularly elusive—"the so-called anguish," "the so-called love," or "What might the prohibited (repressed) be?"—as are verbs: the meanings of such verbs as to love and to hate, to make love and to torture slip indistinguishably into each other. Her experience is conditional, hypothetical, based on a series of subordinate clauses responding to the main clause, the spoken orders of the man: her lover, her torturer, her one friend, the enemy she must assassinate. Her touchstone is her own wounded body—*una espalda azotada* (a wounded back)—which is continuous with her wounded mind, her aphasia: *la palabra azotada,* in which the weight of reference falls not on the noun, but on the adjective, *azotada*. The nameless protagonist, for convenience "the so-called Laura," tastes her bittersweet blood in the slash on her back, the shattered words on her tongue; denied refuge, she has no place to treasure up her scattered bits, no force to bring them together out of their fragmentation. Her story is that of a veiled and unspeakable pornography, rescued through the tentative workings of the subjunctive.

Writing in the subjunctive mood also provides a response to Derrida's query, informed by his reading of Hegelian dialectics, "And if the *relève* of alienation is not a *calculable* certitude, can one still speak of alienation and still produce statements in the system of speculative dialectics? . . . What might be a 'negative' that could not be *relevé*?" (*Margins* 107, my italics). For Derrida, one response might be the machine defined in terms of its functioning rather than its product. In Luisa Valenzuela's word-milk-woman-cow, in her evocation of the madwoman-housewife–torture victim Laura, in Ferré's impassioned

recollection of her own love/hatred of writing, in Margo Glantz's ex-
egeses of women's feet and women's hair and women's missing genita-
lia, we see examples of machines that *work,* and work without calculable certitude and without *relève,* struggling with the old cautionary
rituals, attempting to bypass old myths of the *same* and the *other,* risk-
ing loss (of readers, of self), and forcefully suggesting new kinds of
feminine difference. Puerto Rican Mayra Santos-Febres evokes this
furious commitment, this impatient patience with the old rituals:

> pronto pronto al cuerpo le pasan cosas
> tantas.
> . . . . .
> esquinitas
> por donde la rabia
> se escabulle
> rompe los diques que la mano, mantiene en óptimas condiciones
> la furia
> secreteándose rutas escabrosas que la ensañan más
> contra ésta
> su mano enemiga
> puliéndola, peinándola
> pasándole aceites y sabila.[14]

   Rosario Castellanos calls one variation on such writing adjectival
and defines it as the motivating force behind her novel *Balún-Canán:* "I
wanted to tell about events that, unlike poetry, were not essential:
adjectival events" (Miller 125–26). Prose, let us say, is typically conceived of as a concatenation of nouns and verbs; Castellanos's intuition
of the basically adjectival nature of her work surely deserves note as a
revolutionary transvaluation of prose, rejecting agency and action (the
essential and the essentialist, both touched, for Castellanos, with the
suspicion adhering to typically male preserves) in favor of what is often
downgraded as mere ornamentation: superficial, attractive surely, but
of lesser significance. The title of Valenzuela's story "Cambio de armas," is in the official English translation—Spivak's translation-as-

   [14]From an unpublished manuscript; literally translated: "soon soon things happen to
the body / so many things. / little corners / around which hatred / scuttles / breaks the
dikes that the hand, keeps in prime condition / the fury / hiding itself uneven paths that
enrage her more / against this / her enemy hand / polishing it / combing it / rubbing it
with oils and bitter aloe."

violation—perversely appropriate here: "Other Weapons." In Spanish, ambiguously, *cambio* is both noun and verb: "I change weapons" and "change of weapons." Here we can see another, quite different examination of the deadly significance of this denigration—*la palabra azotada*—as well as the potential for a creative reworking of the stereotypes, by violent means if necessary: changing weapons, taking them up, using them against a repressive order. In Castellanos's work, *la palabra enemiga* is transformed, polished, held close to the body and to the reader, and that reader, Castellanos's ideal reader, knows the precise mechanism of its formal construction, the particular resources and uses of its form. In Valenzuela's work, *la palabra azotada*, the wounded word, serves a similar function, and step by step she teaches her readers to take up this weapon and use it.

Back in the Attic

What room, as Virginia Woolf might ask, does this space leave the woman writer, what theoretical space does it open for the critic? The Latin Americanist must first of all combat the tendency so succinctly described by Jean Franco as the perception, from the first world, of the intellectual underdevelopment of the third: "Anyone involved in Latin American studies knows what it is to be placed last on the program, when everyone else has left the conference. . . . The conclusion is that the Third World is not much of a place for theory; and if it has to be fitted into theory at all, it can be accounted for as exceptional or regional" ("Beyond" 503). Thus, the third world is perceived as neither a fit place for theory to grow nor an appropriate or worthwhile place for theory to be applied. The result is a serious *underdevelopment* of potential in and for Latin America, a lack of recognition of those theoretical positions that do exist, scattered in novels and poems, fragmented in the journalistic occasional essays that sap the strength and energy of so many Latin American intellectuals, collected in anthologies and conference proceedings. This not-so-benign neglect is troublesome enough. By when, as Spivak notes, neglect is accompanied by condescension, the soup becomes a poisonous mess indeed: "It seems particularly unfortunate when the emergent perspective of feminist criticism reproduces the axioms of imperialism. A basically isolationist admiration for the literature of the female subject in Europe and Anglo-America establishes the high feminist norm. It is supported and operated by an information-retrieval approach to Third World literature which often employs a deliberately nontheoretical methodology with self-conscious rectitude" ("Three Women's Texts" 243). This two-tiered system of feminist thought ignores the ongoing interaction among the postindustrial and postcolonial nations of the world, ignores as well the history of intervention and influence that informs Homi Bhabha's notion of the ambiguity residing in a society that is, in his words, "not-quite/not-white" ("Mimicry" 132), a fundamental blindness to the "worlding" of nations that are not merely exceptional, regional, exotic, exploited (but otherwise untouched) outposts of quaint customs mainly of interest to the anthropologically minded.

And yet, the underdeveloping of Latin American theory is as much—or more—a product of internal forces as it is of external perceptions. Too often, Anthony Appiah reminds us, attempts of nativist thinkers to create an alternative to traditional Eurocentric studies fail to take into account the implications of the concepts they manipulate: "Attempts at counterhegemonic cultural analysis are short-circuited by a failure to recognize the historicity of the analytic terms—'culture,' 'literature,' 'nation'—through which the sociopolitical margin is produced as an object of study" (161). Ironically then, failure to deconstruct these cultural models creates, in effect, an embedded counterdiscourse—the implicit Eurocentric contestation to the model intended as a contestatory declaration of independence. "Indeed," Appiah continues, "the very arguments, the rhetoric of defiance, that our nationalists muster are, in a sense, canonical, time tested. . . . Nativist nostalgia, note well, is largely fueled by that Western sentimentalism so familiar after Rousseau; few things are less native than nativism in its current forms" (162). Thus, both Appiah and Spivak point to what might harshly be called an unconscious fetishization of cultural forms which colors the critics' relation to the object of study, which contaminates as well the efforts to construct or reconstruct a literary tradition of/for Latin American women. It is not enough, they remind us, to find refuge in a vaguely defined "otherness" or to decry rational structures in an unspecified manner as theoretically contaminated and hence inapplicable. We need instead to do serious, concrete, and meticulous work that will allow us to learn more about the repressed motor forces of canonical forms, that will help us to deconstruct their *relève*, as Derrida has it, to uncover the way they work.

Says Satya Mohanty: "Notwithstanding our contemporary slogans of otherness, and our fervent denunciations of Reason and the Subject, there is an unavoidable conception of rational action, inquiry and dialogue inherent in this political-critical project, and if we deny it or obscure it we ought at least to know at what cost" (26).

The cost is clear. The traditional rational mode requires coherence as the mainstay of great intellectual achievement. But coherence and profound insight, as Paul de Man reminded us long ago in his *Blindness and Insight*, has a price: the selective forgetting of dissonant elements that is the point of blindness, the dark Nietzschean afterimage of staring into the bright sunlight/insight. This dialectic of blindness and insight is, in the context of a third-world feminist theoretical undertaking, complicated by yet another twist, another uncomfortable turn of analysis. We cannot speak, even of this, other than in a discourse given us by the West, by Western history, Western politics, Western metaphysics. We must use this discourse to open the conditions of possibility for a radical change in discourse.

If such are the concerns of the rational, verging on essentialist, side of the feminist project, the other side—not irrational, certainly—will emphasize the importance of the tropological deconstruction of truth claims. At the risk of replacing a bad old coherence with a bad new incoherence, this side of the feminist project rejects absolutes. We have been too coherent for too long and now take up arms in favor of a willed undecidability in which all the component parts of our theoretical enterprise remain, like the project of Cortázar's Morelli, in a continual flux of constitution and deconstruction, composition and decomposition, distortion and dissimulation. The style is enormously attractive, even though, ironically perhaps, woman herself becomes the major trope, the controlling metaphor for this pervasive undecidability. In Derrida's version, explicating Nietzsche: "Woman (truth) does not allow herself to be possessed" ("Question" 179). If we deconstruct "truth" as one of those iconic figures like "wisdom" and, in the United States, "liberty," if we deconstruct the myth of the inability ever to really possess woman as one of those inexplicable vagaries of abstract Western philosophy, dating at least from the times of courtly love, which is at total odds with the realities of women's existence during the last few thousand years, then we are still left with the figure of woman as a figure of indeterminacy. "Beyond this double negation," of woman as figure of truth or woman as figure of lying, writes

Derrida, "woman is recognized, affirmed, as an affirmative, dissimu-lating, artistic, and Dionysian power. She is not affirmed by man; rather, she affirms herself both in herself and in man" ("Question" 185–86). In this statement, the margin is always withdrawn from control, remains, even when possessed, impregnable. Accordingly, the play of the woman's text is always interminable, as the concept of the correct reading is multiply disturbed from another direction. Not only the laws and conventions of reading a text, the inherited truth claims, are placed into question but also the tenacious claim of a text to establish its own law, in conjunction, as Morelli would say, with a conscientious *lector cómplice*. But what if we take seriously the play of undecidability? Where then does interpretation rest when the fiction of the text becomes our (un)reality and we can be sure only that our reading is in some degree a misreading? The ambiguous task of read-ing becomes in itself a kind of force perpetuating difference through its attention to the literal and literary disturbances in the text, between the text and the reader, between this text and other texts. We must, in such circumstances, abandon the specious security of our rooms for the precarious existence of the itinerant storyteller, with no theoretical room of our own but only a series of temporary situations, a repertoire of useful strategies, our meager handful of weapons.

2

On Silence:
Helena Maria Viramontes

It has become fashionable in recent years to study apparently apolitical works for their latent or unconscious political content. Analogously, those contemporary writers in postcolonial societies whose writing seems detached from concrete political concerns are often looked at askance; there is an undercurrent of criticism and response to criticism flowing through readings of such authors as the Brazilian Clarice Lispector, the Argentinian Jorge Luis Borges, or the South African J. M. Coetzee. Curiously, this interest in political or politicized reading of canonical works has seldom carried over into a deeper interest in overtly political writing, which politically oriented critics still treat with a considerable degree of condescension. Committed writing continues to be damned for too little artistic content and too much topicality or damned for too much attention to art at the expense of concrete political concerns.

The South African critic Lewis Nkosi's much-quoted comment on the relation of politics and literature is apposite. After surveying the situation in his country, Nkosi sums up his response to the recent work of black novelists with the complaint that there is as yet no writer able to respond "with both the vigor of the imagination and sufficient technical resources to the problems posed by the conditions in South Africa" ("Fiction" 211–12). Numerous variants of Nkosi's critique have appeared; in this version, it is accompanied by his carefully hedged suggestion that "it may even be wondered whether it might not be more prudent to 'renounce literature temporarily,' as some have advised, and solve the political problem first rather than to continue to grind out hackneyed third-rate novels" (*Home and Exile* 132).

One might argue that the specific charge made by the South African critic was irrelevant to the Latin America of that time, the midsixties, when that continent was enjoying the full flower of the "Boom"—a movement particularly noted for technical experimentation and imaginative vigor. But this argument misses the point, which has to do with the silencing or the self-censorship (another form of silencing) of politically committed postcolonial writers on the grounds that their intellectual activity is essentially a frivolous pastime. Luisa Valenzuela's response to such critics is to reassert the indirect value of literature as a great social disrupter:

> We are part of this world, and if they invade Grenada or if the Radical party wins in Argentina, we know that for good or ill things in this world are no longer the same, and neither are we the same.
>
> Should we, therefore, write about these topics, to protest or to celebrate? Perhaps in a newspaper article, the territory where concrete opinions have a direct value. Because literature is something else, literature is the crossing of waters—clear waters and muddy waters—where nothing is precisely in its place because we are not familiar with the place, we are searching for it. If we believe that we have an answer to the world's problems, we would be better off to become politicians and try to, or try not to, make a deal with the power that politics provides. Literature does not aspire to solve anything; it is more like a disturber, it is the great agitator of ideas because ideas should not be left to rest until they stagnate and rot. ("Pequeño manifiesto" 81)

In Valenzuela's displacement of the debate to other grounds—other waters?—we can perhaps imagine a more nuanced critique of political writing in Latin America.

There is another response to the concerns raised by critics demanding social commitment, one that is more attentive to the way in which the postcolonial political critic still bases his or her analyses on rejected cultural constructs. Nkosi's critique involves a double and doubly questionable evaluation of literature in terms of its deployment of technical resources (an ominously Eurocentric-sounding criterion), while political activism is narrowly defined and circumscribed as a physical, rather than mental, activity. It is precisely in these terms that J. M. Coetzee, a novelist and fellow South African, questions Nkosi's major premise ("La Guma" 117–18): first, is it valid, even strategically, to frame a literary issue in terms of a specific ideal of political "correct-ness," and second, to what degree does such a prescriptive charge color the question of the social implications of art and the social re-sponsibilities of the artist?

The issue of value is crucial, for its evocation implies a rate of exchange on both literal and literary stock markets. Says Abdul Jan-Mohamed: "Colonialist discourse 'commodifies' the native subject into a stereotyped object and uses him as a 'resource' for colonialist fiction" (64). For Nkosi, writing from the other side of the commodity market, the exchange value of black literature in South Africa is some-what different. He hints that writers cash in their blue-chip literary stocks for investment in the risky potential boom in political activism. There is no doubt that focusing on the dynamics of narrative exchange value offers critics a justifiable method of analysis, one with premiums of its own on the literary-critical market. But can its application be "justified" in these particular articles by these particular critics? Is it the "correct" approach? To what degree are JanMohamed and Nkosi "commodified" by the resources of their respective choices of literary code, by the analytical traditions they so ably manipulate? To what extent does this value system in itself recommodify the native subject into yet another version of the stereotypical object of a Westernized gaze, in this case one in which a non-Western critic inserts himself into a system that many other non-Westerners have, with good rea-son, found to be peripheral, if not totally alien, to their own tradi-tional views? To phrase the question in another way: to what degree, as Nkosi suggests in a later article, is the adulated third-world writer (and, we might add, critic) neatly inserted into a (white) critical discourse through the distortional, patronizing mythologies of the quaintly exotic? (see *Tasks and Masks* 79). In what respect is that critic unconsciously complicitous with such insertion? To what extent, An-thony Appiah would add, is the valued indigenous tradition itself produced and reified, in very concrete ways, by European thinkers and their rebellious postcolonial heirs?[1]

---

[1]Anthony Appiah's thought-provoking reading of the "topologies of nativism" is tellingly pertinent: "British colonial officers . . . collected, organized, and enforced these 'traditions.' . . . Ironically, for many contemporary African intellectuals, these invented traditions have now acquired the status of national mythology; and the in-vented past of Africa has come to play a role in the political dynamics of the modern

There is, furthermore, the problem of linguistic (to set aside for the moment the immensely complex problem of the political) slippage signaled by putting telltale quotation marks around the word "correct." On the most obvious and simplistic level, what is considered "correct" in one age is clear atrocity in another. On another level, as Anthony Appiah reminds us, "this nativism in theory . . . grounds a politics of reading on a spurious epistemology of reading. And the talk of theoretical adequacy—which is both the carrot and the stick—is seriously misleading" because it ignores the multiple "productive modes of reading" in favor of an ill-defined and insufficiently grounded "search for Mr. Right" (171).

Bracketing "correctness" also points to a still more fundamental and unresolved issue relating to the culturally imposed limits set on slippage, what JanMohamed defines as the essential impossibility of comprehending the Other in colonialist texts: "Genuine and thorough comprehension of Otherness is possible only if the self can somehow negate or at least severely bracket the values, assumptions, and ideology of his culture. . . . however, this entails in practice the virtually impossible task of negating one's very being" (65). In cultures so strange as to seem almost completely alien to Western eyes, some residue remains unintelligible; certain crucial distinctions escape notice because they are not amenable to Western categories of thought; innumerable possibilities of interpretation elude our systems of representation. Says Nigerian writer and Nobel laureate Wole Soyinka: "The essentiality of our black being remains untouched. For the black race knows, and is content simply to know, itself. It is the European world that has sought, with the utmost zeal, to redefine itself through these encounters, even when the European has appeared to be endeavoring to grant meaning to an experience of the African world" (769). Nkosi's and JanMohamed's critiques work in terms that suggest their commitment to the revolutionary social and political role of the writer, while ignoring the implicit assumptions of the positions taken—in Nkosi, by his marking, for example, the authority of Jean-Paul Sartre and Lucien Goldman; in JanMohamed, by his privileging of discourse filtered

---

state" (164). Furthermore, "we must not fall for the sentimental notion that the 'people' have held on to an indigenous national tradition, that only the educated bourgeoisie are 'children of two worlds.' At the level of popular culture, too, the currency is not a holdover from an unbroken stream of tradition; indeed it is like most popular culture in the age of mass production, hardly national at all" (160).

through the perceptions of Michel Foucault and Jacques Lacan. Their work, inevitably, is cast in terms of the orthodox Western world view, a narrative context so familiar and so canonical that it passes unquestioned even in journals most attentive to the nuances of " 'race,' writing, and difference."[2] As Gunnar Myrdal writes: "There must still be . . . countless errors . . . that no living man can yet detect, because of the fog within which our type of Western culture envelops us. Cultural influences have set up assumptions about the mind, the body, and the universe with which we begin; pose the questions we ask; influence the facts we seek; determine the interpretations we give these facts; and direct our reaction to these interpretations and conclusions" (quoted in Gould 25). How then, can one even pose the question of the intersections between, to use Soyinka's terms, a culturally defined literary blackness and an essential blackness?

Committed authors write for the present, for an amelioration of contemporary conditions; they transform "mere" journalism into art with their talent. Jean-Paul Sartre's self-critique—"I have undergone a slow apprenticeship of the real. . . . In the face of a dying child *La Nausée* is quite simply lacking in weight. . . . For so long as a writer cannot write for the two billion who are hungry, a malaise will weigh upon him" (quoted in Hollier 103–4)—resonates with Nkosi's militant call to action. These are the most persistent critiques of committed literature: what claims to value or validity can it make as art? what is its weight, its specific gravity in the scale of the real? Furthermore, as Trinh Minh-ha reminds us in *Woman, Native, Other*, putting the question into an explicitly feminist framework, "it is almost impossible for [women writers] (and especially those bound up with the Third World) to engage in writing as an occupation without letting themselves be consumed by a deep and pervasive sense of guilt" (7). She continues later with the wry observation that whereas committed writing helps alleviate this guilt, it involves a simple displacement: "Committed writers are the ones who write both to awaken to the consciousness of their guilt and to give their readers a guilty conscience. Bound to one another by an awareness of their guilt, writer and reader . . . [carry] their weight into the weight of their communities, the weight of the world. Such a definition naturally places the

[2]In saying this, I am merely reiterating Coetzee's point; see "La Guma" 116–17. Henry Louis Gates, Jr.'s poignant recognition (which occurs throughout *Figures*) of the necessary double-voicing of his own academic texts is also highly relevant in this regard.

committed writers on the side of Power" (10–11). Where is the *place* of committed writing in a hungry, violent world? What power does it command?

More specifically, in relation to one particular case much discussed in U.S. political and academic circles, the concept of a politically or morally "correct" response to the problem of Central American refugees is part and parcel of a single reality that includes, as it suppresses, the most typical manifestations of that reality. It involves the entire history of the United States, its cherished national self-image as a nation of immigrants (welcoming the tired, the poor, the huddled masses yearning to be free, and so on, and so on). It involves as well the history of the borderlands and of U.S. intervention in Latin American politics. It also involves debates over the adjective to be applied to particular groups, the legal definition that makes them either "political" (acceptable) or "economic" (subject to deportation) refugees; it concerns the recent history of conflicts with, for example, the Sanctuary movement and the implications of this conflict in relation to the separation of church and state. Such minimally intelligible distinctions as that between the Guatemalan Indian who comes to the United States for fear that the contemporary abusers of human rights in her country threaten her life and the Guatemalan Indian who comes to the United States because historically ingrained human rights abuses in her country threaten her survival subsume the basic questions of value and linguistic slippage and, with the odd displacement, deliver us over to an unthinkable (sub)text that cannot be dismissed or commended as a specific response to the barbarism of a specific regime at a specific moment in the history of a specifically circumscribed and geographically bounded bit of the globe.

I propose to approach these questions, the strategy of silence and the issue of literature and politics in Latin America, somewhat obliquely through a reading of a short story, "Cariboo Cafe," by an American Latina, Helena Maria Viramontes, a Californian now working at the University of California at Irvine. Her work represents one specific writer's response to the implicit call for a moratorium on metaphysics in favor of more "realistic" committed writing and does so in terms that are perhaps the most immediately relevant to this discussion of the value or validity of a certain anguished postcolonialist discourse. Viramontes's deep allegiance to the cause of Hispanic women of color is

unquestionable, and the very fact of her (and other women's)[3] recent but ineluctable presence in a body of writing traditionally identified almost entirely with male authors (the evolving Chicano canon,
up until the 1980s associated nearly exclusively with Rodolfo Anaya,
Rolando Hinojosa Smith, Tomás Rivera, José Villarreal, and other male
writers) testifies to a literary upheaval and official unsilencing of no
mean proportions. Each of the stories in her 1985 collection *The Moths
and Other Stories* provides a nuanced view of some facet of a woman's
struggle against the restrictions imposed by gender roles, of some
dilemma involving a woman's silencing. In the best of these stories, the
overtly feminist critique is sharpened by an undercurrent of unmistakable political commitment.

Silence is an important theme in all these stories, on the levels of
both form and content. They tend to be laconic productions, un-
encumbered by flourishes of baroque imagery. Likewise, characters
speak little, keep secrets, reveal as little of themselves as possible.
Domineering husbands and fathers demand silence, respect, and
compliance from wives and daughters. Daughters, wives, mothers,
and grandmothers find these prohibitions so hard to break that the
smallest rebellion is accompanied by a disproportionately crushing
weight of guilt, and any breaking of silence tends to take extreme
forms—murder, for example. In "The Moths," such silences condition
the narrator's loving relationship with her *abuelita,* her grandmother:
"We hardly spoke, hardly looked at each other" (24). Even in such a
close relationship, these silences are not companionable, and breaking
of the silence is reprimanded: "Regretful that I had let secret questions
drop out of my mouth, I couldn't look into her eyes" (24). Aura
Rodríguez, the incurious homemaker of "Neighbors," has a clearly
established set of limits to her life: she "always stayed within her
perimeters, both personal and otherwise, and expected the same of
her neighbors" (102). Olivia, of "The Broken Web," keeps an unspoken agreement with her children, "a silent contract that they had
with one another, she never played mother and they, in turn, never
asked her to" (54). Olivia's lover's wife, referred to throughout the

[3]I am thinking particularly of contributions to narrative of women such as Lucha
Corpi, Denise Chávez, Ana Castillo, Estela Portillo Trambley, and Sandra Cisneros.
Women's presence in poetry has always been strong, and recognized.

story only as "Tomás's wife," and as the mother of his five legitimate children, floats in a "zombie-like" existence, speaking mostly when no one can hear her, not even the reader of the story, her "puzzle-piece heart" (56) a silent, unresolved mystery.

"The Long Reconciliation" documents Chato and Amanda's brief marriage and fifty-eight-year separation, a marriage conditioned by mutual incomprehension and lack of communication. The only point of contact between them is a toy carousel that each endows with a quite different symbolic burden related to his/her own distinct obsessions, a metaphorical legacy revealed in parallel monologues, overheard by no one but the reader. Chato, the narrator of the story, abandons Amanda without a word after shooting her enemy-lover Don Joaquín—her chosen punishment for aborting Chato's child— and thinks, "We both knew I was never returning; you stood there without a word, immovable as the mountain watching me ride off on a borrowed cloud" (90). Likewise, their long reconciliation is silent, occurring—well, from Chato's point of view at least—on the Day of the Dead, on his deathbed in the alien north, where he has lived during the long years of their separation. "I killed for honor," he imagines telling her, at last unburdening himself; "then I killed for life," is Amanda's imagined answer. But they never meet again in life after that definitive departure during the Mexican Revolution.

In "Cariboo Cafe," this technique of unheard parallel monologues is given its most striking expression; the story provides a third-world feminist's meditation on the function of silence and also offers an overtly sociopolitical commentary on the plight of those individuals displaced by either economic necessity or the horrors of Central America's undeclared wars into those other undeclared war zones, U.S. ghettos. In fewer than fifteen pages it offers a tour of this conventionally unexplored geography, sketching with quick strokes the eliminated inhabitants of these absent regions in our postmodern discourse: the illiterate, the silent, the unintelligible, the senselessly violent, those driven mad by day-to-day life in extreme poverty. The gravity of their plight weighs on us. The refugees, displaced from violence to violence, from the daily fear of repressive regimes in their native lands to fear of the police, the Migra, and the drunks, pushers, and prostitutes that make up their current neighborhood, struggle to survive, to raise their children, and to follow the sometimes labyrinthine code of the new laws of the land: "Rule one: never talk to strangers, not even the neighbor who paced up and down the hall-ways talking to himself. Rule two: the police, or "polie" . . . was la Migra in disguise and thus should always be avoided. Rule three: keep your key with you at all times" (61). Such traces of these existences as eventually reach the eye of the larger public through television reports and newspaper articles tell next to nothing of the destructive daily reality of such violence; history books say nothing at all.

The first crucial concerns inevitably become those of grounding such social and geographical distinctions as these in the graphisms of a politically relevant discourse. Who speaks? From where does speech emit? What is and what can be said? In this land where "freedom of speech" is generally taken for granted, such questions may seem simpleminded. In the context defined by this story, however, it soon becomes clear that these are neither idle questions nor trivial concerns. The story presents itself as a colonialist narrative that is obviously, unambiguously, at least doubly (more accurately, multiply) voiced. Yet, neither of the two dominant narrative voices proposes itself as a theoretical recreation of the voice of the Other, a shadowy presence at best and one that retains an unreadable silence. For example, both in the story and in the "real" world, Central American refugees are taken for illegal aliens subject to deportation; their only safety lies in silence. Shadowy figures stalked by those other shadows, their debilitating fears (64), they have been deprived of the basic human right of speech and, more radically, have learned to shun language as an alien minion of their antagonists. For them, the distorted propagandistic rhetoric of the army and the revolution in their home countries and the incompre-hensible English of the Migra and the police in the United States are equally foreign, equally inaccessible, equally invalid. "Freedom of speech" represents for the silenced refugees a bitterly ironic mockery recalling their lack of freedom and lack of speech. Language is waiting, but not for their voices.

Their fellow inhabitants of the ghetto are almost equally speechless. They are little people, compressed into ever smaller spaces, apologet-ically making their minimal requests, shrinking away, attempting to pass unseen. In Viramontes's text, indicators of smallness serve as stand-ins for what in Spanish would be marked by the ubiquitous use of the diminutive form: the drunk on the bus bench, discarded like the crumbled ball of paper he resembles, the newspaperman who sat in lonely isolation "in a little house with a little T.V. on and selling magazines with naked girls holding beach balls" (63), the illegals from the garment factory who order small cokes and sit to eat their home-packed lunches in silence, the junkie who excuses himself "politely"— "Juice gave him shit cramps, he says" (67)—to go to the bathroom and die of an overdose.

For the writer, the challenge of giving voice to the silent refugees, as well as to such minimally articulate people as the other ghetto dwellers, is great, especially when coupled with the implicitly under-stood requirement that, as committed writing, the work attain a cer-tain weight, a certain gravity. Viramontes's task is further complicated by the need to balance two very different constituencies: those who read, who speak, who enjoy freedom of speech, and those who are illiterate, who dare not speak, for whom the supposedly universal human right to free speech has no more significance than any other phrase of political oratory. In this respect, the Sartrean critic might legitimately address the propriety of writing a complex work in En-glish about (and partially for) people who cannot speak, much less read, even the simplest English phrase.

Who speaks, then, in this story? What is his/her language, sex, age; what are the historical, cultural, psychological, biographical contexts? Where is the place in this story that licenses speech, the demilitarized zone in the ghetto's moral equivalent of war? The easiest answer is that there is no one voice and no clearly localizable place, that Viramontes's story is multiply voiced and ambiguously located, that narrative con-sciousness slips from a near-omniscient third person to the direct reflections of various characters: a lost child named Sonya, an Anglo cook in a ghetto greasy spoon, a Central American woman deranged by grief. It is the child who first expresses the thought that "at least the shadows will be gone . . . at the zero zero place" (64). Yet, in naming the cafe—all the letters of the exotic and ironic word *Cariboo* have peeled off except the two *Os*—Sonya also names its essential charac-teristic. The name is unintentionally appropriate. Name defines place and vice versa; the stuttering emphasis on a mere surcease from fear, the zero zero, represents and performs itself in the act of naming. The story takes place in an empty place, a place that is no place at all. We might go so far as to say that "night" is the essential topographical feature of the ghetto. It is also the fundamental metaphor for the existential question that exercises minds and hearts in this situation. The zero zero, erased remnant of a barely remembered name, is the night's property, a tawdry palimpsest of illegible writing, unintelligibly foreign. What tends to drop out of sight in both stories—the narrator's and the reader's—is, as Lemuel Johnson has reminded me, the *Carib*, the indigenous element that waits, another silent presence, another hidden layer of writing on the scratched surface of the palimpsest, the unrecognized other half of the backdrop against which the transients shuffle, and suffer, and die. What remains undefined is the nameless act of violence that has suppressed the *Carib*, as well as the outline of the form the history of its repression might take.

Likewise, the cafe's "customers" are not customers in a traditional sense. They go to the zero zero cafe primarily neither to eat nor to drink but to seek sanctuary from the streets, to conceal themselves from the immigration authorities, to escape from the police. The zero zero place is an empty signifier, a parody of a no-man's land, an illusory crossroads where characters mistakenly believe the shadows that haunt them can be held at bay. And thus, as the first sentences of the story have it: "They arrived in the secrecy of the night, as displaced people often do, stopping over for a week, a month, eventually staying a lifetime. The plan was simple. Mother would work too until they saved enough to move into a finer future" (61). They, an unnamed they, arrived, and continue to arrive, in the night, in the ghetto, in the double-zero cafe, arriving from Central America, from the wars of the streets, from broken homes and smashed dreams; they, the flotsam and jetsam and refuse of an unwanted humanity, marked and scarred by the wars they have witnessed at first hand; they, arriving with their humble expectations and smaller hopes to confront cultural, linguistic, theoretical, psychological exile.

Who speaks? The readers ultimately. We, who speak for them, who give voice to their unexpressed longings, their inchoate thoughts, their emptied selves, creating text and context in a parodic counterhistorical account of abject beings forced by our conventions into the mold of artistic expression. We flatter ourselves that our attentive ears can hear their silences, that our sympathetic understanding can mediate the distances between their world and ours, can mediate the multifarious violence. "But also, in the end," as Michel de Certeau shrewdly observes, we must try to answer another question: "Where do *we* speak? This makes the problem directly political, because it makes an issue of the social—in other words, primarily repressive—function of learned culture" (135). Here, in this place—let us not pause to define its ruses as yet—we begin our mobilization. Ours is a police action: separating out the voices, bringing law and order, soliciting confessions.

story of my life

"At least the shadows will be gone," Sonya hopes, "at the zero zero place." "The double zero cafe," says the cook-owner of the dilapidated restaurant, in an unintended echo of and response to the little girl: "Story of my life." The name, like the cook, has come down in the world, mutilated from the original *Cariboo* given it by some nameless former owner. The present owner had to look up the word in a library somewhere, and he decided to keep the original name despite its unintelligibility: "It's, well, romantic, almost like the name of a song" (64). He gets, however, not the entire romantic *Cariboo* with its suggestion of faraway lands and exotic music, but only the two *O*s, the *Carib* lopped off and forgotten, the loss made prominent by the sorry remnants. Story of my life. Like the reader of the story, the cook tends to see his life either in terms of the wintery Cariboo scene or, as an unjust and fickle destiny's ironic correlation of his life with the empty double zeroes of his workplace.

"Story of my life," in the commonplace, sarcastic sense, and also the *story*, the story of my *life*, the story of *my* life. The two *O*s of the double-zero cafe recall the cook's double loss, of the wife who left him, of the son who was killed in Vietnam, the wife in occasional twinges of conscience, the son, JoJo, with the incessant pain of an open wound. Two *O*s, JoJo, *ojo*: the cook turns a blind eye to the irregularities of his customers ("Scum gotta eat too is the way I see it" [64]) and a deaf ear to their frenzied pleas for assistance ("Just 'cause they're regulars don't mean jackshit" [68]). The cafe owner is an abject antihero, precariously situated in a marginal business: "I offer the best prices on double burger deluxes this side of Main Street. . . . Okay, so its not pure beef. Big deal. . . . But I make no bones 'bout it, I tell them up front, 'yeah, it ain't dogmeat, but it ain't sirloin either' "(64). The voice of the ghetto businessman, despite his self-justifying insistence on his honesty, is understandably edgy and mistrustful, and his distrust of others reflects a radical personal doubt, his own self-distrust and guilt about the stain that won't wash out of his floor, the evidence of his as-yet-unnamed crime. Always unreliable, consistently self-pitying and bitter, his unvoiced thoughts become increasingly shrill as the story of his life, the story of this crucial day in his life, approaches its climax. The nameless cook feels he is forced into his role as *ojo*, the spectator-spy-denouncer of his clients, and is resentful of the circumstances that move him to *act*, to become the subject of a story, a life, a biography that repeats and reinforces other unspoken, unvoiced, unassimilated biographies of life on the streets.

Briefly and schematically, the events that shape the two days of this cafe owner's life, two typical days in the life of the ghetto, are as follows: The first day is relatively calm. Highlights include the arrival of Paulie, a drug addict and regular customer, who has to be pacified with coffee and yesterday's donut holes; soon after Paulie leaves, more trouble walks in the door in the form of a Latina—"she looks street to me. . . . Right off I know she's illegal, which explains why she looks like a weirdo" (65–66)—who surprisingly has enough money to pay for hamburgers for herself and the two children who accompany her. The next day is more eventful. Paulie OD's in the bathroom and dies. As a result, complains the cook, "I had the cops looking up my ass for stash," and in addition to suffering this humiliation, he still had to clean the vomit and excrement off the walls (67). Then, several illegals hired by the garment factory across the street run into the self-same bathroom to hide from a Migra raid. When the Migra agents arrive, the cook's reaction is to betray the workers: "I was all confused, you know. That's how it was, and well, I haven't seen Nell for years, and I guess that's why I pointed to the bathroom" (68). Shortly after that, the illegal Central American refugee woman returns to the cafe with the two children, whom the cook now identifies as kidnap victims, and once again acting against the dictates of his conscience and his inbred ghetto fear of authorities, he calls the police, because he "doesn't know where [Nell] is at or what part of Vietnam JoJo is all crumbled up in" (73).

The story of the cook's life is constructed around a double zero of these two crucial absences, and furthermore, through the three crucial betrayals of this day, the various wars that have shaped his life coalesce: the war with his conscience (represented by Nell), the war on the streets (Paulie versus the cops), the war against illegal immigration (*mojados* versus the Migra), the war that cost him his son (JoJo versus the Vietcong). The boy-child abducted by the refugee woman becomes for him his own son, a combined identity—JoJo-Macky ("he's a real sweetheart like JoJo"), reminding him in turn of the combined identity JoJo-Paulie ("JoJo's age if he were still alive"; but "I'm too old, you know, too busy making ends meet to be nursing the kid")—all lost in war, in the dirty undeclared wars of the modern world. The plot of this story, the "story of my life," turns, thus, on misreading and misinterpretation, on the error of inserting another face, another body, into the absences left by the doubled zeros of a lost time, of a betrayed conscience, of the inherent negativity of a duplicated guilt: "Children gotta be with their parents, family gotta be together, he thinks" (73). He expends the illusion of control over events in his life in betrayal, in the self-mutilation of a struggle against the power of time, in the effort to recollect and remember his child, to see in others hope for the return of a betrayed, beloved other. The double zero is for him a constant temptation and a continual evasion of responsibility. Drawn by its romance and its emptiness he slips into what Julia Kristeva in another context calls "the vertigo of a love with no object other than a mirage" (*Tales* 104). The empty *O*s of the falsely romantic *ojos* stare out blindly over the urban desert, deceiving the "I": the story, bitterly, of his life. The subtext, then, of the cook's tale of reluctant action is of witness rather than speech. His is an untold tale of a loss remembered in the figure of a silent child upon whom he pours the vertigo of a love loosed from its object by separation and death. In this respect, the cook's story turns on the impossibility of storytelling, while it points to the power of the imagination and "the permanence of love as a builder of spoken spaces" (Kristeva, *Tales* 382). All stories become one story, the story of JoJo and Nell, the end (object and goal) of narrative.

The child Macky, who serves as underlying stimulus for the cook's story, has a similar function in the story of the illegal immigrant woman, who, like the cook, though in an even more immediate fashion, is scarred by war, in her case by the disappearance of her five-year-old boy in a Central America indifferent to the fate of a small child. Macky, the reincarnated Geraldo, the fresh JoJo, represents the intolerable dissonance of hope for both adults, the uncomfortable resurrection of their private dreams. Such dissonance must, in a chilling reminder of the violence permeating the other America, be erased. "In some strange way, [the cook] hopes they have disappeared" as he cooks more hamburgers for the trio of illegals (73). The word *disappeared* echoes with the sinister resonances a thousand newscasts have taught us to recognize. The child forms the bridge between the two stories, between two experiences of war—that of the father and that of the mother—a bridge between two cultures and two languages; at the same time he remains apart, unidentified and unidentifiable. Both object of desire and symbol of the impossibility of its fulfillment, the child's role is best symbolized by the one word he speaks in the story, his only English word, "Coke."

If war is the experience common to all the characters in "The Cariboo Cafe," Coke is its concrete representation, the universal signifier. Coke is the only form of communication common to the inhabitants of the ghetto, the meager, bare transcendental signifier that breaks all their silences. The illegals who work in the garment factory come into the cafe "and order cokes. That's all. Cokes. . . . they mess up my table, bring their own lunches and only order small cokes" (65). The spoken word "Coke" represents as well Macky's hunger and Sonya's fear, providing the motivating force that sends them off through the falling night on the trip to the cafe. Coke, by another slight slippage of meaning, provides solace to the addict, represents the life force singing in his/her veins, the access to poetry, the harbinger of death. Coke is the coin of the realm, the point of contact between worlds; it is nourishment and poison, the ambiguous symbol of the freedom and the repressive violence to be found in the United States. Sweet-sad, ironic-sarcastic, ambiguous-paradoxical Coke: the metaphorical mother's milk of the ghetto. It is also the literary catalyst; through the shadowy figure of Macky, the magic word "Coke" offers passage from the father's tale into that of the mother.

—I saw them—

"Don't look at me," says the cook at the beginning of his monologue (64); another clichéd filler phrase that turns literal in context: don't *look* at me. His story is above all one of a failure of sight, embodied in his inability to see his son and in his lost contact with his conscience, his ex-wife Nell. The illegal woman's horror is the opposite terror of having seen too much. Unlike the cook, whose particular pain comes from not being able to imagine where or how his dead son lies in Vietnam, the woman's agony is that she can see only too well the probable fate of her disappeared five-year-old boy. "I saw them from the window," she says to herself, to us, speaking of the children held by the army in her home country. "Their eyes are cut glass, and no one looks for sympathy. They take turns, sorting out the arms from the legs, heads from the torsos. Is that one your mother? one guard asks, holding a mummified head with eyes shut tighter than coffins. But the children no longer cry" (68). George Yúdice, in a discussion of the Argentinian Mothers of the Plaza de Mayo has incisively underlined the parallels and the crucial distinction between the Central American woman's agony and the more distanced despair of other postmodern subjects:

> It is not concerned with certain cultural practices of Baudrillard-type simulation; nevertheless the same effect is produced: by way of torture, mutilation, and disappearances the past is erased and all identity, even that of the martyr, becomes impossible. . . . In the case of the mothers, it has nothing to do with the invisible logic of a hyper-real postmodernity; the oppressive regimes leave *real* fragmented bodies in public sight, the Lacanian holes (*béances*) . . . are not merely imaginary, but rather correspond to real disappearances. (47, 49)

The point bears repeating. Her despair is of a different order from that of the cook, for she is not allowed the solace of ignorance, is not spared the indecipherable pain of the eyewitness. The insistent visions of her recurrent nightmare strip her bare, denude her of illusions. We readers, voyeurs of her desperation, must distance ourselves from the unimaginable horror of the children: too grotesque to be "true," too true to what we know of oppressive regimes to deny.

The washerwoman's gruesome depiction of dismemberment parallels, as it intensifies, comments on, and reinforces the cook's metaphorical dismemberment of the only other woman described in the story, another mother, Paulie's girlfriend, a prostitute named Delia. Delia exists in the cook's story only as an asymmetrical pair of breasts: "That Delia's got these unique titties. One is bigger than another. Like an orange and a grapefruit. I kid you not. They're like that on account of when she was real young she had some babies, and they all sucked only one favorite tittie." Paulie, her current protector, hangs from the favored breast like another voracious child: "So one is bigger than the other, and when she used to walk in with Paulie, huggy huggy and wearing those tight leotard blouses that show the nipple dots, you could see the difference. You could tell right off that Paulie was proud of them, the way he'd hang his arm over her shoulder and squeeze the grapefruit. They kill me, her knockers" (65). Delia's children are never mentioned again; they are as lost to the story as Geraldo, their only function to provide the mouths that sculpted Delia's dissimilar fruits. Delia's "disappearance" and probable demise, however, is hinted at with a casual offhandedness that chills. The cook sees Paulie walk into the cafe without Delia, and "I open my big mouth and ask about De." Paulie, who is about to explode in the bathroom from a drug overdose, "drinks the rest of his O.J., says real calm like, that he caught her eaglespread with the Vegetable fatso down the block. Then, very polite like, Paulie excuses himself" (67). In this understated suggestion of fierce, silent reprisal, Paulie and the Central American police coincide as perpetrators of senseless violence.

The Central American woman is eventually goaded into action in Viramontes's story, but her role throughout most of the tale is essentially passive. Unlike the cook, whose story is one of apparent reluctance to get involved in the events unfolding around him, followed by a sequence of weakly rationalized actions, she is acted upon by others; only her fiercely protective mother love opens for her the possibility of making the minimal gesture. Losing Geraldo, finding Macky: the one initiates the nightmare, the second takes place in the vaguely realized geography of the dream.

Back in Central America, the humble washerwoman sends her son out to buy a mango; he never returns. She appeals to the authorities, who deny any knowledge of her child but suggest that if he were picked up by them, it would probably have been for distributing enemy propaganda leaflets. No child is innocent, none are too young to be imprisoned, tortured, or murdered, and in the chaotic warfare gripping her country she has no possibility of learning more about her son's fate, much less freeing him from his presumed captors. His disappearance, moreover, makes her an outcast; she is tainted by his presumed guilt. Brought to the United States with the assistance of her nephew, she spots Macky and his sister in the Cariboo Cafe. Ignoring the girl, whose presence never seems to register with her, she attaches herself to the small boy with single-minded determination, feeds him hamburgers and coke at the cafe, brings him home with her, bathes him, gives him milk to drink from a carton, puts him to bed, and the next day, once again at the zero zero place, dies defending him from the police who have come to take her son, as she believes, away from her once again.

No outline can reproduce or account for the extraordinary power of Viramontes's depiction of this Central American Mater Dolorosa, for despite the grotesque hyperbole of her initial vision and the almost staged hysteria of her final confrontation with the police, the suffering washerwoman stands in the text as an icon, a displaced and distorted image of the grieving mother with the body of her murdered son, the suffering pietà relentlessly impressed on our retinas by television cameras and newspapers as the focal image for the price of violence in our culture. The figure of the mother stands silently in reference to and refusal of humankind's frenzied inhumanity, a graphic symbol protesting the loss of individuality in warfare. The mother inhabits a body inexplicably left behind after the death of her child. She continues to exist, her function abruptly truncated, deprived of her rightful claim to the future. Paradoxically, her child, her singular, unique, unrepeatable child, mourned and never forgotten, is in this tale reborn, repeated in Viramontes's text and in the critical text as we merciless bone pickers sort through it again and again. "Writing," says Denis Hollier, "is committed to nothing but the death of a child, the only thing it is absolutely concerned with signing. . . . A dead child, a dead future: two futures that will never have been present, both dead before having seen the day, past before having been present, past without ever having been present" (195, 199).

Furthermore, to what degree is the mother herself particularized in this culture or in this text? To borrow a phrase from Mary Jacobus, is there a text in this woman? Or merely an iconographic image of a body displaced and dismembered by grief? Is there, in the profound sense, a story of *her* life to contrapose to "the story of my life" told by the cook? In attempting to approach this question, I return to the first and most impossible word of the washerwoman's testimonial, "I": "I saw them." What she envisions is an impossible scenario from one of the hidden detention centers for the disappeared: a guard holding up a head (a mother's head, her own head) to a child (her child, a please-God-not-Geraldo child), whom she refuses to recognize because of "eyes shut tighter than coffins." In a few short phrases, the woman presents herself/is presented as subject and object of an anonymous moral tale. She is both witness ("I saw them [the children]") and the horror that is witnessed (the children see/do not see the severed head). In this wavering between witnessing subject and helpless object of aggression she clearly portrays one of the typical reactions to the horrors of war.

The woman's narrative is as scattered and fragmentary as the bodies she evokes: a head here, a torso there, arms and legs tossed together in a gruesome pile, her prose dominated by the seesaw rhythm, the insane logic of horror. "This," says the soldier, sweeping away the tortured moths that fall from the lamp to his desk, "writhing in pain" as they die, "This is what we do to the contras, and those who aid them." "This," says the same soldier, crushing a cigarette butt under his boot, "is what the contras do to people like you" (69). As she looks around her tortured country, she sees the destruction of the people in the name of nationalism: "Weeds have replaced all the good crops. The irrigation ditches are clotted with bodies . . . and we try to live as best we can, under the rule of men who rape women, then rip their fetuses from their bellies" (71). Through the tortured structure of the woman's thoughts, Viramontes is able to show the *effects* of war without the strict literalization of describing actual battlefield scenes. As the collective social body is altered, so too is the earth transformed; irrigation ditches run with blood rather than water, the crops/fetuses/Geraldo are plowed under so weeds can grow.

Likewise, the woman mixes "I" and "she," subject and object, past and present, loss and recovery. It is as if a prolonged encounter with the unmitigated, unmediated fact of violence is more than the woman can bear, and the wavering point of view is paralleled in the text by frequent and jolting leaps from the unmediated "I" to the more distanced, third-person "she." As the story moves to its climax, the shifts in person and point of view become more and more abrupt; each paragraph, sometimes each sentence, moves to other eyes:

I bathe him. He flutters in excitement [direct discourse of the woman]. . . .

He finally sleeps. So easily, she thinks [indirect discourse of the woman]. . . .

All the while the young girl watches her brother sleeping [restricted narrative viewpoint].

Before switching the light off, she checks once more to make sure this is not a joke [omniscient narrator].

The cook wrings his hands in his apron, looking at them [restricted narrative viewpoint]. Geraldo is in the middle [indirect discourse of woman].

She looks so different, so young. . . . He can't believe how different she looks [indirect discourse of cook].

Aw fuck, he says [direct discourse], in a fog of smoke his eyes burning tears [omniscient narrator]. (72–73)

The child is the centering force, the disputed territory in this secret war, the starting point for the twinned narratives of the man and the woman. His is the stuttering tale of a man without words adequate to his solitude. Hers is less a story than a modulated cry of grief, punctuated with the minute hysterical hiatuses of repression, haunted by the reenactment of her loss, imbued with the aftereffects of her maternal incompletion. She offers no seamless surface, no self-justificatory biographical tale, indeed, no story at all since there is no undifferentiated, active "I," despite the irreducible individuality of her loss.

What the washerwoman describes in this broken, hesitant narrative is the reality of loss and the miracle (or fantasy) of repossession. She has regained, however, not her own sweet, obedient son but a child whose resistance to maternal reappropriation and emergence into individuality is signaled by his stubborn repetition of the word "coke." She ignores his resistance, displacing it onto the unseen, unacknowledged sister who retains her grip on the boy's hand in a silent struggle for possession. In this unrecognized tug-of-war, the woman employs her most powerful weapon: the mystique of motherhood itself. She describes her ferocious reappropriation of her child as a metaphor of childbirth: "I grab him because the earth is crumbling beneath us and I must save him. We both fall to the ground. . . . Its like birthing you again mi'jo. My baby" (72). Macky, whose mother disappeared in the Migra raid, is reborn for her as Geraldo, the boy who disappeared in Central America. With swift economy, two losses are made good, two rifts healed and made whole.

Subsequently all the rituals of maternity, of life, are reenacted in swift succession. The newly resurrected mother feeds the boy and bathes him: "I wash his rubbery penis, wrap him in a towel and he stands in front of the window, shriveling and sucking milk from a carton" (72). She croons to him, massages him to sleep; she has become at one with herself again, has recovered her prime function of motherhood, a function that war, with its emphasis on breeding soldiers, can only distort or destroy.

Yet the past is nonrecuperable, and reenactment of childbirth and maternity inevitably leads to a repetition of her loss. The newly birthed child, who shrivels and drinks milk, by a nightmarish implicit reversal becomes once again the child who shrivels and cries—and dies—for lack of care. When confronted by the police in the Cariboo Cafe, she projects a dream of reincorporation, of returning her newborn/reborn infant to her womb: "She wants to conceal him in her body again, return him to her belly so that they will not castrate him and hang his small, blue penis on her door, not crush his face so that he is unrecognizable, not bury him among the heaps of bones, of ears, and teeth, and jaws, because no one, but she, cared to know that he cried. For years he cried and she could hear him day and night. Screaming, howling, sobbing, shriveling and crying because he is only five years old, and all she wanted was a mango" (74). Her abject emptiness betrays her, and bordered by the imaginary father on the one side and the antagonistic girl-child on the other, she gives up her life rather than sacrifice her fantasy. Maternal love, maternal need, is her death sentence. When the police (the army) invade the zero zero place (her home), they bring their official silence with them and arrive "mouthing words she can't hear, can't comprehend." She cannot run and, cornered, must fight with words they in turn cannot hear, cannot comprehend. "She begins screaming . . . , screaming enough for all the women of murdered children, screaming, . . . and he pushes the gun barrel to her face." The distanced narrative clicks one last time into immediacy: "I laugh at his ignorance. . . . I am laughing, howling at their stupidity," as the bullet crashes into her brain (74–75).

The woman's narrative is yet more complex and more poignant. At its heart lies the crucial contradiction between the first-person evocation of birth—giving life and light—and the third-person gesture of concealment, a metaphorical protection that also hints at death and darkness. As the washerwoman herself recognizes, her life parallels the story of La Llorona, and behind the life-giving mother stands the shadowy nighttime figure of that other woman, the hovering figure of death. Laid bare. Unreal. For La Llorona is the counterpart of the soldier, the voice of the unnatural which he knows in himself, the mythic figure of the mother who, having selfishly abandoned her

children, realizes her love for them only after their death and is condemned to search for them endlessly: "It is the night of La Llorona.
The women come up from the depths of sorrow to search for their
children. I join them, frantic, desperate, and our eyes become scrutinizers, our bodies opiated with the scent of their smiles" (68–69). As
a mother, she is vulnerable; as an unwitting, unwilling messenger of
death, she is pitiless. Her eyes, like and unlike those of the soldier, like
those of the doomed children in the detainer, become scrutinizers of
other people's children, are lamps that attract the pretty, doomed
moths, are the moths themselves, fluttering and burning in the flame.
Tragically, there is for her no means of appropriation of the desired
object, no passage to love and life. The loss of her child is a death-in-
life; his recovery is literal death indeed: for her and, perhaps, once
again, for him as well, going into the last darkness, shriveling and
crying or shriveling and silent.

the missing key

The boy's silent presence serves as one apex of a family triangle
characterized by the implicit close combat between opposing forces of
paternal and maternal affection. The two parallel monologues, of cook
and washerwoman, are closely interwoven in the story as a kind of
unrecognized and unresolvable dialogue. Their distinct styles, and the
overall style of the story, operate on the principle of the tape recorder
or oral history. The story is "realistic" to the degree that it presents
itself as true-to-life: actual people using their own words, artistically
organized to create a political, committed prose. Yet this style, too,
obeys an unrecorded wish: the parallel monologues are projected into
a single space, creating the effect of dialogue, a dialogue between the
characters, between the characters and the readers, and between the
characters and the writer who copies down their words and thoughts:
passive, active, unvoiced, unheard. Voices crisscross and mingle in a
heuristically impossible space, a zero zero place of writerly recompila-
tion and readerly reflection. "The art of prose is interdependent with
the sole regime in which prose retains a meaning: democracy," says
Sartre. Adds Lyotard, "In prose, freedoms communicate. But in prose
insofar as it is an art" (Hollier xix). Insofar as the zero zero place
permits freedom of speech.

The story is made yet more problematic through the insertion of a third force into the narrative: Sonya, the "doggie sister," the supplement to the tight family triangle, unwanted by the cook-father, unrecognized by the washerwoman-mother. Hers is the third story, or the first, if we go by strict narratological order, since Sonya is given first voice in "The Cariboo Cafe." In a traditional narrative, her voice would also sound at the end of the story to provide the typical closure, a distanced frame to enclose the reciprocal metaphorization of the man and woman as focused on the boy. Sonya, then, would logically hold the key to a "proper" resolution of the drama, the expected moral principle we readers demand of narratives, political or apolitical.

Yet Sonya's story provides not resolution but a haunting insufficiency. She offers the motive for the story, but it is a motive framed in and conditioned by the negative; she has lost the key to her apartment, she cannot find her way back to Mrs. Avila's house, she cannot orient herself in the maze of back streets of the ghetto, she leads her brother into that quintessential symbol of negativity, "the zero zero place." She is our guide to the zero zero, the keyhole to which she puts her/our *ojo*, a hole in our neat representations of reality, the place that is no place at all. The necessary hole. Says Lyotard: "A hole is needed in every lock because a key is needed in order for it to work. . . . One is not very demanding when it comes to opening the lock. The passkey can be called Stalin, Togliatti, or Mao, as one prefers. What is important is the hole" (Hollier xiv). Sonya gives access to the hole, a hole which for her has many names: hunger, fear, loneliness, pain of loss.

As daylight gives way to darkness, Sonya begins to try to flesh out her desire, her need for shelter, from a chance-seen face on the street:

> She bumped into a tall, lanky dark man. Maybe it was Raoul's Popi. . . .
> Maybe she could ask Raoul's Popi where Mrs. Avila lived, but before she
> could think it all out, red sirens flashed in their faces and she shielded her
> eyes to see the polie. . . .
>   She peeks from behind the poster of Vicente Fernandez to see Raoul's
> father putting keys and stuff from his pockets onto the hood of the polie
> car. And it's true, they're putting him in the car and taking him to
> Tijuana. Popi, she murmured to herself. Mamá.
>   "Coke." Macky whispered. (63)

On the dark street the dark man could bear a resemblance to her classmate, Raoul. From there, the chain of the conditional is forged in the necessary real: A maybe Raoul's Popi becomes Raoul's Popi (maybe guide to Mrs. Avila's) becomes confused with (Sonya's) Popi, who is naturally associated with Sonya's Mamá, and leads (at least in Macky's mind) to the inevitable connection with Coke. Reading between the lines of Sonya's tale, we can see, alternatively, the police making a drug arrest or the immigration authorities capturing an illegal alien. "Coke," perhaps, is Macky's passkey, but Sonya does not trust it to unlock any doors for her. For her that degraded paradise remains somehow absolutely unattainable. This exclusion stands as a figure for other such preordained exclusions, other closed doors: locked out of the family, excluded from the primordial Carib and the exotic Cariboo, released to wander in the dark no-place of the nighttime streets. Without recourse.

Let me repeat: Sonya is the motivation, but she has lost the key, and thus her tale, and implicitly the story titled "The Cariboo Cafe," cannot be plotted through to its hermeneutically satisfying closure but must rest, with Macky and the washerwoman and the cook and Geraldo and Paulie and JoJo and all the other lost children and Sonya's own lost/deported parents, in the tortured dystopia of the zero zero place. Violence become banal, reassimilated as a daily risk in the life of the ghetto, as a constant in the life in Central America, forces the reader and the implicit narrator to evaluate the infinite terrorism of a narrative form that *must not* be closed. Definition dissolves in this shadowy, all-too-real fantasy land conditioned by the exchange of unattended voices, of unspoken, unacknowledged dialogue between maybe-parents, transients in perpetual flight from authority. Around such black holes of an erased geography, of silenced selves, the narrator constructs her story, ambivalently offers her unsettling, ambiguously metaphorical key to those locked doors. The death of the woman forces the cook to speak, the impoverished speech of those whose dealings with words are limited; his self-justification, not surprisingly, is encoded around the edges of that originary silence never meant to be broken. The double zeroes that inflect his story, that are the story, point silently to that ineluctable blank. This mythic masterplot is the necessary fiction that eases the force productive of the dazzling, unclosed, wished-for wound of the layered narration and interpretation of narration, the many-tiered assault on the self. "For the rest," as Barthes acutely remarks, "all we can say is that the object *speaks*, it induces us, vaguely, to think. And further: even this risks being perceived as dangerous. At the limit, *no meaning at all* is safer" (38). Resistance, except to the safely distanced formalizations of myth, is nearly invincible.

Ultimately, we are projected into the text though the keyhole provided by this semiinvisible girl child who understands nothing, who has lost the key and can only grasp, doggedly, doggily, the hand of her brother. Our unheard thoughts are channeled through her and are transformed by the insistent, intermittent force of her silent objection. And in the end, as Mallarmé has it, "Nothing will have taken place but the place" (quoted by Kristeva, *Tales* 135), a zero zero place, an empty space, the unrecoverable locus of the discourse on silence, and on the silenced.

3

Appropriating the Master's Weapons:
Luisa Valenzuela

Not too many years ago, in an essay we might optimistically imagine to be unwritable in this day and age, Clemente Hernando Balmori of the Universidad de La Plata defined women's speech in "a strict, technical sense" (this is an unacknowledged code phrase for "masculine," as we shall soon see) as "a type of differentiated language used by the women of some less-evolved communities" (123). It is clear from the outset that Balmori contends not only that a differentiable women's speech exists in what he might call primitive societies but that such speech is a particular phenomenon of an earlier evolutionary stage of humanity in which the society under analysis and particularly the women integral to it represent the underdeveloped elements. Thus, he concludes:

> One recommendation that all professors make to any student who begins to study a new language is to begin by reading female authors: Sor Juana Inés de la Cruz, Emilia Pardo Bazán, Rosa Chacel, . . . Gabriela Mistral come to mind as examples in our language; just as Virginia Woolf and the Brontë sisters in English, etc. In these women the student of a foreign language will find the most common terminology of that language, in generally simple and clear combinations, without any great danger of encountering obscure or abstruse terms, or difficult and overcomplicated constructions.[1]

[1]"Una recomendación que hace todo profesor al alumno que acomete el estudio de una lengua nueva es que comience por la lectura de autores femeninos: Sor Juana Inés de la Cruz, Emilia Pardo Bazán, Rosa Chacel, . . . Gabriela Mistral se me occuren ahora como ejemplos en nuestro idioma; así como Virginia Woolf y las hermanas Brontë para el

He goes on to discuss intonation patterns and phonemic variation; he mentions frequency of diminutivization and tag questions in women's speech; he talks about taboo words and breadth of vocabulary. And of course, in his study the distinctive postpuberty physiological difference in pitch of men's and women's voices carries its own distinctive value markers, noted by the scientist but left vaguely undefined in Balmori's *por algo:* "Por algo se engendró el refrán que todos hemos oído y celebrado 'Del hombre tiple y la mujer bajón, líbranos Señor'" (130). 'It must have been for some reason that the refrain we all know and celebrate was engendered: "From the male treble or the female bass, save us, O Lord'" (130). After his overview, Balmori finally comes to the conclusion that "all the proof points in the same direction: women specialize terminology less . . . while men demonstrate greater specialization and technical precision and are at the same time more open to the universal." Women are closed and conservative; their more open counterparts, the men, go striding forth into the world, meeting it both with a greater intellectual distance—the propensity to think in technical terms—and with a more receptive attitude toward an evolving society. To support this conclusion, Balmori paraphrases with approbation the finding of Otto Jespersen that "education, therefore, is not . . . the cause of this inequality"; women are just naturally more interested in "the ornamental," whereas men are drawn to "the constructive" (138).

Balmori's conclusions are shockingly parochial, but his 1962 article is a far from isolated phenomenon. He deserves credit for at least recognizing the "technical" importance of women as serious linguistic subjects to a competent investigator's complete analysis of human language use. Not all his contemporaries would agree. Antonio Griera, for example, in his *Linguistic Atlas of Catalonia*, recommended that linguists and their assistants in the field avoid using women as informants, claiming that they cannot sit still long enough to provide adequate samples, their vocabulary is too restricted, and they will not answer the delicate questions investigators must ask (paraphrased from Saint-Jacques 89). Even a cursory review of such papers as these, with their scientific pretensions and protective screen of technical

---

inglés, etc. En ellas el aprendiz de una lengua extranjera encontrará los términos más corrientes en dicho idioma, las combinaciones en general sencillas y claras sin mayores peligros de términos abstrusos, desusados, y construcciones enrevesadas y super-complicadas" (137–38).

vocabulary, serves to remind us that women's right to speech has traditionally been restricted; their right to be listened to, restricted even more. In such studies women are "proven" to be less evolved, less informed, less abstract, less universal, less technical. The disgruntled reader might well conclude that, taken all together, such papers only tend to reinforce a priori stereotypes: men want to sound like men, to meet the world man to man, whereas women want to sound like . . . girls? . . . and to retire to the protected interiors of their real or play houses. I beg the reader's indulgence if I seem to be engaging in an unnecessary argument with an outdated and irrelevant article. My point is not to set up Balmori as a straw man but rather to use his work as a convenient shorthand articulation of popularly persisting assumptions that still provide the basic structure for much social interaction.

At question, as Robin Lakoff teaches us in her seminal article "Language and Women's Place," is not only how women use language but how language uses women and how men and women use language with/against each other in the metaphorical battlegrounds of social interaction. To thinkers like Balmori women's language seems more circumspect and gracious, less charged with the uncivilized variations on emotional expression because of the well-known and documented *pudor femenino* (female modesty and decorum). Why women in particular are more respectful of convention seems, in his analysis, to have something to do with their mental underdevelopment. Thus, their reluctance to employ concrete language relating to sexual functions may be connected to women's greater respect for taboo (134), "maybe because of superstitious preoccupations" (137). Women maintain a linguistic conservatism intimately linked to their greater attachment to tradition and formality. Women, consequently, are "naturally" more retiring, more superstitious, less able to speak directly about their bodies and particularly about their sexuality. Or as Luisa Valenzuela might say, women are charged through their very vagueness with a ferociously satiric repudiation of the norms of what *cannot* be done if a veneer of civilization is to be maintained. As she notes, "Good girls cannot say these things; nor can elegant ladies. . . . Nor can other women, the not-so-ladylike women, utter those words categorized as obscene" ("La mala palabra" 488). For Valenzuela, such linguistic censorship figures other, more directly politicized forms of censorship, and the *palabrotas* (obscenities, big words) are at the heart of a much-needed transformation in language. Men dominate women by dominating the range of expression of eroticism; until women learn to take control of their share of erotic/obscene language, they will continue to be dominated in other realms as well, for by appropriating the language of desire, men appropriate as well what is *propio* to women, what is their very own, though alienated by custom.

It is perhaps to be expected that much of contemporary Latin American women's writing, unperceptively defined from the outside as a "wallowing in disgust," specifically constitutes itself as a refusal of the traditional restrictions and the customary censorship of feminine *pudor* and ladylike *recato* (prudence, coyness) and concerns itself with taking back from men the right to use all the words, including the precise and functional words for the woman's body. When Valenzuela speaks of the need for women to engage in "a slow and tireless task of appropriation [*apropriamiento*], of transformation" ("Mala" 490), she is indicating the important task of taking back the use of the language that uses women. She calls for an appropriation of language that asserts a woman's rights to an estranged linguistic property as her personal possession and is also involved in a making-one's-own of oneself, in realigning alienating categories and creating a new understanding of what is proper in the careful and intentional use of improprieties. *Apropriamiento* is the public assertion of rights to that personal and private space. It is to take that which has been assigned to another for her own, for the first time to take herself and take for herself the woman customarily appropriated by another as his property. "To take" and not "to take back": the original appropriation—of words, of bodies, of power—is credited to human nature. Thus, in Doris Sommer's words, referring to the politically active women of Bolivia's "Housewives' Committee," "these women who take up men's tools also use language in a way that doesn't fall into a 'visceral emptiness' [Elaine Marks's term] but rather adjusts and challenges the very codes they adopted from their admirable men" (125). These women are far too busy and far too committed to worry about emptiness other than the emptiness of their children's stomachs. Nevertheless, they provide a concrete instance of the practice taken up at more theoretical or abstract levels by the Latin American women writers: they take up both tools and language and, in so doing, forge new instrumentalities.

If the contemporary woman writer's subsequent unrestricted reap-

propriation of language is sometimes misunderstood—by the condescending reader who exclaims, "What an excellent novel (or short
story or poem); it looks as if it were written by a man!" (Valenzuela,
"Mala" 491), or the distinguished critic who asks, "titillating voice, full
of insinuation, if it was true that I wrote pornographic stories" (Ferré,
Sitio 23)—the intent is nevertheless clearly other: "Turn back this
weapon, the weapon of humiliating and hotly embarrassing sexual
insult, brandished against us women for so many centuries, against
that same society" (Ferré 25); turn it back in a defiant act of destruction
that is also, obscurely, a constructive act, seeking out and constructing
una voz propia (one's own voice). To appropriate in this strong sense is
an act of hope, a call for transformation of social and political and
linguistic and interpersonal relations, a demand for a different reading, for reading otherwise. To appropriate in this sense also involves,
as Valenzuela and Ferré, among others, openly recognize, the clear
risk of reappropriation and recuperation once again in existing categories, as when a Valenzuela work is read as a transvestite male text,
when a Ferré can be condemned for/congratulated on her pornographic stories.

Appropriation involves entanglement, exposure of vulnerabilities;
in taking over her own voice, the woman writer opens herself to being
taken back (again). And the struggle continues. With the same weapons. Or others. The breach has already been made in the laudatory
statement "it looks as if it were written by a man." As Valenzuela
reminds us, the minimal slippage between "seems" and "is" opens up
the literary canon to a more nuanced questioning of the supposedly
universal character of literature, not now ever preconceived as sexless
but always in terms of a gendered discourse. To write "like a man" in
such a reading is to demonstrate that what is called literature is in fact
men's writing and that writing by a woman is valued according to its
proximity to this dominant male tradition. If such a statement seems a
bit shopworn through overrepetition in the now-standard feminist
analyses of patriarchy and its myths, the implications are not. One of
Valenzuela's most typical textual practices is to appropriate clichéd
words and phrases, marking them and marking off her critical distance
from them through an ironic preface: "la llamada Laura" (so-called
Laura), "su llamada llave" (her so-called key), "el departamento (¿departamento?)" (the apartment [apartment?]), "su pretendida autobiografía" (her supposed autobiography). Valenzuela's remark on

these concepts consists entirely in drawing attention to their traditional uses and connotations, in this manner estranging them from the commonplace and appropriating them for other, yet-to-be-defined usages. Her technique, then, relies on both the reader's and her own steeping in the tradition she decries, so that the alienation from too-familiar, uncontested terms can carry an implicit subversive comparatist thrust.

From the vantage of a literary-critical practice, already in 1981 Myra Jehlen was calling for a radically aggressive feminist comparatist practice in which the critic would examine male- and female-authored texts from the same period together as a salutary lesson in contingency. Here too Valenzuela can help. Her acclaimed and now-canonical texts, with their much misunderstood bifocal vision, are models for this type of analysis and are crucial in suggesting useful tools for just such radically comparatist studies as Jehlen proposes. Certainly in Latin America it is, as Showalter might agree, "far too early and too dangerous to give up the demanding task of reconstructing women's literary heritage, a heritage still unfamiliar to many scholars, in exchange for a one-sided comparison"; still, it is important to recognize yet another mode in which the weapons of a masculinist critical practice are being/have already been exchanged. As Showalter notes, "Jehlen's essay appeared at the beginning of a renewed feminist interest in reading male texts, not as documents of sexism and misogyny but as inscriptions of gender" (*Speaking* 5). In the Latin American context, as Valenzuela reminds us, a subtle transformation occurs with the appropriation of critical weapons—she calls it an injection of estrogen into dominant ideologies—so that when the sensitized readers (male or female) look again at canonical texts (male or female authored), they too begin to appropriate the texts differently. Texts like Luisa Valenzuela's, which subtly employ masculinist assumptions against themselves, require attentive gender-conscious readings with special urgency. It is this type of reading that they were prematurely born to elicit and are in fact eliciting in the interstices of even the most traditional critical discourse, marginally undermined along the double-voiced fault lines of what is said to be, of what is called, of the preemptive "as if" of an incomparable, unexpected appropriation.

The particular form of this appropriative gesture has already been named, in the felicitous coinage of Clarice Lispector, a "fac-simile." "I write you," says the unnamed female artist of *Água viva* to her lover,

her interlocutor, her (male) literary audience, and implicitly the gesture of homage is also a weapon of appropriation: I write (of myself) to
you, and that which I write is constitutive of you. In writing—by
definition "like a man"—she creates a likeness of the man and a self-
likeness, consciously manipulating a style sanctioned by tradition and
undermining its pathological assumptions (when I say this I have in
mind Eve Sedgwick's definition of one of the functions of tradition: "to
create a path-of-least-resistance [or at the last resort, a pathology-of-
least-resistance]" [243]). Tradition can be most effectively subverted
along just such well-worn pathways. At first glance Lispector's narrator hints at an incomplete or distorted autobiographical account; at
second a kind of inept role reversal, Pygmalion to her sculpted lover:
"I write you this fac-simile of a book, the book of one who does not
know how to write" (*Stream* 43). In fact, she is not incomplete, distorted, or inept. The appropriative gesture turns the knowledge of the
other against the lover, she constitutes him as she deceptively in-
scribes a so-called constitution of the self. She appropriates but, with
an injection of estrogen, escapes the confinements of the model in
reconstituting herself as a false copy, a simulacrum, the split simile,
like and not like, that which affirms and negates the model in the same
word. In so doing, Lispector—herself the author of a story with the
resonant title "The Fifth Story"—decries both mimesis and genealogy.
The crucial question, perhaps, is not what the origins of the gesture
may be but to what uses it may be put, and is continually being put: a
way of being that is a way of speaking, or not speaking, or writing, but
which always involves the informed interaction of the reader.

The hormonal charge of a differently gendered discourse is nowise
esoteric, and for clarification I take my example from Luis Zapata's
second novel, *En jirones* (In shreds), the journal of a much-vexed love
affair. At one point in the novel, the (male) narrator explicitly describes
his authorial stance in relation to his work. The severely edited version
of this authorial positioning reads "like a man"; that is, it flows along
the traditional pathways of an archetypally conceived male discourse:
"Independently of the solicitations, of the specifications, of the position taking, and the detailing of desires and preferences, whose author
or designated audience could be anyone, I discover a sentence in the
institute's bathroom that seems to address me specifically." In Zapata's
novel, however, this commonplace phrase is interrupted at each point
by parenthetical remarks that prevent the kind of active misreading

operative in the critical reaction to Ferré or Valenzuela. When the parenthetical remarks are returned to the text, the authorial positioning becomes strikingly, shockingly unconventional, and still, in the Latin American context, largely unacceptable: "Independientemente de las solicitudes (busco verga), de las precisiones (19 años, la tengo grande y cabezona), o de las tomas de posición (soy puto) y la especificación de deseos y preferencias (me gusta mamar, soy pasivo), cuyo autor o destinatario puede ser cualquiera, descubro una frase en el baño del Instituto que parece concernirme directamente: 'Dame tiempo, papacito: llegará el momento en que me la retaques hasta el fondo'" (59). 'Independently of the solicitations (I'm looking for a prick), of the specifications (19 years old, I have a big one with a large head), of the position taking (I'm a hustler), and the detailing of desires and preferences (I like to suck, I'm passive), whose author or designated audience could be anyone, I discover a sentence in the institute's bathroom that seems to address me specifically: "Just give me a little time, daddy-boy: the time will come when you'll really give it to me.'" The reader, shaken from the comfortable pathologies of a neuter reader relationship, is insistently gendered and redefined by sexual preference. Resistance too is subsumed in the prophetic phrase on the bathroom wall, a narration still framed but now out of the closet, the seductive promise of a deferred penetration between men, between a forthright author and a coyly (self-) deceptive reader, without the place-holding, face-saving symbolic exchange of women to mediate the act. Like Lispector and Valenzuela, Zapata also intuits the potency of the fragmented fac-simile, and the charge of his hormonal injection, perhaps even more insistently marginalized than theirs, is equally disruptive of the pathologies of least resistance. In his work, as in Valenzuela's, an apparent "wallowing in disgust" ideologically reframes itself in a violent break from the customary censorship of a highly charged vocabulary.

In the novella "Fourth Version" from *Cambio de armas (Other Weapons)*, the narrator, a frustrated coauthor and editor of the scattered papers of Bella, organizes the fourth fac-simile of the story of the actress and her ambassador lover. At each step the attempt at a rational restructuration of key elements fails. Materials at hand are scarce, key elements are silenced or lost, and what remains seems more appropriate for another genre. The editor, faced with the impossibility of constructing a traditional narrative according to conventional formal properties, eventually breaks down into a fac-simile of a critic: "The papers tell her story of love, not her story of death" (22)—either an indecipherable code or, worse, an incomprehensible reversal of priorities. Later, disgruntled, the editor-critic complains about the difficulty of assigning a genre to the papers—"Verbose Pedro, respecting a certain kind of silence which ended up spreading to Bella too, to the extent that her alleged indirect autobiography, her confessional novel, ended up deflating itself in certain parts" (23)—and finally acknowledges that her preferred reading of events stumbles against a lack of supporting materials: "I don't understand why the crucial information has been omitted regarding this key encounter" (26). Each version—the internal author's, the fourth; the critic's, let us say Sharon Magnarelli's, the fifth;[2] this one, the sixth—carries its own preassumptions and presuppositions; each writes the text as a variation of self-writing (of the critic, not of either Bella or Pedro); each limns another portion of the appropriative field, works another inversion/subversion of the writing of the fac-simile.

In one such variation, "Fourth Version" reenacts in a fictional setting one of the critical moments of Valenzuela's own political activism during the Jorge Rafael Videla regime, when, in her words, "the important thing at that time was the possibility of protecting people" (García Pinto 232–33). It has as its counterpart the final story of the collection, the title story "Other Weapons," told from the viewpoint of one of those to whom the protective net did not extend. "Other Weapons" represents the starkest of these conflictive encounters and also the most extreme case of the appropriative gesture. It projects the limit case of social censorship of women through the unexpected metaphor of a traditional middle-class marriage. Thus, the protagonist, "the so-called Laura," could easily be identified with one of the dissaffected housewives familiar to us from other middle-class fables: those of Clarice Lispector's *Family Ties* and Rosario Castellanos's *Album de familia* (Family album), of Marta Lynch's *Señora Ordóñez* (Mrs. Ordóñez) and Albalucía Angel's *Misía señora* (Mrs. ma'am), of Rosario Ferré's *Maldito amor* (*Sweet Diamond Dust*) and Silvina Bullrich's *Bodas*

[2]Or perhaps the fifth through tenth versions. In her fine *Romance Quarterly* article, "Luisa Valenzuela's *Cambio de armas:* Subversion and Narrative Weaponry," Magnarelli outlines five readings of the novella: political allegory, erotic tale, detective story "on at least two levels," "modern-day rendering of the fairy tale" of Sleeping Beauty, and ultimately, a "synecdoche for the female experience in contemporary society."

de cristal (Crystal wedding), of Cristina Peri Rossi's *Libro de mis primos* (Book of/about my cousins) and the *New Portuguese Letters* of the "three Marias," of Carmen Gómez Ojea's *Otras mujeres y Fabia* (Other Women and Fabia) and Mercedes Salisachs's *Volumen de la ausencia* (Volume of absence) and María Luisa Bombal's *La amortajada* (Shrouded woman), among so many others. Concurrently, however, the reader superimposes another model—that of the hysteric, gone mad among the proliferation of signs detached from meaning—and for this reading the key precursor texts are such works as Freud's *Studies in Hysteria* or the much-analyzed story "The Yellow Wallpaper," by the nineteenth-century American writer Charlotte Perkins Gilman. Still further, and most shocking of all, Valenzuela superimposes on this already over-determined scene of middle-class life the outlines of a specifically political outrage: the disappearance and torture of politically active individuals throughout Latin America.

Says Valenzuela, "Politics has forced itself on us. . . . the time comes when you can't detach yourself from it, the horror was so great that it is worse to keep quiet" (García Pinto 232). This collection of stories is overtly marked by Valenzuela's need to speak out against the "dirty war" waged against Argentinian citizens by its military forces in the 1970s. Foucault has written in *Discipline and Punish* of how, in the past, torture was a public spectacle, and dismemberment took place in the plaza almost as a form of entertainment. In modern times, the scene of torture has moved indoors, underground, and has become anonymous. It is this faceless, capricious torture that Valenzuela so painfully evokes.

The Sábato Commission report on human rights violations during Argentina's "dirty war" documents the forms of that country's terror. Ford Falcons roamed the roadways; people were abducted from the streets, from their homes, blindfolded, and driven to one of the *pozos* (pits). Most commonly, the blindfolds were never removed, and this "walling up" was the first and not the least of the tortures. Its purpose, says the Sábato report, "was to make [the prisoner] lose his spatial awareness, thus depriving him not only of the world outside the pozo, but also of everything immediately beyond his own body. The victim might be assaulted at any time without a chance of defending himself. He had to learn a new code of signals, sounds, and smells in order to guess whether he was in danger or if the situation had eased" (*Nunca Más* 57). Other, more physically damaging tortures followed: wounds, burns, rape; sadistic beatings with rubber truncheons; electric shocks from cattle prods, "the grill," "the machine," or the "telephone"; near drowning (sometimes combined with electric shock) in the "submarinos." Whole families were abducted and tortured in one another's presence. They were tortured less for information than for the pleasure it gave bored officers. As Ronald Dworkin writes in his introduction to the English translation of *Nunca Más*, "At the height of the terror . . . bored junior officers in the torture squads roamed the streets in their Falcons looking only for pretty girls to take back to camp to torture and rape and then kill" (xvii). One piece of testimony is all I have room for; the Sábato Commission has 450 pages more in their report, and those too are selected and incomplete files:

> The next day the interrogation of this person began. First he was tied down to a bed—he couldn't be handcuffed because there weren't any handcuffs large enough to fit his wrists. He was beaten with a rubber truncheon but, seeing that they were not getting any results, they began using the telephone wire on him. One of the wires was tied to the foot of the bed and they applied the other to the most sensitive parts of his body, and to his back and chest. As they still couldn't make him talk, they started hitting him again, until at one point the prisoner asked to go to the toilet, which request was granted. I was put in charge of guarding him personally, which terrified me. I noticed then that he was passing blood, that is, he seemed to have sustained serious internal injuries. When I handed him back to the interrogators I mentioned this, but they dismissed it. Before the torturers went off for the night, they left him tied to a pillar in the open air with strict orders not to feed him and to give him only water to drink. He died hanging there in the early hours of the morning. He had been so badly beaten that he had been unable to withstand the punishment. . . .
>
> Women were interrogated in the same manner. They were stripped naked, laid down on the bed, and the torture session would begin. With women, they would insert the wire in the vagina and then apply it to the breasts, which caused great pain. Many of them would menstruate in mid-torture. With them they only used the telephone, no other device.
>
> On one occasion they brought in a wounded prisoner. One day, out of curiosity, I went up to his window, since I was alone and you could see through the gap. As I got closer, I saw his head had been split open, and when I looked at his hands I noticed that they were full of maggots. (Antonio Cruz, member of the Gendarmería, 1972–1977; *Nunca Más* 37)

Trying to summarize or comment on this testimony, the Sábato Commission stutters on the verge of near speechlessness: one of their most common adjectives is "indescribable."[3]

One especially forceful aspect of Valenzuela's story is her imposition of the political on scenes from everyday life; she reminds us that, on one level, the unequal relationship between the sexes always retains the propensity to slip into a microcosmic dictatorship, or into madness, and recalls as well, on the level of more directed political critique, that one of the horrors of the interactions between a torturer and his victim is the degree to which they rest on and recuperate for the scene of torture the fac-simile of the most conventional domestic arrangements. The scene as initially presented is totally unremarkable. The so-called Laura seems to be the pampered and completely dependent, perhaps even agoraphobic spouse of a loving and understanding man who caters to her whims even as he enforces her dependence and subordination. Yet the attentiveness to her every wish, the anticipation of her unspoken desires, is only the insidiously symmetrical mirror of the ring of prohibitions that surrounds and stifles her. The borderlines of their relationship are clearly drawn, the limits of her field of operation are unmistakable. He, the unnamed husband, is "always leaving" (128), and even when he is present "se queda como ido" (115; English text 107), literally, "it's like he's gone," or more accurately, "he's worried, he's preoccupied." She, the obedient wife, remains behind, on this side of the apartment door. At times, the key

---

[3]Valenzuela's stories, while growing out of the particular circumstances of the brutal police actions in her own country, have a wider applicability: to the Guatemalan government's systematic destruction of whole Indian populations, for example, or to the abuses of power by the military government in Chile. In the latter case, military authorities decided that all women prisoners must be raped, all pregnant women must be beaten until they aborted. Jacobo Timerman summarizes: "The psychiatrists also discovered a tactical decision made by the military: that all women arrested for political reasons should be raped. In those days the rapes were mostly carried out by the officers themselves, but specially trained dogs were also often used to violate women prisoners. . . . The individual who worked out this particular tactic was an intelligent and cultivated man who knew that a woman who has been raped faces great difficulties in rebuilding her emotional life afterwards. He realized, too, that for wives and mothers a sense of humiliation would permeate family life, causing permanent emotional instability. Additionally, the use of rape as simply another police method—a routine part of the system—was a way of overcoming any resistance by the police themselves. A student of biochemistry testified that the man ordered to rape her objected, but was forced to do so by the other carabineros, who then proceeded to gang rape her" (30).

to the apartment seems to call to her, "pidiéndole a gritos que trans-greda el límite" 'begging her to cross the threshold,' but Laura knows too well where the border lies: "But she can't; not yet. Facing the door she thinks about it and realizes she can't, although no one appears to care much" (106). That self-defining border is barrier and shield, that which allows her to extricate herself, confusedly alive, that which, if transgressed, could be either life or death—at any rate, too much of a risk in her present precarious state of consciousness.

At this point the unnamed man has all the weapons, the literal and metaphorical phallic weapons: whip and gun, key and male sex; they allow him to cross the borders and invade her territory without re-course. And yet, curiously, it is in this intimate invasion that the so-called Laura's transgression begins. As Dorothy S. Mull concisely reminds us with reference to another story in the collection, "the protagonist's 'weapon' is not merely the written word, or the spoken one, or fantasy, or amnesia, or a revolver. It is her body itself, and what she does with that body" (95). It is enough for Laura to see herself in the mirrors of her room or the imagined mirrors of another's eyes and, in seeing herself, to absent herself from the eyes on the other side of the peephole, from the brutal construction put on her body by the violent penetration of the man (her husband?): "What good are their eyes, ears, teeth, hands, when those men out there can't cross the line [no pueden transgredir el límite]. Because of that line, drawing it out, he keeps on taking her with fury, without pleasure" (126). Other times and places are lost in the protective amnesia. This time the scene (of the torture?) is triangulated: man, woman, and unidentified violating eyes on the other side of the door. But they (we?) on the other side of the door have no use for their/our bodies, and she—Laura—is inac-cessible to them/us. She is also inaccessible to her husband/torturer. Supposedly his object, his plaything, thrown into an abominable real-ity by his words, his eyes, his sex, she accepts him and in so doing defines the corporeal limit that he cannot transgress. "Woman," says Valenzuela in "The Other Face of the Phallus," "and especially that mythical nonentity called womanhood, has practically always been mapped by men. Ever since the beginning of time we have been told by men what to do with our bodies, and chiefly with that portion of our bodies so full of menaces, so much like the other hidden part: the mouth" (242). The tortured woman/acculturated housewife offers no overt menace; her words and her sexuality seem almost entirely detached from anything that could be described as essentially hers; yet it is exclusively through her words and her sexual life that we readers are able to begin to chart the topography of her life. Hers and his, for like Lispector in the "I write you," she tells not only her own forgotten story but also the untold (abominable, disappeared) history of the man. But as that geography, that writing, like a medieval map, corresponds more to dream and wish than to any concrete knowledge, the woman escapes behind the screen of a superficial appropriation, and the menace redoubles. Laura, in an even more extreme sense than the literary women described in Valenzuela's essay, is able to disappear in the supreme alienation of/from her body, forfeiting her independent existence. In so doing, paradoxically, she ensures her integrity, now repugnant to the man. The "husband" maps Laura's body, but an undefinable surplus escapes his cartography. Her body denies his, even as it welcomes him; he experiences only a fascinated rage and no pleasure in the act of possession, which involves her only as a shattered mirror of his own projections. She is powerless, but her very emptiness drains him.

As he hands the woman her own revolver near the end of the story, the man explains the intent of this charade. He is not only her cartographer but her creator; in the violation of her mind and in the circumnavigation of her body he has constructed a living work of art: "You have to know that now we've come full circle and my task is fulfilled [culmina mi obra]" (134), a hysterical text constituted by a newly achieved understanding of the absences and gaps in the story, of the loss of control and the acceptance of manipulation. But that work of art can be completed only in her recognition of it. In refusing to transgress the limit, she will have defeated him: "Nothing can be perfect if you stay out there on the other side of things, if you refuse to know" (133). She must cross the limit he has drawn; in order for him to emerge victorious in their encounter, she must reappropriate, on his terms, the knowledge he had torn from her mind, must permit him to say, as he has always said, "I write you." Having taken her away from her original purpose and made her over into the stereotypical image of patriarchal domesticity, the unnamable man takes on another role, and another, and another: lover, torturer, psychoanalyst, and writer. The husband suggests the importance of conjugal communication with his wife, the psychoanalyst puts together a case history of a hysterical patient, the torturer demands a confession of the political prisoner, the author requires a rounded story of his protagonist. The blurring of categories reminds us that in each case the woman, objectified, tells not her own story but some version of it as reconstructed by another. Says Elaine Scarry: "World, self, and voice are lost, or nearly lost, through the intense pain of torture. . . . The prisoner's confession merely objectifies the fact of their being almost lost, makes their invisible absence, or nearby absence, visible to torturers. To assent . . . is a way of saying, yes, all is almost gone now, there is almost nothing left now, even this voice, the sounds I am making, no longer form my words but the words of another" (35). The ambiguous and chameleonic "he" asserts himself in these multiple roles by forcing the woman to speak, by censoring the content of her speech, by shaping its intent.

At this point, with deep suspicion, we can look back on the role of the editor/author of the papers collected in "Fourth Version." As Patrocinio Schweickart has pointed out, "Evidence has been accumulating that there are fundamental differences in the 'interactive competence' [Jürgen Habermas's term] of males and females and that these differences are developed at an early age" (303). Schweickart specifies a number of these differences, including a difference in storytelling style: "There is a sharp contrast between girls' well-developed sensitivity to others and their preference for shared storytelling and boys' tendency to 'assert a position of dominance' and 'to sustain a monologue even in the absence of overt support'" (303). Certainly, in "Other Weapons," the coronel's insistent (if ultimately failed) demand to dominate the woman's story fits the masculine style described by Schweickart; he wants the story told, but in his way. What, however, can be said about the more persistently inscribed narrative presence of "Fourth Version," in which the storytelling task seems almost too dispersed?

In "Other Weapons," the coronel reminds the so-called Laura, "I've got my weapons, too" (135); in "Fourth Version," the narrator muses, "And I, who am putting all of this back together now [Y yo, quien ahora esto arma], why do I try to find certain keys to the whole affair when those being handed to me are quite different keys?" (33). *Armar* (to put together) is always a model for potential violence, intuitively pointing toward its opposite: the revolutionary blowing apart of a system or a text. Fellow Argentinian Julio Cortázar's novel *62: Modelo para armar (62: A Model Kit)*, stands as a precursor text for this double meaning of the verb. To write (rewrite) this story is to give it a particular construction, to appropriate its multiplicity for a single point of view, to aim the weapon in a particular direction: "There is no author [autor] and now I am the author [autora], appropriating this text that generates the desperation of writing" ("Fourth Version" 20). The too-easy slippage between masculine *autor* and feminine *autora* is in itself reason for despair, one of the reasons, perhaps, that this markedly feminine author insists on the multiplicity of stories, as if the repeated reminder of the absence of a claim of authority—this the *fourth* in a series of appropriations of the documentary evidence and emphatically and implicitly not the last of such reconstructions—and the admittedly incomplete nature of the editorial enterprise are enough to deflect the critical weapons that may be aimed at it. "Stop talking to me in capital letters," Bella complains to Pedro (41); the crystallization of role and function—the Ambassador, the Actress, the Messengers, the Great Writer—refracts in the multiple mirrors of the layered text as frivolously parodic emblems: arms perhaps, but either sinisterly distanced or singularly ineffective. To identify too closely with them would be to lose the freedom to escape behind the mask, to play with the roles while enacting a subtle *apropriamiento*. What the *autora* fears is the danger that one of a chorus of "las mujeres escritoras" (note redundancy) to whom "they have sold the idea of transexuality" might fall into the text (Ordóñez 518). Most critically, she rejects the pompous and self-congratulatory "Great Writer," who arrives all unaware in the midst of an all-too-real revolution, only to find himself weaponless.

There is, we begin to suspect, an element of the theatrical in this emphasis on mirrors and masks and bodies that react with the discipline of trained mimes. There is, particularly in Bella's repertoire of practiced gestures, the highly overdetermined artificiality of the woman often dismissed as merely decorative. Let us return to Clemente Balmori once again for enlightenment: "Let us begin by noting that the characterization of woman's language has its roots in nature herself. The more spontaneous and natural it is, the more feminine and womanlike will be her speech" (124). Compare this statement with a passage a few pages later which may puzzle us by its apparent contradiction: "In her speech she also sharpens her weapons [ella afina también sus armas], her arsenal of grace and flirtatiousness, to sum up, her anxiety for femininity that will no longer abandon her" (130). After young men reach puberty, Balmori finds, it is a matter of course that they begin to expand their vocabulary through their use of earthy "new terms" paired with a loftier focus on the universal qualities (however defined); but that is another story. Woman's speech is "closer to nature," says Balmori, though this closeness to nature is inexplicably defined through learning to flirt. He specifically relates grace and flirtatiousness to formulas such as "¡Es un encanto de chico!" or "¡amorôoso!" or "¡nnnooo!" 'What a darling child! So lovely!'—what we might consider the linguistic equivalent of the five-inch spike heel. In Balmori's words, women's speech is "always more spontaneous, more emotional, more impressionable *or likes to appear that way*" (my emphasis 133). Women, apparently, demonstrate naturalness through well-defined and highly conventionalized artifices of mock spontaneity. Even more striking, this development is defined, albeit condescendingly, with a military metaphor: "her weapons, her arsenal."

This is, of course, precisely the first image we have of Bella in "Fourth Version." The actress is depicted behind the scenes, "sharpening her weapons, her arsenal of grace," readying herself for the battle, practicing her lines, putting on her makeup for that night's performance on the stage, for the self-representation that is her personal/political weapon in the undeclared war on the streets, declaiming, "My role is to be alive," while "she made herself up carefully to go to the party" (7). For Bella, maintenance of a superficial frivolity is a radical and rigorous form of work. It is, in fact, her life's work, preserving her life to protect others. For Bella, the distance professionally enforced between representation and reality constitutes a shadowy revolutionary praxis. She knows all too well that at any moment the stage set could easily give way to the torture chamber; the theatrical gesture of faked beating might seamlessly merge with the drama of questioning and of pain maliciously inflicted; politically compromised roles could become political reality, the almost pain of self-erasing could slip into the unendurable pain of a reality that recreates the body in destroying it:

De la representación a la verdad, del simulacro al hecho. Un solo paso. El que damos al saltar de la imaginación hasta este lado ¿qué lado? de la llamada realidad. . . . Si vuelvo a mi país y me golpean, me va a doler. Si me duele sabré que éste es mi cuerpo (en escena me sacudo, me retuerzo bajo los supuestos golpes que casi casi me hacen doler ¿es mi cuerpo?).

Mi cuerpo será, si vuelvo. . . . Cuando le arranquen un pedazo será entero mi cuerpo. . . . Y así lo represento y representando, soy. La tortura en escena. (41)

From performance to truth, from simulation to fact. One step. The one we take when we step from the imagination over to this side—what side?—of so-called reality. . . . If I go back to my country and they torture me, it will hurt. If it hurts I'll know that this is my body (on stage I shake, I squirm under the supposed blows that almost really hurt—is it my body?). It will be my body if I go back. . . . When they pull a piece off, it will be my whole body. . . . And thus I perform it; and performing I am. Torture on stage. (39–40)

On the one hand, Bella imagines that her body will become her own on participating in real terror. Paradoxically, she also knows that she *is* only insofar as she *represents*, that her whole being is absorbed in a scene of torture/a drama about torture, that she is herself an embodiment of "torture on stage." To the degree that she enforces this perception she openly identifies herself as literary rather than corporeal. Thus, the fragmentation of her text enacts the scene of physical dismemberment. On the other hand, like the so-called Laura, Bella knows that reality has at least two sides, that in leaping from imagination to the torture chamber she has only crossed the first of the borderlines. Laura would remind her that the second door, the one with the peephole, represents the most ambiguous and dangerous transgression of all and requires another arsenal of weapons to vanquish.

The so-called Laura, too, has been readied for a role, constructed, in the absence of will, in the plastic shape of that most "natural" role for women: the ordinary middle-class housewife. In the absence of will, however, we do not have a representation, natural or artificial, but rather a metarepresentation molded in some synthetic substance: "She only cares about being there, watering her plant, which looks like plastic, putting creme on her face, which looks like plastic, looking out the window at a faceless wall" (117). As Mary Jacobus very acutely observes in another context, "Without representation, there could be no 'self,' and therefore no meaning. The words we learn by rote and repeat to dramatize our (forgotten) stories are all that stands between us and the unraveling of identity" (272).

Valenzuela's genius lies in the brilliant conflation of several stories about women as a single, half-forgotten story. Very simply, one of the terrifying implications of "Other Weapons" lies in its highlighting of the darker side of traditional domestic arrangements, where ties of tenderness or comfort or custom show their hidden affinity with manacles and violent repression and prisons and where the torture chamber mimics the home so as to enhance the charge of horror. For Laura, scarred by the dissection of her identity in the dramatic encounter of the torture chamber, no other representation has the power to move her. Here the unconscious memory of pain is sufficient to announce the conversion of every object—from the more obvious recourse of pistol and whip to such seemingly more innocuous household objects as the photograph, the keys, the peephole, and the mirrors—into instruments of torture. She has been reduced to dumbness, left with no stories, no meanings, no words, or more exactly, with words that dissolve and deconstruct themselves in the moment of enunciation. "Don't torture yourself" says the man, and he (she?) reads the tender request as an autocratic demand: "Let me torture you," asking permission for the impermissible. The threat alone is effective enough; he flamboyantly rids himself of his prop, tossing the whip out the door with a "rather theatrical gesture" (123–24). Her drama is the reverse of Bella's. She once acted without self-conscious representation of her role, and when a piece was torn away from her body/self, her whole self was lost. The man's gesture is studiedly theatrical, Bella's profoundly, if self-consciously, so, but the so-called Laura, reduced to a role, has neither the freedom nor the luxury to meditate on such refinements or to make theatrical gestures.

The woman's habitual mode in the story is, understandably, avoidance: she flees mentally from the drama of life, takes no part even in routine domestic affairs, cannot address herself to the passivity that serves as the precondition and determinant of her current existence. And yet, in her flight from the theater of her current life, the so-called Laura, so-called housewife, has perhaps already achieved a perverse triumph over her tormenter. Martina, the servant hired by the coronel to take care of (spy on?) her, sees her mistress as a madwoman: "Now she doesn't know whether she should leave the poor crazy lady alone or wait one more day or leave forever" (131), and earlier in the story the narrator recognizes but cannot define her difference from other people: "She feels strange. Foreign, different. Different from whom? From other women? From herself?" (110). The room, the self: these are uncontestably real, but the definitions and the connotations of those definitions are unstable, offering the possibility of contestability only in terms that society would consider insane. Madness provides its own relief, its own release from the rage of imprisonment and power-lessness, its own enigmatic self-possession in an inaccessible, inde-pendent realm. As Jacobus reminds us, "Mental illness replaces im-prisonment as the sign of women's social and sexual oppression." In the specific case of the Gilman story "The Yellow Wallpaper," feminist readings teach us "not only to symbolize (reading the narrator's con-finement in a former nursery [in Valenzuela's story the confinement shifts to the bedroom] as symbolic of her infantilization) but to read confinement itself as symbolic of women's situation under patriarchy" and, furthermore, to read into Gilman's depiction of madness a kind of victory over domesticity: "to see in madness not only the result of patriarchal attitudes but a kind of sanity" (233).[4] The insanity that derives from helplessness can convert itself into a fiction of empower-ment. Refusal to recognize the other's weapons becomes in its own way a weapon.

The parallel reading of Gilman's story and Valenzuela's can take us only so far, however, for the two stories differ fundamentally in the form the madness takes. For Gilman, madness presents itself in the figure of a woman creeping behind the patterns in the bilious yellow wallpaper; it is, in Jacobus's words, a madness defined through "the unnecessary maze of sign-reading. . . . Hers is a case of hysterical (over-)reading. Lost in the text, she finds her own madness written there" (231). For the so-called Laura, the case is quite different. She does not "read" at all; her problem is more fundamentally epistemo-logical: "What is the forbidden (repressed)? Where does fear end, where does the need to know begin, or vice versa?" (125) She is at a loss for words to solve the mystery of this "what" and this "where," and fear and confusion keep her silent. Meanwhile, the objects and people around her remain opaque: unintelligible, prohibited, re-pressed. She does not question the material objects around her, nor does she question the reality of her own (fragmented, refracted in

---

[4]Clarice Lispector's story "The Imitation of the Rose" has much in common in this respect with both Gilman's story and Valenzuela's. In the Brazilian's story, a woman named Laura, recently returned to her home after a bout of mental illness, struggles to maintain the flat passivity of domesticity and sanity expected of her by her loving husband, only to slip once again into the self-fulfillment of madness in the contempla-tion of the beauty of a rose.

mirrors) body. What she does question is the subjective possibility of language itself, the ability of an increasingly distanced and distorted "I" to express herself in words and for those words to have any kind of relation to the objects she sees around her. For language plays a crucial role in constructing not only a sense of reality but also a sense of identity and a grounding of self and things in a meaningful system. According to Gerald Bruns, "Having a theory of language means . . . having a theory of meaning or truth, that is, a theory of how language links up with reality. . . . But suppose language doesn't 'link up' with reality, or with anything at all? What if it just stands on its own?" (133). Bruns answers this question with respect to "natural" language and Heidegger's discussion of "saying"; clearly, the so-called Laura intuits another answer to Bruns's very pertinent question. To say and to link things up with language are both dangerous undertakings involved in the expressibility of life and the construction of truth. In this particular case, however, expression is untenable insofar as Laura refuses acknowledgment of the necessary and absurd power play of law and custom. In maintaining her fascinated distance, she perverts language into an utter flatness, the revolutionary impact of which we can perceive only at the periphery of an analytical reading.

The body's needs are themselves defined by the body's nudity, or lack of it:

> Lo llama de vuelta a su lado, para que la cubra con su cuerpo, no para que la satisfaga. Cubrirse con el cuerpo de él como una funda. Un cuerpo—no el propio, claro que no el propio—que le sirva de pantalla, de máscara para enfrentar a los otros. O no: una pantalla para esconderse de los otros, desaparecer para siempre tras o bajo otro cuerpo.
>
> ¿Y total, para qué? si ya está desaparecida desde hace tanto tiempo. (136)

> She calls him back to her side, for him to cover her with his body, not for him to satisfy her. Cover herself with his body like a glove. A body—not her own, obviously not her own—she can use as a screen, as a mask to face others. Or maybe not: a screen so she can hide from others, disappear forever behind or under another body.
>
> And what for, after all? She already disappeared quite some time ago. (127)

The clearly intentional repetition of the key word, *desaparecer/desaparecida*, recalls the circumstances of other cover-ups, other revelations. Political prisoners disappear: unspeakable. Madwomen disappear, ignored by polite society: untellable. Ordinary housewives disappear behind—are absorbed into—the self-representation of the husband, his words, his reading of reality, his interpretation of truth: inarticulate. The so-called Laura disappears from the presumed voyeur's sight behind another body, or is disappeared. *Desaparecida* is action and absence, the body (lost) and the language that defines the screening of the body, the loss of the speaking subject and the speaking of the loss. Has the hypothetical staring through the peephole changed her, reconstituted her? Forced her to reappear, if only provisionally? Foregrounded the conditions of disappearance in the scene of two bodies coupling/covering? Uncovered the nature of the instinctual economy of bodies as an archetypal loss in a masculinist society?

In still other terms, these distinctions, and collapses of distinction, must be reframed in the larger context of the relationship between two groups of men—active/passive, violator/voyeur, and alternatively, lover/husband, revolutionary/military (both armed). This set of connections reflects, of course, the traditional, already-subverted pathways of resistance, but to the degree that Valenzuela's work continues to elicit the criticism/praise that the author writes "like a man," it remains essential to address their permutations. In respect to the so-called Laura, regulation of the factitious marriage bond forms the basis for regulating other societal structures as well. Infractions against political institutions enter the metaphorical realm as marital spats or the disruptive activities of fractious children, and culture itself, in Claude Lévi-Strauss's words, can be described as a system of exchange "not established between a man and a woman, but between two groups of men. The woman figures only as one of the objects in the exchange, not as one of the partners" (115). In this regard, the woman in "Other Weapons" is the object exchanged between the inaccessible lover (her brother or comrade in the revolutionary struggle) and the new husband (the military officer, figure of the paternal order), the penetrable token of their unbreakable bond, their eternal enmity. Caught between their conflicting ideologies, she has already been ground down in the exchange: comrade, wife, whore, lover—in each case she is their constructed object. The lover arms the woman, converts her into a revolutionary, and sends her on a mission: kill the coronel. The coronel enacts the first exchange of weapons, disarms (both senses of the word) the woman, and gives her a new role to play, that of wife. The two actions represent strict corollaries of each other, the woman effaced between them like a screen upon which the two men project their parallel dreams of dominance. In neither case is the choice of weapons the woman's; in both cases her self-ignorance remains enforced by culture, equally constrained by the pathways of convention and of resistance. Another reading of this story, following radically upon the implications of these observations, might well question whether or not there is a "woman" closeted in this claustrophobic apartment with the man, or whether the so-called Laura has so far receded that all we have left is a woman-effect, a woman as the subject of, rather than the subject.

How is it possible, Luce Irigaray asks, framing a series of parallel questions in psychoanalytic terms, that "the active/passive polarity dominating that [sadistic-anal] stage's instinctual economy should subsequently be *split in two,* with one term assigned to the man and one to the woman? The same thing happens with the terms subject/object or again, in the oral and phallic stages, the polarities phallic sex/castrated sex. And all the components of the instinctual economy—see/be seen, know/be known, love/be loved, rape the object/object (liking to be?) raped, . . . pleasure/unpleasure?" (92). The woman's acceptance of her lack of subjectivity complements the male's assumption of his exclusive rights to it. Yet the two are mirror images; the male's dominance propped on female submission, his refusal to recognize her dependent on her self-abnegation. Irigaray comments: "She herself knows nothing (of herself). And remembers nothing. . . . At/as back of the scene of representation which she props up by/without knowing it. She makes no show or display. . . . A lack-luster double of the self-duplication that man carries within him, his 'soul,' when 'she' doesn't stand in the way with her 'body.' . . . Polished surface that will not be scratched or pierced, lest the reflection be *exaggerated* or *blurred*" (345). Laura refuses much knowledge, but she knows this: "The price of knowing the secret is death" (125). Nudity must be covered: by ignorance or pretended ignorance, by self-alienation in the reflective surface or the mirrors, by roles and masks and makeup and ornamentation, in the last case, by another body. Essential knowledge is the intolerable risk. Clarice Lispector suggests a compromise: "We ought to say 'chicken egg.' If we simply refer to 'the egg,' the topic is exhausted and the world remains naked." Similarly, "the universal law so that we may go on living decrees: one may say 'a pretty face' but anyone who says 'the face' dies; having exhausted the topic" (*Legion* 49). To exhaust an object or a life by revealing its essential nudity is a death sentence. Better to be covered, to be mad, to pretend to accept what Valenzuela has called the civilized (male) face of the phallus, to be seen, to be known, to be loved?, to be the object (liking to be?) raped in the abject paroxysms of unpleasure. The voice and all it implies are his; the body, disappeared, hers.

For Valenzuela, the single most powerful image of the screen that uncovers as it discovers and recovers the body is the mirror, in particular, "la máscara de espejos" she invents for her protagonist in *Como en la guerra* (As in war). The mirror-mask takes particular form and significance in that work, but the metaphorical mirror-mask is ubiquitous throughout her other works as well. She tells Monserrat Ordóñez, "This mirror-mask is the other's face. One lives reflecting the other and the only moment in which a person is his/her own mask is when that person holds the mask in his/her hand and sees oneself in that mirror" (511). The specular game intimated in Valenzuela's mirror-mask operates as an exceptional appropriation of the masculine mode of perception by intensifying its hidden signification; he looks and, in his refusal to recognize the other, sees himself, refracted in the more conventional mirror of her submission. In the mirror-mask, however, the submission is turned into a pretence (she hides her face behind his as Laura covers her body with that of the man), while the forms of submission are strictly enforced. The mirror-mask, unlike the time-worn and overused image of the mirror held up to nature, represents not the world-making work of fiction but rather the uncreating of the world, using the word to hollow out the world.

And this operation too suggests a reconstitution, a recuperation or reinvention of what Valenzuela has described under the general term of myth. "I write myths," says Valenzuela, "in order to reinvent myths" (Ordóñez 518). "Myth is a *value*," Roland Barthes has said, but the mythic value, like the desire, has no meaning without self-alienation in what Hegel has described as the unbreakable law of the master who requires a dependent, subordinate consciousness (the slave) to recognize him. In "Other Weapons," the master-slave dialectic is played out as myth, mirror, and mask coalesce under the sign of torture. Torture, as the so-called Laura's tormenter comes to realize, functions only insofar as it enhances the reality of the torturer. In imposing himself on the tortured body of his victim, and in insisting that she watch his possession of her in the bedroom mirrors, he forces recognition of his self, of his desire as the desire of the other. Where this identification falls short, mastery fails, the woman remains inscrutable, inappropriable. According to Hegel's concept of recognition, the self must act, must impose himself on another in order to affirm his existence, but the other must, in turn, accept domination and recognize the other as dominant: the interdependency is inescapable. Alexandre Kojève remarks: "Therefore, to desire the Desire of another is in the final analysis to desire that the value that I am or that I 'represent' be the value desired by the other: I want him to 'recognize' my value as his value" (7). But from the man's point of view, of what value is recognition by a thing of no value, a mirror reflection, a *desaparecida*, pure absence?

There is more. The mirror portends a subtle appropriation in other fields as well. Valenzuela explains: "The mask is a type of defense. . . . It is what we use to hide ourselves and to reveal ourselves. . . . With masks, with the play of masks, we can break the double barrier of censorship. . . . The mask and the human being make this double play of signified and signifier. . . . For me, the mask is a survival" (Ordóñez 512). The mirror-mask, then, mediates the imposition of master on slave, of man on woman, of torturer on victim; she does not want to recognize him and hides herself from him, calling him back, covering herself with his body, transgressing the limits without crossing the threshold of the door. "If there were a definition of *différance*," says Jacques Derrida, "it would be precisely the limit, the interruption, the destruction of the Hegelian *relève wherever* it operates. What is at stake here is enormous" (*Positions* 40–41). Mark Taylor agrees, and he adds a gloss on the importance to Derrida of rewriting the Hegelian principle of the *Aufhebung* in his own mirror-mask text *Glas:* "In rewriting *Aufhebung otherwise*, the writer writes the fissure 'in' Hegel's System. This fault 'is' the tomb in which the 'pyramidal silence' that sounds the 'glas' of Western philosophy forever echoes. *Ecrire autrement: écrire un texte bâtard...récrire gl...gl...gl...Glas*" (Taylor 278). For Valenzuela, (re)writing otherwise is writing out the experience of a woman's primping for her man in front of her mirror, is beginning to intuit the stuttering bastard text of an anguished torture victim whose mirror self has been cracked. It is above all asserting the *différance* in her words, differing from and deferring to the language of patriarchy as she defers her definition of it: "I believe in the existence of a feminine language, even though it may not yet have been completely defined, and even though the boundary between it and the other language . . . may be too subtle and ambiguous to be delineated" ("Word" 96). It no longer surprises us, then, that Bella, the protagonist of "Fourth Version," is an enemy of finding herself in reflections and that she glances obliquely into the mirror only to discover the potential for a *desconocerse*, an "un-recognition" (*Cambio* 4). The intrusive narrative voice informs us that "Bella is one of those people who talk to the mirror because the other alternative would be to look at herself" (*Other Weapons* 5). In contrast, the so-called Laura is endlessly forced to look at herself in mirrors and evinces only curiosity about that plastic reflection, so apparently real, which nevertheless slips almost imperceptibly into something so artificial (113–14).

In Derrida's *Glas,* as Taylor reminds us, the " 'calculated *glissement,'* slipping and sliding, of words, terms and concepts, is repeated as '*gl*... *gl*... *gl*,' " a guttural stop that " 'arrests' meaningful articulation." He quotes Derrida: "But *gl?* His *gl?* The sound *gl?* Then angle of *gl?* His/its *gl?*" The apparently seamless flow of Derrida's punning eloquence confronts the irreducible sound of mutism, the failure of speech or loss of trust in the value of speaking. For muteness can also represent a kind of mutilation of body or mind. With the "*gl*... *gl*... *gl*," the wounded word struggles for expression, eloquence stutters on the edge of aphasia. The *gl,* furthermore, also resonates with the fading of name, self, identity, with corporeal ruin as well as the ruin of language. It is, Taylor concludes, "neither quite animal nor quite human, . . . but somewhere *between* the animal and the human" (300–301).

These difficult and abstract philosophical reflections converge with an unexpected mirror text, *The Little School* of Alicia Partnoy. In this testimonial, Partnoy, an Argentinian poet and ex-*desaparecida*, writes of her experiences and those of her husband in the hidden prison where they were tortured. During the husband's torture, the *gl, gl, gl* returns as the torture victim's unsayable link with humanity—his own fading sense of himself as a human being—precariously retained through his memories of his daughter: "Daughter, dear, my tongue hurts and I can't say *glo-glo-glo;* even if I could, you wouldn't hear me. . . . I've repeated it for a whole day but I still can't sleep. *Glo-glo-glo he sings on the roof...* I won't see you again... The electric prods on my genitals... Trapped, like the little frog... but that's not my scream... That's an animal's scream. Leave my body in peace. I'm a little frog for my daughter to play with... *We all hear him/glo-glo-glo when it rains... glo-glo-glo*" (93, 95).[5] The unspeakable *glo, glo, glo* mediates between animal and human, concretizes the moment in which voice is lost in screams of pain, in which the self and world slip and slide on the verge of nonsense and unintelligibility. "The little school" does not teach its pupils the old anthropomorphizing tales; rather, it enacts a perverse lesson, dehumanizing, decivilizing, unteaching.

For the so-called Laura, the most persistent form of ongoing torture occurs as ritual violation in the repeated rape/seduction of her body on the bed, in the mirror, before invisible witnesses. The enforced recognition (and disrecognition) of the other takes place in this most intimate transgression of her physical boundaries, and it is continually impressed on her that she is merely a thing whose principal characteristic is that of always being pliant and open to the will of her master: "It's an inexplicable multiplication, a multiplication of herself in the mirrors and—the most disconcerting of all—a multiplication of mirrors. The last one to appear was the one on the ceiling, above the big bed, and he forces her to look at it and thus to look at herself, face up, legs spread" (113–14). Thus, through the mediation of the mirror, he maintains his boundaries and transgresses upon hers, insisting on his power and her subordination. Her refracted gaze in the mirror—like the invisible eyes of One and Two behind the peephole—empowers him, reminds him of her fled resistance, allows him to vanquish her former self repeatedly in calling up the image of the woman he has already destroyed. She too is something less than human, something other than animal. If she were in fact only the body on the bed—plastic, artificial—the game would be ended. The "husband" requires something, woman or object, to violate, and though there is progressively less of "her" to rape, the remainder of her original self taunts him to make her will, not only her body, totally his. Likewise, if she had retained the integrity of her original identity as a guerrillera, the violation would be of the body only; her mind would remain intact, hers, not his. It is because she is both his creation and his enemy that he can continue to violate her so ambiguously, because he can still see

[5]Partnoy translates the poem, a popular children's rhyme in Argentina about "El sapito glo-glo-glo," as "Rib-bit Rib-bit Little Frog." I have modified the translation to reinsert the "gl."

himself in the mirrors of her eyes that he can presume to retain his mastery; it is because, in Kristeva's words, "from its place of banishment, the abject does not cease challenging its master. Without a sign (for him), it beseeches a discharge, a convulsion, a crying out. . . . It is a brutish suffering that 'I' puts to the father's account: I endure it, for I imagine that such is the desire of the other" (*Powers* 2). Abjection becomes the first sign of the reemergence of a formerly obliterated self, horrifically eroticized on the threshold of the apartment. She emerges, ignorant and pliant but alive, the bleeding stopped, the hemorrhage of existence halted, scarring begun through her own self-recognition in the eyes/mirrors of the other, in a recognition of self as the object of desire, in the half-stifled aspiration for existence in another, of another. Kristeva again: "There is nothing like the abjection of self to show that all abjection is in fact recognition of the *want* on which any being, meaning, language, or desire is founded" (5). Want is primary, but her ordeal has provoked in her the desire to forfeit want, to want not to want so as to avoid further pain.

This abject self emerges as the by-product of torture, but the arrangement of its modes and effects is similar in outline to that obtaining in hysteria and phobia. Scarry suggests that in torture "the subjective characteristics of pain are objectified" (52), and her use of the passive voice reminds us of the procedures of passivation occurring in these other realms as well. Kristeva, for example, uses terms very similar to Scarry's to write about the slight slippage that can produce a phobic personality rather than merely recapitulate a standard stage in the construction of subjectivity: "In parallel fashion to the setting up of the signifying function, phobia, which also functions under the aegis of censorship and repression, *displaces* by *inverting* the sign (the active becomes passive) before *metaphorizing*" (40). Kristeva speaks of the symbolic threat involved in the syntactical shift from active to passive modes. In the case of the so-called Laura, however, the inversion signals neither a hysteric conversion nor a phobic transformation— though much of the power of the story resides in the potential for confusion with these processes—but rather reinversion of an already displaced sign prior to the recall of a repressed or censored memory. Kristeva describes the sequence by which the phobic manages the threat/fear/fantasy of incorporations as "I am not the one that devours, I am being devoured by him; a third person therefore (he, a third person) is devouring me" (39). For the so-called Laura, the

passivity has occurred during the now-forgotten or repressed episodes of torture and is rehearsed daily in the mirrors above the bed.
Rape and murder are the corollaries to devourment in Laura's version
of the phobic's construction. She has failed to kill; therefore she is
raped in body and mind: "I am not the one that kills/rapes, I am being
raped by him; a third person therefore (he, a third person) is raping
me."

Likewise the corollary to passivity, the tendency to metaphorize,
takes on ominous overtones. For Laura does not "metaphorize,"
though her confusion may lead her to think she is doing so, when she
takes the objects in her cozy apartment for weapons or her "husband's" lovemaking for violation. Instead, she is calling up associations both enforced in torture and repressed by unwanted bodily
memories of relentless pain. Torture, says Elaine Scarry, "is a process
which *not only converts but announces the conversion* of every conceivable
aspect of the event and the environment into an agent of pain" (27–28,
my emphasis). The forgotten or repressed episodes of torture man-
ifested themselves to her in the con/inversion of both signs and sensation. She cannot prevent herself from a so-called metaphorizing but
must resist the pull of metaphor in order to keep from frightening
herself to death. The egg, as Lispector says, must be modified, the face
adorned, for self and civilization to survive.

Words for formerly benign objects are unmade in the process that
"announces their conversion" into weapons. Ordinary household
items have a doubled meaning—one pole forgotten, the other repressed—which retains a vaguely threatening aura: "Then there are
the everyday objects: the ones called plate, bathroom, book, bed, cup,
table, door. It's exasperating, for example, to confront the so-called
door and try to figure out what to do" (106). Scarry explains: "The
room, both in its structure and its content, is converted into a weapon,
deconverted, undone. . . . made to demonstrate that everything is a
weapon, the objects themselves, and with them the fact of civilization,
are annihilated; there is no wall, no window, no door, no bathtub, no
refrigerator, no chair, no bed" (41). For Laura, such conversions result
in the retention of curious sequences of words, seemingly charged
with metaphorical importance, but in fact oddly detached from her
process of living/recuperating. Her lack of memory and the slipperi-
ness of vocabulary to describe her state seem to her to be related to her
occasional headaches ("that pain is the only thing that really belongs

to her"), which distinction in turn leads her to a further discrimination between "that concept of insanity" and "so-called anguish" (107), although she can satisfactorily explain none of the elements in this chain of reasoning. A later sequence, "weapon, street, fist?" nauseates her, although she suspects that both her vertigo and her inability to understand the implications of the words may have something to do with "what they call love" (116). The unintelligible conflation of "colleagues, a little entertainment, for a while" (118) strikes her as merely strange, and strangely incapable of the syntactic elaboration of the sentence, she falls back on inarticulate astonishment. In each of these sequences, the emotional edges have been blurred, so that "love" and "fist," for example, have come, in her muffled reaction, to represent an almost indifferentiable surface. In each sequence, however, the woman's rejection of the conventional understanding of these words signals both the success and the failure of torture. Common objects and vocabulary have been appropriated for torture, and concepts and objects continue to undergo word/world collapse, but at the same time, the so-called Laura unknowingly reappropriates them once again for the reconstruction of her new self, an untrusting zero-degree identity rendered in her stubborn retention of difference, neither challenging nor accepting the interpretation of the man but retaining her distanced not-quite-aversion, her not-quite annihilation, her watchful state of skepticism, of a skepticism that could be interpreted, along the lines suggested by Stanley Cavell, "as the repudiation of language (or reason) itself—and about the recovery from this repudiation as the return, if it is possible, from tragedy, say from the community's repulsion" ("Naughty Orators" 363).

This alienation from and skepticism about the conventional markings of language is a typical feature of Valenzuela's work, highlighted in "Other Weapons" but present in the other stories of the volume as well, a prominent feature of the linguistic defamiliarization and appropriation she advocates. Thus, in "Fourth Version" there is a remarkable, and tellingly marked, slippage between love and fear, or better, between "the word fear" and "the word love." The narrator comments in one of her frequent asides: *Not that Bella is unaware of the word fear, nor did fear paralyze her; but the word love she knew very well indeed, since others had been using it left and right. And she was afraid of the word love* (9–10, Valenzuela's italics). Bella, of course, is an actress, and in her profession the use of words and the distance from words used can perhaps be explained by a strongly developed sense of professional decorum. Still, the marking of the words "love" and "fear" is significant, and evocative of the similarly marked concepts in "Other Weapons." The words themselves are fear producing, quite apart from the acts that spawn and accompany them.

This point is made especially strongly in another story of the collection, the ambiguously titled "La palabra asesino" ("The Word 'Killer'"). The protagonist of this story is in love (?) with a dangerously attractive killer, the man who will destroy her, the man who perhaps sees in her his own destruction. From her point of reference, this destructive capacity involves a profound recognition and ritual pronunciation of *la palabra asesino*—ambiguously, "the word 'assassin'" or "the word, 'I assassinate'" or, uncommonly but grammatically, "I assassinate the word." The unnamed protagonist's link with this man is established through her internalization of this crucial word: "She asks herself how and why she got into bed with a killer, a killer in cold blood. And the astonishment of realizing she has finally acknowledged that word to herself: in her thoughts she has uttered the word killer" (69). By the end of the story we know that her salvation/destruction lies in the exterior enunciation of this forbidden, erotic word. The story ends with her dream of flying out the open window:

> The unbearable urge to jump. Suddenly
> KILLER
> she shouts and the voice finally
> manages to bolt out of her and she isn't calling out or accusing:
> in fact, she's giving birth. (78)

The weapons once again are appropriated and inverted, not through the simple pronunciation of "the word killer" but rather in the use of a woman's metaphor, giving birth, to describe this sudden eruption.

The so-called Laura also has her secret word, likewise a word made flesh in her own alienated body: "Una espalda azotada. Y la palabra azotada, que tan lindo suena si no se analiza" (119), 'A beaten back. The word beaten, which sounds so pretty if you don't analyze it' (111). Slashed back and slashed word, the word that is itself a slash, a wound in language, taking language back into, as language is alienated from, the tortured body. It is a pretty word if muted/mutilated, a word that signals mutilation of self and of world when analyzed carefully. "The beaten word back" persists as the single, radical reminder of a past before this carefully insulated, comfortable middle-class existence, of the shredding of her world before its reconstruction in this reduced space. Torture, as Scarry notes, and it bears repeating, begins as appropriation; the torturer takes over the minimal spaces and objects of civilized life—shelter and human artifacts—for his drama of uncreation and, through the appropriation of the home as the scene of torture, effects the disintegration of comfort and civilization. In Laura's case, the deconstruction is followed by a willfully perverse reconstruction of that world in idealized terms. If the room or the "little school" is the means of uncreation, so then the artificially comfortable new room provides a means for a reeducation and a continuation of the torture on other terms. Only the slashed back, half healed and no longer quite painful, provides a link between the two worlds, the subconscious reminder that she still has something to lose by being uncooperative.

It is a reminder reinforced when Roque one day plays a new game, showing her the whip: "She, who knows nothing about these things, who's forgotten about horses . . . starts to scream desperately, howling as if she were going to be ripped apart or raped with the grip of this weapon" (122). In context, the "as if" construction of Laura's projected fears recalls not a hysterical narrative but an unraveling of one of the mysteries surrounding the woman's present circumstances, how she came to live in this apartment, an amnesiac with a wound on her back. There are to be no surprises, after all, only a repetition of events that happened earlier: severe whipping and rape. And the whip and the penis become equivalent generators of a single blurred emotion: the so-called love, the tormenting fear. The fear, however, no sooner appears than it is bracketed off in discourse by the counterfactual "as if" that permeates the all-too realistic terror with an elusive nonmateriality, cutting her off once again from that which is intimately known, yet necessarily unapproachable. The threat, as the woman in "The Word 'Killer'" knows all too well, comes only partly from the outside; it also comes, most tearingly, from within. For the woman in "Other Weapons" is, as Partnoy hints in her ambiguously powerful narrative of the "sapito glo-glo-glo," turned into an animal by the very force she uses to protect herself; pain produces the scream, but the human scream disintegrates in the cry of a wounded animal under the whip: "scream" becomes "howl."

Later, in Laura's violation before the eyes of One and Two, and others, intuited on the other side of the peephole, the same transformation obtains, or at least is elicited: "He redoubles his thrusts to turn her groan into a howl." Metaphorically the unsuccessful effort to induce an animal howl in her turns back upon and infects the man. He leaves the woman and begins to pace the room with the barely contained rage of a "caged beast," an "unsatisfied animal." "Roaring," he tears back and forth until the woman calls him back to her to serve as her blanket, until finally, "tired of bellowing, he goes back to her side and starts caressing her in a surprisingly different mood" (126–27). Her very weakness, her passivity is turned against the man in an unexpected and stunning reversal of roles. Finding in her nothing to master, no reflective mirror of his desire, he becomes, temporarily, what he never was/will be: the loving husband.

The man's emphasis on the importance of eliciting animal cries from the woman he has destroyed demonstrates yet another aspect of the language-destroying work of torture: the relative insignificance of the content of the victim's answer to "the Question" in comparison to the importance of the visible and acknowledged progressive deconstruction of the victim's voice. Is the question, ultimately, even an interrogative or is it something else, some rhetorical construct that asks only for an answer rather than for any specifically signaled content? Scarry explains that

> what masquerades as the motive for torture is a fiction. . . . [The questions] are announced, delivered, *as though* they motivated the cruelty, *as if* the answers to them were crucial. . . . But as the content and context of the torturer's questions make clear, the fact that something is asked *as if* the content matters does not mean that it matters. . . . while the content of the prisoner's answer is only sometimes important to the regime, the form of the answer, the fact of his answering, is always crucial. (28–29)

Laura's answer is likewise crucial to the man in "Other Weapons," and the content he requires now has nothing to do with the insurrection against his government. His question, insistently, is some variant of "What do you remember?" The only acceptable answer from his point of view is her story, in his words. Indeed, his most powerful weapon is her own story, his most exquisite torture her lost (and presumably regained) memory. For his torment to be complete, Laura must take up once more the weapon she earlier tried to wield against him and fire it again, in full knowledge of what he has done to her, deconstructing and reconstructing her most intimate self. The essential weapon, then, is not the weapon of violence—gun, whip, penis, or its metaphors—but the capacity for word making and word manipulation. The man has appropriated her weapons and her words; in giving them back to her at the end of the story he is giving her back her own story, transformed through his appropriative gesture as his story about her. "Other Weapons" represents, thus, a limit-text of the most extreme variation on a well-established trick of patriarchy. Men chart women, make them up, and acknowledge no essence but that of their own creation. Valenzuela writes, "Women are on the uncharted face of the phallus, that which has not yet been named. Men are on the safe side, the 'civilized' face, where each thing and sentiment and behavior has its own name." For women writers, the work necessarily becomes an unwinnable struggle against the power of these preimposed names: "Women are forced to use these names and so, finally, express men's ideologies" ("Other Face" 243).

How then, can/do women reverse the charge, appropriate and make the word-weapons their own? "Names are irreplaceable," says Valenzuela, "so what we must enforce is our own compound . . . , inject estrogens in our writing. That is far from being a mild thing to do. It should be done with force and subversion—with fury if necessary" ("Other Face" 243). For the so-called Laura, ironically, her forced seclusion from language provides her with the essential attribute for resistance to her tormentor's version of the story. Her resistance to meaning, any meaning, feeds her passivity but also establishes her non-co-optability. She has discovered/recovered an intrinsically corporeal sense of self in her recognition of the *espalda/palabra azotada,* and if language seems to dissolve and re-form ambiguously in the realm of nonsense or of the impossible/intolerable reality in which she finds herself, it does so in reference to or in spite of this irreducible bodily self. The violence done her serves as a radical reminder of the consequences of physical and grammatical domination, a knowledge too often ignored or undermined by forgetfulness or the mystifications of power.

In the Bengali Mahasveta Devi's story "Draupadi," Gayatri Spivak explains, the word *counter* is used deceptively with reference to a doubly mystified coding: "It is an abbreviation for 'killed by police in an encounter,' the code description for death by police torture." The protagonist of the story, an insurgent woman who neither speaks nor understands English *does* understand the euphemism and by the end of the story "comes mysteriously close to the 'proper' English usage" in her challenge to her torturers (Foreword 391). Her laughter and her challenge to the police officer who ordered her torture and gang rape serve as an intolerable challenge, an unexpected appropriation and reversal of his words, his methods, his official story:

> Draupadi stands before him, naked. Thigh and pubic hair matted with dry blood. Two breasts, two wounds.
> . . . Draupadi shakes with an indomitable laughter that Senanayak simply cannot understand. . . . You can strip me, but can you clothe me again? Are you a man? . . . What more can you do? Come on, *counter* me—come on, *counter* me—?
> Draupadi pushes Senanayak with her two mangled breasts, and for the first time Senanayak is afraid to stand before an unarmed *target*, terribly afraid. (402)

The point, of course, is not that Draupadi is an unarmed target, though in conventional terms she cannot be considered anything else, but that she is *differently armed,* and her arms, appropriated from his arsenal, are fearsome when turned back upon him because they derive from his making but are bonded to the unerasable core of her own identity: two mangled breasts and his own foreign code word used against him. Her sexuality is all the more potent for having been forcibly desexed, her uterus destroyed by rape, her breasts torn away. She has been appropriated, but rejects appropriation, refuses shame. In confronting, and countering, Senanayak, her laughter and her fury serve her as her submission and tears would not.[6]

The so-called Laura's key words, highlighted in section headings, reflect a similar demystification of the cunning ideologies of civilization, their injection with estrogens and their rewriting in the fury of a woman's appropriation. Estrangement from the commonplace items in a standard household—"the photograph" "the plant," "the mirrors," "the window," "the colleagues," "the peephole," "the keys"—points toward an implicit revaluation of the "civilizing" features of daily life in less ingenuous terms. "The well" and particularly "the whip" remind us of the carefully nurtured horror behind a superfi-

---

[6]Catherine Den Tandt provides a fuller analysis of the parallels between the Bengali and the Argentine stories in an unpublished paper on Valenzuela's "Other Weapons."

cial facade of civilized behavior. "The words," "the concept," "the names," "the voices," "the secret (the secrets)," "the revelation," and "the ending"—all point to a careful deconstruction of the signifying system undergirding (implicitly masculinist) assumptions of narrative. Laura, a meaningless name, is applied to the woman whose most crucial identifying characteristic is her wounded back. She exists, essentially, as her wounded back—all else torn away. She of the almost-closed wound takes as her first and most critical act of rebellion the passive refusal of the name, hers or his, and in so doing rejects signifiable identity. Feminist critique, notes Jessica Benjamin, "has demonstrated that the concept of the individual is really a concept of the male subject. Likewise . . . the principle of rationality which social theorists since Weber have seen as the hallmark of modernity . . . is in fact a male rationality. Rationalization . . . dovetails with the oedipal denial of woman's subjectivity, which reduces the other to object" (184–85). The presence of women in what remains the social construct of a "man's world," therefore, has essentially no effect as long as the basic assumptions remain uncontested, as long as the protean and elusive hegemony of impersonal organization remains undisturbed. Rationality, subjectivity, and the name (that is, recognition of individuality) are all male; for the denouement of the story he is writing, the so-called Laura's torturer requires of her exactly and precisely that recognition of his name and function. The countless names she gives him, however, resolve not into recognition but rather into petrification. On the photograph, the signature reads "Roque," and the woman comments, "Something hard, like granite. It suits him, it doesn't suit him" (111); it is, perhaps, "for the first time, his real name" (115), but the appelation and the identification are as offhand and ambiguously empty as any of the other defamiliarized key words. In "Fourth Version," the narrator asks, "Who throws the first stone?" immediately before introducing "he who was already Pedro . . . with an identity all his own" (12–13), an identity recalled in Bella's admonition "Stop being so superficial, Pedro, stop being so petrous" (45). The name, even the rational, proper name, is already injected with a charge of estrogens.

At the very end of her book *Powers of Horror*, Julia Kristeva asks herself a question highly pertinent to Valenzuela's enterprise: "Is it the quiet shore of contemplation that I set aside for myself, as I lay bare, under the cunning, orderly surface of civilizations, the nurturing horror that they attend to pushing aside by purifying, systematizing, thinking; the horror that they seize on in order to build themselves up and function?" And she answers her question with a phrase that reminds us of Laura's *espalda/palabra azotada*, of Draupadi's mangled breasts, even of Bella's self-conscious construction in the actress's mirror; "I rather conceive it as a work of disappointment, of frustration, and hollowing—probably the only counterweight to abjection. While everything else—its archeology and its exhaustion—is only literature" (210). Valenzuela too knows of the work of disappointment, the fury and frustration of hollowing out an as-yet-undefined space for difference, the "well" or the abyss of a reappropriation of an irremediably alienated language, making it one's own. But "only" literature? Kristeva's echo of Verlaine's famous line seems almost unbearably precious and conventionally intertextual. I would say rather that everything—the horrifying surface of civilization and its counterpart, abjection—is countered by the force of literature, by *la espalda azotada* that marks the physical effects of the exhaustion of language, by *la palabra azotada* that signals the place of what has seemingly been canceled, hollowed out until nothing that is hers remains, nothing at all familiar except for the blurred shadows of an untrustworthy memory.

María Inés Lagos-Pope, then, is both inaccurate and incomplete in her conclusion that "these stories give witness to a transformation, but it seems that the weapons have not yet changed hands" (83). The arms have been changing hands, albeit imperceptibly, but the essential change has not been taking place in the appropriation of whips and guns; it has occurred in the appropriation and *apropriamiento* of language itself. Valenzuela alienates commonplace terms like "photograph" and "plant" in "Other Weapons," creates surprisingly apt new compound words such as "bolastristes" for Amanda's lover in "Rituals of Rejection," puns furiously and seriously in "Fourth Version" with such inventions as "proctocolón" and "embajodernos," inserts words and phrases in English ("correr el amok," "las etapas del cold turkey"), Portuguese, and other languages. In each case, Valenzuela demonstrates her control over her chosen weapon and also calls attention to its natural/artificial constructions, reversing the charge of the linguistic arsenal placed in her hands by tradition. In her seminal article "Making up Representation: The Risks of Femininity," Jacqueline Lichtenstein comments on the topos of associating such rhetorical flourishes with a critique of women: "From antiquity to the classical age, the seductions of makeup were thought to correspond, in the hierarchy of representations, with the aberrations of femininity. It was as if the luster added to appearances could only be thought through categories designating a sex whose essence, it was said, consists precisely of the deprivation of essence—since its nature, ontologically deficient, is necessarily exhausted in its simulation of appearances" (78). In Valenzuela's work, women like Bella manipulate the simulation, making appearances work for their own purposes, and the so-called Laura, lusterless, exhausted, deprived of essence, can still describe the indomitable force of an unwilling skepticism in her very emptiness.

It is not a coincidence that Bella, the actress and political activist, sees filing her nails as a version of sharpening her weapons, sees putting on makeup as putting on her armor. In each case, she is preparing herself for battle, creating a version of herself for public consumption, a modification of the self, in all its various connotations, to present to a potential enemy. *"Makeup, woman,"* says Lichtenstein, "two terms signifying the same substance, or rather the same absence of substance—as La Bruyère wrote, 'a kind of white lie'" (78). Bella plays with the lie self consciously, performs it as a strategic ploy: "Bella,—quite beautiful but hardened— . . . Bella, the actress, playing her own waiting role. Filing her nails" (5). Bella anxiously awaits a message and, to camouflage her anxiety, self-consciously plays the role of the actress anxiously awaiting a message; the mirror, the nail file, the makeup are her props. After her performance is interrupted by a messenger (instead of a "Messenger with a capital letter"), Bella returns to her mirror and her nails, her alibi perfectly prepared for a flawless performance:

> Y si alguien más adelante insinuara la sospecha de que se las había estado afilando, Bella sabría responderle:
> —Nada de afilarme nada. O al menos por fuera. Yo me afilo por dentro. . . . Por fuera sólo soy la que soy con ligeras variantes y con las menores asperezas posibles. No tengo por qué afilarme de manera alguna. (6)

> And if later on anyone hinted that she had been sharpening them, Bella would have answered:
> "Would I do such a thing: Anyway, I don't sharpen anything. At least on the outside. I sharpen the inside. . . . On the outside I'm just what I

am, with slight variations and the least possible roughness. I have no reason to sharpen anything." (6)

It is a scene that repeats itself again and again in this version—these various versions—of Bella's life, "with slight variations" and mirror reversals, until the military forces finally see through the makeup to the subversive intent of the performance going on in the ambassador's house and, with a single shot, end it.

The single shot echoes through to the end of the collection of stories, and Bella's slow, interrupted fall is recapitulated in the mirror reversal of the final moment of the final story in the volume, a story in which the so-called Laura, forced to take possession of her own revolver once again, "begins to understand a few things—what that black instrument is for, that thing he calls a gun. So she lifts it and aims" (135). Throughout this final story, Valenzuela constantly plays on the closeness of the two verbs *armar* and *amar*. Love is a weapon; the man certainly uses it as such against the woman he has destroyed and remade, and the so-called Laura has only his so-called love as her own weapon to relocate and rearm her sense of self. In returning the gun to the woman who tried to kill him once before, the coronel announces, "I've got my weapons, too": the whip and the revolver, clearly, diminish in importance to the status of props in this other, domestic war. His principal weapon has already been deployed: his confidence that he has succeeded in undermining or depriving her of her own voice by interpreting her. Just as clearly, the dead (assassinated) lover from her former life has little influence on the motivations of this other Laura, who aims a revolver at her new lover, old enemy. "No, don't leave me," she begs just before she takes aim; ambiguously, her motivation for this new, unconsummated act could as easily be jealousy as politics.

And yet, this minor mystery is not the point either. For if at the end of "Fourth Version," the soldiers fire the single shot that kills Bella, at the end of "Other Weapons" the resolution is by no means so straightforward. The story of the so-called Laura ends as she raises the weapon; no shot is fired in the text. Thus, the appropriation/reappropriation of weapons occurs only in the context of the minimal change involving not the image of death but the figure of recurrence, more powerful in that it does not merely end, as does Bella's story, with (in the fourth version, at least) the performance of her graceful swoon into death in the arms of her lover. In "Other Weapons," the figures are frozen, the confrontation does not end simply, or happily, or tragically. It does not end.

The coronel wants to deprive the woman of voice and volition, to decreate her by deploying his voice and his weapons to torture her out of her mind, so that her loss of confidence in language leads to a loss of reason as well. But not only that. As much as he wants her silence, he also wants her voice. He wants to ventriloquize, like so many generations of male authors; their bitter love/hate affair stands as a paradigm for the perversions and seductions of the competition for control over the narrative. He wants her to forget and requires her to remember. Thus, she becomes his compulsion, the subject of his narrative, the elusive object of his quest, as much as he is the subject of hers. Insofar as his existence outside the apartment is also outside the text, he is trapped behind the deceptively unlockable door as much as the woman is, closeted with her in this artificial space of his own construction. Stanley Cavell reminds us that one way to understand such closeting "is as the maintaining not of the place the man cannot leave, the space of what is not his to say, but (also, before that) the place he cannot let the woman leave, the space of what he does not want, and wants, her to say" ("Postscript" 277). At the end of the story, when Laura does use her voice in the plea to him not to abandon her— "don't leave me"—her voice is the mad voice of his construction used against him, and only he is positioned to understand the nuances of her assumed or real madness, her voice of the jealous wife, in his self-construction. His training particularizes and aims her weaponry, her heartfelt? mad? feigned? refusal to abrogate their spurious contract. Her refusal to play the game by his rules slyly appropriates the scene to her ends, effectively inverting (but not only that) the structure of domination. The revolutionary soldier would kill the enemy before her eyes, the housewife would weep at his defection, but only the madwoman could presume to conflate the two, pleading for love and aiming the revolver, uncoupling the narrative from its planned denouement. Such decoupling or unhinging reminds us that the narrative exchange, as if between two men by way of the object-woman, must take into account the effect of this third element. By extension, the effect of the woman's appropriation of voice and arms in literary exchanges is not to bridge discourses, not to mediate exchanges, but to act on the pivot of the exchange itself, to unhinge its component elements.[7] Ruth Salvaggio writes: "There is not a subject continually reaching for an object, not the one eternally in quest of the other. Instead, women write the unhinging of this dangerous pivot. Subject meets subject not at a closed door, but at the frame where the door opens" (160). Valenzuela is less certain, or perhaps less optimistic, more Latin: for her, to dislocate narrative frames may offer new vistas; it also risks unhinging in the second, colloquial sense of madness.

Valenzuela's tactic does not involve a vision of liberation; she is not a utopian writer. Her struggle is more primary. Against the euphemistic subterfuges she counterposes an image of the unforgettable wound. And if the typical literary figure of the woman's response to, or mediation by, literature is that of Bovarization, Valenzuela proposes instead the initially unattractive concept of bovinization: "cow-words like cow-women," chewing, digesting, lactating. The contact with cows is a painful identification, combining attentiveness and intelligence with a knowledge of sacrifice and submission: "Nonetheless, it is our body, *our* body, and we produce it with our own juices, sometimes called saliva, sometimes not" ("Word" 96). The body's needs dictate the literary form in the desire for appropriation, unresolvably, but necessarily, otherwise. Potentially unhinged.

> If when I was set free someone had asked me: did they torture you a lot? I would have replied: Yes, for the whole of the three months. . . . If I were asked that same question today, I would say that I've now lived through seven years of torture. (Miguel D'Agosino, *Nunca Más* 20)

[7] I borrowed this idea from Anne McLeod, who describes the effects of feminism for women as unhinging, imaging "antithetical relations between the parts in such a way that the ontological framework within which they have been thought comes unhinged" (59).

4

Surfacing: Rosario Ferré and
Julieta Campos, with Rosario Castellanos

Literary critics tend to see interpretation as excavation. We search for "hidden meanings," enjoin our students and colleagues "to dig deeper," acknowledge our preference for the "profound." Great literature, accordingly, is that endowed with "creative depth," that which "probes below the surface" of daily life in search of universal values and eternal verities. What is "real" and "true" and "valuable" is what is underground, hidden behind veils, sunk in a postmodern *mise en abyme*, discovered at the end of arduous delving by the enterprising critic as archaeologist. In this metaphorical model, although the critic is not always male, the truth that must be uncovered has an abstractly feminine quality, and "women" tend to be relegated to the domain of the superficial. This division between an abstract feminine quality and an abstracted female nature is essential, for oddly enough, the superficial beauties of a text's manifest discourse have frequently been associated with the artifices of feminine beautification as a kind of rhetorical cosmetics; after uncovering/unveiling/digging through these superficialities, the critic arrives at an abstract, ultimately unknowable quality: "truth," *la verdad*, Sophia. The female, safely distanced, represents in this manner both the essential truth and the inevitable bad faith of falsification. Woman is the ethereal; she is also the earthy. She is artifice personified and man's hidden dream. It would be both unnecessary and tedious to review the entire history of such representations; instead, let me remind you by way of a story, one archetypal story chosen from many, of similar injunctions given in all seriousness by respected thinkers; this description of women and their function is from Søren Kierkegaard's *Either/Or:*

> A woman comprehends finiteness, she understands it from the bottom up, therefore she is beauteous. . . . Woman explains finiteness, man is in chase of infinitude. So it should be, and each has one's own pain; for woman bears children with pain, but man conceives ideas with pain, and woman does not have to know the anguish of doubt or the torment of despair. . . . But because woman thus explains finiteness she is man's deepest life, but a life which should always be concealed and hidden as the root of life always is. For this reason I hate all talk about the emancipation of women. God forbid that ever it may come to pass. (quoted in Flax 135)

Kierkegaard masks self-serving pomposity as a natural good. Woman, he says, needs to be protected not only from emancipation but also from any activity that might involve thinking, from any conception other than that related to the reproduction of the species, so that she can continue to serve as man's anchor, his contact with the earth, his deepest and most hidden life. The place of woman is concealed within man's heart, hearth, and home; her function is to represent beauty (a quality denied man), to serve as a display object in the niche assigned her. What remains to be examined is why Kierkegaard feels he must confine woman to the depths and subsume her practice of femininity within a male signifying theory, evoking women only in a fantasy scenario that superimposes an abstract, philosophized imaginary over the social norm of an unlearned, often superstitious practice of repression. Furthermore, and here is the most interesting and perhaps most revelatory aspect of all, only through exclusion of the feminine can a male signifying practice be defined at all. Fulfilled by the physical act of childbearing, women are complete in and of themselves, but at the same time they represent the unfulfillable void at man's center. Only by defining himself as the eternal seeker after these (or other) impossible, perhaps nonexistent depths can man, according to Kierkegaard, begin the agonizing process of mental conception and philosophical birth. In this manner Kierkegaard unwittingly reveals the fragility of philosophical speculation in this area, which can only reaffirm the symbolic preeminence of intellectual pursuits by setting up a metaphorical barrier: "No women here." This philosophical "here" is valorized precisely because it admits "no women"; women are permitted only elsewhere—in the depths, on the surface—but not in the space the philosopher identifies and polices as his private domain.

Readers may mistakenly object that such statements, though perfectly typical of the prefeminist era, are no longer possible in these more aware modern times. One depressingly pertinent observation is that Kierkegaard can still be attacked; his continuing relevance is in this manner confirmed. I can also offer a more contemporary example. I am, of course, taking this selection out of the author's context and inserting it into my own; nevertheless, Jean Baudrillard's statement cannot fail to strike certain resonances, although where Kierkegaard sees women as man's "deepest life," Baudrillard imagines women as triumphantly superficial:

> Now woman is but appearance. And it is the feminine as appearance that thwarts masculine depth. Instead of rising up against such "insulting" counsel, women would do well to let themselves be seduced by its truth, for here lies the secret of their strength, which they are in the process of losing by erecting a contrary, feminine depth.
>
> It is not quite the feminine as surface that is opposed to the masculine as depth, but the feminine as indistinctness of surface and depth. Or the indifference to the authentic and the artificial. . . . The masculine, by contrast, possesses unfailing powers of discrimination and absolute criteria for pronouncing the truth. [Later Baudrillard adds that men "have depth, but no secrets" (68).] The masculine is certain, the feminine is insoluble. (10–11)

Despite its postmodern feel and somewhat ambiguous deployment of the metaphors of depth and truth, Baudrillard's elegantly posed allegory reinstates the old, old tradition of the seductive (female) text and the male reader who triumphs over the polished superficiality of discursive game playing to uncover the abysses of a text's unconscious secrets. As for Kierkegaard, beauty (seductiveness) belongs to the female realm, and the signifying practice remains unremittingly male. If the certainties supposedly uncovered in this adventure of exploration represent more of a seduction by the reader's own unconscious than an unassailable revelation of a transcendental truth, well then, the "insoluble" superficialities of the feminine discourse—the shiny surface of signification—must be held responsible.

On a less abstract level, much of traditional feminist scholarship is also ruled by the metaphor of surface and depth. New writers and forgotten voices are "dredged up from the depths" and "brought to the surface" where they can be recognized and inserted into an evolving canon. Given its long history of validation, there is, it seems to me, a certain inevitability about the appropriation and deployment of this metaphor and a good deal of discomfort with any alternative model. As Rena Fraden says, "I wonder whether it is inevitable that the embrace of multiplicity means that I must concede hierarchy or metaphors of depth to the traditional humanists. Depth may not be something I am willing to give up altogether—at least with respect to morality and politics, if not aestheticism" (277). An aesthetics of the superficial may be forgiven, but in Fraden's view it is something quite different, and quite reprehensible, to speak of a politics or morality of the surface.

It is in this context, then, that Rosario Castellanos's striking proposal to Latin American women novelists to celebrate and polish the superficial as their particular charge in the world of letters sounds a radically subversive call to reexamine an entire system of inherited values. First of all, she takes back knowledge of women from men, asserting her own property rights. Second, she suggests that real women, constantly confronted by the male-constructed image of femininity, do not necessarily have to recognize themselves in it, and at the same time she gives us license to play with that fantasy product:

> Cuando la mujer latinoamericana toma entre sus manos la literatura lo hace con el mismo gesto y con la misma intención con la que toma un espejo: para contemplar su imagen. . . .
>
> Las novelistas latinoamericanas parecen haber descubierto mucho antes que Robbe-Grillet y los teóricos del *nouveau roman* que el universo es superficie. Y si es superficie pulámosla para que no oponga ninguna aspereza al tacto, ningún sobresalto a la mirada. Para que brille, para que resplandezca, para que nos haga olvidar ese deseo, esa necesidad, esa manía de buscar lo que está más allá, del otro lado del velo, detrás del telón. (*Mujer* 144)

> When the Latin American woman takes a piece of literature between her hands she does it with the same gesture and the same intention as that with which she picks up a mirror: to contemplate her image.
>
> Latin American women novelists seem to have discovered long before Robbe-Grillet and the theoreticians of the *nouveau roman* that the universe is surface. And if it is surface, let us polish it, so that it leaves no

roughness to the touch, no shock to the gaze. So that it shines, so that it sparkles, so that it makes us forget that desire, that need, that mania for seeking out that which is beyond, on the other side of the veil, behind the curtain.

In Castellanos's proposal, reading is no longer identified with excavation, where the more important discoveries come as a result of digging deeper, nor is "woman" the icon of a veiled truth. Moreover, this inherited value system operates, as Castellanos reminds us, in severe disjunction with the aesthetics/ethics of the feminine beauty system based on preservation of the surface, traditionally seen as an activity both necessary and frivolous. Castellanos suggests a radically different model in which both reader and writer are metaphorically feminine, and the issue of an "in-depth" reading no longer arises. No "deeper" order invalidates the superficial discourse. The realm of appearances is not decried as merely frivolous, nor can the details of a text be read as an attractive symbolic mask. To try to attach the concerns of profundity to its lacquered existence is dangerously misguided.

Implicit in and emerging from Castellanos's celebration of superficiality are a number of difficult questions. By breaking the hierarchy of surface and depth, she interrogates not only their binarism and other binarisms constitutive of the Western concept of self—male/female, mind/body—but she also asks the far more difficult question of why such distinctions exercise our minds and why we assume they are necessarily meaningful. Furthermore, in positing a self that changes at will through a skillful manipulation of appearances, Castellanos directly confronts a Platonic philosophical tradition that defines truth as unitary and as deceivingly veiled, posing instead a polyphonic model of linked and mutually interactive stances or theories that can be adopted and abandoned without penalty. Truth, then, is no longer something to be found under an illusory appearance, in the depths of profound reasoning, but something that has been and will continue to be constructed and interpreted. The writers' and readers' commitment, then, becomes linked to something like conversation rather than something like domination, to the production of an evolving series of transformations rather than to the discovery of a hidden jewel of knowledge.

In short, Castellanos is engaged in rethinking the rules for all sorts of human exchanges, including sexual exchange, at their most basic levels. Her project represents not a superficial politics, in the reductive sense that Rena Fraden might have feared, but an ideological stance in its purest form; her questioning opens a free space for a different, virgin exploration. Reading this excerpt in conjunction with others of her essays, such as "Language as an Instrument of Domination" or "Herlinda Leaves," reminds us as well that for Castellanos this project of clearing a space for the display of the many and multifarious forms of life is not exempt from considerations of social class. She refuses the easy answer or the utopian vision, and never blindly dismisses the incongruencies—roughnesses?—in her own program with a high-handed disregard for unpleasant "details." Advocating the strategies of polish and pluralism, at the same time she signals their limitations both as theory and as practice in Latin American societies. It is, clearly, the upper-class woman whose body "is dressed in silks and velvets, adorned with precious metals and jewels"; likewise, it is leisure that allows for the elegancies of reading and writing. In "Language as an Instrument of Domination," she notes the particular ideological signif-icance of surface manifestations for the Spanish-speaking criollo in colonial times, a value that has not been surrendered in modern Mexico: "The most important thing then was to display signs of dis-tinction that demonstrated at first glance, and in the eyes of any passing stranger, the rank that one held in society. The color of one's skin said a lot but not everything; one had to add the purity and antiquity of faith and something else: the command of the oral means of expression" (Ahern 250). Even purity of skin and faith and language was not enough, of course; the American-born Spaniard also needed ample time, the by-product of luxury: "Leisure offered the *criollo* the chance to refine, polish, embellish himself with all the adornments that wealth offers and cleverness can procure: the decorative quality of language, skillful word matches, verbal fencing" (Ahern 251). In "Herlinda Leaves," Castellanos poignantly adds a tacit acknowledg-ment of her own contemporary complicity in retaining such privileges in her hands and in unconsciously refusing these refinements to her own servants (Ahern 268). Implicitly, intimately, Castellanos ques-tions the binarism she herself has proposed—the binarism rough/smooth—and the ideological mode of an oppositional style that oper-ates by offering only a smooth surface (smooth to *whose* touch?) that does not offend the gaze (*whose* gaze?).

Francine Masiello has explored these questions at length in her superb article on nineteenth-century constructions of women in Argentina. She finds, interestingly enough, that in relation to fashion magazines the significance of surface and gaze is weighted differently, in ideological terms, depending on how that discourse is produced. Male-organized fashion journals (the bulk of such products) create "the image of a coquette; the women's journal avoids fixed definitions for females and creates a private identity for women that insures both self-insulation and safety" ("Civilization" 531). Before Castellanos, the female editors of the fashion journal *La Camelia* were able to propose a reformulation of the laws of the beauty system to benefit women:

> the editors of *La Camelia* propose an appropriation of discourse on dress, taking charge of the world of style and cosmetics to invent a language of their own. Thus, through descriptions of wigs, evening gowns, and accessories, a social subject dominated by men is reformulated in the language of women. . . .
> At the same time, by reversing the semiotic markers available in the discourse on beauty, women use the advantage of cosmetics and dress to protect themselves from the immodesty of the social sphere. Using the disguise or false persona created by fashionability, the women are able to create a mobile, elusive subject, which in its peculiar ways inverts the icon-fixing patterns belonging to the idiom of style. (530)

The principle of self-transformation, derived from the predominant male-defined gaze, is in this manner retransformed and restructured as a particularly feminine product, gaze, or discourse. In any case, what slips away in this self-restructuring is the "elusive subject" beneath the false persona, itself a product of the fashionable disguise provided by cosmetics and dress. The mask of fashion is still in this nineteenth-century formulation a prop and not an intellectual property in any sense; it is this further transformation that awaits Castellanos's insight.

At the end of Castellanos's drama *The Eternal Feminine*,[1] Lupita, the bride-protagonist, offers several options for the liberation of Mexican women from their historical subordination: "First, defend traditions,

---

[1]The concept of the "eternal feminine" is borrowed from Nietzsche, who talks about men as multiple and plural but woman as a singular being, with the only proper form being the "eternal feminine."

modernizing them, of course, in order to update them. . . . Second, break with the past as our Yankee neighbors have done." In response to the "lady's" query "Isn't there a third way for those of us who belong to the Third World?" Lupita proposes the most difficult option of all: "The third way has to reach the heart of the problem. It's not enough to adapt. . . . It's not enough to imitate models proposed for us that are answers to circumstances other than our own. It isn't even enough to discover who we are. We have to invent ourselves" (Ahern 356). How? Language, the instrument of domination, is also the potential liberating tool. Latin American women writers, says Castellanos, have been unconsciously polishing their craft for generations; what is exciting about the contemporary moment is that they are also beginning to invent new possibilities for self-definition in the *conscious* deployment of these instrumentalities.

The myth of the Mexican woman—so ably outlined in her various facets in that nearly unproduceable drama *The Eternal Feminine*, as well as in her many essays on the topic—provides the overriding semantic axis for Rosario Castellanos's critique; its particular effect is felt through her struggles with the almost overwhelming background presence of the saintly and self-sacrificing mother. If in recent years the rhetoric has changed from that used in Castellanos's youth to hold women back from education and careers, still virtually everyone knows the ideal of womanhood proposed. The icon of the *ama de casa* is still held in enormous respect, and current women's magazines and advice columns continue their general mission of preparing young women to catch and retain a man through modest and decorous behavior, to keep house for him and the children, to keep quiet when he strays, and to prepare tasty meals against his eventual arrival. This hoary myth still provides, thus, the grounding against which a practice of liberation must define itself. (I am thinking here not only of common domestic arrangements but also of the way these arrangements are underlined and perverted in limit situations. Eva Forest, for example, has done magnificent work in deconstructing the rhetoric of domesticity as deployed in the scene of torture.) In "The Liberation of Love," Castellanos speaks directly and forcefully to her complacent counterparts, the comfortably passive "informed" women of her own country:

> You, madam, self-sacrificing little Mexican woman, or you, self-sacrific-
> ing little Mexican woman on the road to emancipation: what have you

done in the last few months on your own behalf? I can imagine the obvious answer: you have reviewed Simone de Beauvoir's now classic text, either to disagree or to support your own arguments. . . .

Of course you closely follow the events that document the existence of Women's Lib. Of course you pretended not to understand . . . and it never occurred to you that it applied in the least to the situation that concerns us now. . . .

. . . in any case, you deeply regretted that the example of North American women is impossible to follow in Mexico. Our idiosyncrasies are so different, as well as our history and our traditions! The fear of being ridiculed paralyzes us. (Ahern 264)

In the sarcastically laudatory description of the Japanese model of a "women's love" movement which follows, Castellanos holds up, as she reminds her readers, "a distorted mirror" to their own practices. In so doing, she suggests a straightforward critique of the roles women are traditionally taught to play and their complicity with these roles that trap them in a complacent, manipulative, destructive, eternal childhood. As Ingrid Muller incisively comments, "Castellanos' strategy thus allows the reader to recognize for herself the insidiousness . . . of the role of tradition as an ideological tool. . . . The 'Liberation of Love,' then, has nothing to do with love, and if that were possible, even less with liberation" (quoted in Ahern 48).

The typical woman's reading of others and of herself has been "lethetic" (I borrow the term from Clayton Koelb), that is, a reading that "takes place when the reader acts as if he or she does not believe the text being read and thus deliberately ignores what the text seems to be trying to say. . . . Reading in the lethetic mode is not interested in what a text means, only in what it says—or rather *that* it says" (Koelb and Noakes 305). Castellanos asks this "self-sacrificing" woman to come to terms with the fact that her own lethetic reading of her family is not innocent, that it reflects neither naïveté nor Christian forgiveness but a complicitous exploitation and radical reshaping of the text itself. In order to reread the hieroglyphics of her life alethetically, she has to accept her own hypocritical passivity, she has to take on the hard task of self (re)invention.

In Castellanos's critical/theoretical writings, this process of self invention derives from what Maureen Ahern calls a resemanticization of the rituals of domesticity (53) as ideological constructs. One essay, from the time of Castellanos's service as Mexican ambassador to Israel, begins, "As I was putting on my makeup to attend the dinner that the Israeli government is offering President Nixon" (*Uso* 269). Ahern points out that this is a typical tactic on the part of the Mexican writer, whose texts commonly begin "with an utterance by an autobiographical I, who tosses out a provocative personal detail or an aside on a domestic event that sets up the discussion of an issue of cultural, political, or artistic importance" (52). These provocative details are never meant to be shunted aside, however; like theatrical asides, her apparently discountable prefaces are anything but trivial. "I was putting on my makeup" introduces a homely task, and yet one that describes the essential function of the domestic woman, concisely defining the field of operations of the woman as subject ("*I was putting*") and the woman as object of display (properly coifed and made-up). Moreover, the fissure between Castellanos, whose artifice is in the cosmetics she applies, and such politicians as Richard Nixon and Henry Kissinger, whose makeup is less visible but no less potent, is also subtly suggested and ironically, diplomatically, decried. The naked truth is not served in large quantities at diplomatic dinners; instead, politicians tend to prefer the verbal equivalent of cosmetics, the kind of rhetoric that Quintilian calls, in Jacqueline Lichenstein's paraphrase, "debauched, vulgar, seductive, and excessively made-up." Lichenstein continues: "such wanton elegance decidedly bore the stigmata of dissolute femininity, or rather of a dissoluteness which is that of femininity itself" (79). In both politics and the women's beauty system, the overriding function is the same: the creation of an attractive, impervious surface. The value of these superficial representations is not negligible: "As a paint company has pointed out . . . often 'if you preserve the surface you preserve all' " (Lilly Daché quoted in MacCannell and MacCannell 221). And as Castellanos hints, neither is the process wholly innocuous; for good or ill, by means of careful rhetoric and carefully constructed faces, manipulated appearances construct what we accept as the real, and depth is turned inside out.

Makeup, literary or literal, seduces. It seduces women, first of all. The complex rituals of achieving and maintaining a beautiful face and body can give women with excessive leisure a concrete and socially approved way to spend their time. Dean and Juliet Flower MacCannell find that "the most self-sustaining achievement of genderism is the normalization of *boredom* for women. In all beauty books, it is taken for granted that most women will be agonizingly bored most of the time; that when they are alone, they will occupy themselves preening and

their heads will be empty" (210). Primping, then, becomes only secondarily other-directed and much more immediately motivated by the
well-to-do woman's need to fill endless empty hours. Nevertheless,
whereas such books might assume that women's heads are mostly
empty and that beauty is a concrete objective a woman can achieve
after a specific, productive expenditure of time, the MacCannells'
analysis shows that far more is at stake. In a culture that essentially
decrees that naturalness = ugliness = nothingness (214), "the beauty
system provides the only cultural place where a woman can exercise
power *as a woman*" (223): thus, artifice = beauty = essence, and this
equation constitutes a covert will to power. Castellanos's gesture of
putting on her makeup, then, offers a concrete instance of the practice
of superficiality as an alethetic act of self-invention.

There is, of course, a further and more sinister implication in the
beauty mandate. "Cover girl" is frequently a cover-up, and the power
of beauty is only the power beauty is allowed to exercise, a particular
look valued in the male gaze. For beauty has only an attenuated and
weakly enforced property right and right to privacy in public practice,
if not in law (but also in law, where statutes governing rape differ from
those for other crimes of violence). Walter Benn Michaels describes an
early lawsuit brought in 1902 in support of Abigail Roberson, who
objected to having an unauthorized photograph of her face used to
advertise Franklin Mills Flour. Roberson, says Michaels, was "left with
nothing but what a New York judge called the 'compliment' to her
'beauty,'" but the case established a precedent for a Missouri judge in
1912 to rule that "the possessor of a 'peculiarity of appearance' that
could be made 'a matter of merchandise'" should indeed have the
right to profit from this valuable personal property (501). The concept
of appearance as an aspect of personal property with an ascribable
value flies in the face of the common notion that "beauty is in the eye
of the beholder" rather than an attribute the person so beheld, and it is
through that (implicitly male) gaze that property relations and value
are established.

There is another cover-up, too, in which value is twisted and distorted. "Being beautiful," the MacCannells explain, "is the only socially acceptable cover for having no heterosexual relationships, for
beauty alone can convey the impression that the woman is without
a man by choice" (227). This perception holds even more force in societies like those in Latin America, where public and professional life is

still more male oriented than that operative in the Euro-American scene described in the MacCannell essay. If, on the one hand, the woman who plays the beauty game is condemned for her superficiality, on the other, the woman who does not play or who refuses to play the game is ascribing herself to "a genderless, zero category" (MacCannell and MacCannell 223), hinting at her unwillingness to subordinate herself (to men, to discipline); she is superficial again, possessor of an all-too-present material body. For the MacCannells, then, the constructed authenticity of the beautifying rituals recovers a specific ideological charge that, curiously, would set such rituals and the women so constructed in absolute opposition to the notions of female conduct implied in the beauty manuals. Beauty is not merely the gauge of attractiveness to the opposite sex; it is also a means of establishing a power base and even a degree of independence. We could go so far as to say that for Castellanos at least such rituals have an unrealized revolutionary potential to combat other traditional notions about women as well.

Significantly, such notions are often framed in images of surface and depth. Thus, one common reading of the phenomenon rejects the empty-headed society woman, traditionally valued for her display of the constructed attractions of face, form, and ornamentation, for the "merely superficial" attractions of her dazzling (but implicitly false) beauty. This criticism of self-serving or frivolous women is practically unassailable if we accept the basic underlying premise. Curiously, however, Nancy Armstrong has discovered that such condemnations of aristocratic superficiality have often been extended to the woman who writes, a connection that makes most of us uncomfortable but that continually resurfaces in critical texts in one form or another. As Armstrong notes, "A woman who wrote poetry could always be accused of indulging in a form of aristocratic display" (Armstrong and Tennenhouse 117). The woman who writes, if she displays any talent, is analogous to the empty-headed beauty; her rhetorical attractions can be dismissed as mere cosmetics without profundity. If, however, her prose lacks elegance, she can of course be dismissed as a second-rate writer, or perhaps a merely journalistic one, of some slight historical interest but with no lasting beauty to delight the reader from future generations. Rhetorical flourishes and cosmetics once again cross-reference each other, this time in a claustrophobic space. Nancy Armstrong specifically studies the rhetorical mode of the eighteenth-century conduct manual (still with us, she maintains, in the form of advice columns and how-to books) in the construction of the middle-class domestic woman. Conduct books, she feels, invent a spurious depth specific to women as a control mechanism to ensure their continuing subordination; such books "suggest that the female had depths far more valuable than her surface. By implying the essence of the woman lay inside or underneath her surface, the invention of depths in the self entailed making the material body of the woman appear superficial. The invention of depth also provided the rationale for an educational program designed specifically for women, for these programs strove to subordinate the body to a set of mental processes that guaranteed domesticity" (114). Women, seduced by the illusions of depth, allow themselves to be repressed. It is unsurprising, then, that so many feminist writers urge the need to get beyond the domestic sphere and adopt other tactics in their struggle.

Makeup, obviously, also seduces others. That, clearly, is precisely the point of the elaborate game playing of Gioconda Belli's aristocratic architect as she prepares for a job interview, anticipating how to manipulate the boss, attentive to his rules:

La observó de arriba-abajo, midiéndole el ostensible *'pedigree,'* el largo de la mini-falda, el pelo desordenado en rizos. Era un hombre cuarentón, de ojos alertas y actitud pragmática, pero con la necesidad de seducción propria de los hombres latinos a esa edad. . . . Ella no tuvo remordimientos de conciencia por usar todas las armas milenarias de la feminidad. Aprovechar la impresión que causaba en los hombres las superficies pulidas, no era su responsabilidad, sino su herencia. (15–16)

He looked her up and down, measuring her ostensible pedigree, the length of her miniskirt, her artfully disordered curly hair. He was a fortyish man, with alert eyes and a pragmatic attitude, but with the need to seduce typical of Latin men of that age. . . . She did not have a guilty conscience about using all the millenary weapons of femininity. To take advantage of the impression caused in men by her polished surfaces was not her responsibility but her inheritance.

Lavinia, the capable young architect, correctly presumes significant sexism in the workplace and plays to those expectations, downplaying her intellectual accomplishments and highlighting her natural beauty, her social savoir faire. She gets the job. Says Baudrillard: "Men, moreover, are never seduced by natural beauty, but by an artificial, ritual beauty—because the latter is esoteric and initiatory, whereas the former is merely expressive." According to this French thinker, even natural beauty needs to be organized and defined. Makeup makes no pretense at uncovering a law of nature; rather, it organizes a cycle of appearances (90); that is, its very nature is desire driven and essentially fictive, ineluctably akin to the writer's or the painter's art. In their most radical mode, cosmetics erase the beautiful face so that a natural-seeming beauty can be drawn on the tabula rasa of that face's regular features. How could others *not* respond to such careful constructions?

Furthermore, says Baudrillard, through the use of cosmetics, "the body is made to signify, but with signs that, strictly speaking, have no meaning. . . . The body is covered with appearances, . . . not in order to dissemble, nor to reveal, . . . nor even just for fun. . . . What is involved here is an undertaking that Artaud would have termed metaphysical: a sacrificial challenge to the world to exist" (91). Through the rituals of making herself up for a state dinner, Castellanos is undergoing one of the commonest metaphors of self-invention; erasing or effacing one self in order to produce another, superior version of the self, to produce, in effect, an official self, a certain appearance (that in official circles will once again efface itself in the commonality of other made-up faces). "I was putting on my makeup": theatrical, self-conscious, producing nothingness but making it shine.

The underlying assumption, still, is that the woman's gaze is directed only at herself, in the mirror, as she applies her face; men, in this economy, are licensed to gaze at women, and this license to stare is nonreciprocal. It is only recently that artists and theorists have begun to analyze how these typical experiences predispose human relationships and enable/disable both men and women. One midseventies experiment in the direction of restating subject-object relationships included visual artists' concretization of fantasies about the self with only the self as ostensible audience. Lucy Lippard gives examples:

> "How others see me" and "how I see myself" are two of the basic themes that lend themselves to Conceptual media. Makeup (Pretend) is in turn one of the basic tools. In 1972, "Léa's Room" at the Cal Arts Feminist Art Program's *Womanhouse* was occupied by a lovely young woman sitting before a mirror, day after day, putting on makeup, wiping it off in discontent, beginning again, dissatisfied again. When [Jacki] Apple had herself

"redone" as an artwork at a department store in a free cosmetic advice session, she came out looking just as she makes *herself* up. (106–7)

In this overt posturing, the woman artist, like Castellanos's woman writer, ostentatiously turns herself into an appearance in order to disrupt and question the concept of appearances, thus directly politicizing the act of putting on makeup, counteracting the voyeuristic gaze. In such works, the artist introduces a formal approximation to a woman's autobiography, rehabilitating the "I" and insisting on the face, only to proceed slowly and deliberately to wipe out both insistence and face, before reconstructing that fact? fiction? once again. "Only falsehoods alienate the truth," says Baudrillard, "but makeup is not false, or else (like the game of transvestites) it is falser than falsehood and so recovers a kind of superior innocence or transparency. It absorbs all expression within its own surface" (94). Perhaps the conceptual artists also intuited this analogy between cosmetics and a transsexual(ized) identity; one of the works Lippard discusses is Martha Williams's photographic series, *Posturing: Drag* "in which she first transformed herself into a man, and then into a man posing as a woman" (106). In each of these projects, the common element is an autobiographical gesture—"I was putting on makeup"—that concentrates on a consciously constructed self, a staged performance that comments on, challenges, or exposes role playing and posits life as a staged aesthetic performance, a production valuable not for its hidden depths but for its style of presentation. Likewise, the theme underlying all these productions is not the uncovering of a buried origin; rather it is the reduplication of a social ritual—makeup, the elegant cosmetics of language—that represents (if the concept of "representation" can still be used in this context, even metaphorically) the rereading of a stanza of the body's poetic topography.

Deeply problematized in such productions as these is the role of the reader or viewing public. I have hinted that the audience's gaze upon these public/private spectacles is hypothetically voyeuristic. The issue is more complicated, however, because the circuit of exchange involves a recognition of the audience as voyeur looking upon a primal scene of narcissistic self-contemplation that is, nevertheless, a staged scene, meant to be overlooked. Rosario Castellanos's direct address to "you, madam, self-sacrificing little Mexican woman," is only the most overt of such gestures. We might also say that what is most seductive about the conceptual art works Lippard describes is precisely their pose of mortal self-absorption, their apparent extreme narcissism, which nevertheless can operate only as indexed by the ignored response of an implicit but vitally essential audience. Or in Vincent Descombes's formulation, "What seduces is not some feminine wile, but the fact that it is directed at you. It is seductive to be seduced, and consequently, it is being seduced that is seductive. In other words, the being seduced finds himself in the person seducing. What the person seduced sees in the one who seduced him, the unique object of his fascination, is his own seductive, charming self, his lovable self-image" (quoted in Baudrillard 68). The fact that for Descombes the "you" is necessarily a "he" is not gratuitous. It merely reproduces the archetypal economy of the man (lover, writer, critic) reading (seducing/seduced by, writing, interpreting) woman (the mistress, the work of art, the text). But what happens when that "you" is a female reader? Is the text unreadable? Does the reader automatically reposition herself as a transvestite? Is the female reader, like Martha Williams's self-portrait in drag, a she posing as a he posing as a she?

One of the most extended and concrete explorations of this problematic can be found in Julieta Campos's novel *Tiene los cabellos rojizos y se llama Sabina* (She has red hair and her name is Sabina). In this novel, written almost entirely in the conditional tense and subjunctive mood (as Alicia Rivera Potter has already observed [905]), writers, critics, editors, readers, and commentarists proliferate around a single character, a woman, and a single action, looking out to sea. One of the voices tells us that the only certainty in the novel is that given in the title, that is, that the woman has red hair and her name is Sabina (177). Readers external to the text are inclined to believe this voice, if only because the assertion reappears in both French and Spanish and is reinserted on the cover and title page of the book. There is certainly no other reason for accepting this one over any of the other contingent, inconsistent, and contradictory assertions made in the book about the woman, her present circumstances, and her past. My own inclination would be to discount the assertion "she has red hair and her name is Sabina," together with all the other parallel assertions made in the text about the woman, her life, attitudes, genealogy, and so on, as totally gratuitous. In fact, I would argue that the primary narrative node generating the text is not the title phrase but another, also seemingly straightforward statement, also frequently reiterated, this one couched in the first person instead of the third: "I am a character that looks out to sea at four in the afternoon . . . from a scenic overlook in Acapulco." This single assertion is the crucial starting point for the adventure of reading and writing, what Stephen Heath calls the "scriptural" of narrative in this text. From this statement depends, first of all, a nonsystematic sequence of relationships among the various agents of the verb: "I" refracts into "you" (both the informal *tú* and the formal *usted*) and into "he" and "she." The "I," "you," "he," "she," and intermittent "we" and "they" in turn serve as nodes organizing a proliferation of other characters, or character-positions, some of whom carry on dialogues with each other, some of whom ignore each other's existence, some of whom contradict each other or logically cancel each other out, some of whom occupy the space of the subject in near simultaneity: "the novel that she, I, you would write begins at last to displace the other, the one that he would be writing (73).[2] Likewise,

---

[2]All the characters are at least double, a feature perhaps to be expected in the work of an author whose other publications include a volume titled *La imagen en el espejo*. "I" refracts into: (1) the character who looks at the sea (sometimes also referred to in the third person, "she," by one of the narrators), who is further refracted into (1a), a character that looks at the sea in the present from a scenic overlook in Acapulco, and (1b), a character who looks at the sea from a dock in Havana twenty-two (or thirty-nine) years before (perhaps also referred to at some points as "she"); (2) the autobiographical character who imagines another character, who is in turn refracted into (2a), a character sometimes called Julieta Campos, and (2b), a woman on the promontory steps, who is in turn divided into (2b1), a writer who takes notes, and (2b2), a photographer who may or may not actually take any pictures. There is also "I"3, a woman novelist working on a novel from her maple writing desk, and "I"4, identified as Celina (like one of Julieta Campos's characters from another book), who cannot find the words and is associated with cats. "I"5 shares a hotel room with her husband, Marcuse, and "I"6, an old woman from the Caribbean, lives in Paris, etc. What the "I"s seem to have in common is that they are all women, mostly writers, all self-consciously aware of their fictive natures.

The variations on "él" (he) lack such self-consciousness, are mostly voyeurs, and are often distinguished from "I" as Robbe-Grillet-ish male narrators whose methods, style, and theories of narrative place them at a considerable remove from the female narrator(s). (Things get complicated: for example, this novel "could only be written by a female writer because only women attach themselves so obstinately to any absolute fiction" [55] sounds like a statement made by one of the "he" characters, rather than one of the "I" characters.) The "he"s also have distinguishing characteristics, however. "He"1 is a voyeur; "he"2 is the potential author of an objective novel, perhaps even a best seller, "he"3 is a character from Robbe-Grillet's *Dans le labyrinthe* and is closely associated with the author of one of the novels about the woman who looks out to sea. This particular "he" is one of the most prominent narrators, frequently contrasted with the woman novelist of the maple desk and the potential novelist of the promontory by the Julieta Campos character. "He"4 is one of the readers (there is also at least one reader identified as "she"); "he"5 is Marcuse (a red herring). "Tú" and "usted" offer refining

the concept of "character" itself serves as another juncture. At one extreme, the reader could suggest that the novel has only one character, the woman who looks out to sea and whose entire fictional existence is consumed in that gaze; at the other, the various novelists, readers, critics, editors, and characters from other novels (by Campos, by other contemporary Latin American and European writers: the novel is to some extent a postmodern literary detective's delightful garden of allusive clues) impinge and infringe on this space, gazing (voyeuristically) at her, defining and interpreting her look, situating her in a particular fictional construct that says more about the needs and desires of the narrator/reader/critic/literary canon than it does about the simple action of gazing out to sea. In the same manner, the sea becomes, at different moments, the Pacific Ocean, the Atlantic Ocean, the Caribbean, the Mediterranean; four in the afternoon indistinguishably fades into other times, "It's twenty to ten. . . . It is midnight and/or it is noon" (45); the overlook may be a dock, a hotel window, or an imagined/remembered scene; Acapulco is Havana, New York, Venice, a movie backdrop.

For Campos, the operative metaphor for the surface/depth discussion can be found in her obsession with the sea. One could attempt to argue that the sea is both feminine and explicitly maternal in her work. *Sabina,* for example, is dedicated "to Terina de la Torre, my mother," and the dedication page is followed by an epigraph from Chateaubriand: "Je reposerai donc au bord de la mer que j'ai tant aimée" 'I will rest beside the sea I loved so much.' The juxtaposition of dedication and epigraph suggests the familiar and much exploited play on *la mer* (the sea) and *la mère* (the mother). Such a reading is plausible but requires nuancing. At this point, let me just say that whereas the images of the sea, repeated throughout Campos's work, are associated with the female characters, the sea itself, though beautiful and strangely compelling for Campos's female characters, is not itself particularly feminized. It is in no wise a metaphor for an imagined mater-

---

and critical commentaries from various directions. "Tú"1 is the "I"1's double, the other self that contributes dreams, fantasy, the irrational component of the self, and the remembered. "Tú"2 is feline (perhaps the conversational other of "I"4, Celina). "Tú"3 is the voice of command in the text: correcting, demanding changes, making equivalences, shifting directions. "Usted" is the critic/interlocutor, at one point ejected from the novel (23–24) but returning as a critic addressed in the informal "tú."

Similar genealogies could be constructed for the "she" and the "we" characters.

nal depth; rather, it speaks of the more generalized *human* need to surface from meaningless voids. The sea, simply, is the place where a human being must remain afloat to live, and the depths of the sea bring not enlightenment but death: "And it involves telling something as it is because one supposes that things happen that do not explain themselves and that look for words in order to come to the surface [para salir a flote], as one, on the point of drowning, looks for a piece of wood to grab onto and hold oneself up" (*Sabina* 11).

The same contradictory voices that determine the labyrinthine structure of the self-conscious text constantly call upon the reader to respond to the experience of reading: "The reader's confusion should surpass, by this point in the novel, that of the character: the reader will have to lose himself . . . in order to find, if it is possible to find, a caricaturesque index of his own image. You are mistaken. The reader, by then, will have abandoned the reading, leaving off being, in consequence, the reader. Therefore, in the improbable case that he has allowed himself to be devoured by the avalanche of words . . ." (121). Clearly, this novel, like many contemporary "elite" novels with which it might be compared, highlights the process of a novel's creation: how to structure a beginning and an end, how to repress or emphasize stylistic quirks. It includes debates on the use of symbols and concerns itself about whether or not to leave in or take out all punctuation: "Take out the commas, the periods, the semicolons, all the signs of punctuation, of interrogation, of exclamation, and allow the interior discourse to flow. Make the reader work a little. Forgive me. . . . I think in periods and commas" (127). At the same time, it plays with these postmodern obsessions, these eminently readable confections of a now-established, and highly stylized, tradition of unreadability, the contemporary novelist's verbal equivalent of the conceptual artist's makeup. By insisting on this saturation of fictional techniques, this dizzying declension of narrative possibilities, Campos underlines the constitutive importance of the process of reading to the creation of the fiction, as well as the unretrievability—or ultimate irrelevance—of any kind of originary or founding statement.

In the case of Rosario Ferré's short stories "When Women Love Men" and "Isolda's Mirror" (the original Spanish title, "Isolda en el espejo" [Isolda in the Mirror], suggests a somewhat different, and even more relevant, play of image) as in Campos's hyper-confused text, this play of unreadability is posed in the text as a problem and as part of the project of the work, in which the issue of making up for a particular audience becomes part of the message of the text. Ferré, however, skirts the dangers of a certain too-knowing glibness that could be ascribed to Campos's 1974 novel, a perceived facileness that threatens to collapse Campos's very real interrogation of the conditions and contracts of reading into a bag of tricks. To call "When Women Love Men," for example, "unreadable" or "pornographic" (as a few critics have done) is to refuse the invitation of the text to reflect upon a specific ideological value that the very structuration of the story itself precisely refutes. "When Women Love Men" ostensibly addresses itself to an absent seducer—"you, Ambrosio"—the man who oppresses the two women in his life, his wife and his mistress, in the most traditional and intimate ways. Now dead, Ambrosio wills his house to both women jointly, perhaps in revenge for unstated discomforts they have caused him, perhaps as a joke. Ultimately, elaborately, Isabel the wife and Isabel the mistress find their liberation from his presence and from his instructions by following his will (both senses) exactly and thus subverting Ambrosio's intent. Rather than declare war, the two women coalesce like two surfaces gliding over each other. The objective correlative for this process is, for each of them, a particular shade of violently red nail polish they both prefer, and this unexpected merging "was our most sublime act of love" (177).

Likewise, "Isolda's Mirror," formulates itself as the image of a woman looking at her constructed (painted, made-up) double in the mirror of her husband/lover's eyes. Don Augusto Arzuaga loves the much younger Adriana Mercier for her resemblance to a work of art. Her face has an astonishing similarity to that of Isolda in his favorite painting, and in order to complete the transformation of the living woman into an art object, Augusto has carved a state of Venus that creates an exact reproduction of her own body (*Sweet Diamond Dust* 152). Adriana's revenge, like that of the women in "When Women Love Men," like that of the commentary of the conceptual artists, like that of the Latin American woman writer described by Castellanos, is a precise and exact reduplication of the reproduction. Adriana destroys Don Augusto by making up her face and body as exact replicas of painting and statue; she reproduces his terms exactly, without comment. In both stories, then, the woman reader is invited into the textual structure as coconspirator with the female protagonists, is asked to look over the shoulder of the ostensible, male-identified reader-creator (Ambrosio, Don Augusto) and to reconstruct the tale in the polished surface of a series of cosmetic transformations. In both stories, the cosmetics applied are decisively literal. Even more: as Lucía Guerra-Cunningham has so acutely noted, cosmetics in the work of Rosario Ferré serve not only as mask and adornment, not only as weapons in gender conflicts, but also as markers of social class and individual identity: "The adoption of a feminine identity deriving from the lower strata implies abandoning the exquisite refinement of cosmetics and items of clothing that, in Rosario Ferré's narrative, function as important indices, since her representation of woman correctly includes them as signs of identity" ("Tensiones" 21). Any reading of Ferré, therefore, is incomplete if if does not take into account the more than symbolic significance of, for example, Cherries Jubilee nail polish, or the lip-smacking relish to be enjoyed in the more than rhetorical flavor of "Hersheybarskissesmilkyways."

In her lacquering over of surfaces, Ferré attempts to reveal the magic in any superficial and all-too self-evident manifestation. Her technique might be said to approximate the "crystal" photographic technique perfected by Tina Modotti, a method that "consisted in the double development of the negative," resulting in a photograph characterized "by an absolute clarity of expression, that takes the image to the level of the abstract" (*Arbol* 46). In double development, one level of superficiality—what Ferré elsewhere calls the "anterior surface or secret of the text"—slides over and under a second surface, "the posterior and evident surface" or textual form (*Arbol* 10). Her job as the artist is not just to create the double and deceptively clear surface of a crystalline expression but, more important, to capture the slippage of surface over surface in action and, in so doing, to free textual mystery (the image) from all that would keep it shadowed, muddy, obscure.

Ferré attributes to Alfred de Musset the neologism *emancimatriz*, which he used to describe George Sand's recognition of the power of desire and control over sexuality as the woman's most effective weapon against oppression. *Emancimatriz*, Ferré notes, signals the "emancipadora de la matriz" (*Sitio* 65), and Musset's French invention takes on a new twist in Ferré's Spanish: emancipator *of* the womb, but also *from* the womb. Like Campos, Ferré accords no particular primacy or mystique to the female's ability to reproduce the species. On the contrary, more essential is precisely that liberation from the task of forced childbearing she salutes in George Sand. Luz María Umpierre

perhaps unintentionally shifts ground once again and goes even farther when she suggests that for Ferré, "la liberación de la mujer es la
'emancimatricidad' y que ésta debe ir acompañada de la revolución de
orden político-social" (120) 'woman's liberation is "emancimatricide"
and should be accompanied by a revolution in the sociopolitical order.'
Ferré becomes, in this reading, more than the emancipator of the
womb, from the womb; she is also the liberator of/from the mon-
ster/mother, by matricide.[3]

I want to juxtapose these two Caribbean writers (Ferré, Puerto Rico;
Campos, Cuba), from two different generations, whose major works
conform to two different genres (short story, novel—and I will use for
this exercise Campos's first novel, *Muerte por agua*, where the mother-
daughter theme is more explicitly broached). Reading them alongside
each other sharpens the contrast between two different ways of eman-
cipating the womb, two very different styles of producing a feminine
countertext to the rhetoric of depth, two forms of patri/matricide, two
modes of surfacing and celebrating the surface.

In *Sitio a Eros* (Besieging Eros), Rosario Ferré recalls how difficult it is
for a man to write in a world indifferent to his labors; for a woman,
however, these difficulties are multiplied: "El mundo no dice a ella,
como les decía a ellos: 'Escribe si quieres; a mí no me importa nada.' El
mundo le dice, con una risotada: '¿Escribir? ¿Para qué quieres tú
escribir?'" (149).[4] Perhaps the lingering aftereffects of this inhibition
are partly responsible for Ferré's preference for the short forms—
essay, story, poem, novella (as she says, "the novel demands time I
still do not have" [García Pinto 94])—and it is certainly a factor in the
anger that permeates the entire body of her work. The anger, Ferré

[3]Mothers too are often displaced in Ferré's fiction, as, for example, in the priggish and
sanctimonious "reverend mothers" that deform little girls' lives in the convent schools of
"El regalo" ("The Gift") from *Sweet Diamond Dust* or "Sleeping Beauty" in *Papeles de
Pandora.*

[4]Ferré here echoes (quotes) Virginia Woolf's formulation in *A Room of One's Own:*
"Accentuating all these difficulties and making them harder to bear is the world's
notorious indifference. It does not ask people to write poems and novels and histories; it
does not need them. It does not care whether Flaubert finds the right word or whether
Carlyle scrupulously verifies this or that fact. . . . But for us women, I thought, looking
at the empty shelves, these difficulties were infinitely more formidable. . . . The indifference of the world which Keats and Flaubert and other men of genius found so hard to
bear was in her case not indifference but hostility. *The world did not say to her as it said to
them, Write if you choose; it makes no difference to me. The world said with a guffaw, Write?
What's the good of your writing?"* (53–54, my emphasis).

notes, had a double purpose: "On the one hand, it threw itself against the muteness imposed by our society on certain topics up until then considered taboo . . . , and on the other it also attacked the terror I felt about my own muteness, about my own tendency to censure what I so desperately needed to say" (*Sitio* 194). In the specific case of Puerto Rico, the silencing makes itself felt as a personal and social silencing of censored topics and as a muting of women's issues. It also, says Ferré, shows itself in the more pervasive linguistic silencing of Puerto Rican youth as determined by Puerto Rico's peculiar relationship with the United States: "The sad thing is that they have forgotten Spanish and never learned to speak English. They are becoming mute" (García Pinto 72). Thus it is that, in Guerra-Cunningham's words, the "figuras cosificadas" 'thingified figures' of Ferré's stories enact their "ornamental passivity" in a "ritual of communication" ("Tensiones" 16–17). Her silenced and objectified women contain in essence a comment on the Puerto Rican situation in general; for her female characters in particular, few other options beyond the ritualistic are even remotely conceivable.

Yet these women do resist, and they resist precisely at the textual level. By fixing the reading on the Cherries Jubilee nail polish ("When Women Love Men" 178, 180, 185) or the "Coty facial powder in the 'Alabaster' shade" (the English text 155 offers a somewhat different version; I cite the Spanish text "los polvos de Coty tonalidad 'Alabastro' " 160), Ferré unbalances conventional expectations: the tension is not buried deep within the women, as Guerra-Cunningham suggests, but displayed prominently and unexpectedly on the surface. Nail polish and facial powder are not even symbols to be decoded; because their function is decisively literal, they are all the more potent. Cosmetics, then, along with race, serve as the fundamental visual clues of social class. It is with cosmetics and—as Castellanos noted—with language, that emancipation must begin, and if the stories represent Ferré's verbal praxis, it is through a revolutionary use of makeup that her characters in "When Women Love Men" and "Isolda" stage their rebellion. Instead of making themselves up for a man, they are making themselves up as a form of emancipation that serves along the way as a potent demystification of the myth of everlasting love in its conventional forms. In a parallel vein, Ferré's takes her title *Sitio a Eros* from a 1923 book by Soviet writer Alexandra Kollantay, *Sitio a Eros alado* (Besieging winged Eros), which proposes, in Ferré's summary, a revisionary view of the role of love and marriage in the proletarian state. For Kollantay, and for Ferré, "the recognition of love as an an essential ingredient in marriage had profound economic and class reasons" that are no longer valid in a proletarian society, where the myth of fidelity and the fiction of legalized love no longer have any basis (111–12). As Ferré notes, her own project in both fiction and essays is similar: to explore "how woman . . . finds herself irremediably divided between her need to negotiate [transar] with socially imposed formulas . . . and her need to persist in the search for an ideal love, which has as its goal not the possession of the beloved but rather self-transcendence and self-perfection" (*Sitio* 196). In this ongoing project, "When Women Love Men" and "Isolda's Mirror" have distinct but complementary roles. In both, "love" has a very different meaning for the male and female characters; linguistic and sexual encounters depict at best an asymptotic approximation to the ideal of physical and spiritual love described by Kollantay and Ferré.

"When Women Love Men" was originally published in Ferré's short-lived journal, *Zona de carga y descarga* (Loading and unloading zone) as one of a pair of stories (the other by Manuel Ramos Otero) printed together as a memorial to Isabel Luberza, the famous prostitute from Ferré's home city of Ponce, who had recently been killed in a drug raid.[5] In Ferré's story the white woman, the wife of Ambrosio, is incongruously named Isabel Luberza, and the black prostitute, Isabel la Negra, has no last name—already a statement about social, as well as racially determined, class distinctions. The two women imagine themselves and each other, before meeting, by means of contrasts that already depend from a certain generalizable connection. Each is "bewitchingly beautiful" (184), but one has the porcelain beauty of a doll, the other the earthy beauty of an overwhelming sexuality. Each is shaped by the pressure of a man's hands sliding over her, forming her to his requirements, one to enforced and conspicuous daily laziness, the other to nightly labor, one to the mechanical reproduction of the necessary male heir for the propertied husband, the other to frenzied

---

[5]Manuel Ramos Otero's story is reprinted in his collection, *El cuento de la mujer del mar* (The story of the woman from the sea). The story, "La última plena que bailó Luberza" (The last plena that Luberza danced) has several points of contact with Ferré's story but describes an aging woman always addressed as "Frau Luberza Oppenheimer," who has attained her significant power not so much from her considerable sexual attractions as through the intercession of prayers to traditional African gods: Ochún, Changó, Obatalá, and Eleguá (59–60).

but sterile sensuality. Each finds herself trapped in the house he has
built, one on the balcony, where she can be observed, the other in the
bedroom, where she can be hidden away. For each, clothing makes the
woman, one in her "dress of silver lamé," the other "barefoot and
dressed in rags" (180). Hatred and fear define the standard relationship between the two classes represented by the two Isabels; only in
the catastrophe of their joint inheritance of Ambrosio's mansion can
we see some kind of comprehension and unification. In the wake of
that unexpected disaster comes a final realization, that class distinctions have less to do with the one's straight blonde hair and alabaster
skin and the other's kinky black hair and dark skin (although that is the
starting point) than with what the Isabels recognize as the way that the
light/dark self is presented: the "stiff, rich icing" (179) on their bodily
cakes. The realization of this fundamental similarity of oppression
serves as the neutral point that separates and unites these shifting
duplications, the blank (black?) space that lies between body and
clothes, nail and polish, face and cosmetics. Appearance and being are
crossed and recrossed in each other's (their own) reflections about
language and self, in the two women's mutual desire to be without
foundation for each other.

Isabel la Negra speaks with pity and fury of the white women
destined to be wives of the men she services, "those blobs of custard
that rich girls probably look like in bed, because it is not proper for a
good girl to thrust her pelvis, because good girls have vaginas of
polished silver and bodies of carved alabaster" (181). Good white girls
have to be stiff and proper, have to observe the proprieties, because
they are the visible sign of the property of the white men. Wicked,
black girls, on the other hand, have the freedom to enjoy sex but, as
the invisible property of the white man, must be prepared to suffer the
more unpleasant assaults on their bodies as well as the pleasurable
ones. The black woman's hold on the man resides in her accession to
his demands to share her sexual expertise with his friends; her revenge is to charge them for her services. The white woman's only
weapon to win Ambrosio back is a futile display of domesticity (183).
When he ignores these efforts, in revenge Isabel Luberza begins to
imagine what form a frenzied, rather than passive, sexuality might
take, begins to allow her alabaster skin to become tanned, so that
upper-class society will suspect her of having mixed blood, a suspicion
that will reflect on Ambrosio's social standing (184–85).

Isabel Luberza's hatred and impotence is no less than that of her counterpart: "So many years of anger stuck like a lump in my throat . . . so many years of painting my fingernails every morning . . . with Cherries Jubilee" (178). The hatred flows through her veins and becomes pure love in "this confusion between her and her, or between her and me, or between me and me" (178), and when one of the Isabels takes the face of the other between her hands and kisses her, they both realize that they are wearing the same shade of nail polish (182). For Isabel Luberza, the nail polish and the red heels effect the interpenetration into her husband's mistress: "Swaying myself now back and forth on my red heels, through which come down, slow and silent like a tide, that blood that was rising from the base of my fingernails from so long ago, my blood polished over with Cherries Jubilee" (185). Her fascination with her rival reflects, as José Blanco might say, "the traditional fascination of the bourgeoisie (who are 'less body' . . .) with the bodies of misery," a fascination that resides, he notes, "in that, in effect, these bodies are the Great Carnal Interpretation without mediations" (126).

Isabel la Negra, who does not envy the white woman her "polished silver vagina" does dream of "her dress of silver lamé . . . spilling down my back like a cape of ice," cooling the sensual heat she is tired of simulating. She dreams of her rival's "perfume Fleur de Rocaille," of replacing the too-familiar smells of semen and bodily wastes with Luberza's ineffable virgin smell of sanctity, dreams of covering her dark body with her white counterpart's "powder, Chante D'Aromes," simulating her rival's skin, so white that there can be no suspicion of even the smallest taint of black blood (179). Isabel la Negra is tired of dancing to the sensual music written in "her" honor. She has recognized the trap in being identified with rich and scrumptious chocolates; little brown boys sell "Hersheybarskissesmilkyways" for white men to gobble up. Isabel la Negra dreams most of all of the luxury of sitting on the balcony, sharing in the mandated leisure of rich women. "The Great Carnal Interpretation" is for her another tired myth of the same oppressive bourgeois society that has made her body a trash receptacle for its poisoned desires. She has lived the life of that "body of misery," so fascinating to rich men, and now would like some of the advantages of those others who are "less body" because "they fulfill their personality above all in the material or symbolic extensions of property, capital, state, commerce, religion, etc." (Blanco 126).

José Blanco's critique of the generalized whiteness of official "civilization" and of that self-proclaimed civilization's romance with the racially other, is well taken. Blanco claims exemption from this rule by virtue of his overt homosexuality, Ferré by way of her sex. And yet, the very propositions laid out in Ferré's story, as in Blanco's essay, raise the question of whether or not the "white," indefectibly, returns in their work. This is not to say, of course, that a privileged white woman cannot write convincingly about a poor black woman, but as has been suggested to me, the point remains that "Ferré's story is written and usually read from a white woman's bias. . . . could a black woman imagine as easily that she were being confused with a white one? Or is the confusion a possibility prepared by a liberal and privileged position that enjoys imaging race blindness?"[6] In this sense Ferré's story might be compared with works such as Mexican Elena Garro's much-anthologized story "It's the Fault of the Tlaxcaltecas" or Nicaraguan Gioconda Belli's novel *La mujer habitada* (The inhabited woman). Both Garro and Belli participate in what I uncharitably consider a developed longing for a reverse *mestizaje*, an attempt to recuperate the Indian "soul" through the spiritual repossession of a criolla's body. Garro's staid housewife is taken over by the still-living anguish of an Indian woman, a betrayer of her people, and is condemned to relive the taking of "la Gran Tenochtitlán" (Mexico City) and the death of her beloved cousin-husband. In Belli's novel, by means of a glass of orange juice infected with a pre-hispanic spirit, the aristocratic architect is taken over by a sixteenth-century Indian guerrillera named Itza and, through the operations of this benign possession, is influenced to take the laudable and politically correct step of joining, and dying for, the revolution in her home country.

Isabel la Negra, however, is no blind dream-spinner who will adopt upper-class values with her upper-class income, nor is she a romantic who will dedicate her remaining years to volunteer work for charity. She will, with Luberza's full cooperation, turn Ambrosio's stately mansion into the greatest dance hall and brothel in the country and will display on the surface what has always been the dark underlayer of that privileged existence: "Sitting on the balcony of my new brothel . . . , the balustrade of long silver amphoras now painted shocking pink, aligned in front of me like happy phalluses, the white

[6]I am indebted to an anonymous reader for Cornell University Press for this insight.

plaster garlands adhered to the façade, that gave the house that romantic air and feeling of excessive respectability of a wedding cake" (179). The house, too, has been made up, and the deceptive icing on the wedding cake has been openly paired to the "happy phallus," the abstract symbol of power, which Kollantay and Ferré interpret as the signal of the most pernicious effect of the bourgeois mixing of love and marriage. There, hidden in plain sight on the balcony, impeccably made-up, the composite Isabel awaits her customers, the unstoppable revolution already underway.

Throughout *Papeles de Pandora* (Pandora's papers) the ideological valence of makeup remains constant. Decent women wear alabaster powder and subtle perfumes to emphasize their porcelain-doll-like fragility and helplessness, while strident colors underline the robust sensuality of their rivals. In "The Youngest Doll," for example, all the young women in this particular family of the hereditary cane aristocracy are given a life-size doll-replica of themselves on their wedding day, and in "Marina y el león" (Marina and the lion) the aristocratic protagonist gives a costume party in which she is dressed as a doll and put in a cellophane-covered box: "Through that surface both hard and viscous at the same time, Marina watched the world pass by that night as if she were covered by a coat of varnish" (109). Rebellious María de los Angeles, in "Sleeping Beauty," like Isabel Luberza, marks her rejection of high society by adopting the bright colors of the lower-class women. She paints her face and hair before prostituting herself, and she finds the heavy makeup strangely liberating: "She had her eyes surrounded by zinc rings, against which were prominently displayed her enormous black eyelashes. The pancake makeup on her cheeks was so thick that it looked like it was going to detach itself in slabs."[7] In "Isolda's Mirror" from *Maldito amor (Sweet Diamond Dust)* the terms and method of critique shift. This time, the demythification of social conventions does not take place in the shifting of surfaces and classes and races over one another through the polishing of nails or the inversion of cosmetic schemes; rather, it occurs in the unmistakable literalization of white society's preference for what the Isabels call "bodies of carved alabaster."

Andrew Bush has recently suggested that in *Maldito amor*, the

---

[7]"Tenía los ojos rodeados por dos chapas de zinc, contra las cuales se destacaban sus inmensas pestañas de charol. El pankake de sus mejillas, de tan grueso, parecía que se le iba a desprender de la cara en tortas. Pensó con alivio que por primera vez iba a poder ser ella" (*Papeles* 180). Ferré and Vélez's English version of the story abridges this section.

Puerto Rican woman has not only rescued but practically invented a Puerto Rican romanticism, "for as ironic as it may be, the romanticism there represents an effort to define the national identity in its own terms" (81). Much of *Maldito amor* (Ferré's choice of *Sweet Diamond Dust* as her title for the English version conveys a very different organizing principle) indeed demonstrates a rewriting of nineteenth-century romanticism and twentieth-century (*novela rosa*) fantasies as well, in Ferré's now-familiar deconstruction of the lives and loves of rich and spoiled sugarcane aristocrats. "Isolda's Mirror," however, opens with a scene that seems to be drawn less from the romantic tradition than from the tradition of the great late nineteenth-century realist novels of Benito Pérez Galdós. Like the works of the Spanish novelist, Ferré's story begins with a similar leisurely recounting of the genealogies of the prominent families, the same gradual approximation to the picturesque (though squalidly polluted) town through the uncharacteristically transparent air of Don Augusto Arzuaga's wedding celebrations when, for the first time, "northern bankers and the town's industrialists and businessmen would get together with the old sugar cane aristocracy of the valley" (122). After this traditional introduction, however, the story shifts styles. The slightly archaic opening clearly reproduces Don Augusto's view of the world—a museum piece consistent with his collector's mania—but the story quickly escapes his control. Not immediately, of course, or overobviously. Don Augusto had the foresight to see that the rum barons were losing ascendancy and that good relations with the new North American investors were essential to his continuing personal prosperity. Accordingly, he has made himself rich (and the town dirty and choked with dust) in the cement business, building new facilities for U.S. army bases. Adriana Mercier, the much younger bride, a cabaret singer and former lover of Don Augusto's son, is an army brat: "They kept eternally floating, displacing themselves from country to country, from military base to military base, enclosed in their unbreakable soap bubble" ("ellos seguían eternamente flotando, desplazándose de país en país . . . dentro de su irrompible pompa de jabón." Spanish text 135; the English text omits this sentence). The need to maintain good relations with the United States, more particularly with the U.S. bankers, at whatever cost, informs one of the story's crucial concerns; the other is the importance of a beautiful woman to decorate an upper-class home. Don Augusto needs a loan from the Americans to keep his business afloat ("floating" is a frequently used metaphor in this story); he is convinced that his tastefully furnished and impeccably decorated home will send the proper message about his business acumen and that the charm and grace of his beautiful new wife will seal the agreement.

Adriana, who has grown up speaking perfect English in an American army bubble, is much less sanguine than Don Augusto. She knows that in Puerto Rican high society—half of the distinguished wedding guests—white skin is highly prized as sign of pure blood and aristocratic leisure. She also knows firsthand of the North Americans' differently evoked and even more intense intransigence in matters of race. Her warm brown skin, no matter how beautiful, would never pass, and if in Europe her perfect English and French-sounding last name served as a key to open doors in all levels of society, on this side of the Atlantic Ocean things are not so simple: "In the Old World, the continental surnames had helped them. . . . But in North America it was a different story. Perfect English and an exotic last name weren't enough. They were caught out by their skin, by their color" ("Pero en Norteamérica había sido otra la historia. El inglés perfecto y el apellido exótico no habían sido suficientes. Los sacaban por la piel, por la pinta." Spanish text 139; the English version omits this section).

What happens when the pace of the storytelling accelerates and this volatile mixture is shaken together is still a matter of discussion among the townspeople: "Taking advantage of the privilege of their visibility" in the temporarily dust-free air of their city, "Santa Cruzans began immediately to spin stories, adding and subtracting details to facts that were already well known to all" (*Sweet Diamond Dust* 121). A few things seem clear, however. Don Augusto's interest in Adriana is exactly parallel to his passion for paintings of female nudes; he likes his women made-up, distanced, artificial, and existing by and for his pleasure. He likes to pretend that the paintings/women depend on him, that he is subject to their whims. He tells the young woman in explanation:

> Without the light of day a painting dies smothered, and ladies' portraits are the most temperamental of all. They fade, grow scales, shed their varnish like sunburned skin without vitamins. The visitor's eye nourishes their vanity, gives them a reason to go on living. One must be constantly restoring them; cleansing their faces of centuries-old dirt with Castile soap; spreading them on stretchers and tightening their wedges; varnishing and waxing them. My ladies are like divas, they like to be pampered. (144)

These beautiful women who make up Don Augusto's "harem," presided over by his favored painting of the death of Isolda, eventually replace his first wife in his affections and in his life. Margarita conveniently dies when her aging face can no longer be restored to pristine loveliness, opening a space in Don Augusto's private gallery for her successor, Adriana, the image of the painted Isolda. Don Augusto is determined to have her for his collection. The old man wants the young woman to represent the favorite painting come to life, to become Isolda's simulacrum, altering the Isolda story so that the beautiful woman remains with the old man (King Mark) instead of pining for the young heir (Gabriel or Tristan). Moreover, he specifically and slyly requires her to be unchanging—he calls it "fidelity"—and enforces his decree by ordering a statue of Venus, bearing an anatomically exact relation to Adriana's body, which he places on display in his newly constructed "Temple of Love" (151).

Up to this point the story has the familiar contours of those collected in *Papeles de Pandora*, that is, the society woman as decorative/decorated doll, a lesser, because impermanent, work of art. In a startling denouement, however, Adriana brings together all the themes of the story, reveals them to be a hypocritically dusted-over tale about domination and exploitation, and then escapes, intact. The cement dust that chokes the town and the "Coty facial powder in the 'Alabaster' shade" (Spanish 160), the Hispanic demand for pure blood and the North American preference for white skin, the work of men and the work of art, the metaphorical prostitution of Puerto Rican men in search of American dollars and the society marriages of Puerto Rican women in need of male support—all condense to a single image, that of Adriana impersonating the woman that Don Augusto sees when he looks at her, Isolda-Venus:

> As the bullets began to fly in every direction, Adriana's surprise was finally revealed, that scandalous spectacle which caused not only the bank's ruin, when the northern investors decided to sell their shares and get out of Santa Cruz, but unwittingly that of her husband, as well: the vision of her naked body, an exact copy of the Venus of the Temple of Love, under Isolda's dress. (159–60)

In Adriana, Ferré creates a resemblance of a resemblance, a woman (Ferré, Adriana) reflecting the idealized image of a cultural artifact (a story, a painting) that in itself pretends to comment on a well-known mythic story (of colonization, of love). Yet, finally, it is a reproduction without foundation, a styled resemblance as resistance literature. Masiello says that in works like those of Ferré, Latin American women authors "describe a body that resists the tactics of naturalization, a body that eludes the careful and predictable anticipatory level always accompanying repressive discourses. . . . At the same time, this new body offers itself as denunciation of civil and political authority insofar as it untangles the trap of a language established by law and tradition" ("Discurso" 56). It is this richness in the transformative valences of makeup that distinguishes "Isolda's Mirror" from other Ferré stories, such as "The Youngest Doll," in which the doll's rebellion is much less multifaceted.

It is essential at this point to rejoin the question of the reader. If this is a literature of denunciation, as Masiello suggests, to whom is the denunciation addressed? Ostensibly, all the women in Ferré's stories are making themselves up "for" men. Ostensibly, then, the denunciation would be of a male power base that turns women into dolls and sensual playthings and mute works of art. That is part of it, of course. But the men in Ferré's stories are too defeated, too unmanned by other circumstances to bear the weight of a nuanced cultural critique. Her male characters, while seemingly prepotent, are curiously caricaturesque or easily discounted as forces of civic and political authority: the rum barons are drunken has-beens, Ambrosio is dead, Don Augusto is old and bankrupt. Likewise, while the Yankees loom on the horizon as the new masters of economic power, their power is still felt only distantly, and their effect on social interactions is minimal. We could even say that if the women are surfacing in these stories, the men are drowning. Evidently, too, Ferré's concern is as much with empowerment (of men as well as women) as with denunciation. It is in this respect that the author of these stories asks women to look at themselves, to see themselves making themselves up in the mirror of her text, to see their own complicity in and responsibility for their subjugation. It is here that the slipwise mediation of the male gaze allows the female reader to reflect on the shifting dynamics of male-female relationships; it is in the mediation of the textualized male gaze that she is protected from a self-critique too devastating to be helpful. Rosario Castellanos suggests polishing the surface, making it shine, slipping in a space for an evolving, transformative self; Rosario Ferré offers a buffered (male-coded) space for mediation between the transformative surfaces of the female narrative and the constantly self-displacing, transforming surfaces of the female reader.

Unlike Ferré, who reads through the explicitly textual male audience to the female reader, tempering her fury with a positioned critique of contemporary gender relationships, Julieta Campos utilizes the fiction of reading through the textual establishment—the elite reader of the French *nouveau roman* and subsequent exercises in postmodern self-conscious textuality—to a specific female reader who no longer exists. Campos's reader, then, is to some degree blocked and blocked out on the surface of the text. Alicia Partnoy's concept of the *lector enemigo* (the enemy reader) helps define this relationship more precisely. In concrete terms, the *lector enemigo* is the prison official who reads all letters and manuscripts before allowing their release to the intended audience; in a broader sense it refers to the shaping of narrative for a particular audience to which the woman writer must write, in the full knowledge that the *lector enemigo* may be the only audience she will ever reach. For Campos, the educated reader, who too easily mistakes her works for superficial and merely brilliant verbal games in the style of the French new novel, embodies that *lector enemigo,* the antagonistic reader who is indeed intended to misread the complexity of such games as an ideologically free surface.[8] Thus, what Ferré outlines in the concrete use of textual cosmetics, Campos reserves for the more intangible makeup of linguistic structures rubbing up against literary history. Ferré's is the realm of *emancimatricidad:* liberating women, killing off the repressive reverend mothers that serve as the pillars of patriarchy, taking apart outworn uses and customs; her style, though outwardly fragmented, stresses cohesion, wholeness. Campos knows that most of her readers will be *lectores enemigos* and knows that her writing will be warped insofar as she has to write through them and to them at the same time: thus the "layered look" of the text, thus the slippages between its lacquered surfaces, thus also (given an academic audience trained to look for depth) critical misunderstanding, accusations of inadequacy of text to the (presumed) form, general puzzlement over the stylistic elaborations, and so on.

Campos's work is far more highly fragmented than Ferré's; yet she

---

[8]Identification of Campos with the *nouveau roman* is already a cliché in recent literary histories. See for example, Sefchovich 1:27.

stresses that for her, "writing interests me as a way of integrating, in words, something that in the world is disintegrating" (B. Miller 87). Hers is an ethics of fragments shored up against the ruins of a post-modern culture. Furthermore, for Campos the lost mother represents the ideal reader to whom she directs her work. Earlier in this chapter I said that the sea was not particularly maternal in *Sabina*; let me compli-cate that statement now by suggesting that the novel's dedication, "a mi madre," and epigraph "Je reposerai donc au bord de la mer" entails not an identification of *madre* with *(mère)/mer* but rather a story about "the vacuums we writers feel, the difficulty in finding valid interlocu-tors, so that writing is not just a solitary monologue" (Campos, inter-view B. Miller 91). It is as if in writing *madre* (mother) Campos is already writing *muerte* (death), the void, and in writing "mer [mère] que j'ai tant aimée" she is writing of the confusion that gives rise to the story and to the uncompletable dialogue with the mother, who is the only possible interlocutor for her work. She ciphers, then, multi-lingually, the confusion between *la mer/la mère → amor* and *la mer/la mère → la mort*, where love, death, and writing are inextricably inter-twined:

> Yo buscaba en las novelas que otros habían escrito una manera de llenar un vacío que la realidad me dejaba y que sólo empezó a llenar para mí, personalmente, cuando escribo mi primera novela, *Muerte por agua*.
>   Mi madre estuvo muriéndose de cáncer en el pulmón durante dos largos años. La muerte . . . fue como si se hubiera abierto una grieta enorme en el suelo, una fisura del tamaño del mundo por donde de escapaba toda la vida. El libro, la novela, fue un intento de llenar ese hueco. (B. Miller 82)

> In the novels that others had written I searched for a way of filling a void that reality left in me and that I began to fill for myself, personally, only with the writing of my first novel, *Death by Water*.
>   My mother was dying of lung cancer during two long years. Her death . . . was as if an enormous crack had opened in the ground, a fissure the size of the world through which all life escaped. The book, the novel, was an attempt to fill that hole.

The death of the mother is the stimulus for a kind of writing that can arise only from this unwelcome emancipation. Yet there is guilt. For the mother is not only the ideal reader, against whom all other readers are discounted as *lectores enemigos*; the mother is also the occasion for writing. Her death and the text's birth have an intimate and tortured relationship, as the writer figuratively cannibalizes the mother's body to create the phantasmal body of the text (in saying this I am paraphrasing Campos [see "Vocación" 467–68]). In Julieta Campos, the cannibalization is also literal, and loving: "My mother kept a diary in which I have discovered, I believe, the origin of my literary vocation" (B. Miller 86). "Holes" and "voids" haunt Campos's work, as does her much-repeated sense that the function of the novel is primarily that of installing itself "in reality's cracks" (*Función* 31). This need to fill a void is common to all writers, says Campos, but it is especially acute when the writer also happens to be a woman: "Accentuated when the novelist is a woman is the dispersion of self, the fragmentation of the person, who has to divide herself among numerous demands, demands the world makes to donate herself, to hand herself over." For this reason it is both more difficult and more essential for her to find "her place in this work, which becomes for her, much more than for the male writer, 'the room of one's own' of which Virginia Woolf spoke with a much more concrete connotation" (*Función* 141).

But still the guilt returns with redoubled force, paired to the concern that, painfully, death itself, in its effort to fill the void, can be fragmented and polished into a brilliant surface, can be made to shine, can be isolated and made manageable and superficial. And yet the void remains, both in the writing and in the reading. This is precisely the danger and the attraction of fictive rituals of mourning or fictive constructions of a woman's room of her own. It can also, says Baudrillard, serve as the locus of irresponsible reading: "What discourse must fight against is not so much the unconscious secret as the superficial abyss of its own appearance; and if discourse must triumph over something, it is not over phantasies and hallucinations heavy with meaning and misinterpretation, but the shiny surface of non-sense and all the games the latter render possible" (54).

What rescues such works as Campos's from the (enemy) reader's recuperation and codification of their transgressive moves is not the shiny superficiality of nonsense but the smooth and aligned surface of an elusive "scriptural"[9] of writing that leaves nothing concrete for that

[9]The word is Stephen Heath's: "The alignment of these elements horizontally, in the play of repetition and variation, produces a kind of 'declension' of the elements of fiction, giving what was called at the beginning of this chapter a *scriptural* of narrative (as Leibniz talked of the *geometral* of an object) that invites the reader to read the writing of the text" (*Roman* 136).

reader to grasp. Language carefully runs along the surface (but there is the void, papered over), naming things, describing them in detail (but the void persists, unnameable), defining a world of great linguistic complexity that nevertheless manages to encode a certain despera-tion, a subtle silence—"la mère que j'ai tant aimée"—mutely inscribed against the backdrop of an antitraditional readability.

For Francine Masiello, Latin American women's writing at its best displays what she calls, following Mikhail Bakhtin, a "double dis-course," a hybrid language "that recognizes the structures of power at the same time that it offers an alternative" ("Discurso" 56). In Campos's work, the discourse is never solely double, never offers only one alternative. Then too, her best work links to the recognition of social and political structures of power to a forceful recognition of the equally significant rhetorical structures that are among power's essen-tial building blocks. Thus, her story "La ciudad" (The city), a fable that could be read allegorically or ironically or politically (or, if the *lector enemigo* prefers, as a hermeneutic game), takes into account these hereditary literary powers and turns them to new use. A note at the end of the text informs us that the story was largely constructed from bits and pieces taken from books including Cirilio Villaverde's classic romantic novel *Cecelia Valdés*, Alvaro de la Iglesia's *Tradiciones cubanas*, and the now-canonical Cuban "Boom" novels: Alejo Carpentier's *Siglo de las luces*, Guillermo Cabrera Infante's *Tres tristes tigres*, and José Lezama Lima's *Paradiso*. Some of it, she tells us, has been "pulled out of her other works, some from texts included in this book, others from the novel *Muerte por agua*" (119). Campos steals the words about Havana—words that in essence construct, and have already con-structed, Havana for most readers—and reinserts them into her own context, robbing the city to save the city, in other terms. The operation is strictly parallel to the fragmentation of the maternal body: "It is necessary to keep on looking for the words, words that steal some of its being from the city in order to deposit it in a safe place, a place as invulnerable as the pages of a book, any book, could be (could be?); words that return the city to us, enclosed in the contours it had, has had, has at some point: the city, a strip of scurrying substance" (117). In order for us to grasp the city intelligibly, Campos suggests, its slippery substance must be fixed in the words that redeem and kill it. The question, then, is not just the choice of the words but the hovering or hesitating over the variant forms of discourse as they operate in a tension of solicited interdependence. Furthermore, it is precisely Campos's intent to offer these quotations from her predecessors, these confections, as substantiation for her sense that the postmodern reader-critic has long since become adept at dealing with fragmentation, has indeed newly constructed the conventionalism of strategic interventions ruling even the most contemporary modes of reading fragmented tests. She reevaluates the hubris of that modern reader, who faithfully (Cortázar might say complicitously) reproduces a fiction of the illusion as an illusion of the truth as it might be, will have been, perceived at some moment in time. Such readers, and such texts, share a delight in the intersecting surfaces of game playing as a mode of reality construction.

For Campos, in contrast, the illusion is quite other, not the illusion of truth but the illusion that words on a page reproduce something other than syntactical structures. Furthermore, her reader is not complicitous but embattled, engaged in a struggle for control within the universe of the fiction. The novel, says Campos in her *Función de la novela* (Function of the novel), "is a reality created by the word and the fabula, a constant gestation of . . . an *estar siendo,* a gerundial universe where the author, the characters, and even the reader fight incessantly for life" (66). The point here is precisely the unorthodox and untranslatable play between the two Spanish verbs of being, *ser* and *estar.* English uses the gerund *being* to represent the noun; in Spanish the infinitive is employed: *el ser* (never *el estar*). Campos's proposition of a gerundial form, *un estar siendo,* brings together the two modes of being, both the gerundial and the infinitive, responding to cultural as well as linguistic imperatives, and brings together as well two nuances of existing, a peculiarly Spanish shade of meaning, one the shadow-dream-reflection of the other, and does so in a world that slips in and out of conventional fictional illusions or slides from the illusions of fiction to the illusions of "reality." From "La ciudad" once again:

Empieza a producirse lo insólito: un habitante de una casa en la parte vieja de la ciudad penetra por la noche y se duerme; al día siguiente, cuando sale a la calle, encuentra que se ha producido alguna modificación difícil de precisar, un cambio que no podría describir ni siquiera en ese momento, viéndolo como lo ve. . . . Sin embargo . . . la única prueba es la sensación vaga, indefinible del hombre que pensaba, piensa, salir de su casa como todos los días. Y ese hombre, por mucho que yo quiera, no está aquí para dar su testimonio. Y aunque estuviera, ese testimonio no serviría. Porque el hombre, inventado por mí, dejaría de tener la más mínima realidad necesaria para reclamar el derecho de la existencia si en este momento se encontrara "realmente" fuera de esta página, aunque ese sitio fuera el quicio de la puerta . . . de su casa en la parte más vieja de la ciudad. (111–13)

The unexpected begins to happen: an inhabitant of a house in the old part of the city penetrates through the night and falls asleep; the next day, when he goes out into the street, he discovers that some difficult-to-pin-down modification has taken place, a change that he could not define, not even in that moment, seeing it as he sees it. . . . Nevertheless . . . the only proof is a vague, indefinable sensation of the man who thought, who thinks, he is leaving his house just as he does every day. And that man, no matter how much I might wish it, is not here to bear witness. And even if he were, the testimony would be meaningless. Because the man, my invention, would have ceased to retain the most minimal degree of reality necessary to claim the right to exist if at this moment he were to find himself "really" outside this page, even if that place were to be the threshold of the door . . . of his own house in the oldest part of the city.

Like the woman who looks out to sea in *Sabina*, the character in this story is present, but without either perspective or the trappings of an illusory validation, hidden from the reader in his visibility to us. Economically, Campos sketches a scene, creates character and plot (the unforeseen and vaguely menacing undefinable change), then, with a swift sleight of hand, reveals the plot's basis in a human desire to cover over some other void (boredom, loss, lack of control, sense of impinging chaos) before restoring that merely fictional construct, that character, in another lapidary phrase. The fiction, Campos tells us, does not (should not?) create a mimetic reproduction of reality; instead, to some degree it proposes a parallel, more mathematically exact, and controllable artifice. It is no wonder then, that characters in her story miserably latch onto "personal objects, especially watches, as a guarantee or final trapping of a personal existence" ("La ciudad" 113); ritually objectified things help maintain a slippery sense of identity, a minimal hold on a state of being, however attenuated or contingent.

Campos's warning has a specific social and political charge for her fellow women, in whose lives the attenuated sense of self is not only fictionally but also literally operative. Already in the essays collected in *La imagen en el espejo* (The image in the mirror, 1965), Campos has charged women with the responsibility for taking an active role in their own lives. She warns that it is insufficient to construct a sense of identity around a husband and children; a woman needs to "produce something that transcends her and makes her really exist" (115), or she will be left in the illusory doorway of someone else's story, a fictional construct without power to give testimony or even to vocalize her unease. All her books, from the early collection of essays on contemporary writers—including Nathalie Sarraute, de Beauvoir, and Woolf—to her more recent metafictions *Sabina* and *El miedo de perder a Eurídice* (Fear of losing Euridice), have as one of their central focuses Campos's ongoing exploration of the forms taken by feminine sensibility and female creativity. All her books offer eloquent testimony to her own commitment to and ambivalence about giving voice to a particularly feminine authorial presence. Of all her books, it is still *Muerte por agua* (Death by water), the first novel, the novel created in the aftermath of the loss of the mother, which speaks most directly and specifically to these concerns.

Julieta Campos has lived in Mexico since her marriage in 1954, but the first twenty-three years of her life were lived as a Cuban, and it is Cuba that marks her fiction most strongly, another void, a kind of nostalgic atmosphere that permeates her work: "In my stories, in my novels, one can feel everywhere the stamp of my childhood, and especially of the sea, the landscape par excellence, the most vital, the most suggestive, the most stimulating setting" (B. Miller 85). The sea is that room of one's own that is the literary enterprise, and like the sewing room occupied by Laura and her aging mother, Eloísa, in *Muerte por agua*, the sea has its most secret and concrete nature defined by the labor of a female invention: "Now she knew. She knew she had not invented that atmosphere or at least that she had only invented it as this room itself, which was her work" (67).

The plot of *Muerte por agua* is extremely simple, involving the desultory conversations and tired silences of Laura and Andrés, a middle-aged married couple, and Laura's mother on a rainy day in October 1959. The relationship between the two women is foregrounded in the dialogues, and although Andrés has the last word in the novel, it is Laura and, secondarily, her mother who share the scene as the major point-of-view characters. Despite, or perhaps because of, the conventional outlines of her life, Laura is plagued by a nagging sense of her own superfluity, "this impression of being in the way [estar de más]. Of not being needed. Of having been left outside" (133). Curiously, she is left out because, like her mother, she has always been the one to stay within, to remain behind when other family members left to experience life, to disappear into death: "They were the ones who left and the ones who came back. I always stayed behind. Someone had to shut the door. . . . One house, and then another house before this house, my house" (140). As the housewife looks back over her life and her mother's life, she is vaguely aware that hers is a being in excess, "un estar siendo," of accumulated, still accumulating futility that layers over her gerundial universe in translucent sheets, as the rain layers over the surface of the window, preventing her from seeing outside.

Laura's dreams are uncomplicated ones, conditioned by her lack of experience. She wishes to imitate the birds, the messenger pigeons and pelicans and seagulls that fly back and forth over land and sea; she dreams of planes that fly fixed routes. Birds and planes, like the people she greets at the door of her house, can come and go, sailing over the surface and returning to the nest. She also imagines herself as a fish in an aquarium or a fish in the sea, "which can be seen during the day, swimming very rapidly close to the surface" (72), because in her life, as in the imagined life of the fish, everything seems light and floating, weightless. But these homely metaphors, embodying her dreams of flight and her dissatisfaction with floating, metaphors that multiply throughout the text, seem to her inadequate to describe her weightless floating, her sense of helpless incompleteness before life: "There must be other things but, after all, she did not have much imagination. If she had not been so enclosed…" (112). Laura's imagination is caught up short before the concept of the open door, unable to project what might lie beyond the threshold. The enclosed life has dusted her over, like an abandoned piece of furniture, coating her with a layer of atrophied will, and between the metaphorical layers of dust and water, Laura—neither burrowing animal nor fish nor soaring bird—feels both buried and drowned.

Inevitably, Laura probes the significance of these layers and finds in them the replica of her body, her superficial and hollowed self. Again, she has various metaphors for this uncovering of the hidden self, this meticulously surfaced-over void. She imagines that she is a Russian doll, the innermost doll of the identical nested dolls that compose the layers of her world. It is, she says, "as if everything had been constructed in the same way as those Russian dolls that store other progressively smaller dolls inside, and the smallest one of all was the table with the cards and themselves around it, and after that the walls of the room, and then the rain, and the street, and the city, and the sea, and the world, all the rest of the world, behind the line of the horizon" (84). Alternatively, she imagines the day as her own well-worn and wrinkled dress, which she could slip off and hand to Andrés across the table with the playing cards she is holding in her hand, slipping him the keys to a kind of minimally imagined paradise. She imagines that Andrés "allows himself to be rescued, allows himself to be literally covered in that avalanche of love" (81). And again, she imagines herself as an archaeologist and her personal history as a hidden treasure awaiting discovery:

> Resulta que uno a acordarse de cosas tristes, debajo de todo eso como otros tantos niveles engañosos, como los que despistan a los arqueólogos en las exploraciones de palacios enterrados, estaba el motivo auténtico, lo que se buscaba, el tesoro intacto, protegido por todas esas capas superiores. . . . Laura cree estar allí, en ese nivel profundo y resguardado, limpiando todos los restos de yeso y de polvo, para contemplar por fin la superficie pulida. (80)

> It turns out that when one begins to remember sad things, underneath it all, like so many other deceptive levels, like those that throw archaeologists off track in their explorations of buried palaces, was the authentic motive, what one was seeking, the intact treasure, protected by all those layers on top. . . . Laura believes she is there, in this deep and protected level, cleaning all the bits of plaster and dust, in order to contemplate at last the polished surface.

What Laura hopes to find in the polished surface of the hidden treasure is something like an authentic self, something like the avalanche of love she pours over her unaware husband. Yet she is aware that the archaeologist is more likely to find deteriorated artifacts than an intact treasure, and what Laura contemplates in the polished surface of recovered authenticity is something more like a mirror reflection of her ordinary, inert self than a princess in disguise under an everyday dress.

Although she dreams of flying, Laura knows she is housebound.

She knows as well that even her husband's comings and goings reflect less a voyage of exploration than a daily ritual no less compelling than her own cycle of household duties. As Andrés says, thinks: "After all, one can fill life with ceremonies and that simplifies things" (13), and later, "It seems to him that everything can be reduced to that, to a few very simple gestures that one makes without reflecting, which are repeated every day" (100). These rituals can fill a life, can make it seem busy and useful, and Eloísa, at least, finds comfort in such minimalist ceremonies. Laura, despite her confessed lack of imagination, is less easily convinced. She knows that the ritualistic quality of daily life serves as a self-imposed screen to vitiate critique. Her mother too easily defers uncomfortable situations or too-acute perceptions. "Luckily," says Eloísa, "the two of us have a lot to do" (23). "The truth is," answers her daughter belatedly, mentally, "she doesn't have anything to do" (99), or rather, those few repetitious housewifely tasks that need to be done can be broken up into ritual gestures of dubious value and less transcendence. Laura has to decide, for example, whether to get up or to stay sitting in the rocking chair (37) and once that decision has been made, whether to sit quietly or lean her head back and rock (116). And there are always the dolls, waiting to be dressed and decorated with ribbons. More abstractly, the women have the task of convincing themselves that they have tasks to complete, of "filling up the voids, the little ones and the big ones, again and again. Just like Penelope. Very attractive. Knit up the hours every day and then unravel them and start over. Always in the same place. At the same time. On the same day" (124). A housewife's efficiency and a housewife's metaphor: everything is neat and ordered and in its place, and since only clocks and calendars theoretically disturb this polished perfection, they too must be co-opted into the unchanging rituals of the day.

The woman's role is precisely this: to be vigilant, to be attentive, to keep things in place and orderly. The floor must be swept, the dust cleaned away, the dishes and chairs placed in their appropriate ranks, the flowers maintained in a state of plastic perfection. Likewise it is her job to make sure memories are polished and ordered, that conversations stick to ritual exchanges of commonplaces and favored clichés. She must remember to mend the clothes and the lives and to pull together threads, to keep the physical and metaphysical rooms free from literal and figurative insects, "avid to devour, to tunnel under the order of the world surreptitiously, to take over the house, to crumble it down" (40). Eloísa in particular distributes order wherever she passes with a practiced and unreflective hand; order, she knows, creates time—"time to fill her pores with patience, like a white layer of wax on the furniture" (126)—and so she creates a polished surface that is the illusion of permanence and beauty, that resists decay and the incursions of metaphorical termites. There are no alternatives and no dilemmas.

Laura, less ordered internally, tries to imagine—only imagine—a world in which things are permitted to arrange themselves in other patterns or are allowed to fall as chance dictates: "And what if she started to embroider something else, isolated words, chosen by chance, and what if she were to write daylilies in yellow, for example, or mimosas in indigo, or lilacs in rosewood or corn tassels in sky blue?" (58). What would such a room be like, such a world? Laura dreams of a memory/book/room with another hierarchy than that she and her mother impose, by inertia, on their shared household,

> un sitio de cosas inútiles, trastos inservibles, muñecas sin cabeza, mesas quebradas, sillas desfondadas, teléfonos desconectadas, espejuelos rotos, bañaderas oxidadas, violines sin cuerdas, columpios arrumbados, bombillas fundidas, máquinas descompuestas. . . . Y es igual que imaginar un cementerio de palabras, como si las palabras le tendieran a los pies un pendiente suave hecha expresamente para deslizarse, mientras que las cosas, sin sus nombres, sin las palabras, pierden el equilibrio y se quedan flotando, liberadas de la gravedad, a la deriva, girando sin detenerse en un espacio infinito, sin atmósfera. (52)

> a place of useless things, of unserviceable dishes, dolls without heads, cracked tables, unstuffed chairs, disconnected telephones, broken eye-glass lenses, rusted bathtubs, stringless violins, taken-down swings, blown-out light bulbs, out-of-order machines. . . . And it is exactly like imagining a word cemetery, as if the words spread out at her feet a gentle slope expressly made for her to slide down, while things, without their names, without the words, lost their balance and stayed floating, freed from gravity, drifting, spinning without stopping in an infinite space, without atmosphere.

Laura's projection of a disordered room, the counterpart to the too-neat shared rooms in her family's house, calls to mind the similarly, if more extensively, evoked lists in the Uruguayan Cristina Peri Rossi's ubiquitous museums: the empty and eerily resonating nonrefuges in *Los museos abandonados* (The abandoned museums), the dusty archive in the title story of *El museo de los esfuerzos inútiles* (The museum of futile efforts), a museum presided over by the gentle presence of a suggestively named curator called Virginia.

Both Campos and Peri Rossi, in their different modes, describe the woman's task of ordering and sweeping out lives and rooms, a labor not unrelated in kind to dictionary writing or other more generally conceived projects of syntactic organization. Both of these women, in foregrounding the cluttered back rooms of the mind and of historical reconstruction, also stress that the liberation from ritual housekeeping forecasts a linguistic aperture. Furthermore, in prizing the image of a "place of useless things," things without names, Laura implicitly sets herself in a theoretical stance at the opposite end of the spectrum from the well-known and influential Cuban writer and theorist Alejo Carpentier, who, in *Tientos y diferencias,* sounds a call to Latin Americans to exercise what he considers their legitimate and essential perogative to the baroque, as conditioned by their need to give names to their reality so as to format it for universal consumption. In "Problemática de la actual novela latinoamericana" (Problematics of the current Latin American novel) he writes:

> Enrique Heine nos habla, de repente, de un pino y una palmera, árboles por siempre plantados en la gran cultura universal. . . . La palabra *pino* basta para mostrarnos el pino; la palabra *palmera* basta para definir, pintar, mostrar, la palmera. Pero la palabra *ceiba*—nombre de un árbol americano al que los negros cubanos llaman "la madre de los árboles"— no basta para que las gentes de otras latitudes vean el aspecto de columna rostral de ese árbol gigantesco, adusto y solitario, como sacado de otras edades, sagrado por linaje, cuyas ramas horizontales, casi paralelas, ofrecen al viento unos puñados de hojas tan inalcanzables para el hombre como incapaces de todo mecimiento. . . . Esos árboles existen. . . . Pero no tienen la ventura de llamarse *pino*, ni *palmera*, ni *nogal*, ni *castaño*, ni *abedul*. San Luis de Francia no se sentó a su sombra, ni Pushkin les ha dedicado uno que otro verso. . . .
>
> No temamos el barroquismo, arte nuestro, nacido de árboles . . . barroquismo creado por la necesidad de *nombrar las cosas*, aunque con ello nos alejamos de las técnicas en boga: las del *nouveau roman* francés, por ejemplo. (33–34, 36)

Heinrich Heine speaks to us, suddenly, of a pine and a palm, two trees that have always been planted in the great universal culture. . . . The word *pine* shows us the pine; the word *palm* is sufficient to define, paint, show the palm. But the word *ceiba*—the name of an American tree the Afro-Cubans call "the mother of trees"—is insufficient to show people from other latitudes the beaklike trunk of this gigantic, austere, and solitary tree, as if taken from another age, sacred by lineage, whose horizontal, almost parallel, branches offer to the wind only a few hand-fuls of leaves as unreachable to man as they are incapable of any sway-ing. . . . These trees exist. . . . But they do not have the good fortune of being named *pine,* or *palm,* or *walnut,* or *chestnut,* or *birch.* Saint Louis of France never sat in their shade, nor did Pushkin ever dedicate them a line of verse. . . .

We must not fear the baroque, our art, born of our trees, . . . a baroque created out of the need *to name things,* even though with it we distance ourselves from other fashionable techniques, those of the French *nouveau roman,* for example.

Campos's work, neither *nouveau roman* nor neobaroque, fits into nei-ther of the two categories of description Carpentier defines but, rather, points toward a third type of writing, in which *pine* and *ceiba* are set free to drift in the same sea, neither falsely universal nor narrowly local, of unbalanced, free-floating words.

Laura's attitude, her mother thinks, can be defined, obscurely, as "that lack of impatience," which, she recognizes, is different from patience: "One cannot quite say '*Laura is patient*' because that would be something else." In Laura's case, the lack of impatience manifests itself in sitting in a chair rather than going out, in dropping herself into the drifting currents of the sea of useless things, in "the impression she gets of erasing herself in what surrounds her, of assimilating herself, of looking too much like everything else" (110). Eloísa does not pre-tend to understand what has happened. She, by her own account, "has not lost her impatience," and yet Eloísa believes that she (unlike her daughter) is patient, "and it doesn't surprise her that things don't look like her" (110). Nevertheless, it is not Laura but Eloísa who suffers from a perpetual skin irritation, visible even under the heavy, too-white powder she wears, the angry red shadow of a potential eruption that never quite reaches the surface of her skin (113–14). It is Eloísa who impatiently covers the tables with wax, her face with powder, the termites with a skin of sound wood. It is Laura, quietly rocking in her chair, who patiently begins to erase herself, the walls, the rain, the words, and the city. From their two unreconcilable extremes, their two voids, Laura and Eloísa enact their daily rituals, their empty conversations, and their unheard parallel monologues.

Whereas Laura is concerned with surfacing and soaring, Eloísa's interest is in tending fixed appearances. Laura is drawn to disordered back rooms, her mother to the impeccable front rooms where guests are received in a setting of timeless, inhuman perfection. Her talismanic objects are not birds and planes but the photographs and the mirrors and the shiny surfaces of all sorts that she preserves from harm: "Eloísa moderately distributes an order that is within her. Things become compact and fixed. The walls of the house, around her, are eternal. . . . There is no vestige of vertigo or of broken glass. More like a common luster over all the peaceful, invulnerable things" (68). Since Eloísa not only distributes but *is* order, her emotions (those powdered-over eruptions) remain trapped somewhere under or behind the homogeneous surface she presents to the public, her human fears locked inside a glass bubble or lost in a mirror-maze. Like the undressed dolls, with their staring ceramic faces, piled naked on the workroom table, Eloísa resembles one of those diminutive, "monstrous, scandalously made-up corpses, like infants dead before birth" (66). The termites in the wood, the pimples on the face, the fury behind a doll's eyes—all these are relegated to the forgotten storeroom of useless things where her daughter labors but in which Eloísa does not set foot. Hers are the walls of the workroom, filled on three sides with innumerable photographs of family members, "which covered the walls almost without leaving an empty spot, as if because of an elaborate horror of the void" (61). The fourth wall of this room, significantly, is a defective mirror that, because it is not perfectly flat, reflects back into the room a distorted image of the woman, who, by the act of walking into the room, integrates a version of herself into the gallery of pictures while serving as the cynosure of all those painted and photographed eyes, filling walls and room at the same instant. And in the same manner that the mirror reflects her distorted image, so too the pictures reflect other distorted images of the order she creates, the stories she constructs, the family members (distorted mirrors of her image), all now dead except for her and Laura, whom she remembers. In the end, the room, terrifyingly, becomes a room totally and claustrophobically of her own. "There were no longer mirrors all over," she says in her final, unheard monologue. "They all surrounded me. I am alone" (141).

And Laura? She is an Alice who cannot get to Wonderland, who feels that there is magic behind the mirrors but has no idea how to reach it. The similarity of her life to a photograph or still life stifles her, and the rhythm of her last, stichomythic sentences reflects the gasping for breath of this progressive asphyxiation: "I see you. Drinking coffee without breathing. I see her. Covering the cup with one hand. . . . And it is like I see myself. Turning the spoon over and over. As if we were posing. The three of us, posing. For a picture that fixes, traps, immobilizes us" (142). Incapable of freeing the words from the scene she sees and imagines representing in eternal rehearsal for some never-to-be produced drama, Laura recognizes how life creates itself in a perfect replication of something that never existed, what she calls "that carbon copy . . . of a forgery, that mascarade" (59). These arti-ficial poses become the pictures on the wall and the representation of the self in the mirror, as people conform themselves to expecta-tions and half-recalled, half-invented memories that time has con-verted into truth. Experiences mount up, she says, experiences that later "continue to compose themselves, enrich themselves, transform themselves, until the moment comes in which one remembers a dif-ferent scene, superimposed on the one that really occurred, or, better, when one remembers something that is no longer very clear . . . and that ends up being, definitively, the only true version of what hap-pened" (70–71). This definitive version, however, belongs to Eloísa; Laura is the custodian of the forgotten, what has already drifted away into the no-name cemetery of words.

Despite her affinity for the nameless, Laura feels, however, that if at that particular moment, sitting around a table on a rainy evening in October 1959, she could see and name her mother, it would represent something like endowing a minimal datum with signification and, from that basis, formulating the initial step in a chain of something like meaning, something like a lifeline in the drifting sea "of seeing herself and Andrés and Eloísa (calling her mother that, by her name, and not mommy, or her, or mother, is to let her be, not to take away anything from her self, to return her identity to her after so many years of not being anything but the mother of her and her siblings)" (86). It is unmistakably a utopian dream to believe that she can return to the old woman a prior identity, for the chain of signification that is Eloísa is an *estar siendo*, a gerundial rather than a substantive being, "Eloísa" and "mother" and, for good measure, the aged widow. Yet Laura's intention is clear; though she may be defeated by life, by the still lives and rehearsed conversations and replicated poses, she intends to be unsatisfied with the static task of keeping things in their place, intends, as Campos suggests, to try to create something outside the round of housework and family, to surface from their suffocating (another term heavily employed in Campos's vocabulary) embrace and swim free in the free-floating surface of words not anchored to the cemetery of meaning. More important, the name of the mother is a prohibited term, which in some essential sense cannot be spoken; it holds, as Campos has already reminded us, the name of the death-of-the-mother, the death by water, the actively forgotten fictional death that, although forgotten in the no-name sea of the disordered back room, keeps the text alive and struggling with its *lector enemigo*. Yet the no-name struggles to the surface. It is this unachieved or only ambiguously approximated ambition to communicate the censored no-name that is Campos's linguistically denoted parallel to the literal cosmetics of Ferré's fiction: the evocation of a polished surface and the translucent superimposition of a progressive series of transformations on its lacquered stillness.

5

Negation: Clarice Lispector

Commentary on most authors begins with a demarcation of territory; discussion of Clarice Lispector's works more often opens into a process of progressive subtraction, the negative limning of her figure through the detailing of dubiously valid "facts" about an author and an oeuvre that eludes the critic, far in advance of efforts at elucidation/effacement. She was born in transit to Brazil, in Ukrania, of parents who had already left their homeland, and she arrived in Brazil at the age of two months. This fact, a mere curiosity or accident of birth which Lispector considered meaningless, is generally mentioned by way of explanation for one facet or another of Lispector's astonishing talent. She is not, by implication, *really* Brazilian. An otherwise perceptive Emir Rodríguez Monegal writes, for example, "Clarice was two months old when her parents settled in Alagoas. Because of this fact, this writer—one of the most important writers Brazil has produced—had to learn Portuguese as a foreign language" (237). The implication is that no native speaker would have arrived at Lispector's markedly original deformations of Portuguese syntax. She is not, say the critics, *typically* Brazilian: "No one writes like Clarice Lispector. And she doesn't write like anyone" (Alceu Amoroso Lima, quoted in Jozef 252).[1] Certainly for many of her contemporaries she is not Bra-

---

[1] In the larger Latin American context I would say that this assertion is not strictly true. And since we are talking about negation, Tita Valencia offers an interesting counter-Lispector. Hers is also a woman's negatively encoded writing about negation, but Valencia writes from the point of view of a refusal of liberation, in her *Minotauromaquia*, for example: "Es cierto que hay mujeres que luchan con esas armas impersonales,

zilian enough (Fitz 1, 26); she is not a feminist (Fitz 23); and though her central concerns are ontological, she writes in neither an autobiographical nor a psychoanalytic mode (Sá 272). The words she uses are not particularly informative (Jozef 250). She rejoices in a non-identity. The Lispector/Specter evoked by Rodríguez Monegal is dressed up in conventional, fashion-page terms for the mysteriously (mystery is the definition of the genre) attractive woman of society: "a beautiful woman, with deep and unfathomable eyes, high Slavic cheekbones, and a mouth like a painful sensual wound, . . . a mysterious surface" (Rodríguez Monegal 231–32). This is the language typically used to describe the infinitely interchangeable and languishingly seductive femme fatale of B-movie and pulp-novel fame.

Likewise, the terms used to describe her work recall not so much the Wittgensteinian exhortation to express the inexpressible as Roland Barthes's variation on the phrase—to unexpress the expressible—or perhaps, yet more confusing, to unexpress the inexpressible. The rather loosely defined ab/objects around which she structures her narratives seem to operate less like centers of gravity for a transcendental signifier than as placeholders for the black hole left by the implosion of signification. Puzzlement and a valiant effort to define this elusive type of nonsymbolic fiction dominate the criticism dedicated to Lispector. She is frequently described in terms that recall the nausea of Sartre or the existentialism of Camus; the moments or perceptions around which her fictions are structured are often called Joycean epiphanies or, less frequently, antiepiphanies. To many readers, says Olga de Sá, her work may seem monotonous; but her style could more appropriately be described as oxymoronic (273). "Insanity or mysticism?" asks María Luisa Nunes, "androgynous artist or writer?" But the terms of both of Nunes's mutually exclusive either/ors are strikingly inappropriate. Lispector, says Antonio Candido in 1943, on his first discovery of her, is not a great writer, perhaps not a perma-

---

privilegio de hombre: llevando una retaguardia de Dalilas, Carlotas Corday, Georges Sand. No fue mi caso" (146); or later, "En mí no convergen esas pioneras de la liberación femenina que tú mencionas, rencoroso. No tengo nada que aportar a su fatigante e ilusoria heroicidad. Ni siquiera, ni siquiera tengo nombre propio" (164) 'It is true that there are women who fight with those impersonal weapons, the man's privilege: they include a rear guard of Delilahs, Charlotte Cordays, and George Sands. That was not my position. . . . In me there is no convergence of those pioneers of women's liberation that you mention rancorously. I have nothing to contribute to their fatiguing and illusory heroism. Not even, not even my proper name.'

nent one, but one who comes close "to breathing in an atmosphere that approximates greatness" (131). Other critics struggle in other ways, almost always resting, helplessly, on an evaluation couched in the negative. Marta Peixoto, Naomi Lindstrom, Emir Rodríguez Monegal, Bella Jozef, Olga de Sá, Hélène Cixous, and Earl E. Fitz, among others, all find it expedient to describe her work by what it is *not*.[2] For all these critics, "Clarice Lispector," both the person and the works

[2]See, for example, the following kinds of critical statements, pulled out of context and set to speak to/against each other in a deliberate chorus of negation:

Marta Peixoto: Lispector's "abstract formulations . . . at times elude the rational intelligence" (287). "Lispector preferred to think of herself as a writer unmodified by the adjective 'female'" (287; Fitz's comment that "it is demeaning to speak of 'women writers'" [129] reminds us that the qualifier "woman" has generally been taken to be pejorative in Latin American literary circles). "The negative terms that often describe these moments [of epiphany]—'crisis,' 'nausea,' 'hell,' 'murder,' 'anger,' 'crime'—convey the guilt and fear that accompany the questioning of conventional roles. . . . They more or less pull back, returning to a confinement they can't or won't change" (289; also Sá: "Negative adjectivation indicates a critical epiphany" [259]). "The power a woman wields within the family has a negative, constricting side" (291). "The tendency to redefine words and concepts, to reverse traditional metaphorical associations or draw images from negative and antithetical realms supports and furthers Lispector's questioning of a 'woman's destiny'" (299).

Naomi Lindstrom: "Glimpses of nothingness and absurdity and ruses to evade" ("Daydreams" 7). "She is facing nothingness and meaninglessness" ("Daydreams" 10). "Especially telling, in this respect, is the fact that the narrator assigns no names to those with whom Ana speaks: they remain *o marido, o filho, os irmãos, a empregada*" ("Articulating" 49).

Emir Rodríguez Monegal: "The first impression that Clarice Lispector left on me was this: that there was no access, or that the access might be in some other part (in her texts) made no difference to me" (232). "The mystery consists not in *writing* . . . but rather in *being written*" (236).

Bella Jozef: "The meditation concludes with adherence to silence and renunciation of language. . . . If to write meant, for Clarice, to live, to write without style" (245). *Água viva* "is not a novel . . . but rather a cosmic creation, a human mirror of infinite reflections" (247); *Um sopro de vida* (A breath of life) can be classified as "nonmemoirs" (251); both could be defined by what Jozef might call, conflating and condensing two formulations, a baroque vacuum.

Olga de Sá: "In Clarice's novelistic universe, if this perspective does not properly constitute a parody, it will be, at least, a pause, the necessary respite to celebrate happiness. It is not, clearly, a solution" (271). "The silence here announced is not the amplified, hyperbolic silence of rhetoric. Neither is it an emphatic silence. Clarice's discourse points toward silence as a 'zero degree' of writing" (277). It points toward a zero-degree writing, but does not reach it: "Clarice distrusts 'zero degree'" (278).

Hélène Cixous: "Woman is: woman-is-other. An impersonal, living togetherness, that cannot resolve itself. Or make history" ("L'approche" 415).

Earl E. Fitz: "It is within this shadowy realm of uncertain and hidden meaning, of off-center ambiguity within the territory of the imprecise, vague, unnamed objects and impulses that Lispector chooses to operate" (44–45).

published under that name, is the very figure of negativity, the mysterious and untouchable abyss of negativity as such. Similarly, the protagonists of her stories and novels, generally middle- and lower-class urban women, are frequently described as mutilated, fragmented, incomplete, incoherent, evasive, escapist, voiceless, and incapable of self-determination. All true. This general inclination to discuss Lispector's work in terms of negative categories is clearly pervasive and equally clearly cannot be dismissed as the limited or inappropriate impositions of unsympathetic or imperceptive critics. The consequences and stakes of this general perception, however, remain to be discussed.

Curiously enough, despite Lispector's radical and far-reaching revelations about the mental and moral cost of the oppression of women in Brazil, she is generally considered strangely aloof from contemporary social and political problems. Fitz's summary is quite correct, if oddly redolent of a national self-image that excludes half of Brazil's citizens: "Lispector's narratives have with very few exceptions had little to do with re-creating the 'authentic' aspects of Brazilian culture or national identity. . . . This general (though not, as we shall see, total) absence of nationalistic concerns was what set her early work apart" (26). Clarice Lispector would agree. In one of her brief essays she writes, "Ever since I came to know myself, the social problem has been more important to me than any other issue: in Recife the black shanty towns were the first truth I ever encountered. . . . I tend to be straightforward in my approach to any social problem: I wanted 'to do' something, as if writing were not doing anything. What I cannot do is exploit writing to this end, however much my incapacity pains and stresses me" (*Legion* 124). The seriousness with which critics must continue to take this criticism, or self-criticism, relates to the problem, focused both from the inside and from the outside, of wanting a usable tradition for postcolonial struggles and relates as well to the intellectual difficulties in reconciling this desire, this need, with an abiding concern about the legitimacy of the writer's role in contributing to the construction of this tradition. Thus, Clarice Lispector's novels, though highly praised for their technical complexity and dazzling originality, persistently seem to inspire charges of a lack of commitment on the author's part to the Brazilian reality. Lispector's ambiguous, anguished narratives are faulted for being too tenuously connected to specific social and political issues. Right thinking is not enough, the accusation goes; it must be accompanied by right action or the work gives evidence of bad faith.

The typical response to such criticism is to accept the major premise and attempt to disprove the conclusions drawn as related to the specific writer under analysis. This is the approach taken by Earl Fitz, who acknowledges the potential for mystification in Lispector's better-known work but argues powerfully that not all Lispector's fiction is subject to the charge. The more straightforward narration in her "simple" children's stories (she wrote four) Fitz argues, is, neither simple nor exclusively intended for children. He asks, "Are Lispector's 'children's stories' meant only as a pure diversion for young people or do they contain messages that demand (or allow for) decoding on a more socially and politically sophisticated level?" (120). He answers, emphatically, that the sharply political reading is indeed licensed by these texts. Thus, "O mistério do coelho pensante" (The mystery of the thinking rabbit) can be read as an allegory of the need for politically aware citizens to rebel against the military dictatorship; "A mulher que matou os peixes" (The woman who killed the fish) offers a stern lesson on the sufferings of the dependent when selfishly neglected; "A vida íntima de Laura" (Laura's intimate life) could be read as the story of racism and of the abuse of women in Brazil; and "Quase de verdade" (Almost true) provides a model for rejecting oppression and demanding basic human rights (117–21). Lispector, according to Fitz, does respond conscientiously and committedly to the specific problems raised by the conditions in Brazil.

Another response to the persistent charge of lack of commitment would be to expand the terms of analysis, for as Griselda Gámbaro, the Argentinian playwright, quite rightly observes, "as far as I'm concerned, a work is feminist insofar as it attempts to explain the mechanics of cruelty, oppression, and violence through a story that is developed in a world in which men and women exist" (18–19). In this respect, too, Lispector can be considered a political activist, for her stories of the stifling entrapment of her countrywomen in the restrictions of their role as wives and mothers are pointed reminders that women do indeed exist. Clarice Lispector is the representative of this hitherto unspoken spectral life, the documenter of the way in which her society codes itself for confrontation—or avoidance of confrontation—with the feminine. "I perform incantations during the solstice," says one of her characters, "specter of an exorcised dragon" (*Stream*

57). No mystic ecstasy here; Lispector's writing points to another style of approaching the unnamable, through the difficult, rock-hard process of coming to terms with the recognition of the specter as specter, in expecting little and receiving that little as the only possible joy. Thus Lispector warns potential readers of *A paixão segundo G. H. (Passion according to G. H.):*

> Eu ficaria contente se [este livro] fôsse lido apenas por pessoas de alma já formada. Aquelas que sabem que a aproximação, do que quer que seja, se faz gradualmente e penosamente—atravessando inclusive o oposto daquilo de que se vai aproximar. Aquelas pessoas que . . . entenderão bem devagar que êste livro nada tira de ninguém. A mim, por exemplo, o personagem G. H. foi dando pouco a pouco uma alegria difícil; mas chama-se alegria. (3)

> I would be happy if [this book] were read only by people with fully formed characters. People who know that an approach, of whatever sort, must be carried out gradually and laboriously—traversing even the opposite of that which is being approached. They . . . will understand that this book exacts nothing of anyone. To me, for example, the character G. H. little by little began to give a difficult joy; but it is called joy. (v)

This difficult happiness is not unlike that contained in the enigmatic smile on the face of the smallest woman in the world or in the insane self-possession of Laura in the presence of the roses, both from stories in the collection *Laços de família (Family Ties):* the fleeting happiness of transitory possession, of beauty ciphered in the minuscule, the evanescent, the happiness of minimal creature comfort, of not being devoured—yet.

One could sketch, based on such considerations, the outline of one or several contentious socially and politically aware readings of the thematics of Lispector's work. One reading would insert Lispector into the postcolonial dialogue about human rights, another would study her covert commitment to addressing the concrete political realities of Brazil, and another such reading would clearly have to include the articulation of a broadly conceived feminist stance in relation to Lispector's work. Still another would read Lispector's fictional practice as a concrete example of Theodor Adorno's "negative aesthetics," the dialectical critique of inauthentic cultural products and the positing of a more authentic production in the "determined negation" of traditional forms. In all these accounts, negation on one level would, in Adorno's words, "create something like meaningfulness in the second degree" (quoted in Birus 146). There is, however, an alternative reading, one that takes as its point of departure the unaccountability of Lispector's work to the standard methods of thematic analysis, one at which Lispector's critics have already hinted in their implicit recognition of the resistance in her texts to such readings. For this kind of nonthematic reading, we will have to take into consideration the workings of the negative in Lispector, the way in which the subject of discourse is marked off not by the contours of a critical topography but by a desire satisfied in the hard process of gradual deprivation, by the unfolding lie of identity. For this kind of reading, negation cannot serve as a fundamental principle or an index of meaningfulness; indeed, it would be impossible to consolidate negation into any appropriable form at all. At one extreme, we witness the power of (literary) language to negate language and its evocative power.

We listen to the words of an unnamed female character, an artist, who tells us: "I'm not to be trusted" and "This is the word of someone who cannot" and "Never is the impossible. I like never" and "I know no limits. . . . I labor with the indirect, the informal, and the unforeseen" or "I'm taboo to myself, untouchable because forbidden" or "Discoveries, in this sense, are unsayable and uncommunicable. And unthinkable" (*Stream* 25, 27, 31, 61, 72). We compaginate these assertions with the sometimes identical words of the author in her essays: "A palavra pescando o que não é palavra. Quando essa não palavra morde a isca, alguma coisa se escreveu" (*Legião* 142, *Água viva* 25). 'The word fishes for something that is not a word. When that nonword takes the bait, something has been written.' Or this, which resonates in different versions throughout all her prose: "I am incapable of 'relating' an idea or of 'dressing up an idea' with words. What comes to the surface is already expressed in words or simply fails to exist. . . . I should avoid using words. This might prove to be my solution" (*Legion* 211–12). Writing, then, is like fishing for a nonword between the lines. Did the fish get away? All the better; Lispector can then throw the word away with relief. Salvation is not in fishing out the word but in writing absentmindedly enough to refuse monumentalization. To use another of Lispector's metaphors, only what is green and unfinished evokes life; that which is polished and finished is death's own carapace.

In his brief essay "A Note on Writing," South African J. M. Coetzee discusses a paradigm of writing reflected in the sentence "I | am writing | a note." For Coetzee, the figure conceptualizes a lack of relation between subject and verb, between subject and object (12), which strikes me as highly relevant to Lispector's work, where the writer is, despite herself, written into the text as the only space left for the one who writes, and yet she remains adamantly apart from the word-fish, the word-idea, the word-object so constructed, emphasizing, if there is to be emphasis at all, the fragmentary and wholly tenuous nature of the standard narrative fictions ("I am writing a note") in which the action exists primarily in reference to the acting self. For Lispector, the copula must be sublated into (1) whatever is between the lines in the place of the verb or (2) the words or nonwords that appear inexplicably on the surface as figures of the grammatical object or (3) the fictive and infinitely diminishing fraction of herself that echoes in the insistently open negatives of the subject position. All such possibilities are reflected in the practice of a narrative form that *must not* be closed and infinitely hopes for closure. The options are limited to a choice of voids. "I | am writing | a note" becomes "I | am writing | death"—G. H. tells her invented interlocutor/lover, "I advanced with the determination not of the suicidal but with that of the self-assassin" (*Passion* 158)—or simply, hopefully, "I am death," or impossibly, in the future conditional tense, "I desist, and I will have been a human person" (*Passion* 171).

How then, to take what Cixous calls the "Clarisque," to read, as Rodríguez Monegal might have it, spectrally, subversively, taking the side of the enemy against the establishment's James Bond? I return once again to the strategy outlined in Josefina Ludmer's seminal article on Sor Juana Inés de la Cruz, in which she outlines the operation of the essential textual machine of Sor Juana's letter to Sor Filotea:

> La escrítura de Sor Juana es una vasta máquina transformadora que trabaja con pocos elementos; en esta carta la matriz tiene sólo tres. . . . Modulando y cambiando de lugar cada uno de ellos en un arte de la variación permanente, conjugando los verbos y transfiriendo la negación, Juana escribe un texto que elabora las relaciones, postulados como contradictorias, entre dos espacios (lugares) y acciones (prácticas): una de las dos debe estar afectada por la negación si se encuentra presente la otra. (48)

Sor Juana's writing is a vast transformatory machine that works with very few elements; in this letter the matrix has only three. . . . By modulating and changing each of them in an art of permanent variation, conjugating the verbs, and transferring the negation, Juana writes a text that elaborates the relations, postulated as contradictory, between two spaces (places) and actions (practices): one of the two ought to be affected by the negation if the other element is present.

The essential elements of Clarice Lispector's transformatory machine are likewise few: in each of her fictions, there is, first of all, a subject or placeholder for that elusive position, frequently "I," sometimes another woman (Laura, Ana, the grandmother); second, a common object (egg, apple, rose, cockroach, or in its most abstract form, "it"); third, a limited repertoire of essential verbs (to be, to need, to love); and, finally, the operative principle that sets these various elements in motion—the negative. Each story or novel, then, could be set up as a sequence of Coetzee's barred sentences; generally, the initial statement is gradually refined through the progressive operations of the negative. In the case of one of Lispector's more conventional stories, "The Imitation of the Rose" from *Family Ties*, for example, the tale of the timid housewife protagonist, Laura, could be schematically depicted as:

Laura | needs | love.
Laura | loves | a rose.
~~rose~~
Laura | is/not | a rose.

Similarly, a later, more abstract work, *Água viva*,[3] could be schematized as a successive deletion based on the construction:

I | love | it.
I | love. |
(I) | am. |
| é |

This fiction, then, is not based on description, or on the primacy of the noun; it is a stripped effort to reduce fiction making to a neuter "it" that

[3] I prefer to retain the Portuguese title for this novel when I cite it, although quotations will be from the English edition. The term *água viva* more literally translates as living water, and suggests a whirlpool or white-water rapids; *água-viva* (with a hyphen) is a medusa or jellyfish: both significations are more accurate than "stream of life." I thank Luiza Moreira for her reading of this chapter and for this insight.

acknowledges the uneradicable "is." "I" becomes a mere placeholder for any grammatical subject: "E se eu digo 'eu' é porque não ouso dizer 'tu,' ou 'nós,' ou 'uma pessoa.' Sou obrigada à humildade de me personalizar . . . mas sou o és-tu" (*Água* 14) 'And if I say "I," it is because I do not dare to say "you," or "we," or "a person." I am limited to the humility of self-personalization . . . but I am you are' (*Stream* 6). "Is" reduces being to its narrowest limit. This is a literature based on the absolute essence of the thing, perceived in all its superficiality, which goes far beyond anything imagined by the French new novelists, paring language down to the essential, minimal "is"—in Portuguese, the single-letter word "é," with the unstated subject left implicit rather than explicit—on the verge of dissolution. As Cixous writes, "Clarice tries to be as essentialist as possible, even if there is, of course, no essence" (*Stream* xix). She extracts the maximum value from this no-essence, questioning the possibilities of language, reducing phrases and words to the irreducible final element.

To focus such refinement of the essential, Lispector generally chooses a cliché or the cliché's visual counterpart, a common household object, as her pre-text. It would be wrong, I think, to say with Jozef that Lispector's art serves to revitalize these inert forms (250); I suspect that revitalization is quite the opposite of Lispector's intent. She tells an interviewer: "I wanted to write something that was tranquil and unstylish, something like the remembrance of a tall monument that seems taller because it is remembered. . . . Really, I do not know what the word monument means to me. And I end up writing entirely different things" (Gomes xvii). Lispector's art is not to revitalize the monument, even in the distortions of remembrance, not to reproduce it but rather to try to understand the word *monument*, to know, if only tentatively and interlinearly, what the perceived word-monument, the found object can do, what it is—not what it represents—in relation to a monumentalized, inert life. And then to remember these fragments of something that never existed as an ongoing process in her prose.

Simple things, often things with a shell or a peel, take the place of the monument in Lispector's writing: egg, oyster, apple, cockroach, rose. It is as if Lispector has an obsession with the permeable/impermeable membrane, the thin protective space that provides the carapace against existence. But she will not seek symbolism in such objects. As Cixous writes: "There, there is an apple. . . . And then there is *this* apple" ("L'approche" 412–13); or later, "But for Clarice . . . in order to 'see' an egg, it must be un-seen [dé-voir]: to try not to break the egg with a glance, not to see-swallow [ver-gober]. But to wait for the hour of the egg, keeping careful watch, it will render itself into the tranquil, disinterested, open expectation, which allows it to come or not to come, into the day, according to its method. Sometimes the egg arrives (—but something else could arrive; or nothing)" (414). Such things cannot be taken as monuments, even as monuments to negativity. Nor do they represent epiphanies of heightened awareness. Nor do they offer access into the Sartrean nausea of existence. The thing does not arrive, as in Sartre, burgeoning with the soft decrepitude of life; rather, it is already protected by a shell, fragile but impervious in its fragility.

The thing is, ultimately, the book itself, but more abstractly, Lispector figures the essential object as an undifferentiated "it," a word she gives in English so that Portuguese grammatical gender markings can also be stripped away: "Eu sou puro it que pulsava ritmadamente. . . . História não te prometo aqui. Mas tem it. . . . It é mole e é ostra e é placenta" (*Água viva* 45) 'I am pure, rythmically pulsing it. . . . I do not promise you a story here. But it has it. . . . It is soft and is an oyster and is a placenta' (*Stream* 28). *It* is the writing between the lines in invisible ink. *It* is the word for a helpless ignorance or an equally helpless knowledge. *It* is the consciousness of a force, a power, of something ending and something coming to life. *It* destabilizes all formalisms. *It* infects history and points to history's surfeit. *It* motivates this account of a time figured by the movements of a musical piece and a space that is the geography of the page—or of the mother's womb. *It* is the only possibility for happiness—an atonal joy, says the narrator of *Água viva*, "uma alegria atonal dentro do it essencial" (112)—and the only name for the search for happiness. *It* is the game we decide to play when reality no longer stands up to the thinning out of names. *It* is I. It is. É.

The first step in Lispector's most unconventional masterpieces will be, as Cixous writes, a delicate "ne-pas" (*Stream* xiv): a nonstep, a do not. Cixous's formulation is reminiscent of Lispector's own language, typically characterized by a constant structural antagonism between component parts of the sentence, which creates the appearance of a violent convulsion of language, torn against itself, and, alternatively, sets up a paradoxical incantation of strophe and antistrophe which is, for Lispector, the only guarantor of existence. Take, for instance, these examples, all from the opening pages of *The Passion according to G. H.*:

> Perdi alguma coisa que me era essencial, e que já não me é mais. . . . E voltei a ser uma pessoa que nunca fui. (9)

> Estou desorganizada porque perdi o que não precisava? . . . É difícil perder-se. É tão difícil que provàvelmente arrumarei depressa modo de me achar, mesmo que achar-me seja de nôvo a mentira de que vivo. (10)

> Tôda compreensão súbita se parece muito como uma aguda incompreensão. Não. Tôda compreensão súbita é finalmente a revelação de uma aguda incompreensão. Todo momento de achar é um perder-se a si próprio. (14)

> I have lost something that was once essential and is so no longer. . . . I have gone back to being a person I never was. (3–4)

> Am I disorganized because I have lost something I did not even need? . . . It is difficult to lose oneself. It is so difficult that probably I will organize a way to find myself, even though to find myself would be once again the lie that I live. (4)

> All sudden understanding looks very similar to an acute nonunderstanding. No. All sudden understanding is, finally, a revelation of an acute nonunderstanding. (8)

In each of these examples the text itself sets up a strategy of resistance, text and antitext compressed in the space of a single sentence mediated by the minimalist copula of the verb "to be": "I" | is | "not-I"; understanding | is | nonunderstanding; finding | is | losing. To retain the delicate balance of the step-that-is-not-a-step is the most difficult of isometric exercises, doomed, G. H. suspects, to the eventual failure that breaks apart the copula, leaving the individual with one-half of the proposition—"I am"—followed by the substitutionary mechanism of description, explanation, and elucidation: the lie, the traditional narrative of a life. Jacques Derrida could as easily be writing about Lispector as Heidegger in these comments from "How to Avoid Speaking: Denials":

Twice, in two apparently different contexts and senses, Heidegger *explicitly proposed* to avoid (is there denial, in this case?) the word *being*. More exactly, not to *avoid* speaking of Being but to avoid *using* the word *being*. Even more exactly, not to avoid *mentioning* it . . . but to avoid using it. Thus he explicitly proposes, not to avoid speaking of Being, nor in some way to avoid mentioning the word *being*, but to refrain from using it normally, one may say, without placing it in quotation marks or under erasure. And in both cases, we may suspect, the stakes are serious—even if they seem to hold to the subtle fragility of a terminological, typographical, or more broadly, "pragmatic" artifice. (56)

Lispector's fragile threshold space allows only for the most minimal coexistence of "I" and "am," of self and being, and even this fragile compromise is endangered by the inevitable appropriations of literary language and a literary audience which will turn the typographical evocation of "being" into a monumental form, speaking negativity and erasing the sign of erasure.

G. H. negotiates the difficult pressures of the monumental form by forcing herself to remain in the realm of the antisentence, to retain the consciousness of that other life hidden under the carapace of understanding and to witness its slow opening into knowledge. It is the process precisely captured by the double meaning of the verb *to realize*— to open into comprehension, to make real—which is in Lispector's work accompanied by an unblinking awareness of the necessary fictiveness of the process of realization. "What I want is an invented truth," says the protagonist of *Água viva* (*Stream* 14). And in "To Lie, to Think" Lispector provides the second half of this truncated antisentence: "What am I, in fact, trying to think? Perhaps this: if a lie were merely the negation of truth, then that would be one of the ways (negative) of telling the truth. But the worst lie of all is the *creative* lie" (*Legion* 119). The invented truth, the truthful lie that is merely truth's negative side: these are prized values. But the creative lie, Lispector aesthetically, ascetically eschews:

Vou criar o que me aconteceu. Só porque viver não é relatável. Viver não é vivível. Terei que criar sôbre a vida. E sem mentir. . . . Criar não é imaginação, é correr o grande risco de se ter a realidade. . . .
    Até criar a verdade do que me aconteceu. Ah, será mais un grafismo que uma escrita. (*Paixão* 19)

I am going to create what happened to me. Only because living is not tellable. Living is not livable. I will have to create upon life. And without lying. . . .

I will create the truth of what happened to me. Oh, it will be more a graphism than a writing. (*Passion* 13)

Life, imagination, memory, knowledge, truth, lie: these are the conceptual centers of energy in her texts. Such concepts are not treated analytically, however. Lispector's art is the "graphism" and not the "writing," and we as readers, as the unnamed interlocutors in her texts, are constructed in the shifting patterns of her elegant formal designs. Her attention to the graphisms on the page extends to her hyperconsciousness of the shape of the word and to both the artistic possibilities and the hard intransigence locked in a single letter. "Mas eternamente é palavra muito dura: tem um 't' granítico no meio," says the narrator of *Água viva*, and later, "Mas a palavra mais importante da língua tem uma única letra: é. É" (31–32) 'But "eternally" is a very hard word: it has a granite *t* in the middle. . . . But the most important word in the language has but a single letter: *é*. It is' (*Stream* 18–19). Likewise, by extension, sentences are for her things that recuperate a concrete identity in space and time, and the musicality of her phrases remind us that her works are put together with a consciousness of the aural consequences of her rhythms. But we are initiated into not only the music but also the dance, with all its stops and starts, leaps, and delicate mincing steps. Her work partakes of this evanescent and permanent physicality. The search for *le mot juste* is a cliché of literary life, and Lispector, though clearly obsessed with such definition as she can make, is likewise certain that the search, like the idea of the literary life, is fundamentally flawed. The fictional existence of *le mot juste* would be a violation of the principles of dance, a betrayal of living life itself. Lispector settles instead for the graphism marked as such and for the consciously embraced facsimile, the placeholder: "Living is not tellable. Living is not livable" (13). We can legitimately suspect that in Lispector's work all such references to "life" retain the mental reservations she notes in her reflection on the word-monument: the word-life, the word "life," the word-lie, living the word.

Few authors are as attentive to the details of sentence construction. At times, the dancer pauses, holds a position for an impossibly long time, as in this from *Água viva*: "It is as if life said the following: and there simply wasn't any following. Only the colon, waiting" (*Stream* 70). "It is as if": another version of the antisentence, the counterfactual "as if." "It is as if life said": but by definition life did not say; we are explicitly asked to enter into the realm of fantasy, of the dream, of the creative, created truth of a temporal dance of living (verb) crystalized into the static form of a life (noun). "Life said the following": what life said—or, radically, what life *is*—is the colon itself, the pause, the wait for a meaning that cannot ever materialize. "Life said": and what follows is unsayable. And alternatively, what life said is precisely that "there wasn't any following." No constructions of life adequate to the ongoing, untellable living? No life following life? No life following death? "Only the colon, waiting." Cixous asks herself and us about the function of the colon in Lispector's work in her foreword to the English translation of this novel: "It can be said that the colon is not the period, it is the period of the period, the canceling of the period. It is a moment mute and marked; it is the most delicate tattoo of the text" (*Stream* xxx). And yet, the colon is itself a principle of order, separating the two discrete movements of call and response, statement and elucidation. To the left of the colon is the abstract, general category, to the right the concrete details, the elements of the list, that which provides an opportunity for elaboration and clarification. But when the left side is problematized and the right remains blank?

The second nonstep is the concatenation of antisentences in the field of the fiction, which responds less to an ordering principle than to a practice of dishevelment. In general, the antisentences are combined in a narrative form ruled by what we might call, following David Hayman, macroparataxis: "Parataxis is more than a list, however, since it occupies both space and time . . . while belonging to neither. Whether it is included in or imposed on narrative, it contributes a static element, a bulk and density that appears to be immobile. In other ways, it may contribute a dynamism, a jagged dance of interacting and even clashing forms" (149). The tactical advantage of parataxis on the level of whole fictions is precisely captured in the oxymoronic juxtapositions of Hayman's definition: immobile dance, static dynamism, jagged bulk. In Lispector's short stories, the impingement of such paratactic arrangements on the more conventionally hypotactic coherence of the text produces the interstices of unreason, the underground awareness of life, waiting, in the static dynamism of the colon, for recognition. Such moments are traditionally defined as epiphanies in Lispector criticism: the conjunction of self and three mirrors in "The Daydreams of a Drunken Housewife," the blind man chewing gum in "Love," the tranquilly beautiful rosebuds awaiting recognition in "The Imitation of the Rose," the incongruous humanity of the smallest woman in the world. These are moments of incoherence consciously suppressed by the protagonists in these narratives in favor of an ordered life, an idealization of existence in which incongruous elements are flattened out, smoothed over, or ignored so that conventions can be maintained. These women are well aware of the intolerable constrictions of the role that society wanted for them, that they have accepted and even now desire, but they are not forceful enough to break down the overarching pattern of small coherences. Thus, the orders of housekeeping provide the structure for a civilization now recognizable also as coercive, indestructible, and irrelevant. The disease these paratactic elements introduce at the level of text, however, infects the entire structure, implying the subversion of the text of life at its most fundamental level.

In longer fictions such as *The Passion according to G. H.* and *Água viva*, these paratactic arrangements move to the foreground, no longer the interruptions in the text but the dominant mode of the text itself. In *The Passion according to G.H.*, for example, the event that induces the first disorder is the unidentified happening prior to the opening of the text: "Did something happen, and did I, because I didn't know how to live it, live something else? It is that that I would like to call disorganization." This happening has changed the shape of the narrator's world: "If I go forward with my fragmentary visions, the entire world will have to transform itself for me to fit into it" (*Passion* 3). She has no choice but to go forward and change the world to the shape of her vision. In this new world, the interstices of the prior organization are estranged from the text through the distanced references of alienation—I, that woman: "I got up from the coffee table, that woman. . . . I would engage in the kind of activity I liked best: picking up. I have always liked picking things up. . . . In ordering things I create and understand at the same time. . . . Picking up is finding the best form. . . . Picked up form?" (*Passion* 25). Yet the form-giving repetition is a forbidden pleasure; the attraction to the comfortable orders of housekeeping must be resisted as the price to be paid for a nearly intolerable and fearful freedom. That woman, the sculptor, might have been able to shape and order the circumscribed fiction of her life;

this woman, the present G. H., can only rearrange the graphisms on her page and watch the transformatory mechanism of the text produce the paratactic increment of fragments that never resolve themselves into a disciplined structure. The quite intense labor of producing these scarce and minimalist disorders, however, these original created truths, counters and comments on the fluencies so easily available to others who choose to retain the illusion of control provided by an acceptance of limitation to the creative lies of human relationships.

Interestingly enough, Lispector's own writing practice as detailed in biographies reproduces a similar paratactic split: this woman | that woman. *This* woman defines her practice of constructing fictions out of fragmentary and partial notes she can no longer elaborate further: "I take notes upon notes, file them away, and then comes the terrible job of mounting them into some kind of meaningful structure. That's when I get terribly lazy. For me, the most interesting part is taking notes" (Lowe 36). Rather than tie the loose ends of her notes together in the fictions, her structure likewise follows from a macroparatactic practice: "I would interrupt a sentence in chapter ten, let us say, in order to resume the writing of chapter two, interrupted in its turn for months while I devoted myself to chapter eighteen. I found that I had the necessary patience and it taught me a great deal: for example, how to bear the frustrating discomfort of disorder, without any guarantees" (*Legion* 211). *This* woman accepts the challenge of disorder, slips back and forth from one section to another, compiles notes with minimal transitional material to provide conventional linkages; *that* woman, on the other hand, worries about the discomfort and needs the reassurance that her work will respond to some kind of inner cohesion (Fitz 7). *That* woman is the one intermittently visible in G. H.'s un-acted-upon desire for clear organization; *that* woman is the writer who needs to invent an interlocutor (16–17) as a buffer against the terror of coming face to face with the unknown qualities of living.

The third no-step directly follows upon the second: Lispector's work, while more precisely and obsessively aware of the passage of time than that of almost any other writer I can think of, yet abrogates time in the burning nowness of the inescapable first event that existed, exists, and will exist only in the perpetual present of the writing and the reading: "To write is to prolong time, to break it down into particles of seconds while giving each of them an irreplaceable life" (*Legion* 190). Thus, *A paixão segundo G. H.* not only can be translated as "the passion according to G.H." but also carries the buried and uncommon second-ary resonances of "the passion-second," and the book becomes the word-monument to the prolonged, insubstantial, infinitesimal instant of passion, meticulously dissected and deorganized in the space of 182 pages (in the English version, 173 pages). "What I write you," says the narrator of *Água viva*, "has no beginning; it's a continuation" (*Stream* 37), and the careful paradoxes of G.H.'s deployment of temporally disjunctive nouns also bear out this insistence on an instantaneous eternity, fluid and granitic: "Prehuman divine life is of a burning nowness" (*Passion* 93), or "I was living the prehistory of a future" (*Passion* 99). Words continually slip out of key, escaping the repressive formulations of a conventional history that slides from past to present and looks toward an unformulated future. Likewise, the writing has no ending, which does not mean that stories are obliterated. The reader and writer are condemned to stories still, if infinitely deferred, exquisitely painful ones: "I was condemned never to die, for if I died, even once, I would die. And I wanted not to die but to keep per-petually dying like a supreme pleasure in pain" (*Passion* 113–14). The permutations of the verb *to die* in the sequence of tenses—I will not die, if I died, I would die, I am perpetually dying—offers a concise summary of the operations of macroparataxis on the level of the story that cannot ever, cannot simply die.

Not

We have not yet, it will be noted, arrived at a topic for this chapter. That the topic has been deferred is, I would argue, in itself a playing out of the chapter's announced theme—negation—as it pertains to Clarice Lispector. Nevertheless, as even Cixous would remind us, the awaited egg sometimes does hatch. Let me hasten to offer a specific instance of interpretation now, to conclude this chapter with a brief analysis of *The Passion according to G.H.*, a work that is considered one of Lispector's masterpieces—"one of the most singular Latin Ameri-can novels of the 1960s" (Fitz 79)—and one I consider transitional between the more conventional narrative structures of popular and widely read stories like those collected in *Family Ties* and the more abstract, atonal music of her other recognized masterpiece *Água viva* ("Just as *A paixão segundo G. H.* must be considered one of the most powerful Latin American novels of the 1960s, so, too, must *Água viva* rank as one of the outstanding achievements of the 1970s" [Fitz 86]). I propose to examine *The Passion according to G. H.* as the detailed unraveling of the ramifications of a single simple sentence couched in the negative: "I am not I."

I

The first word of *The Passion according to G. H.* is *estou* (I am); the last, *adoro* (I adore). The contraction of the novel between these two poles would yield an expansion on the Cartesian formula that moves from the realm of thought to that of feeling: I think, therefore I exist becomes I am therefore I adore. As a model for the text, this contraction is both neat and superficially correct; however, the "I" at the beginning of the novel is a far distant self from the "I" at the end, so different as to suggest two entirely different orders of being. From G. H.'s own words we can begin to draw a portrait of this initial "I," to understand what has happened to make this narrative necessary, beginning from first principles. Says G. H.: "I have to at least make the effort of giving myself a prior form, so I can understand what happened when I lost that form" (16). The anterior form is, however, in some ways quite conventionally formless. G. H. informs the reader that because she has never chosen to marry or have children, she has not had to "wear or break shackles: I have been continuously free" (21), free from the usual types of roles women choose or have chosen for them. With no husband to define/circumscribe her, no children clinging to her fashionable skirts to give her existence weight, she evades the standard responsibilities and the more common categorizations of her sex. By implication, of course, those other women—wives, mothers, lovers— have somehow taken a less aesthetically pleasing path. They have slipped into mediocrity, and her faintly ironic tone decries the choice. She, in contrast, has experienced neither love nor suffering nor any definable intimate life: "I lived mostly inside a mirror. Two minutes after I was born I had already lost my origins. A step from climax, a step from revolution, a step from what is called love. A step from my life" (20). She is a woman of leisure, an indifferently talented and properly unambitious sculptor; the most consistent effort in her desultory artistic career has been the sculpting of a smoothly plastic identity for herself, a mannequin of a life that retains just a hint of socially acceptable self-parody: "I have always kept a quotation mark to my left and one to my right" (23). G. H. presents herself to us directly, concisely, in that phrase. She is the ageless, carefully groomed, elegant woman of society whose role and function and entire effort in that society consist in the creation of that meticulously groomed facade she presents to her small world. Her beautiful, tastefully decorated, and well-ordered apartment creates the frame that reflects and is reflected by the woman living within. Bad taste or excessive emotions are the only real sins; cool imperturbability and an ability to smile self-consciously at her own extravagances—the protective quotation marks to left and right—embody her entire code of behavior and encapsulate the approved virtues she has adopted as her model.

Yet this freedom, too, represents, as G. H. acknowledges, a happy prison routine. She is afraid of passion and any other strong emotion, afraid of silence, afraid that her life is plotless, afraid that one day she will look in the mirror and see not the witty statement of a bracketed and carefully constructed self between quotation marks but nothing at all. The quotation marks are her carapace, her protective shield, but also the walls of her prison. "That image of myself between quotation marks satisfied me," G. H. informs her reader, "and not just superficially. I was the image of what I was not, and that image of nonbeing fulfilled me: one of the two strongest modes is to be negatively" (24). With a slight twist, the witty negativity unravels. Being for G. H. is related to having—a luxurious apartment and the things that fill it, a maid, a free life, a dilettantishly practiced profession as sculptor. But at some point, having becomes being once again and defines it: "It is enough to see the initials G. H. on the leather of my luggage, and that is me" (16). "G. H." on leather suitcases: a statement of conspicuous consumption. That is she, and conversely, frighteningly, she is that. She has created herself as the mask of a woman, abandoning, almost from the moment of birth, an active being for the static personification of life. The initials on a dusty, unused suitcase signal not the willingness to learn and experience but the insanity of the name, the imprisonment in a lifestyle, philosophy, or fixed identity that the act of naming represents. Within the security provided by the name, G. H. has no need every truly to recognize or acknowledge any existence outside herself, no need to accommodate herself to any incongruous new fact. Every bit of new knowledge can be subjugated to the old pattern; whatever she encounters can be assimilated into her usual frame of reference. But if the suitcases were to go traveling, where would the confirmation of her conspicuous nonidentity be, the other side of the coin of the empty "I"? On what can identity depend if G. H. is forced to look beyond initials on a suitcase, beyond the mental bracketing of her existence between quotation marks?

This realization is, in some respect, the motivating impulse that sends G. H. off on her search for passion, propelling her into her passionate encounter with another side of herself, escaping from the neutral projection of an overripe superficiality into the green, vital present: "It was finally now. It was simply now" (72). With this fortunate fall into the "nowness" of existence, G. H. can begin painfully to examine the conditions of her living. Something has happened, subjectively if not historically, and from this point on G. H.'s world has to change.

not I

The maid and the cockroach: these are the figures of the not-I in this novel, and they too are separated from the "I" by mental quotation marks. Neither the absent maid nor the all-too present insect represent the Other against which G. H. plays her game of identity or nonidentity. Such a solution would be too facile, too much like the neat orders of freshly dusted knickknacks in a recently tidied room. Rather than a hypostatized, monumentalized other, the maid and the cockroach point to the order of passionate existence which G. H. is just beginning to intuit, and they do so as images in the mirror that is G. H. They are the I-not-I, the repressed alter egos, hated and desired, the creative fiction of the self, slightly twisted and defamiliarized in a foreign shape.

Thus, whereas G. H. expects and hopes to find in the maid's room a jumble of existence, a distant empire, a disorganized storage room temporarily and messily housing a foreign life, instead she is shocked to discover something quite different. She had planned to assert her existence to herself, her difference from her middle-class counterparts, and her superiority over her maid in the act of picking up and organizing the room; she opens the door and "my eyes had to squint in reaction and physical revulsion": the room is perfectly neat. G. H. continues: "From the door I now saw a room that had a calm, empty order. . . . It was a clean, vibrant place" (30). Not only has the maid taken over the storage room as if it were hers, an implicit invasion of the resting place of G. H.'s essential self—the imprinted luggage—she has imprinted upon it the stamp of her will. This back room, the storage room of G. H.'s hidden disorders, has become a facsimile of the rest of the house: clean, ordered, neat, empty, its original character erased in the impersonality of an impersonation of a hospital room. G. H., unsurprisingly, feels violated by this anticipation of her plans; the picking up was done, but not by her.

The room, however, is only apparently empty, only characterless at first glance. For the maid, again shockingly, has occupied one wall with a charcoal drawing: "And it was on one of the walls that, recoiling in surprise and revulsion, I saw the unexpected mural" (31). Once again, the shock is less at the content of the mural than at the un-welcome anticipation of G. H.'s own actions. For G. H. has just begun her journey to passion, a trip already completed in the maid's mural and in a form that makes G. H.'s soul-searching look belated, and also pompous. G. H. has announced her intention of creating a work that will be more a graphism than a writing, more a painting than a biogra-phy, and she asks herself, "Will I stay lost amid the silence of the signals?" (13). G. H. loves this phrase and allows it to roll off tongue and pen repeatedly, with slight variations, drawing attention to its beauty by enclosing it in quotation marks. Clearly, through her atten-tiveness to the balanced form and studied elegance of this phrase, she is posing for her anti-self-portrait, anticipating the creation of herself which signals but does not violate the comfortable quotation marks within which she has always lived her acceptably rebellious, conform-ist middle-class life.

The maid's drawing is quite different. In the first place, the maid does not reside among the silence of signals, does not take studied poses, does not have the leisure to practice her self-presentation in front of a mirror. If G. H., inauthentically, takes on the bourgeois anguish of a contrived silence, the maid, by background and social usage, is silence. Period. If G. H. proposes to encode this silence in a graphism, it must now be done with reference to and in the context of her revulsion at the originary graphism created by the maid. "The drawing was not a decoration," says G. H. on first seeing the three figures on the wall, "it was writing" (32): a writing and an indictment, an inscription of a passion that, had it not been so indifferentiable, would be called hate. It is, furthermore, a writing that demands a response:

Um chiado neutro de coisa, era o que fazia a matéria de seu silêncio. Carvão e unha se juntando, carvão e unha, tranqüila e compacta raiva daquela mulher que era representante de um silêncio como se representasse um país estrangeiro, a rainha africana. E que ali dentro de minha casa se alojara, a estrangeira, a inimiga indiferente. (43)

It was the thing's neutral screeching that made up the matter of its silence. Charcoal and fingernails join, charcoal and fingernails, calm, compact fury of that woman who was the representative of a silence as if she represented a foreign country, the African queen. And there in my house she lodged, the stranger, the indifferent enemy. (35)

The room and the drawing are, in the first place, as G. H. readily recognizes, a violation of her quotation marks, "of the marks that made of me a quotation of myself" (34). The drawing and the aggressively neat room itself are silent commentaries on this indulgent practice of self-quotation; at the same time they cite G. H. indirectly, putting another's quotation marks around her quotation marks, as it were, or stripping away the quotation marks altogether. Second, the furiously mute pointing of the drawing signals a practice of writing as graphism always already in existence, "much more simple," as Lispector writes in *The Foreign Legion*, than the complex process of stripping away selves and words outlined in the text of the novel. And she asks, "If in life he is a silent man, why did he write as if he were speaking?" (114). The project, as G. H. will discover, is to unspeak, to unname, to unexpress, so as to arrive, finally, at her own version of the mute pointing, not now in hatred or disgust but through love and adoration.

"Passion," "adoration": such words seem to allude to a religious experience, perhaps a mystic one, and critics of Lispector's work have already explored in great detail the possible mystic referent of Lispector's text. It needs to be noted, however, that the passion and adoration, accompanied in Lispector's text, as may be expected, with frequent references to the divine, is motivated not by the vision of God's face but by the sight of a cockroach scurrying from closet in the maid's otherwise immaculate room. The vision is less immediately recognizable as mystical than as Buñuelesque.

It is the cockroach, rather than the absent maid's charcoal drawing, that motivates the most sustained meditation in the novel. In Fitz's formulation, the encounter with the insect is the moment of epiphany stretched to encompass two-thirds of the work (80). Briefly, G. H.

opens the closet, is startled by the appearance of a large cockroach, and kills it. In killing the cockroach, however, she kills something of inestimable importance to herself or something in herself that has now lost its false transcendence. The cockroach comes to take on a perverse beauty, a seductiveness, and a sacramental quality. G. H. feels that her action is not complete, her joy unfulfilled until she takes some of the oozing cockroach mass and eats it. She moves, thus, from fear to ecstasy in slow increments of contemplation and barely perceptible action: an antimystical experience.

G. H.'s first reaction on opening the door and seeing the roach is her standard one of fear and loathing, of a disgust made more intense by her fear and her realization that such fear is unjustified: "Nothing, it was nothing—I immediately tried to calm myself in the face of my fear. It was just that I had not expected, in a house meticulously disinfected against my dread of cockroaches, I had not expected this room to have been left out. No, it was not nothing. It was a cockroach" (39). Implicitly, the cockroach, like the charcoal drawing, signals defiance, an eruption of the not-I from the hidden storage room into the meticulously disinfected, artificial existence of the rest of G. H.'s carefully ordered house and life. The cockroach is dreaded, however, not only because it is inappropriate and unexpected in these carefully ordered realms, not only because it is repellently ugly, but also because its interruption serves to bracket those other, artificial orders and to permeate all her comfortable life with nonexistence.

The roach reminds her, first of all and unpleasantly, of the discordant prehistory of her present middle-class life, of her childhood poverty, of the insects, rats, and leaky roofs that made that existence so hellish. In this realization the first unwanted identification is made: "I had looked on a living cockroach and had discovered in it the most profound identity of my life" (49–50). This, then, is the life of the "I" that existed before the willful construction of the face presented to society between mental quotation marks, the primordial mass from which that self was sculpted. That mass, restrained by the quotation marks, is still present, wriggling in its need to free itself from the constrictions of the carapace that no longer suits it, the world that no longer fits. The insect is the concrete image of that other, repressed self struggling to escape, that other, denied self scuttling away in corners, disinfected out of the front rooms of the mind. "A cockroach is an ugly, shining being," she tells her imagined interlocutor. "A cockroach is inside out. No, no, she herself does not have an inside or an outside:

she is that. What she had on the outside is what I hide: I have made my outside into a hidden inside" (69). In her later work, *Água viva*, Lispector will use the letter X and the English word *it* to figure a parallel, if more abstractly denoted, experience of insight as the stripping of transcendence down to the neutral bone of existence; here, G. H., more burdened with words, strays into the territory of the animal and maintains and strengthens the coincidence provided by grammatical gender: she, the cockroach of G. H.'s buried early memories, easily slips into the she of *essa mulher* (that woman).

The cockroach, then, while embodying everything that her present existence would deny, is also that indestructible and strangely necessary, if repressed, core of herself, which brackets and dissolves the language and spurious reality of "that woman." But the insect does not impinge on her life as a symbol or a transcendental signifier. The cockroach simply *is*, as Lispector might say. It *is* now, in the ongoing flow of a nowness ineradicable and unbreachable by either past or future. Language itself loses its autonomy and fades like a mirage when confronted by this solid being-in-the-moment. Primal revulsion and fear are erased by the momentary apprehension of the (created) real. And it is here, at last, that the "I" begins to shift and change, to become more nearly itself in becoming more profoundly identified with the corporeal not-I:

Sabia que havia lutado, que havia sucumbido e que cedera.

E que, agora sim, eu estava realmente no quarto.

. . . pouco importa que não eu pròpriamente dita, não isso a que convencionei chamar de eu. . . .

Eu, corpo neutro de barata, eu com uma vida que finalmente não me escapa. . . . Sou o silêncio gravado numa parede, e a borboleta mais antiga esvoaça e me defronta: a mesma de sempre. (65)

I knew that I had been fighting, that I had succumbed, and that I gave in.

And that, right now, I was really in the room.

. . . it mattered little that it was not I properly speaking, not that which I customarily call I. . . .

I, neutral cockroach body, I with a life that at last does not escape me. . . . I am the silence scratched in the wall, and the most ancient butterfly flutters in and looks at me: the same as always. (57)

The I is changed, and begins to take form in the unshakably stable territory of the fluid, dehumanized object: inert cockroach body, oozing slimy body mass through a split shell; fluttering butterfly body, ancient and observant; personified silence, inscribed on an otherwise impeccable and depersonalized wall alongside the maid's charcoal figures created in rage and indifference. We are, as Kristeva tells us, at a boundary point: "We are no longer within the sphere of the unconscious but at the limit of primal repression that, nevertheless, has discovered an intrinsically corporeal and already signifying brand, symptom, and sign: repugnance, disgust, abjection. There is an effervescence of object and sign—not of desire but of intolerable significance; they tumble over into non-sense or the impossible real, but they appear even so in spite of 'myself' (which is not) as abjection" (*Powers* 11). As the I is changed, removing quotation marks, so too is the fact of being, and the act of seeing: "But if its eyes did not see me"—in the conventional sense of the verb *to see* as used by middle-class women whose existence is bound up in the reflections of their mirrors—"But if its eyes did not see me, its existence existed me" (*Passion* 68). The phrases enact a delicate balance of signification—either seeing or existing, and both—which, as Kristeva reminds us, is and is not abjection: "Not me, Not that. But not nothing, either. A 'something' that I do not recognize as a thing. A weight of meaninglessness, about which there is nothing insignificant, and which crushes me. On the edge of non-existence and hallucination, of a reality that, if I acknowledge it, annihilates me" (*Powers* 2). Through confrontation with these others, insect and drawing, these nonobjects of her painfully constructed utterance, the non-subject, G. H., conceives of herself again, as a not-I, painfully transmuted.

I am not

At this point G. H. is ready to begin the deconstruction of herself, to inaugurate the progressive removal of accreted existence, stripping the shield of superficiality from her superficial existence to bare the minimal essence of her life. For Kristeva, "The abject confronts us, on the one hand, with those fragile states where man strays on the territories of *animal*. . . . The abject confronts us, on the other hand, . . . with our earliest attempts to release the hold of *maternal* entity even before ex-isting outside of her" (*Powers* 12–13). The liminal humanity of the maid, reinforced by the terrifying familiarity of the cockroach, provide the material for the first confrontation; G. H.'s meditations on the other prehistory of the self, her impossibly early memories of nursing at her mother's breast, provide the other.

"This is my body," G. H. tells us again and again with slight variations as she takes the cockroach matter in to her mouth, enacting a desacralized version of the Catholic mass in which Christ's body and blood are transubstantiated from the bread and wine of the ritual offering. Here, at the asymptotic limits in which her social identity meets the antisubjective self, G. H. initiates the ceremony of consecration without sublimation. The literal quality of the transubstantiation practiced in the mass is preserved—don't bite the host, I remember the nuns telling us, and we schoolchildren told each other in whispers that biting must hurt Jesus—and inverted; it is her own body she eats and drinks and no metaphorical simulacrum. Inevitably, in this taste of the cockroach, her prehuman self, she is led to recall the taste of her mother's milk, sign of the original separation of self from self, ambiguously human and protohuman on her lips: "And mother's milk, which is human, mother's milk is much prior to the human, and it has no taste, it is nothing, I have already tried it." Mother's milk, like the drawing, like the cockroach, is at the far limits of self-definition; mother's milk, unlike the drawing and the cockroach, exists prior to representation in the space where bodies, sights, and the symbolic are all meaningless. "I have already tried it," says G. H., groping for a metaphor: "It is like the empty and expressionless sculpted eye of a statue, for when art is good it is because it has touched the inexpressive" (136). G. H., glutted on the tasteless nothingness of her mother's milk, falls into this inexpressiveness in which the single referents are intense need, deep wanting. There is not, and cannot be, a place, a grounding to define this need in language. G. H., like the infant, recognizes only one quality, being (under erasure), and only one emotion, wanting.

For the case of this fiction, the logic of her essential self-recognition requires passivization. In fact, critics frequently describe Lispector's style in terms of her predilection for the passive: not to write, as Rodríguez Monegal reminds us, but to be written (236). Lispector would not object to this description. In the brief essay "Two Ways," she ascribes the passive mode of existence entirely to her writing self: "When writing I have insights which are 'passive' and so intimate they 'write themselves' the very instant I perceive them almost without the intervention of any so-called thought processes. For this reason I make no choices when writing" (*Legion* 191). Likewise, Peixoto, among others, points to the essential passivity of Lispector's female characters (see 291, for example), and French critic and philosopher Hélène Cixous advocates radical passivization as a model for one mode of reading Lispector's works: "I let myself be read according to C. L., her passion has read me" ("L'approche" 409). Thus, too, G. H. performs the second of the two actions in this novel (killing the cockroach is obviously the first) and eats the cockroach as she drank her mother's milk—passively: "For I had taken away all my participation before I did it. I did not really want 'to know.'" And then G. H. generalizes to all of life: "Was that, then, the way things are done? 'Not knowing'— was that the way, then, that the most profound things happen?" (159). G. H. signals the impossibility and the necessity of writing while knowing nothing, a babe at the breast, at the same time negotiating the granite obduracy of the knowledge of nothingness which is her hard-won prize. Any appeal to transcendence, spiritual or secular, would be an evasion of this imperative. We, in turn, allowing ourselves to be read by what has been written under the name "Clarice Lispector" are also preerased in the wordlessness, in the futility of adding our "I am not" to hers.

"I am not," this new G. H. reminds us, I am not an active agent in the story of my life My existence exists me. My cockroach self was eaten by me. I want, but I do not have the words, nor do I want the words. Not knowing and not saying: these are the two sides of the unexpressed/inexpressible. G. H. takes in this nothing, enacts this nonevent, with great attentiveness. The goal, clearly, is to sweep away the accumulations of what "we know," to strip the accretions from the face and the body, to approach as nearly as possible the wordless and impossible "I am not." She recognizes the weightiness of "our hands that are gross and full of words" (152) but gropes toward another state: "But it is I who should keep myself from naming things. The name is an accretion, and it inhibits contact with the thing. The name of the thing is an interval for the thing." Nevertheless, she is aware that this call to namelessness, to unword the world or simply to desist from the perpetual action of giving names, requires a huge effort of voice. Silence is not given easily: "The will to accretion is great—because naked things are so tedious" (133).

What is left, or what is left out of this expressionless sculpture? "Much remains to be told," G. H. warns her readers near the end of the novel, just after giving us an outline of the conventional biography she pointedly will not tell—she is not, among other things, a story-teller after all. She will not tell (*contar*) all; nevertheless, she has one reminder of her persistent and ineluctable need, her need to need, which it is imperative for her to state: "I will need for the rest of my days my sweet, good-humored light ordinariness, I need to forget, just like everyone else" (155). Along with all those other words, including her own name, which G. H. will need to forget in order to find the word *passion*, she will need to forget heroism, and along with her active forgetting of the word she will also need to forget this experience that ambiguously changed the shape of the world (if only temporarily). In abandoning that expectation of heroic stature along with all other expectations, G. H. is finally able to begin to speak about desisting, if not actually to desist, and she calmly states the final sequence of paradoxical antisentences: "By not being, I was. To the end of that which I was not, I was. What I am not, I am. Everything will be in me, if I am not; for 'I' is merely one of the world's instantaneous spasms" (172). This is not a mere idle ticktock of passing time and playful antitheses but G. H.'s manner of grasping, in an almost physical sense, the neutral nowness of her existence while leaving her hands, empty of words, folded loosely in her lap. The particular and very concrete "I" slowly and insistently gives rise to the universal, and then, spasmotically, both the insistence and the universality are swept away.

I am

G. H. has stripped herself to the essential core, while retaining at the end of the novel, the proximate end of the words, reference to an "I am" that cannot be imagined as an "I am."—with the period indicating a final resolution. Rather, we have the tentative nonconclusion of "I am:"—where the colon comments on the continuing construction of the self in the difficult labor of waiting, and not waiting, which ensues beyond the pages of the text. And which has no existence outside the text, because the hypothetical interval it opens is unbounded. G. H., self-reduced beyond initials to namelessness, is compelled by the final constraints of language, something similar to the crisis of metaphorical signification Kristeva notes in "Throes of Love": "*Being like* is not only *being* and *nonbeing*, it is also a longing for *unbeing* in order to assert as only possible 'being,' not an ontology, that is, something outside of discourse, but the constraint of discourse itself" (*Love* 273). Exactly so. For Lispector, however, discourse stands alone, not as a metaphor, not as a speaking of, or even a speaking to, but as an act of discourse released from that which is outside it. In G. H.'s final revelation, both "I" and "am" are severely problematized as a so-called I that can be signaled in discourse only by a so-called verb of being, but more than ever the only possible reference begs the reader/interlocutor/other self/lover to read between the lines of what can be said for the essential unsayable that is beyond speech.

But G. H.'s last words are not given to the continuing existence; rather, they point to its transformation into some amalgamation of need and being: "All that is missing is the coup-de-grâce—which is called passion" (165). Passion, or what is called passion, the word *passion*, is not only the missing element toward which the entire text strives, it is also that which, named even tentatively, exerts the killing blow. Her "I adore" is, in this killing power, as far removed from her prior experiences of "I love" as the initial from the final "I." Previously, tediously, love was marked for her by the interval. In her devastating critique of the conventional decorum of "being in love," she defines love, or "o que chamávamos de amor" 'what we called love,' presumably in counterdistinction to what she later identifies as the missing passion. Love for G. H. has been experienced, in the passive, as "the neuter of love, that is what we experienced and despised. What I am speaking of is when nothing happened and we called that nothing happening an interval" (110). This nothing of being in love is a bounded interval defined by another arbitrary arabesque of discourse: of simply no longer being in love, another merely grammatical gesture like that drawn around her name by the mental quotation marks.

Her final gesture has a doubly displaced core in its faintly sketched allusion to the Cartesian motto, and in its own bifurcated semierasure. In Gerald Bruns's acute observation, "The loss of subjectivity means self-annihilation only if we hold to the Cartesian outlook of the pure subject. . . . Descartes' motto . . . carries with it the angelic corollary that thinking, and therefore being, can do without the body. . . . The body, in the modernist or Manichean view, is a negative entity" (129). For Lispector, however, the essential thingness of the body comes into its own as the speaker speaks, for "passion" is not the rational intellec-tualization of "love" but the commitment of the body to the dance of mutual appropriation in the recognition of the body's being-mortal. The final transformation of "I am not I" can, thus, be read as "(I am: therefore) I adore" or "I am: (therefore I adore)." G. H. is no longer interested in the intervals, although this novel is undeniably an interval, a long discursive one, bounded by idiosyncratic ellipses at beginning and end rather than by conventional quotation marks. She can no longer imagine the compartmentalization of existence into before and after, I and not-I, subject and object, knowing and not knowing: "The world interdepended with/from me, and I am not understanding what I am saying, never! never again shall I understand what I say. . . . how will I be able to say except timidly, like this: Life is be-ing me" (173). This is the extreme passion, not only stripping away the accretions of a bracketed self but sweeping away as well the nothings of dead intervals and the notion of interval itself. It is a passion that responds to the need to speak, not, poetically, to say the unsayable but rather, or in addition, to unsay altogether, and to do it in words.

Água viva takes off from this point, emphasizing the unbounded fluidity, the unprocessed continuum of living writing, while clarifying that such writing has, inevitably, its own diamantine shape and form. "What I write is round" (5) 'escrevo redondo' (11), says the nameless narrator. "E antes de mais nada te escrevo dura escritura. Quero como poder pegar com a mão a palavra" (13). "Meu 'it' é duro como uma pedra-seixo" (35). 'And above all else I write you hard writing. I want to discover how I can grasp the word with my hand' (5–6) 'My "it" is hard like a pebble' (22). Negation is not easy, not irrelevant, not soft and fluid. For at the same time that Lispector speaks of a fluid writing, she gives to her art an attention as disciplined and as harsh as the cutting edge of a jeweler's saw. "Há uma linha de aço atravessando isto tudo que te escrevo," says the narrator of *Água viva* (45). There is indeed a line of steel traversing everything that Lispector writes.

6

Writing in the Margins:
Rosario Castellanos and María Luisa Puga

There are margins, and there are margins: incongruent, overlapping, discontinuous, parallel. To the non-Spanish-speaking Indians of provincial Chiapas, the Mexico City–educated, white, upper-class Rosario Castellanos must seem the very embodiment of the center. Yet for Rosario Castellanos, her condition as a woman was sufficient to marginalize her, both personally and politically, to such a degree that her space was analogous to theirs. In the national culture represented by the norms and mores of the city, Castellanos's sex limited her access to the inner circles of professional activity; her vocation as a writer marginalized her yet further. As Poniatowska notes, although all women writers feel compelled to excuse themselves before a hypercritical public, "Rosario goes even farther because she throws herself into begging forgiveness." A professional woman is tolerated— barely—and society in general refuses to acknowledge her potential for commitment to a profession: "Single women work, as do divorced or abandoned women, or at any rate, the feminists, who in order to be feminists have gotten divorced. . . . Respect for their careers? Women still have not conquered that in Mexico. A woman who works is an object of compassion." In the case of the writer, this grudging commiseration dissolves into distaste: "Moreover, they fear that writing might marginalize them, as in fact it does marginalize them" (*Vida* 101–2). Marginalization is not a philosophical position but a hard fact of daily life.

Unlike the provincially bred and born Castellanos, María Luisa Puga was born in Mexico City, the very center of national cultural identity.

Although she always scribbled in notebooks, she feels she did not become a writer until she left Mexico, at age twenty-four and in the portentous year of 1968, for Europe and Africa, where she lived for ten years before returning to Mexico and publishing, in rapid succession, half a dozen novels, starting with *Las posibilidades del odio* (The possibilities of hatred), as well as numerous essays, and the antiautobiography *La forma del silencio* (The form of silence). It is as if Puga had to leave the national center, recenter herself in Europe, and then find the most eccentric position possible, marginalized as a foreigner in the marginally existent continent of Africa, before returning to her own eccentric center, Mexico.

And then to go forth again. In "El lenguaje oculto" (Hidden language), her contribution to *Itinerario de palabras* (Itinerary of words), Puga defines, from Mexico City, the themes of a series of thirty-four lectures she proposes to give in a tour of the north of the country. Her themes are "the appropriation of language," in her definition, how language acquires a voice of its own when literature begins to appropriate the history of the nation; "how we are taught to read," the delineation of a general practice of miseducation which presents language and culture as alien objects of detached study rather than integral components in the ongoing construction of the self; "what we read," that is, disconcertingly, *El mío Cid* in school and American best sellers at home; "how language colonizes," an examination of how people are taught to speak "correctly"; and "identity through language," that is, the manner in which a personal self-concept is created in stories told us and stories we tell about ourselves (12). She soon realizes that her well-intentioned project is hopelessly naïve and absurdly reductive. In the small provincial town of Vícam, she prepares to give her talk to the junior high and high school children, who have been bused in, many without breakfast, for the occasion. She wants to converse with the students; they hesitate and hide their faces. Such extreme shyness blunts Puga's attempts to create an atmosphere of open discussion. "Please remember," says one of their teachers, reminding the well-intentioned writer that these young people lack a common ground for discussion with a well-dressed, well-connected, well-fed woman from the center of the nation, "recall that these are Yaquis; they have to translate into Spanish as they go along" (16). One language for school, as Castellanos might say, and one for dreams. Puga struggles on valiantly:

Eran no sé cuántos. Estábamos en la biblioteca del CBTA de Vícam, en donde lucen sus lomos los libros de siempre, ya saben: Sor Juana, Alfonso Reyes, Octavio Paz, Carlos Fuentes. . . . gracias a ellos somos internacionales, pero no logramos que la gente de nuestro país nos lea. . . . A los chavos de Vícam eso no les servía. Clases de literatura habían tenido, sí. Algunos recordaban haber leído *La Celestina, El cantar del mío Cid*. . . . Con razón odiamos tanto leer. . . . Nos ocuparon el lenguaje; lo llenaron de gestos que no son nuestros, que no nos dicen. (17)

I don't know how many there were. We were in the CBTA library in Vícam, in which we could see the same book spines as always; you already know: Sor Juana, Alfonso Reyes, Octavio Paz, Carlos Fuentes. . . . Thanks to them we are international, but we can't get the people of our own country to read us. . . . None of it was of any use to the kids from Vícam. They had had literature classes, of course. Some remembered having read *La Celestina, El cantar del mío Cid*. . . . No wonder we hate to read so much. . . . They took over our language; they filled it with gestures that are not ours, that do not speak us.

Puga's difficulty with the Yaqui students is captured succinctly in the morass of her pronoun references: we (the students and I) were in the library, we (Mexicans) achieve an international presence in the works of our best writers, we (the best writers: Puga implicitly includes herself in the canonical roll call) are not read in Mexico. Then, more distanced: it (the library) has no relevance to Yaqui speakers from Vícam; it is not their culture or their language, after all. Implicitly Puga asks why they should want to read the canonical Mexican authors. They (the students) have been compelled to read other canonical Spanish works; we (the students and ex-students) find them boring: worse, they (such works) are imperialistic. Such national masterpieces do not feed Yaqui souls; they seem written for external consumption only. In these works, says Puga, shifting ground once again, "our" (Spanish) language has been occupied as if by an invading force. Yet still, the specific case of the Yaquis has been left unaddressed. Even granting that the Spanish of canonical texts rather than "our Spanish" occupies the space of learning, with all the available interstices filled in with roughly translated versions of American best sellers, Puga has still not focused on the central issue: Spanish is a foreign tongue for the Yaqui schoolchildren. All these struggles between competing armies remain irrelevant, for none of them has left any place for the

Yaquis, who not only must read *El mío Cid* but must also awkwardly translate it into their own language. And without breakfast. The implications of this half-unacknowledged internal colonization of Mexico's own people are vast, if unexplored.[1] Such half-pursued insights and blurred distinctions are the very essence of Puga's writings.

Both Rosario Castellanos and María Luisa Puga take the fact of this marginalization, and in their very different manners, write from the margins of official discourse, consciously choosing the painfully reconstructed intersections between two types and intensities of marginalization, inscribing in their first novels the broken remnants of an oral culture struggling to maintain its unique identity against the pressure of encroaching official historicization. In both *Balún-Canán*[2] and *Las posibilidades del odio* the effort results in a strangely hybrid text, written for those oppressed and marginalized classes who have neither the available spending money for books nor the leisure to read them, even if, which is frequently not the case, they have the level of education necessary to decipher the Spanish words. Castellanos's most intensely colored scenes are saved for women like the nana and the *cargadora* (carrier), who have served white women like her almost invisibly for generations, and for the Indian wives and Indian mistresses who remain, unheard and almost unseen, on the fringes of existence, marginal even to marginalized cultures. In Puga's case, the alienation between writer and implicit audience is, if anything, even more extreme, for Puga writes, in Spanish, of the Gĩkũyũ-speaking people of Kenya, whose reality is accessible to her only at the double remove of a common second language—English. We have, then, with either novelist, the odd contradiction of a writer whose ideal readers cannot read her work, the writer who must instead cast her text into the hands of those inhabitants of the center who do indulge in the luxury of book reading.

This situation threatens, as Jean Franco might tell us, a kind of

[1] I feel compelled to note that all the foregoing discussion depends on a cultural heritage shared by Puga, me, and you, the reader, premised on a German model of education whose goal is, in Jeffrey Sammons's words, "the cultural formation of the self so that it might reach the fullness of its potentialities" (14). It is this shared heritage from which we cannot distance ourselves that makes the discussion possible, even as the (silent) presence of the Yaquis denounces it.

[2] In my discussion I quote from the 1959 British translation of *Balún-Canán* titled *The Nine Guardians*. I have modified the translation where necessary, and I have retained the original title of the novel, an untranslated, non-Spanish place-name.

double, or triple, treachery, first, as Franco notes, "on the level of the enunciated—that is, in the space where plot, character, and novelistic time are interwoven. These novels therefore register the first type of treachery, that which takes place in the shift from the community bound by orally transmitted culture to the nation" (*Plotting* 132). To write the oral tale is to betray the very nature of that tale and, by extension, to betray the community itself—in Castellanos's and Puga's cases, by a recognizably incomplete knowledge and by an acknowledged inability to translate accurately from one language to another, from one culture to another.

The treachery may take place on other levels as well, for by abandoning the implicit public (nonreading) for the other, mainstream public, the writer betrays herself once again, establishing a contract with a reader that is not her reader, making a space for the ineluctable reappropriation of the margins—as anthropological study, as exotica, as the obscure other whose only function is to circumscribe or define the center—for other purposes. "Indefectibly," says Mallarmé, "the white blank returns" (quoted in Derrida, *Dissemination* 257). Efforts to deconstruct the unitary myth of the nation inexplicably, unexpectedly, simultaneously contribute to the reinscription of that rejected concept. The blank returns. And as the sonorous spaces are ambiguously filled, remarkably the insistent counterhegemonic negation "not I" "not that" becomes the compass point for the return of the white as well: the latifundista's daughter who will never enter the world of the Tzotzil- or Tzeltal-speaking Indians; the displaced Mexican tourist, forced to recognize that in Kenya she is not embraced by the nonexistent great sisterhood of third-world women of color but ignored as yet another suspect white outsider.

To weigh the valences of the atomized margins involves a third denial of marginalization, a third betrayal, for to the double betrayal of language and cultural context is joined that of the writing self. As Trinh Minh-ha writes in *Woman, Native, Other*, the postcolonial woman writer, ironically, "usually writes from a position of power, creating as an 'author,' situating herself *above* her work and existing *before* it, rarely simultaneously *with* it" (6). To write "well"—like a (postcolonial) man—is to jeopardize or forget or transcend her originary source of strength and her primary sense of difference forged in her self-identification as a writer from the margins. It is actively to seek *his* acceptance, *his* power, *his* authority. In the voices ricocheting, as Doris Lessing once said, like machine gun bullets, "I, I, I," her voice is too easily lost: co-opted or silenced, lauded or disregarded. Thus, Rosario Castellanos presents the all-too familiar case of the token woman as canonical writer, unread except for the standard anthology pieces, dismissed in the vague eulogies of a faintly supercilious and condescending public. María Luisa Puga, of course, remains a curiosity outside of (and perhaps even within) Mexico.

Words on the Wind

In a recent *New Yorker* article, John Updike notes "the curious but widespread autobiographical impulse in men still enjoying middle age" and theorizes that this Eurocentric, male, midlife need to testify to the progress of life in the midst of living it "possibly stems from a desire to set the record straight before senility muddles it, and a hope of lightening the ballast for the homeward leg of life's voyage" (92). Almost every word of Updike's tongue-in-cheek comment would sound hopelessly foreign to a Latin American woman, whose hard-won and precariously held right to literary expression does not allow her a place either so central or so confident. Her life story is nothing so simple as straightening out the misprints or filling in the details in an extended curriculum vitae. It is not just, as Doris Sommer would agree, that "for women their 'condition' was female rather than human and hardly described or acknowledged" (68), although this concern is felt. Rosario Castellanos recognizes that in writing from the margins of accepted literary culture, the woman writer must continually and on all levels renegotiate the implicit contract between the subjective realms and the social and ideological imperatives. In so doing, she stretches the limits of autobiography as traditionally defined and also asks us to think about the cultural assumptions behind all such apparently "universal" generic categories. In her poem "Pasaporte," she writes:

> Mujer, pues, de palabra. No, de palabra no.
> Pero sí de palabras,
> muchas, contradictorias, ay, insignificantes,
> sonido puro, vacuo, cernido de arabescos,
> juego de salón, chisme, espuma, olvido. (*Meditación* 215)

> A word-woman, then. No, not word.
> But of words:

many, contradictory, ah, insignificant,
pure sound, void, sifted with arabesques,
parlor games, gossip, foam, forgetfulness.

Castellanos rejects the neat orders of a rationalized, self-justificatory tale. She is not single, not a word-woman, but a woman of many, and contradictory, words. Accordingly, her intensely personal writing, whether in poetry, prose, or drama, refuses to enact the autobiographical pact that would reduce it to a single, if highly elaborate, thread. Her identification of herself and, by extension, all Mexican women with the cause of other marginalized peoples, especially the indigenous peoples of Mexico's peripheral provinces, would prevent such reductionism.

In addition, the tradition of women's participation in Mexico's national culture is extremely thin. Women have been discouraged from the public arena for centuries; their role in the literary and political debates surrounding their male counterparts has been obscured or denied; and their voices are only now finding entry into the national discourse. Thus, when Rosario Castellanos in her various articles on autobiography looks for Mexican foremothers, she can identify only two: Sor Juana Inés de la Cruz, the brilliant seventeenth-century nun whose impassioned "Reply to Sor Filotea" includes a two- or three-page autobiographical sketch, and the marquesa Fanny Calderón de la Barca, the English wife of a Spanish ambassador to Mexico, whose memories of her two years in that country (1839–1841), *Life in Mexico*, one of the most cherished historical documents of the nineteenth century, was written and published in English. The lack of access to the written word was such that one of the heroines of Independence, doña Josefa Ortiz de Domínguez, "wanted to let Father Hidalgo know that they had been discovered, but could not write out her message because she did not know how to write" (*Mujer* 27). In 1946 Mexican women were officially given citizenship, including the right to primary (now junior high) education, but economic factors still affect actual literacy rates.

Rosario Castellanos, damned with faint praise as "the most solid example of a literary vocation we have had among us" (Poniatowska declares that hard work rather than high quality was Castellanos's principal virtue [*Vida* 47]), spent the first sixteen years of her life in the town of Comitán in the state of Chiapas, a community that was completely isolated from the central government until the Panamerican Highway reached it in 1951. The Revolution of 1910 passed by it; the 1934 agrarian reforms of president Lázaro Cárdenas took years to arrive, and when they did, in 1941, the neofeudalistic lifestyle of Castellanos's family was swept away almost entirely. Her father lost his ranches and the economic and social power that went with them, and the family emigrated to Mexico City. Rosario Castellanos eventually returned to Chiapas for several years as an employee of the Instituto Nacional Indigenista; by all accounts, these later experiences confirmed her early sympathy for the Tzeltal- and Tzotzil-speaking Indians of the area and inspired almost all her prose work. Says Aurora M. Ocampo, "Rosario Castellanos knew how to listen to the voices of the dispossessed because she too was dispossessed, to the voices of the oppressed because she too was oppressed, and to the voices of the executioners because she too had been one on occasion" (201). Castellanos never forgets that by writing her story and the story of the Indians in Spanish, a language historically prohibited to them, she is making herself complicitous in one of the most tortuous ambiguities of the *palabra enemiga* (alternatively, the word-enemy, the enemy word, or as Suzanne Jill Levine translates Fuentes's use of it, "The Enemy: Words"), alternately victim and executioner, giving voice to herself and to them in the language of the oppressors, in a form and a style inaccessible to the people she represents.[3]

Rosario Castellanos was essentially a poet, whose best-known, best-appreciated works are her volumes of poetry, and she was an artist who could not permit herself the facile distinctions other writers and thinkers maintain between art and life. For her, personally, literature was in a quite literal sense her life; not only did she encode every aspect of her life in her poetry but her work induced her to continue living by saving her from the abysses of impotent anxiety. Politically, she believed that literature carried the power of changing reality through the act of naming. Unsurprisingly, *Balún-Canán*, although "essentially an autobiographical book," according to María

[3]Besides land redistribution, the other highly disputed element of Cárdenas's agrarian reforms was to require landowners to teach Spanish to the Indians. This measure was considered almost blasphemous, for one of the major means of control over the Indian population was to discourage them from learning any more Spanish than absolutely required to follow commands. Since their own language, of course, had no official recognition, the Tzeltal speakers were thus effectively disenfranchised.

Luisa Cresta de Leguizamon (10), violates almost all the normative requirements of the autobiographical genre as traditionally conceived. Castellanos elaborates: "It is the *narration* of my infancy; it is, at the same time a *testimonial* to the events I witnessed at a particular moment in which attempts were made to effect an economic and political change in the places I lived during that time . . . but of course, these events are told as *literature,* not as a chronicle or in the way it might have been told on psychoanalyst's 'couch'" (Cresta 3, my emphasis). In another interview, Castellanos adds, "strictly speaking, this work cannot be considered *prose*" (Miller 125). Briefly then, to recapitulate the disjunctions with traditional expectations: it is a narration but not, "strictly speaking," a prose one. It is a testimonial but not a chronicle of events. It is a literary autobiography but not psychoanalytical one. If it can be said to follow any established form, *Balún-Canán* seems to fit in best with that protean variety of feminine autobiography described by Françoise Lionnet:

> It should not be surprising for an autobiographical narrative to proclaim itself as fiction: for the narrator's process of reflection, narration, and self-integration within language is bound to unveil patterns of self-definition (and self-dissimulation) with which we are not always consciously familiar. . . . the female narrator . . . exists in the text under circumstances of alienated communication because the text is the locus of her dialogue with a tradition she tacitly aims to subvert. (92–93)[4]

The tradition she wishes to subvert is triply her own: hers by right of class, race, and access to education. All three terms are problematized

[4]In the Latin American context, it is important to salute Doris Sommer's seminal article, "'Not Just a Personal Story': Women's *Testimonios* and the Plural Self," which provides one of the most concise approximations of some the issues vexing a theorization of third-world autobiography. Since Sommer deals with the testimonio, however, and not with either autobiography or fictional autobiography, much of what she has to say cannot be transposed to an analysis of Castellanos's work. See, for example, her concluding assertion that "autobiographers can enjoy the privilege and the privacy of being misunderstood, whereas those who testify cannot afford or even survive it" (130) (Castellanos's skillful deployment of ambiguity suggests that she shares this aspect of the autobiographer's privilege) or Sommer's discussion of testimonios as making no pretense "of universal or essential human experience." Furthermore, in such works, she finds, "singularity achieves its identity as an extension of the collective," for testimonios are "strikingly impersonal" (108–9). These statements are extraordinarily helpful in understanding the oral testimony of such activist women as Domitila Barrios de Chungara and Rigoberta Menchú but are less pertinent in the analysis of Castellanos's very personal, very artful, very *written* text.

in this poetic novel, inasmuch as it is precisely in respect to this privileged position that Castellanos grounds her critique, intentionally confusing the distinction between autobiography and fiction so as to call attention away from the failed ideal of a meaningful, complete, and self-directed life toward the (for her) more essential contribution of an ideological critique of a society that actively prevents self-direction in a significant majority of its citizens.

Rosario Castellanos's tale begins and ends with the social upheavals both in her own landholding class and among the Indians following the tardy arrival of Cárdenas's land reforms during her seventh year. The closure of this abbreviated life is marked by the girl-child-narrator's access to the written word, for it is by means of the very fact of writing that the child unwittingly inserts herself into the rejected conventions of devalued tradition and, moreover, confirms her identity as property of the male. This oral tale, finally and inevitably lost, is paralleled by a second tale, that of the Tzeltal-speaking Indians, also oral, also a story of loss and expropriation of the word that spoke identity and so gave it being. For the Indians, the idea of an individual autobiography is, however, incomprehensibly alien; their mode of telling the self is not personal but communal, the story of an interrelated identity forged by the voice of the storyteller, "el hermano mayor de mi tribu," the Elder Brother, the embodied tribal memory. This tale, too, was once put into Spanish and into writing at the demand of the landowners; frighteningly, it was preserved by the male heirs of the landowning family as documentary proof of their legal claim to traditional Indian territories. The girl's story incorporates and recuperates this tale alongside and tangential to her own, but the older and wiser Rosario Castellanos is clearly aware of the potential for co-optation of her dual text as well—hence the elusive poetic style that seems to operate in flight from all such potential betrayals, including those of generic conventions.[5] For all these caveats, I would argue nevertheless that Castellanos's poetic novel provides a truer plumb line, given the only partially Westernized cultural context, into the autobiographical

[5]*Balún-Canán* is actually divided into three parts, the first and third of which are narrated from point of view of the seven-year-old child, the second, from the point of view of an omniscient third-person narrator. The work develops as a series of confrontations between oppressor and oppressed sparked by the new government requirements: César Argüello, the landowner father, versus Felipe, the Indian leader; César versus his wife, Zoraida; Zoraida versus the girl-child; the brother, Mario, versus the girl; the girl, finally, versus the Indian nana.

impulse as adapted to an eccentric member of the landowning class, a class that is at the center of its own provincial concerns but definitely on the periphery of national life and consciousness.

"Underreading" describes the most common critical reaction to *Balún-Canán*. When the work first came out in 1957, it was safely classified as an "indigenista" novel and read as an elaboration on the traditional political commitment and social consciousness of that particular politically charged variation on the more general exoticist recuperations of "costumbrismo." Such readings are plausible, if narrow, but in order to function they must repress the most arresting and original features of the narrative as imperfections in the author's achievement of the indigenista form. Because her second novel, *Oficio de tinieblas* (Tenebrae service), with its stock characters and stereotyped good and bad guys, was much more easily recuperable to the indigenista model, many critics saw it as confirmation that Castellanos was able to correct the mistakes and infelicities of her first prose work and produce a more polished, more categorizable second.

Recent reevaluations of both novels often attempt to recuperate them for a content-based protofeminism by focusing on the figure of the woman in the text; curiously, in relation to *Balún-Canán*, most of these readings ignore the most central female—the seven-year-old girl—and all of them ignore the Indian nana, who disappears, ironically, into the invisibility that she had bitterly predicted as her tribe's communal fate.[6] *Balún-Canán* opens in medias res with the voice of the nana as she *dresses* but pointedly does not *address* the child, raising at the very beginning of the narrative the suppressed question that will haunt and destabilize the whole of the succeeding text. At this point I permit myself the luxury of a long, essential quotation.

> —… y entonces, coléricos, nos desposeyeron, nos arrebataron lo que habíamos atesorado: la palabra, que es el arca de la memoria. Desde aquellos días arden y se consumen con el leño en la hoguera. Sube el humo en el viento y se deshace. Queda la ceniza sin rostro. Para que puedas venir tú y el que es menor que tú y les basta un soplo, solamente un soplo…

[6]Examples of the first, indigenista reading, include Benedetti, Franco (*Introduction*), and Sommers. Fiscal, Frischmann, and MacDonald are typical of the protofeminists. Cypress's fine discourse analysis does take into account the importance of the girl-child as narrative figure.

—No me cuentes ese cuento, nana.

—¿Acaso hablaba contigo? ¿Acaso se habla con los granos de anís?

No soy un grano de anís. Soy una niña y tengo siete años. Los cinco dedos de la mano derecha y dos de la izquierda. Y cuando me yergo puedo mirar de frente las rodillas de mi padre. Más arriba no. Me imagino que sigue creciendo como un gran árbol y que en su rama más alta está agazapado un tigre diminuto. Mi madre es diferente. Sobre su pelo—tan negro, tan espeso, tan crespo—pasan los pájaros y les gusta y se quedan. Me lo imagino nada más. Nunco lo he visto. Miro lo que está a mi nivel. . . . Y a mi hermano lo miro de arriba abajo. Porque nació después de mí y, cuando nació, yo ya sabía muchas cosas que ahora le explico minuciosamente. Por ejemplo ésta:

Colón descubrió la América. . . .

—No te muevas tanto, niña. No puedo terminar de peinarte.

¿Sabe mi nana que la odio cuando me peina? No lo sabe. No sabe nada. Es india, está descalza y no usa ninguna ropa debajo de la tela azul del tzec. No le da vergüenza. Dice que la tierra no tiene ojos.

—Ya estás lista. Ahora el desayuno.

Pero si comer es horrible. Ante mí el plato mirándome fijamente sin parpadear. Luego la gran extensión de la mesa. Y después… no sé. Me da miedo que del otro lado haya un espejo. . . .

—Quiero tomar café. Como tú. Como todos.

—Te vas a volver india.

Su amenaza me sobrecoge. Desde mañana la leche no se derramará. (9–10)

"… and then, angrily, they dispossessed us, they tore away what we had treasured: the word, which is the ark of memory. And since that time they have burned and been consumed with the wood in the fire. The smoke rises on the wind and dissolves. All that remains is ashes without a face. So that you can come, and the one that is younger than you, and with a breath, with only a breath…"

"Don't tell me that story, nana."

"What makes you think I was talking to you? Do people talk to anise seeds?"

I am not an anise seed. I am a girl and I am seven years old. Five fingers on the right hand and two on the left. And when I stretch up I can look straight at my father's knees. No higher. I imagine that he grows upward like a tree and that in his highest branch crouches a diminutive tiger. My mother is different. Above her hair—so black, so thick, so curly—pass the birds, and they like it there so they stay. I'm only imagining. I have never seen it. I look at things on my level. I can look at my brother from top to bottom. Because he was born after me, and, when he was born, I already knew lots of things that I now explain carefully to him. For example, this:

Columbus discovered America. . . .

"Don't move so much, child. I can't finish combing your hair."

Does my nana know I hate her when she combs my hair? She doesn't know. She doesn't know anything. She's an Indian, she's barefoot, she doesn't wear anything under the blue cloth of her tzec. She doesn't care. She says the earth has no eyes.

"You're ready. Now breakfast."

But eating is horrible. In front of me the plate stares up without blinking. Then the long stretch of table. And then... I don't know. I'm afraid there might be a mirror on the other side. . . .

"I want coffee. Like you. Like everybody."

"You're going to turn into an Indian."

Her threat chills me. From now on the milk will not spill. (13–14)

The nana's frightening tale of an ongoing conquest is twice interrupted: once in the white space before the beginning of *Balún-Canán*, once by the child's imperious demand that the nana not tell that particular story. The nana's incomplete story is further displaced by the child's "knowledge," her counterhistory, complete in one simple sentence, which erases the native Americans from the tale: "Columbus discovered America." And this unreliable child-narrator once again complicates the nana's message in the tangled interweavings of the voices of the subordinate adult and the ignorant child, the former dependent on the latter for her very life and livelihood, the latter on the former for maternal care and attention. The love/hate relationship of mutual dependence and the shifting lines of power between the white child and her Indian nurse are exquisitely captured in the war between storytelling styles: the metaphorical, lyrical mode of the woman, cut off by the petulance of the child and obliterated by the matter-of-fact European version of Spanish arrival in the Americas; the child's petty assumption of the nana's ignorance, the nana's revenge in suggesting the metaphor of an eyed earth to the child's mind so that plate and table become leering faces or horrific mirrors; the childish demand for coffee, the nurse's menacing response couched in the simple declarative sentence of the whites, foregrounding the child's secret fear: "You're going to turn into an Indian." The work opens, then, with two competing author figures battling uneasily for control over the text—

the girl child, the least-valued individual of the dominant class, and the nana, the most marginalized member of the communal culture—a battle, from one point of view, for the lowest possible stakes.

This is no traditional autobiography that begins with some version of the sentence, "I was born." The opening gesture invalidates such trite phrasings. Instead of the emergence of the individual self as a function of the acquisition of language, we are thrown into contact with a primary and soon-eradicated "we" that defines itself through the historicomythic account of an originary loss of language, which has come to endow reality with its present form. Without ever leaving their homeland, the natives of Chiapas have been disenfranchised, morally exiled, dehumanized, marginalized, silenced, and then readmitted once again as barely tolerated semislaves on the fringes of a geographical and historical space that was once their own. As Doris Sommer says of the Central and South American women who share their voices with us in the testimonial form, "conscious of working in a foreign language, they do not have to be reminded of the arbitrary nature of the sign. They live the irony of those linguistic disencounters" (121). Like them, Castellanos's fictional nana, channeling her fury, has to live and work and express herself in the conqueror's tongue. Furthermore, the nana's tale, pointedly NOT one of those other stories she tells to amuse the child, functions most importantly as a kind of narrative revenge. "What makes you think I was talking to you?" erases the child as much as possible and in the same manner as her people have been erased: by denying her access to or participation in the storytelling cycle, the history of the nation. See me, she seems to be whispering to her charge, see *us*, if only in the ashes left by your burnings, see us in the traces that slaveholding leaves in the faces of slaveholders. And at the same time, shouting, these faces, these remnants of words are not for you. I am contemplating my private wordself, and you have no right to intervene. And yet again, insinuatingly, I am watching you listen/refuse to listen to me as I tell myself (but implicitly you) this story, and you are angry because you want me to hear you. But in seeing me you see the unwanted, unspoken, rejected side of yourself and refuse that story, that mirror. The child is caught up in this seductive, tangled plot. "For listening," says Gerald Bruns, "is not the spectator's mode; listening means involvement and entanglement, participation or belonging for short" (127). As we read this novel (eye work) we are forced to recall the entirely different work of the ear that, helpless, cannot turn away from the story. But cuts it off. "Don't tell me," says the child, though the expropriation of the ear has no recourse. The child, however, has become the woman, has rejected the ear for the power of the written word, the "Columbus discovered America" that silences the nana's speech.

From yet another vantage, the essential issue in such an exercise in self(selves?)-writing is to point to the operative questions that guide a sensitive reader of the text. Of what significance are traditional distinctions between "fact" and "fiction"? How valid are the kinds of conventional demands we are likely to make of a work of this sort; for example, Is it authentic? Is it correct? Is it complete? What does it tell us about the author? And, for third-world texts, is it politically useful? The double lines of the initial act of storytelling—two individuals, two cultures, two traditions, and implicitly, two languages—imply an ambiguous textual space and an uncomfortable textual reality in which such problems and questions become, at best, undecidable, at worst, irrelevant. Basic tenets of knowledge which anchor reality—Columbus discovered America—are revealed in context as purely fictional, laying open the flayed knower to other fictional perversions: eyes in plates, metamorphosis into an Indian.

Philippe Lejeune observes that "we cannot write 'I was born the . . . ,'" any more than 'I died the . . .' Not that autobiography should give up narrative; but it must put it back in its place, and not allow it to decide, by means of a cliché, an undecidable question, the question of origin" (235–36). The novelist is necessarily haunted by a sense of her personal and communal past, but she realizes as well a double thrust to the question of origins. On the one hand, she (the child) has no history, did not exist, until Columbus arrived in 1492 and discovered the Americas. On the other hand, she (the nana) has a past that is the story of the loss of history, of a past that was uprooted and destroyed by the same historical cataclysm that brought the white child into her world. The beginning of history is also the end of history or, at the very least, the interruption of history into two discontinuous moments, of which one consists of the remembrance not of the other but of the tale of its disappearance. The essential core of the narrative, that toward which the narrative strives, is impossible, unsayable, irretrievably alienated. And yet, that forgotten, unspeakable lost time returns again and again as the absent memory that subverts the text of the present. All this writing, then, in some sense stands in place of that which can never be said, which the nana has started to say: the alternative, eccentric, marginal history that has been wiped away and relegated to children's tales by the official, nation-making truths. The nana, though given the first word, can be silenced at any time. Furthermore, she is licensed to speak only in the form and the language authorized by her capricious child-mistress. And still further, to what degree is Castellanos's assumption of a childlike voice, the recuperation of her personal past, not only a clever act of ventriloquism but a troubling ruse to abdicate responsibility for exploitation (of words or people) through a pose of powerlessness?

Castellanos was well aware of her own blindness in this regard. She wrote feelingly about both her actual nana, whose name was Rufina, and about her *cargadora* (carrier), María Escandón, the woman and the child whom her parents handed over to her as if they were playthings. Her behavior, if not extraordinarily exploitative, was not exemplary either: "I don't think I was exceptionally capricious, arbitrary or cruel. But no one had taught me to respect anyone else except my peers. . . . The day when it was revealed to me in a blinding way that the thing that I made use of was a person, I made an immediate decision: to ask pardon of the person whom I had offended. And I made another vow for the rest of my life: not to take advantage of my position of privilege to humiliate another person." This realization of the essential humanity of a plaything is both wrenching and horrifying, and Castellanos did dedicate much of her life to the cause of indigenous Mexicans. Her dedication, nevertheless, had a curious and inexplicable omission, a blind spot or, harshly, a hypocritical element. After María Escandón had passed thirty-one years at her side, Castellanos, at the time of her marriage, released her old companion to the service of another woman. By Castellanos's own account, that new mistress, Gertrudis Duby, was amazed that during those thirty-one years, Castellanos never found the time to teach her servant to read or write. As Castellanos herself notes, "There I was off playing Quetzalcoatl, the great white civilizing god, while right next to me someone was consumed by ignorance" (Ahern 267–68). The commitment was inconsistent and unreliable at best; the risk, if such a word can be used in this context, no risk at all.

The metaphorical/spiritual "word" ripped away from the Indians in what looks to Western eyes like a translated version of the biblical rape of the Ark of the Covenant later appears in *Balún-Canán* in concrete form as the document composed in Spanish by the embodied memory of the tribe at the command of the landowner and preserved by César Argüello as proof of his rights to the lands of Chactajal. In this document the genealogy of the Argüello family is an incidental detail in the landscape of oppression. "Those who were destined to come, came," says the Elder Brother of the tribe. "They preserved us to humiliate us, to make use of us in servile tasks. They separated us like the chaff from the grain. Good for burning, good for trampling, that's the way we were made, my brothers. See how the cashlán diffused everywhere the splendor born of his skin. See him here, able in demanding tribute, powerful in punishment, walled up in his language as we in our silence, ruling" (56–57).

The Elder Brother's tale forces us to reevaluate the nana's story, which has the same metaphorical base in its focus on issues of memory and silence, on the coming of the Castilian whirlwind, the burning, and the dispersed face of the tribe; it forces us to read the nana's second "they" ("they have burned and been consumed") more ambiguously than we first imagined: they (the cashlanes) burn in a metaphorical hell for their blasphemy; they (the Indians, "good for burning") burn with humiliation and oppression; they (the words) burn away, leaving only silence, dispersed chaff, ashes without a face. The Elder Brother's words suggest as well the degree to which the nana's charge, the seven-year-old girl, has unwittingly absorbed the Indian conquest stories she consciously rejects; her lyrical imagining of her parents' inaccessible faces has the same tone as the Elder Brother's reference to the shining splendor of the Castilian skin, a tone quite different from the matter-of-fact voice used for official knowledge.

It is the persistence of this "knowledge," moreover, rather than the child's rather petulant "Don't tell me that story" that poses the essential narrative dilemma in foregrounding the existence of a force so strong that it leaves no place for the nana's voice, no room to trace her tribal silencing back to its inexpressible origin, no space in which the erased face of the Indian can meet the blinding features of the Castilian. It is this dilemma of the impossible confrontation that drives the narration, that requires the intervention of the reader in order to project and reinscribe it elsewhere, here perhaps, in the political act of bringing it into existence by naming it.

Furthermore, the concrete "ark of memory" of the tribe comes to be reinscribed in the text of *Balún-Canán* through the girl's secret theft of the word, in the reappropriation of the Indian's writing as the genealogy of the Argüello family, the history of abuses which is the family's story in the eyes of the oppressed, which is, in this book, the only full accounting of the girl's ancestors. Significantly, it is the mother who interrupts the girl's reading, barring her way to the dangerous pages of that potentially subversive, unofficial history: "Don't play with these things," she warns her daughter after giving the pages her own surreptitious skimming. "They're the inheritance of Mario. Of the boy" (59). The male, clearly, is the sole occupant of the legal and the literary spaces, displacing the female from both realms entirely. In denying her daughter's right to the papers, Zoraida repeats the age-old tradition of repression, handed down from mother to daughter from time immemorial. As Castellanos writes in *Salomé*, "My mother instead of milk gave me submission" (141). Repression and further marginalization are her heritage, just as the papers are the heritage of her brother.

One of the more interesting aspects of this byplay is the refracted role of the *lector enemigo*. The Elder Brother tells the story for his own people, so that the memory of his people can be preserved. Nevertheless, told at the command of the white landowner, in Spanish, and in writing, the history takes on some of the qualities of a forced confession. Tacitly, hopelessly, the Elder Brother cannot help but know that his text, like his people, has been co-opted for the service of the conquerors in order to justify the Indians' disenfranchisement. The fact that the only reader of the Elder Brother's text in the text of *Balún-Canán* is precisely the disinherited girl-child suggests that within the ranks of the *lectores enemigos* there are also hierarchies and subdivisions. The child, then, represents both oppressor and oppressed and unwittingly serves as a *lectora enemiga* to both the white texts and those of the Indians, from which she is equally estranged. At the same time, life, the silenced lives of the girl and the Indians, continues, as Sommer says in another context, "at the margins of Western discourse, and continues to disturb and challenge it. . . . this return [of the repressed] occurs at the margins of the same imperializing language that it challenges, [and] it helps to define that language by showing what has been excluded" (111).

The central issue in relation to *Balún-Canán*, then, is not historical correctness or congruence with verifiable personal experiences; it is not even a question of philosophical or intellectual adequacy. Rosario

Castellanos turns aside from such traditional expressions of value, for they tend to short-circuit discussion. In an article on Simone de Beauvoir, she states her dissatisfaction with both the traditional male value of lucidity (in its standard definition) and the traditional female value of intuition (a second-rate substitute awarded virtuous females by their condescending male counterparts). Simone de Beauvoir's distinctive quality, for Rosario Castellanos, is poetic: "She discovers, little by little, the most hidden aspects of things" (*Juicios* 22). It is this quality, rather than strictly defined veracity or even verisimilitude, which is most outstanding in her own text as well, counteracting the impacted, overdetermined murmurings of official history. To uncover the hidden aspects of things and name them represents, for her, the primary use value of the double-voiced text as a recontextualization of specific reading and writing practices as political strategies. The story of the self is defined partly by the historical abuses and the continuing imposition of one culture on another and partly by the incongruous and unexpected infiltration of Indian discourse into the very founding gesture of the dominant class, while the two languages and two cultures retain their mutual incomprehensibility. The juxtaposition of the two creates not a harmonious whole but a strategic positioning of an entire set of resistances to repression. To bracket the child and the nana, as critics of this text have traditionally done, is to ignore its most radical contribution, is, in Lionnet's analogy, "acting like the surgeon who blithely 'cures' feminine hysteria by doing hysterectomies" (205). In what follows, then, I would like to undo the hysterectomy, to explore the various conditions of marginalization and responses to oppression (and to repression) in this text, and to examine its implicit criteria for value in naming the undiscovered.

Silence, the traditional characteristic of the indigenous peoples, is not, as the nana has reminded us at the outset of the work, properly speaking a response to oppression; it is, rather, a condition of that oppression itself. Marginalized peoples are excluded from the great conversation that makes up national discourse; their voices and their very being are erased as an unpleasantly dissonant background. The Indians, says the Elder Brother, are walled up in their silence at the time of the conquest; the contemporary landowners continue to enforce this historically established linguistic tradition: "No self-respecting white man," says César, "will condescend to speak in Spanish with an Indian" (177). To speak to the Indians, the landowners employ a few limited phrases of Tzeltal, ignoring with the impunity of those in power all but the few phrases they expect to hear in response, effectively reducing their debt-laborers to a status little removed from that of the horse or the dog, who are also conditioned to respond obediently to a few spoken phrases. The landowners are as uninterested in the conversation and domestic arrangements of their servants as of their cattle; or perhaps the cattle, since they provide meat, interest them somewhat more.

The females of the dominant social class, likewise, are condemned to silence and invisibility. Unheard and unseen, they offer, on another level, the dominant class's unacknowledged counterpart to the repression of the Indians. The child's mother, Zoraida, accepts the traditional role allotted her in exchange for the material comforts accruing from her husband's name. " 'Zoraida de Argüello.' I like the name, it fits me" (89), she tells herself in the single extended interior monologue she is given in the novel, trying to convince herself that her family's decision was the correct and only possible one. The name and the status are what has been chosen for her, what she chooses, what she wants, what she has to tolerate. She maintains her minimal hold on her marriage rights through abject self-humiliation, even though she knows she was sold into marriage like a hen and is about as highly appreciated as one, even though her husband now ignores her since she cannot produce more children, even though she knows of his Indian mistresses and unrecognized children, even though the rest of the family and society at large follow his lead, walling her up in an official silence as profound as that imposed on the Indians, if of a different sort. Her alternatives at this point are strictly circumscribed by custom; to put an end to the continuing humiliations of her marriage by leaving her husband would be to fall into an even less enviable situation: "I don't want a separation, like Romelia has. A woman's a hanger-on everywhere then, and fits nowhere. If she dresses up well and goes out on the street they say she's being a coquette. If she shuts herself in, they think she's up to mischief. Thank God I have my two children. And one is a boy" (90). Self-annulment is the price she pays for the social standing of respectable matrimony; her son is the sole acceptable sign of her tenuous ability to retain this status, distinguished only by being less undesirable than its alternatives. A deromanticized distancing of the feminine and a repressive silencing of her needs are still at the heart of the control mechanism.

Castellanos was always interested in these parallel marginalizations, these two variations on silencing. In her second novel, *Oficio de tinieblas*, the parallel is, if anything, more sharply drawn. One of Zoraida's counterparts is the bitterly unhappy Isabel, whose only child is the daughter of her first marriage and whose relations with her second husband are shadowed by her dreams of liberating herself from the man who flaunts his mistresses before her, from the man to whom she is tied by an incomprehensible passion, from the man who, perhaps with her complicity, killed her first husband, his own brother. The other, more important counterpart is the silent, almost invisible, and only briefly mentioned wife of German immigrant landowner don Adolfo. This woman's fugitive evocation strikingly collapses the implicit linkages of woman and Indian through their parallel marginalization. Doña Ifigenia is an Indian woman, and her duties correspond exactly to those Castellanos defined as her own during her brief, unhappy marriage: "I have to take on all the responsibilities and tasks of a maid. I have to keep the house impeccable, the clothes ready, meals infallibly on time. But I am not paid a salary, I do not get a day off once a week. And I cannot change masters" (Poniatowska, *Vida* 65). Such are the only concessions to humanity awarded don Adolfo's wife. According to the landowner, she has had the supreme good taste to erase herself almost completely from the family's awareness. Her domain is the ranch's kitchen and the ironing board, and "she had the good sense not to pass down to her children," the blue-eyed, white-skinned young women who live in the city, "her skin color (dark, from a Zoque Indian), or the coarseness of her intellect, or the roughness of her customs" (55). Furthermore, doña Ifigenia "never attempted to establish equality with him, and the linguistic barrier had imposed, from the very beginning, a real and tangible limit on their intimacy" (56). She represents, therefore, the perfect wife, hardworking and uncomplaining, silent by necessity since she does not speak the same language as her husband. Any words she might speak, any thoughts she might conceive go unheard and unimagined; her husband's denigration of the "coarseness of her intellect," for example, is a theoretical supposition, a generalized racist insult that obviously can have had no basis in experience. Doña Ifigenia is a woman with no options, no alternatives, not even theoretical ones; she can only wait for fate to return her to usefulness by making her a grandmother. Her position in the household is such that she must continually beg forgiveness for continuing to exist.

In *Balún-Canán*, such official silencing is subjected to resemanticiza-tion. In a first, striking use of the properties of silence, neither the child nor the nana is named, and this silencing of their "proper" names leaves them free to act as markers or position holders while escaping implication through the definition of their functions. This silence as to name marks a transferral of value, the substitution involved in taking charge of silence as the power of concealment, the necessary and elided missing element (nana, child, *hermano mayor*) carving out the path for narrative. "Since it is necessary to write," Clarice Lispector reminds us, "at least do not smudge the space between the lines with words" (*Legion* 114). Castellanos, too, keeps the spaces between the lines clear of reductive clutter. "Daughter," for example, means child of no value, a perceived mistake, a familial burden to be passed on to the future husband, who will (finally) give her a name, his name. The son, Mario, however, encodes the hope of the family for persistence of the name and the heritage. The girl, then, as a thing of no account, has a freedom not allowed the boy; as long as she maintains her passive exterior she can engage in the subtle hypocrisies of invention and storytelling, creating a space for the quietly subversive counterknowl-edge that is this book, the expanded counterpart to the nested tale of the Elder Brother, the gloss on the doubly interrupted story of the nana.

"Who are the ñine guardians," the child asks the mysteriously unattached wandering wiseman, or fool, tío David. His response is to enforce silence once again. "Don't be so inquisitive, child. The elders know, and that's why they call the place Balún-Canán. They give it that name when they talk among themselves. But we, little people, it's better we keep quiet" (28). Too much knowledge may, in fact, infringe on the possibilities encoded in this productive silence. Too much knowledge for the little people, the marginalized people, may also be unsafe. Unlike the nana and the *hermano mayor*, tío David silences his story entirely, but his appearance at the beginning and reappearance at the end of the novel underscore the importance of his untold tale. Toward the end of the novel, after the child has witnessed death and revolt and responsibility for the first time, the old Indian returns; at this point he offers to answer the girl's question of a year before and to take her up the mountain to the "very heart of Balún-Canán, to the very place where the nine guardians live. You'll see them all just as they are, with their real faces, and they'll tell you their true names" (256). The child, perhaps wiser now, refuses such intimate knowledge, turning away the invitation with a lie. She has learned that names told her by others are less significant than the names she tells, in her own way, with her words or with her silence, with her own truth that is the product of her imagination.

As the girl finds her own voice, a new voice, so too do the Indians. Like the Elder Brother, the new speaker for his people uses Spanish, but this time the language of the dominant class is deployed as a conscious political strategy. When Felipe Carranza Pech confronts César over the dining table, the Indians' new voice cannot be as easily dismissed or ignored as those half-understood voices speaking in Tzeltal, cannot be as simply co-opted as the *hermano mayor*'s tribal history. The mechanics of the exchange deserve attention:

> Zoraida muestra a César un rostro contrariado y que exige una explica-ción. César habla entonces al intruso dirigiéndole una pregunta en tzel-tal. Pero el indio contesta en español.
> —No vine solo. Mis camaradas están esperándome en el corredor.
> Zoraida se replegó sobre sí misma con violencia, como si la hubiera picado un animal ponzoñoso. ¿Qué desacato era éste? Un infeliz indio atreviéndose, primero, a entrar sin permiso hasta donde ellos están. Y luego a hablar en español. Y a decir palabras como "camarada", que ni César—con todo y haber sido educado en el extranjero—acostumbra emplear. (97–98)

> Zoraida turns a vexed face to César, mutely begging for an explanation. César speaks to the intruder, asking him something in Tzeltal. But the Indian replies in Spanish.
> "I didn't come alone. My comrades are waiting on the veranda."
> Zoraida starts violently back as if a venomous insect had stung her. What disrespect is this? A lowly Indian presuming first to burst in on them without leave, and then to speak in Spanish! And using words like "comrade," that not even César, with all his foreign education, is ac-customed to using. (95)

Felipe Carranza Pech refuses to be negated as a human being and underlines the fact of his rebellion by speaking to the landowner as an equal, in the landowner's language, the language of access to power, with, as Zoraida quickly notices, the unfamiliar vocabulary of a dif-ferent ideological mode. The confrontation, typically, is between the two men; typically, Zoraida remains the silent spectator, recognized by

César only, and belatedly, in her superior servant-function—she is sent for more coffee. Equally typically, Zoraida's unspoken reaction to the scene is to align herself with her husband in defense of the status quo; her silence and her repression will remain untouched by events. Significantly, however, in terms of the narrative strategy, César's very real power is symbolically undercut. Silent Zoraida is the point-of-view character in this scene, and it is the Indian's words, rather than the landowner's, that are highlighted on the written page corresponding to her record of the exchange.

Like the Indian leader, the girl-child, in order to combat repression, must eventually break silence and speak or write, negotiating the tricky domains of the said and the unsaid, the words written down, as Lispector would have it, smudging the page and the words left, for whatever reason, between the lines. If her first written words, "Mario, Mario, Mario," filling the pages of her first notebooks seem as "cramped and halting" (271) as the hand that writes them, we know that she will go on to other words, will become, as she reminds us in the poem "Pasaporte," a woman of many and contradictory words and of many and devious stories in which the story of Mario, the apparently central story, becomes another code for the many silenced stories, and his name, the spoken, written name, fades into insignificance, into ashes on the wind, in the face of those graver, unspoken names.

When the silence of the marginalized is broken, its first and most essential form of expression is by negation: "just say no." And from this primary oppositional strategy the consolidation of an independent self and a concrete political strategy begins to emerge. Ludmer's seminal discussion of Sor Juana Inés de la Cruz's letter to the bishop of Puebla traces what we might call a symbolic logic of minimalist transformation: A not-A, B not-B, in which the negative functions as the performative metaphor of difference, setting the stage for the emergence of the "I." The negation represents the signal mark of internal division of the field, creating the signifying gap but also motivating potential reconstruction on other terms. To know and to say, mediated, as Ludmer reminds us, by the "no" displays the concealment of both knowledge and speech as the presence of the irrecuperable other.

Silence and distance are only one step of the process Ludmer defines; the next step is the displacement and deferral organized through the agency of negation itself. One could suggest that this tactic operates not only through what she calls the "reorganization of the field of knowledge in function of not-saying (to keep quiet)" (48) but, more important, in a reorganization without functionality, as a negation infinitely represented, infinitely deferred, which could be called, at some remove, an affirmation. Says Castellanos of her most directly experienced familial repression, "I affirmed myself through people who at all times wanted to destroy me. By reflex I said: No longer. But it was a very guilty 'no longer'" (Poniatowska, *Vida* 119). Her guilty and silent refusal of her mother's repeated negation, the *no*'s that limited her activity and circumscribed her opportunities for experience both at home and outside it—the negation of the negation—becomes the essential core of her identity: she is that which, negated (*ninguneada* is the felicitous Spanish word for this condition), has negated the negation and affirms herself as that dangerous essence rejected, marginalized, denied, but nevertheless undeniably present in the energies expended to preserve the status quo.

In *Balún-Canán* the doubled storyteller at the opening of the work suggests a doubled field of operations; the elements involved, however, are exactly those defined by Ludmer: "to know," "to say," and "no," with the permutations defined through the unstable relations of the nana and the child and their mutual ability to limit knowledge and speech in the other. The first and last speech of the opening chapter is given to the nana; in the first case, the child's "no" interrupts the speaking; in the second, the nana's implicit "no" silences the child and ensures obedience. Between these two instances, the narrator weaves the shifting, and destabilizing, patterns of knowledge and speech as relative positionalities rather than absolute concepts.

The nana's opening tale is a story of negation, of memory as the memory of loss. Accordingly, her language figures the violent institutionalization of racial difference as a primary division between saying and not saying. What the nana tells, therefore, is nothing less than the tale of forcible silencing: "They dispossessed us, they tore away . . . the word," later, "leaving ashes without a face." No face, no word. For the nana, no name, no genealogy, no story but the interrupted story of the loss of name, genealogy, story, speech, a recognition confirmed, chillingly, from the other side of the vexed relationship by the girl-child at the end of the novel, when, thinking to recognize her nana in the crowd, she realizes, "Never, even if I see her again, I will never be able to recognize my nana. . . . Besides, all Indians look the same [tienen la misma cara]" (271). The worst of racist clichés, that all Indians look alike, represents, in the context of this work, the nearest approximation the young white girl can make to the most profound reality of Indian life—the loss of face, which is their irremediable historical tragedy, the loss of face, which makes a mockery of the narcissistic impulses of conventional autobiography. In this book, accordingly, the collective "no" of the Indians profoundly complicates any other individual's speech.

What is lacking is the essential, unequivocal knowledge of the Indian's nature, established by the framing of the Balún-Canán with reference to the nana and by markedly denying the nana identity and speech. It is clear in the novel that such a lack and such knowledge urgently require interpretation, but interpretation is impossible because of an act of willful disfiguration and effacement: the silencing of the other. Castellanos's work, uncomfortably, opens with a tale of silencing and closes with a strictly parallel act of silencing; the negation turned against itself.[7]

The nana's uncomfortably effaced knowledge is repeatedly rejected in favor of the child's own set of things she knows. First, however, the child uses her own negation ("Don't tell me that story") as a way of interrupting the telling and discrediting the teller ("She doesn't know. She doesn't know anything") before inserting the list of her own, highly controversial bits of counterknowledge: "Columbus discovered America," "Swiss means fat" (10), and later, "all Indians look the same." The first and third "facts" in the child's list represent cultural clichés so deeply ingrained that they represent the essential cornerstones of knowledge at the basis of the construction of the national identity. The defamiliarization operative in juxtaposing such truisms to the nana's deeply disturbing tale reveals their profound flaws and makes a political statement of considerable force. By placing these bits of knowledge in series with the statement "Swiss means fat" as facts of similar incontrovertibility, the narrator also implies their absurdity.

The same pattern is repeated when the child steals into the father's library and gets access to the forbidden tale of the Elder Brother.

---

[7]In this sense Castellanos's work is quite different from other fictional texts with which it might superficially be compared, works such as Garro's "It's the Fault of the Tlaxcaltecas," or Belli's novel, La mujer habitada (The inhabited woman). Castellanos refuses either to ventriloquize for or to recuperate the Indians even for a politically liberal paradigm.

Again, knowledge of loss is the basis of the Indian's tale, again, the telling (reading) is interrupted by the authoritative "no"—"Don't play with these things," says the mother. Again, the negation is followed by the controverted knowledge of the dominant society implicitly rejected in this context: "They're the inheritance of Mario. Of the boy." In such a context, the idea of knowledge about a person as revealed through a background of concrete, individualized, and objectively verifiable historical fact, which is at the heart of traditional autobiography, demonstrates itself to be either insufficient or distinctly distortional. The negation operates across the board.

Although her discussion of Sor Juana does not develop the implications of the insight, Ludmer also points to another possibility for resistance which goes beyond both silence and negation as tactics of the weak and marginalized. This tactic, she suggests, "consists in that, from the assigned and accepted place, she change not only the meaning of that place but meaning itself of what is installed in it" (53) and, I would add, the meaning of meaning as well. In such a practice, negation does not serve only as an oppressor's means of establishing difference, recuperated for other reasons by the oppressed. Negation allows a space for mental reservations, for unspoken distancing, while suggesting the potential for a creative reappropriation of the negated elements. Thus, the woman artist can effect a transvaluation of values, bridging the gap of difference *on her own terms*, giving substance to the rather abstract principle of self-affirmation adduced by Castellanos in her rebellion against parental pressure. The logic of such reappropriation is neither symbolic nor political but poetic, based on the affirmative and constitutive power of the metaphor. One concrete result is that already theorized by Ludmer as the necessary reinvention of domestic space: "The regional spaces that dominant culture has extracted from the quotidian and personal and has constituted as separate realms (politics, science, philosophy) are constituted in the woman as derived precisely from what is considered personal, private, and quotidian. And if the personal, private, and quotidian are included as the point of departure for these other discourses and practices, they disappear as personal, private, and quotidian" (54). Negation in the first, simple sense neglects the possibilities for individual or communal agency in effecting such reciprocal adjustments. The double negation—refusal of subsumption in the dominant, refusal of alienation in the marginal—creates a disturbance in the fields of discourse.

The crucial element that Rosario Castellanos would add to this two-

step reversal is her realization of the essential fictiveness of experience, her understanding that a system of signs, recognized as arbitrary, remotivates itself in the retelling, engendering a literary self
from the crumbling remnants of the purely personal. To accomplish
this remotivation, however, she needs to forget the rules of the game
of autobiography, "overstepping," as Derrida says, this "*pas* of forgetting" with her own work, in her prose and in her poetry, recovering
as she violates the profoundest sense of the genre. "*Pas* is forgetting" (quoted and trans. in Fineman 140), stepping forward into a
story of what is long lost, long forgotten, long relegated to the realm of
old wives' tales and kitchen fictions. She thus frees herself in the
heady independence that, although fictitious, is lived as real and thus
negates negation itself. The prose/poetry, autobiography/fiction of
Balún-Canán is a natural product of this impulse. Consider the dynamics of this exchange, part of which I quoted earlier out of context:

> Interviewer: ¿Hasta qué punto la poesía ha influído en tu prosa?
> Castellanos: Este influjo se nota fácilmente in *Balún-Canán*, sobre todo en
> la primera parte. En forma estricta, esta obra no puede considerarse
> prosa. . . .
> Interviewer: ¿Cómo llegaste a la prosa?
> Castellanos: . . . Escribí dos cuentos: uno de ellos, "Primera revelación,"
> que es un germen de *Balún-Canán*. Deseaba contar sucesos que no
> fueron esenciales como los de la poesía: sucesos adjetivos. . . . Así,
> casi sin darme cuenta, di principio a *Balún-Canán:* sin una idea general
> del conjunto, dejándome llevar por el fluir de los recuerdos. (Miller
> 125–26)

> Interviewer: Up to what point has poetry influenced your prose?
> Castellanos: This influence is easily noticed in *Balún-Canán*, especially
> in the first part. Strictly speaking, this work cannot be considered
> prose. . . .
> Interviewer: How did you come to prose?
> Castellanos: . . . I wrote two stories; one, "First Revelation," is the germ
> of *Balún-Canán*. I wanted to tell about events that, unlike poetry, were
> not essential: adjectival events. . . . In this way, almost without realiz-
> ing it, I began *Balún-Canán*, without any controlling idea, allowing
> myself to be carried along by the flow of memory.

Castellanos's declaration of the basically adjectival nature of her work
operates as a revolutionary transvaluation of prose, rejecting, im-

plicitly, the tyranny of agency and action, of nouns and verbs, in favor of what is often downgraded as mere ornamentation: superficial, attractive surely, but of less significance. In a move similar to her transvaluation of the transformatory power of the Latin American woman before her mirror, she opposes the adjectival to the essential, reversing the categorical frameworks of modern imagination.[8] In Castellanos *la palabra enemiga* is transformed, polished, held close to the body and to the reader, and that reader, Castellanos's ideal reader, knows the precise mechanism of its formal construction, the particular resources and uses of its form. I do not want to imply that the interviewer, in this case Emmanuel Carballo, is insensitive to these issues because he is a man; I do want to pose the hypothesis that his program, his apparent unwillingness to depart from his prepared script for idiosyncrasies of the writer, is typical of a certain common misunderstanding that is in itself culturally determined by concerns about proper behavior, definitions of a literary property, and examinations of how specific property relations are negotiated linguistically.

In English the connection is almost too direct. Plot, as Lennard Davis reminds us, "has no relation to traditional myths or storytelling. . . . The origin of the word 'plot' is related first to a plot of land, and subsequently to describing that bit of land—that is, plotting its dimensions" (201). In Castellanos's metaphorical history of language as an instrument for domination, she writes, "Perhaps property/propriety [the word *propiedad* means both] was originally understood as a linguistic correction. . . . Speaking was an opportunity to exhibit the treasures of which one was proprietor. . . . But to whom or with whom did one speak?" (*Mujer* 177). Castellanos's *lector hembra* has another value for property/propriety, another program, another face, another place, another force, another interlocutor. Perhaps, as Jean

[8]An alternative reading of Castellanos's preference for the adjectival would be to see it as a feminist appropriation of a male-oriented quality of multiplicity in contrast to a woman's supposedly singular essence. Colette Guillaumin writes: "In whatever context, professional, political, or otherwise, every appropriate qualifying noun is omitted or withheld when denoting agents of the female sex, whereas of course it is these qualifiers alone that are used to designate all other agents. These phrases, for instance, which I collected over the last forty-eight hours: 'a student was punished by a month's suspension, a girl was reprimanded,' . . . 'A company president, a croupier, and a woman,' . . . 'They murdered tens of thousands of workers, students, women.' . . . These phrases, whose imprecision regarding occupation, status, and social function when speaking of the women concerned we find so exasperating, are not mere lapses due to lack of information" (6).

Franco suggests, the heritage of the photonovels has exercised a sinister and deep-rooted influence on writing, as well as on the reading practice of women (*Plotting* 133, 135), who, accustomed to imagining themselves in the glamorous photographs of mass-market fiction, look for their romantic counterparts in noncentrist politicized works as well. Perhaps, as Castellanos suggests, the process is more complex. She would agree with Franco to the degree that she also notes its narcissistic component: "When a Latin American woman takes a piece of literature between her hands she does it with the same gesture and the same intention as that with which she picks up a mirror: to contemplate her image," and this image, true to the photonovel form, "is dressed in silks and velvets, adorned with precious metals and jewels." But Castellanos adds a disquieting rider in the form of a question: the adornments "change her appearance as a serpent changes its skin to express . . . What?" (*Mujer* 144).

It is in this undefined "what" that Castellanos hints at the potential for a revolutionary recuperation of the form in the service of those marginalized members of society: "Latin American women novelists seem to have discovered long before Robbe-Grillet and the theoreticians of the *nouveau roman* that the universe is surface. And if it is surface, let us polish it, so that it leaves no roughness to the touch, no shock to the gaze. So that it shines, so that it sparkles" (*Mujer* 144). Suggestively, Castellanos points to the startling possibilities of a feminine aesthetics as a model for feminist politics, in her evocation of the unmistakable image of the bored upper-class woman as the model for the woman writer. Her polished prose can never be mistaken for a masculine attention to style. Instead, she inverts the photonovel's message of being-for-a-man and revalorizes its typical image as the expression of an irreducible femininity.

The plot has everything to do with what society considers proper. Lennard Davis notes that "whatever period we are discussing, the necessity for considering location as replete with ideology and serving the purposes of a social defense has to be considered. Property is always *there* of course, but in novels it is *there* with a vengeance. . . . These places, that pretend to be open spaces of the real, are actually claustrophobic encampments of the ideological. As such they are not ancillary to but the absolute concomitant of the novel's discourse" (101). Does the traditional novel pretend to present a dimensionless boudoir? Castellanos will respond with a boudoir relentlessly high-

lighted, its ideological underpinnings displayed in the pitiless in-
tertext. Is the woman marginalized as frivolous, merely intuitive,
childlike? Castellanos offers a narrative of an unwanted, untutored,
thoughtlessly cruel girl-child, whose irresponsible and frivolous act
causes (she believes) the death of her brother and the destruction of
her world. *Balún-Canán* does not provide a model to imitate or a
mimetic reflection to contemplate; it creates a polished surface to
triangulate desire (nana, *niña,* and a third term, the female reader), a
free space for self-invention. It is also an ideologically charged act to
reject such elaboration as trivial or decorative.

Back in Comitán, in the provincial schoolroom, a tired schoolmis-
tress displays before the bored little girls under her tutelage the catalogue of her meager knowledge, permitting "each of us to choose the
knowledge that best fits us. From the beginning I chose the word
'meteor.' And from that time on I have worn it on my forehead, sad
from having fallen from the sky" (16). The sun emanating from the
Castilian skin of the conquerors shines, blinding the Indian; the child's
light is a nighttime light, a fugitive, "fallen" track across the sky. Her
identity is never meant for monumentalization in a bulky history.
Instead, we note her passage briefly and she is gone, age eight, almost
before we have time to register her existence, restored and effaced/de-
faced in a single gesture. "I'm afraid," says the child in the opening
pages of the book, "that there might be a mirror on the other side of the
table," a mirror that might reveal, for example, not only that Indians
do all have the same face but that the single face of the Indian is one
she too shares—that all oppressed people, not only Indians, share the
same mirror-face. And so she invents herself in the metaphorical
slicing of a fugitive word across her sky: "meteoro" in the beginning of
her schooling, deformed to "Mario" in the last untold story, the story
of her brother's short life and premature death, the beginning of
writing.

Rousseau ends his *Confessions* with the act of reading his *Confessions.*
It was, as H. Porter Abbott says, "a shrewd idea" that initially resolves
the thorny problem of the slippage between property and propriety,
positing a specific audience to whom the work is directed or with
whom this prize possession is to be shared. Abbott continues: "Rousseau selected for this event an audience of the highest breeding and
most exquisite sensitivity. Yet the observable effect of this reading
(silence, disturbed only by the enigmatic trembling of Madame d'Eg-

mont) . . . only heightened the pathos of his effort to control response through the control of form" (610). I am disturbed by the silence and the "enigmatic trembling" of exquisitely sensitive Madame d'Egmont; however, since my topic is not Rousseau but Castellanos I merely point out the careful negotiation of the issues of self-writing and the reception of that writing as acts of self-possession and repossession. Castellanos's work ends, as the nana began it, with the image of empty hands. The child is dispossessed, deprived of voice, and in enforced muteness she finds the strength to take up her pencil and begin to write: "With my awkward, unsteady handwriting I began writing the name 'Mario.' Mario on the bricks of the garden. Mario on the walls in the hall. Mario in the pages of my notebooks. Because Mario is far away. And I want to ask his forgiveness" (271). Ironically, the story is, as her mother predicted, the posthumous inheritance of someone else, if not of the son, Mario—for he has, in death, gone far indeed—then of some other heir, equally beloved, equally hated, equally foreign. Although very different from Rousseau's concluding gesture, Castellanos's final words also offer an implicit commentary on the communal/self-portrait she is drawing/erasing: that the conflictual rescue of buried memories is as much a decomposition as a recuperation, that it is all but impossible for the forgotten trace to speak of more than the process of its repression, that it is as much her torment as her salvation that the reader, male or female, mirror or reflection, must complete the shifting disenvelopment of appearances, that what we do with this property, this *Balún-Canán*, is, by her license, a matter for our own sense of decorum.

Tales from the Dark Continent

María Luisa Puga's narrative presence in her first novel is limited to a secondhand reference in passing. Nyambura, a Kenyan postgraduate history student, meets an unnamed earnest young Mexican woman in a literature class and accepts an invitation to coffee. She is bored and distrustful of the Mexican woman's ambition to write a novel about Africa, and she immediately decides that they could never be friends. The Mexican woman wants intimacy; the Kenyan woman is repelled: "(I don't know what I am going to do if I don't see anything. I don't feel anything, she said) while Nyambura for her part, looking for her own feet, her tone, her world, knew that if she saw her hostess in the street she would pretend not to know her." The Mexican woman's perception of a parallel between the Latin American and the African experiences of colonization and liberation, she suggests, offers her a privileged position from which to stand in describing Kenya, "and I know, I know very clearly, that I do have to write the book and try to establish bridges that do not cross through Europe" (276). Nyambura looks around the hotel room, inaccessible to her people except as maids cleaning up after the tourists, looks at her hostess and sees not her counterpart from across the ocean but another white face.

In these few pages at the end of the novel, Puga reveals the intent of her effort, but also how shallow and unrealizable that effort is. Indefectibly, the white returns, to establish bridges, to set the pace for cultural approximation, to define marginality with reference to the acculturated self. The white returns, but problematized and marked as such. In traditional novels, the bridge is a given of the superior white culture, beyond remark. Any alienation can be overcome by the aesthetic approximations of art. In Puga's novel, however, alienation clearly cannot be overcome; it is the constant condition of the work itself to struggle against alienation while enforcing recognition that the conflict is, essentially, unresolvable. The black, inevitably, remains a blank; the white is doubly marked, marked in both senses: as witness to inscription and as the only possible inscribed object. It is wholly understandable, and practically inevitable in context, that the African woman would find the Mexican's conversation boring, her project only intermittently insightful. The two margins meet, and despite superficial resemblances between their individual political pasts, find they have very little in common after all.

Puga does not, curiously, go to Ngũgĩ wa Thiong'o, the Kenyan writer and political prisoner to whom she dedicated her first work. Ngũgĩ, writing from the standpoint of the indigenous peoples, more clearly defines the political repercussions of the linguistic stakes undergirding the kind of scenario Puga describes in the whirlwind literary tour of the north of Mexico which takes her to the impoverished Yaqui-dominant provincial town of Vícam. "To choose a language is to choose a world," he writes in one of his many articles on the topic of African languages. And he continues: "If you write in a foreign language, French for instance, you can reach only a French-speaking audience; if in English, an English-speaking audience; in practice, foreigners and those of your people who know that foreign language. . . . If a Kenyan acts a play in English . . . he cannot possibly be assuming a truly Kenyan audience" (*Writers* 53–54). In this manner, he says in a later work, in using the languages of colonization, "the African novel was further impoverished by the very means of its possible liberation" (*Decolonising* 70). The works of such great writers as Chinua Achebe and Wole Soyinka are not, he finds, African at all, strictly speaking, but Afro-European, direct products of an unquestioned and unproblematized cultural imperialism embedded in African peoples through their most primary educational structures.

To correct the kind of miseducation Ngũgĩ describes in Africa, he counsels revising educational mores and seriously reevaluating the pertinence and usefulness of the European canon to the present and future education of African students. Instead of a continued concentration on Western European masterpieces, Ngũgĩ advocates an emphasis on (1) indigenous literatures, both the traditional oral forms and the contemporary works written in African languages; (2) "antiimperialist literatures from Asia and Latin America and literature from socialist countries," which depict parallel historical struggles against racism, colonialism, and the various forms of imperialist domination; and (3) an informed and rigorous reevaluation of all works of art, both foreign and native, in relation to their potential contribution to the positioned critique of repressive social structures (*Politics* 30, 38). Only in such a manner, he suggests, can African peoples, slowly and with great difficulty, begin to speak to each other without the mediating influence of those remnants of colonial power encoded in the linguistic structures of the language.

Las posibilidades del odio (The possibilities of hatred) in some sense attempts to rise to the challenge of Ngũgĩ's call for an antiimperialist dialogue with Latin America.[9] It is an unusual novel, as distinct as possible from such bastions of Mexican literature as the canonical works of Paz and Fuentes and other writers whose nuanced explorations of the nature of Mexicanicity have been greeted both at home and abroad with recognition and applause. It is striking on first glance because in setting the novel in Nairobi, Puga implicitly comments on the inward-turning nature of almost any other Mexican novel one can bring to mind. She expands the horizons of center and margin and

---

[9]The original paper, "Literature and Society," was read in a conference of teachers of literature in Nairobi in 1973, predating by several years the dates of composition (1976–77) of Puga's novel.

redefines the periphery in an entirely different way. It is striking also in its ambitiousness and in its internal recognition of the impossibility of achieving its goal of speaking about Africa to Africans as well as Latin Americans. Puga eventually comes to the unhappy realization that the history of Kenya inscribed in the pages of her novel does not differ markedly from the tourist guide's superficial patter, because sympathy and desire are not enough to bridge the abysses of incomprehension between the writer and her subject. The bridge that the Mexican woman of the final section of the novel dreams of extending between the two continents will be crossed only in one direction, if at all, and imperfectly at that. Her reconstruction of Nyambura's struggle against the forces of a Eurocentric writing of history is admittedly a flawed fictional account. Likewise, the Kenyan student Jeremiah sees Mexican student José Antonio as a tourist and an employer, not as his third-world counterpart and even less as a comrade in the struggle; Julius, the embittered and rebellious friend of the establishment black in another vignette, dreams of the University of California at Berkeley, not the Universidad Nacional Autónoma de Mexico; and Nyambura takes her scholarship to Rome, not the New World.

The novel consists of six vignettes of varying length alternating with a schematic chronology of important events in Kenya's history, from 1888 to the last entry, which corresponds to 1973. Each vignette takes the form of a dialogue, or implicit dialogue, between two characters. In the first, a white tourist guide provides the visitor from Europe with a counterintroduction to the African setting, feeding his tourist companion a vision of Kenya that is patently inaccurate, incomplete, intentionally filtered for foreigners, a picture in which smiling natives and quaint customs predominate. Overall, this is the Africa of safaris and dancing natives, the fuzzed and beautified Africa commodified for external consumption, like some exotic dessert. The guide's own ignorance and bigotry and dislike emerge only gradually in drunken ramblings and parenthetical asides. These comments provide another side to the picture—not *the* other side, since both sides of the guide's depictions are equally reductionist and clearly distortionary: "It never occurred to him to think about the blacks, the Asians, or themselves, the whites, because even in his school there had been some black students. Not Kenyan blacks, but ambassadors' children from other parts of Africa, but still, blacks after all" (14). Or later, "And if one looks at the thing straightforwardly, Aren't they one more tribe? A white tribe? What fault is it of theirs to be the best?" (17). The white Kenyan makes the seemingly unanswerable argument from experience in his exposure of what he must consider the dark underbelly of the dark continent. If in his minimal schoolboy non-contacts with the children of foreign ambassadors he never actually met a Kenyan black person, child or adult, well, as Castellanos might ironically remind the reader, all blacks have the same face.

In the second vignette, the narrative voice and point of view shifts abruptly to the invisible population ignored in the tourist guide. A twenty-six-year-old beggar watches and listens indifferently to the innocently cruel comments of a child who passes by every day with his mother. The beggar, for his part, has come to accept and discount hunger and other discomforts as permanent conditions no longer deserving of note. For him, time, like hunger, like the concept of hope, has no meaning: "But time did not exist. . . . It was not even a vigil for death. There was no time for death. . . . This particular minute was all there was" (28). The beggar's story, then, suggests not only an implicit dialogue with the hope and well-being and orientation toward the future represented by the middle-class child; it is also a commentary on and critique of that other Africa depicted in the tourist guide. And yet, from another point of view, the Africa of the beggar is no less a stereotype than the Africa of the safari. While apparently showing us the poverty from the "inside," Puga also shows us the Africa most familiar to us from our newscasts: the Africa of the starving millions: helpless, hopeless, with no recourse. The mediation of his all-too-familiar poverty by the well-fed child who happens to register his presence as a feature in the daily landscape, suggests a very real filter for distancing and buffering the impact of the beggar's tale.

In the third tale, the tourist guide returns, transmuted into the young black student, Jeremiah, who agrees to take the conventionally leftist, rich, young, pseudo antitourist, the Mexican student José Antonio, to see the "real" Africa. José Antonio despises the safaris and the native dances usually included in the standard package tour and seems to define reality as drinking in the working-class bars that the wiser Jeremiah would like to avoid, lying on proletarian beaches that working people have little leisure to visit, and having sexual relations with a real African woman (when he finally accomplishes this adventurous undertaking, he is shocked and grieved to discover that the woman, though not a prostitute, is quite happy to take his money and leave him without regrets). José Antonio wants to be friends; Jeremiah wants to pay his father's hospital bills. José Antonio complains about the insensitivity of gringo tourists in Mexico, their superficiality, their lack of interest in the uglier side of Latin American life—all of which he has tried to ameliorate: "He had helped Doris. . . . He took her all over Mexico. He had intentionally thrust her into everything so that she would lose her fear—her disgust—so that Mexico would become real to her" (78). Jeremiah dreams of the day when he can abandon the Mexican who is making his life so difficult, so dangerous, and so humiliating: "I am learning to ask for what I don't want in order to get what I want; for this reason my father asked me if I was learning how to be truly poor" (72). Jeremiah recognizes the oppressiveness of the Kenyan system and his own marginalization within it; he recognizes with an impotent hatred the doubly humiliated oppression of his present interaction with the Mexican student. Like the beggar, however, he does not dwell on his congenital discomfort; his concerns are more immediate: his father's poor health and his own powerlessness to assist. José Antonio's impassioned appeals, couched in the rhetoric of the well-informed, right-thinking, politically conscious human being, are somehow all the more intolerable for their shortsightedness and well-fed patina of concern. Jeremiah simply cannot imagine himself in the scenario of transcontinental solidarity José Antonio tries to create.

Jeremiah's counterpart in the fourth episode is the pathetically eager-to-please establishment black, an administrative supervisor raised to that level by his willingness to buy into the white man's myth of the happy native, assisted in the task of self-improvement by a beneficent white colonization. Unfortunately, the narrator is not able to enjoy the benefits of his position and instead lives perpetually anguished. His English is not good enough for him to understand clearly or follow completely the instructions from the white man who gives him orders, and he has to fumble along in constant fear of making major blunders through mistranslation. The supervisor is effectively isolated from both blacks and whites; appropriately, his monologue is directed at his friend Julius, the missing interlocutor. Julius has had all the advantages of good schooling and a thorough training in English; his friend finds it incomprehensible, crazy, that Julius has not put these talents to work in order to rise in the company hierarchy. The climax of the story is almost inevitable. Misunderstanding the English instructions, the supervisor loses his job for not performing a simple errand. His former employer blacklists him and he is unable to get another job.

Each of these tales is a moral parable, meant to serve as counterpoint and counterpart to the complementary histories ciphered in the schematic lists of names and dates. In the fifth story, however, we move more obviously into the territory of the fable. We return once again to the point of view of a white man, this time an expatriate British teacher who comes to Kenya with a detailed plan to teach and organize the blacks, eventually to use his own carefully planned assassination as catalyst for revolutionary confrontation. The man's complicated plan involves reducing all the individuals touched by it, including himself, to emblems: White Oppressor, Black Mother, Revolutionary Student. And the hatred spawned of this reductionism also feeds into his plan. As he says at the outset, echoing the inbred consciousness of superiority voiced in more blatantly racist terms by the tourist guide, "I knew from the time that I was very young that I belonged to the dominant race" (145). His instinct is to reject—albeit incompletely and in bad faith—the concomitant sense of white superiority while retaining the impulse to dominate. By the end of the tale, he is able to tell his student/stepson/assassin Makini, "You are doing the right thing in killing me. It will be your purification. The beginning of true liberation. Although, do not forget, you can only kill me when I decide that the time is right. That is the trick of superiority" (181). Thus, even the promised liberation is tainted, and the emblematic colonizer demonstrates that for the black peoples of Kenya, nothing can be achieved independently or on their own terms. "One truth at home and another abroad," says Trinh Minh-ha, to which I might add, one truth for whites and another for blacks. Trinh continues, "the same logic compels the native to endure the enculturation process and to resist acculturation" (*Woman* 58). Even in killing the white man, Makini follows the white man's script, is inscribed in the white man's concept of revolutionary activity, is excluded from equality with him.

Nyambura, the central character of the last and longest of these six tales, almost a novella, must pull together these emblematic presences. They all—from tourist guide, to establishment black, to radicalized students—represent some integral part of herself, some crucial element of the contradictory set of complexes and reactions that is her own tenuously knotted identity. Like the tourist guide, Nyambura has been shaped and deformed by her education: her "history," shockingly, is not far distant from his. Like the beggar, Nyambura knows "the real Africa" from the inside, but she knows that it is knowledge too scant and fragmentary to be of service in confronting official historians. Her mother is long dead, and her father's symbol of his authority under a Westernized regime—the ever-present pens in his shirt pocket—is more solid to her than her mother's stories. Then, too, like the other young black Kenyans in the novel—the struggling student, the unidentified supervisor, the activist—Nyambura has been shaped by the structures of colonialist imposition, even when that imposition wears its most benign mask. The native culture she retains has been both overdetermined and impoverished. Trinh Minh-ha again: "With a kind of perverted logic, they work toward your erasure while urging you to keep your way of life and ethnic values *within the borders of your homelands.* . . . Tactics have changed since the colonial times and indigenous cultures are no longer (overtly) destroyed (preserve the form but remove the content or vice versa)" (*Woman* 80). These assigned and unsurpassable limits are drawn historically as well as individually. Looking back over the stories, we can imagine a paced chronology as well as a superimposed synchronicity of scenes. The white man arrives and invents Africa in Western terms (tourist guide); later, he allows the "real" Africa (the beggar) to impinge on his consciousness marginally as local color. Reinterpretation in third-worldist terms follows (Jeremiah and José Antonio). Subsequently, various international interests discover the potential for African investment through white-run companies (chapter 4), and leftist theories of liberation are imported with the white revolutionary.

Unlike Makini, however, who has been trapped by the discourse toward which he looked for liberation, Nyambura rejects all colonialist discourse even in the certain knowledge that she cannot get outside its historical structures. Her values and sense of self are inextricably bound up in her love for her Westernized father and non-Westernized mother; in her resistance to acculturation, even as the educational system codes her culturally and allows her no other access to the greater discourse of the nation; in her weakly motivated and half-committed support for her brother's political activism. What is left for a native rewriting of history? For Nyambura her only recourse is to continue the thankless job of filling in blanks that she herself has torn in the seamless fabric of historical discourse, in the difficult labor of unsaying one story so as to create the space for another. For you, the white boyfriend complains bitterly, "everything is colonization" (188). Chris means the statement as an accusation, perhaps an exaggeration; for Nyambura, however, "everything is colonization" is a simple fact, a tragic fact of African existence. Nyambura looks around: at herself, with her Europeanized background, her white boyfriend, her Italian companions; at her circumstances, studying for a postgraduate degree in African history in Rome, of all places. And she is forced to ask herself, "Did Africa really exist?" (243). The only assurance of its (and her) existence she can seem to find is in her own loneliness and hatred, the only common conditions she can identify in her people and her country.

Kenya in this novel is a place of muted hatreds, filtered almost inarticulately through the six vignettes, refracted at some unpredictable remove of ignorance or misunderstanding. *Odio* (hatred) is, unsurprisingly, the most obsessively repeated word of the novel; yet it escapes comprehension. Each of the vignettes points to concrete injustices that cry for redress, that validate and define the hatred. Yet "hatred" is what is thought and felt, not said; the word somehow eludes speech, and the reader is left with the impression that even if shouted it could not be grasped (must not be grasped; the hatred is directed at us).

The work, then, is constructed around and takes the form of these modified case histories. They feel less like chronicles than like short stories, but Puga enacts an uneasy compromise with their very literariness, which is felt as somewhat peculiar, perhaps even inappropriate to the form. It is as if Puga's intention is neither veracity nor verisimilitude, as if she does not intend to make her tales psychologically convincing or even persuasive. She is offering us exemplary texts. There is no debate, no in-depth study of characters or issues, no concerted attempt at psychological portrayal. The voices of her characters are not so much quoted as ventriloquized—and all the more marginalized from their incipient particularity because of it. Perhaps, as Nyambura and the Mexican woman in the sixth vignette would agree, such overdrawing is inevitable, given the Latin American woman's abyssal remove of ignorance; perhaps it is even necessary as a first step in the literature of social struggle. All the characters are representative types of one sort or another, with the heightened colorings that belong to what Georg Lukács has defined as the typical. We could, in fact, hypothesize that Puga's goal is to construct a historical novel of the Lukácsian sort, in which typical characters are set in motion on a field, like paired marbles that intersect and collide with other marbles, creating a shifting portrait of an evolving society.

Essentially, then, the crucial concern of the novel is black Africa's relation in and to history, but it is a relation to history marked and charged by a particular omnipresent sense of belatedness, of always arriving in the world's attention in a secondary, subordinate, or derivative role. History, even for Nyambura, who has dedicated her professional career to its disentanglement, is the ultimate colonizing weapon. To stand outside history is impossible; to remain inside the constructions of history allotted her even more impossible. She shuttles back and forth, advancing little. Her intuitive history is the history of the appropriation of history, of the collective loss of self-determination of an entire continent. Official history is the decomposed and remembered tale of an Africa immaculately conceived with a word from outside—with a "Let there be . . ." pronounced by the first white explorers to set their impressions down on paper—and then hauled into being, a monstrous birth, the child of miscegenation. It is unsurprising then, that history betrays itself in Africa, mutilates itself, becomes liable to self-forgetfulness, displays itself as unknowable. It is unsurprising that "politics," "chronologies," "history" are distrusted as rhetorical games, as the refusal of other types of knowledge, as a kind of shield held up against a reality one does not want to have to comprehend. It is precisely fitting that the sole sympathetic white figure in the book, the British revolutionary, reminds his students of the lessons of history by enforcing eternal remembrance at the very moment of their supposed triumph over him and what he represents. It is instantly comprehensible how the dissolution of her certainty as to the purity and necessity of historical studies leaves Nyambura mistrustful, embittered, increasingly solitary, and full of self-doubt. History is, in the ultimate analysis, the constellation of all the multifarious possibilities for hatred evoked throughout the text.

The most striking and problematic image in Puga's text for this undesired, unrejectable history is the aborted child. Children haunt the narrative, but it is only in the last two chapters that the image crystallizes into the figure of the unborn, never to be born child of miscegenation. Before arriving in Kenya, the white activist lays out his plan of action:

a] Conseguir un empleo en una secundaria. . . .
b] Casarme con una local. . . .
c] Hacer un escándalo en algún sitio público que cree un conflicto con la
   posición blanca. . . .
(No cometer el error de aprender la lengua local. Hay que ser aceptado,
   no asimilado. Parte del truco de la superioridad es que la masa siente
   que el superior es distinto y no viceversa.) (152)

(a) Get a job in a high school. . . .
(b) Marry a local woman. . . .
(c) Cause a scandal in some public place that creates a conflict with the
   position of the whites. . . .
(Do not commit the error of learning the local language. It is essential to
   be accepted, not assimilated. Part of the hoax of superiority lies in the
   fact that the masses feel that what is superior is different and not vice
   versa.)

His plan succeeds marvelously well. As he predicts, provincial schools
are eager to hire a real Brit, and he has no difficulty finding an appropriate school as a base from which to launch his subversive activities.
Likewise, proposition b is easily accomplished; he proposes marriage
to a chance-met black prostitute and is mistrustfully accepted. Creating a scandal, in a country full of racial tension, is even easier. But how
to get himself killed? His wife, Flavia, provides the motive. She becomes pregnant and, against her wishes and the wishes of her brother,
the white man's protégé, has an abortion, providing Makini with the
personal motives for assassination:

—Tiene que comprender. Debe comprender. La superioridad es un
   truco.
—No entiendes. Quería ese niño.
—Sí, me doy cuenta. . . .
—¿Por qué dejaste morir a mi hermano?
—No era su tiempo. Hay todos los otros por ahora. Ésos son tus her-
   manos.
—Te mataré.
—Ya sé. Espero que tú no lo olvides. (179–81)

—You have to comprehend. You must comprehend. Superiority is a
   hoax.
—You don't understand. She wanted that baby.

—Yes, I realize that. . . .
—Why did you let my brother die?
—It wasn't time for him to be born. There are all the others right now.
 They are your brothers.
—I'll kill you.
—I already know that. I hope you don't forget it.

The revolution profits from and is tainted by the death of this child, the child it fails to produce, the child it buries, aborted. And this foreclosing of the future stymies the potential thrust of history, infects history, denies it. For the history of Africa is, cruelly, a hoax, the sleight of hand of an ingrained sense of superiority meeting a conditioned inferiority complex: the white man's imposition on a black female, the center's domination of the margin. What ought to be, is not. What might have been, cannot be. What will be, is not yet. Reality is contained and programmed by covert control over its means of reproduction. Puga's white instigator of revolution, furthermore, can be directly inserted into the model Doris Sommer so succinctly adduces of the Latin American intellectual, for whom "the privilege of education often brings with it a combination of guilt, social responsibility, and a kind of superiority that breeds messianism. . . . To be an intellectual is precisely not to come from the people, or . . . to return to them" (112–13). In the case of Puga's revolutionary agitator, the split is reinforced and dramatized.

In Nyambura's case, the roles, though not reversed, shift slightly. Chris wants her to stay in Europe, to subscribe, as he does, to middle-class British values. Nyambura rebels. Imagine, she tells him, speaking quickly, knowing that she is going to leave him, imagine that they were to get an apartment, buy plants, ask her father's forgiveness, invite her brother to visit, begin to have mixed-race children, go to the beach in the summer, watch the children grow up speaking Italian and maybe going to the United States and joining the black power movement. Yes, he answers, just like that. "Oh, no," she responds, "I don't want to. It horrifies me. I don't want a future. I don't even want very much present. . . . I don't want to be happy" (301–2). No less than the activist of the previous tale, Chris wants to write Nyambura's history for her, to tell her tale and put an artificial happy ending on the final page. Yet her entire experience of history has led her, on the contrary, to this moment of rejection, which she cannot help but see in terms of a continuing colonization. She rejects in one action, then, the investigation of the past (the confusing and misleading formal studies of the historical record) and the projection of a future based on this lie of a comprehensible, learnable, if not common, history, drawing herself inward until the present moment becomes the focus of her attention. No genealogy then. No children either. Death of her mother and brother on the one hand; anterior death of her potential children on the other.

Unlike Lispector, neither Puga nor Castellanos rests on the "now-moment" of scrupulously refined negation. Both Puga and Castellanos end their novels with the beginning of the telling, in writing, of the story. Both emphasize that their story is not a history but something like and something else, as fits a concentration on a people victimized and marginalized by history. In Castellanos, the child laboriously begins to fill notebooks with the word "Mario"; in Puga, the black woman listens to the Mexican woman discuss the potential outline of her projected novel. In both cases, then, the novel we have just read is, simultaneously, the past and the future of reading, at the same time emphasizing its presence, here and now, in the precise moment of its conception. This unresolvable dialogue with historical boundaries is one of the interminable conversations of writing on the margins.

7

In a Subjunctive Mood:
Denise Chávez, Maxine Hong Kingston,
and the Bicultural Text

Luisa Valenzuela, trying to write about feminine language and about the body and writing, comes upon the image of the "cow-word" and in her short story "Other Weapons" brilliantly works through the painful symmetries of *una espalda azotada* (a wounded back) and *la palabra azotada* (the word-wound, the wounded word). Alicia Partnoy, the Argentinian poet, speaks from bitter experience of *el lector enemigo.* Each of these formulations presupposes a fiercely antagonistic struggle or a bittersweet alienation from the languages these women speak, and must do violence to, and from the languages that speak, as they violate, their most intimate selves. Gayatri Spivak refers to the "structure of certification we cannot not want to inhabit" when she writes about the simultaneous operation of resistance to and seduction by the appeal of the dominant discourse in a postcolonial writer/critic. It is this type of intersection between violation by the other and betrayal of the self which undergirds all these formulations, forcing the complex and subtle double-voicing of the literary text. It is, however, a delicate operation to study these sliding structures of violence, and the boundaries, as Valenzuela writes, "may be too subtle and ambiguous to be delineated" ("Word"). For that same reason, when two languages and two cultures are involved, this double-voicing is forced into the foreground, making it somewhat easier to mark in the bicultural work the textual site of the functioning of translation-as-violation.

We could call the study of these interstices semiology or phantasiology or, following Nicolas Abraham and Maria Torok, cryptonomy, though only in a value-neutral sense. I choose to begin with the

Whorfian hypothesis: briefly, that the perspective of each individual language determines (and overdetermines) our view of reality. Benjamin Whorf's conclusion, derived from his work with the Hopi people in the 1930s, has been largely discredited. Philosophers and linguists point to the circularity of its logic; anthropologists complain that it is merely intuitive and that experimental verification is impossible.[1] For literary studies, however, Whorf remains suggestive, particularly in relation to ethnic minority texts, as a cautionary voice. We critics work daily with some version of the insight credited to Whorf, as we confront continually and with uncompromising force the necessity and impossibility of carrying one set of cultural assumptions across to another linguistic-cultural complex, aware at all times, if we are honest with ourselves, of the slippery and marginal tenability of our mediatory positions.

One consolation, one bit of relief, comes to us from theory. In "The Pit and the Pyramid," Derrida writes: "This entire logic, this syntax, these propositions, these concepts, these names, . . . this very language are engaged in the *system of this unpower*, this structural incapacity to think without *relève*. To confirm this, it suffices to make oneself understood within this system. For example, to name a machine a machine, functioning a functioning, work a work, etc. Or simply to ask *why* one has never been able to think this, to seek its causes, reasons, origins, foundations, conditions of possibility, etc. Or even to seek other names" (*Margins* 107). At issue in this structural incapacity is a conception of language that buries most deeply its most critical natural necessities, a system of power (or unpower, of blindness) characterizing the hidden history of rhetoric and metaphysics. The problem is, I think, well posed by Derrida. I would like to displace the complexities of the Derridean analysis of Hegel, however, to work in the interstices of another striking, if illicit, conjunction. For Abraham and Torok, cryptonymy is characterized by a displacement of words "arising from the lexical contiguity of the various meanings of the . . . *allosemes* as they are catalogued in a dictionary. . . . the real originality of the procedure . . . lies in replacing a word by the synonym of its alloseme." This displacement, as Abraham and Torok describe it, is not a metonymic transfer of representations but rather a

---

[1]See for example John B. Carroll's introduction to Whorf's *Language, Thought, and Reality* and Robert Miller, pp. 103–20.

disfigured translation, "a metonymy of words" in which "the word itself as lexical entity constitutes the global situation from which one particular meaning is sectioned out of the sum total of meanings" (19). Whorf comes to an interestingly parallel concept through his study of comparative linguistics: "A covert linguistic class may not deal with any grand dichotomy of objects, it may have a very subtle meaning, and it may have no overt 'reactances' with certain overtly marked forms. It is then what I call a *cryptotype*. It is a submerged, subtle, elusive meaning, corresponding to no actual word, yet shown by linguistic analysis to be functionally important in the grammar" (70). By means of this distinction, Whorf hopes to clarify the difference between a figure of speech or a formality, used, for example, for ritualistic reasons, and a deeper structure unconsciously projecting a particular linguistic construction as a world view. His cryptotype helps resolve the questions of the ethnographer or linguist interested in why, for example, the Hopi use an animately marked plural form for "clouds" but can also begin to address the more abstract concerns of concepts of time and space in other cultures (57–58, 70–79, 153–58). From their very different perspectives, Whorf and Abraham and Torok join Derrida in emphasizing the function of what Whorf calls the covert—in other terms, the resistances to analysis which in their obstructiveness serve to situate evaluation. For our purposes, Whorf complements Abraham and Torok in his recognition of the cryptotype as part of a syntactic field; for Abraham and Torok, the cryptonym is an elided segment in an associative sequence, reconstituted as a "verbarium."[2]

Whorf, Derrida, and Abraham and Torok, in their different vocabularies and different modes of analysis, suggest ways other than the thematic to begin to describe the different "feel" in women-authored bicultural texts. They help to circumscribe the field that will allow us to look at the operation of subtle displacements in the work of Denise Chávez and Maxine Hong Kingston. To their arguments, I wish to add one more, derived from Spanish grammar: the subjunctive mood of the verb, a mood that of necessity takes its cue from context and encodes a delicate interdependency and careful distinction between two fragments of a discursive structure.

[2]The full elaboration of this conjunction would require more space than I have available here. I leave it to my idealized *lector complice* to imagine the potential theoretical implications.

The subjunctive mood traditionally carries another freight of signification and recalls a history of relationships—linguistic and social—
ordered and arranged according to a well-defined institutional hierarchy: of the sentence, of the society. "Subjunctive: Mood of the verb
that indicates an action is conceived as subordinate to another, as
doubtful, possible, or desired" (*Larousse*). "Subjunctive: That which is
subjoined or dependent; designating a mood the forms of which are
employed to denote an action or state as conceived (and not as fact)
and therefore used to express a wish, a command, exhortation, or a
contingent, hypothetical, or prospective event" (*OED*). The subjunctive then, has no independent existence in standard grammar; it is
other-directed in the modes of request, subordinated in complex structures as a reaction or as a secondary action existing only in relation to
some other act. It has traditionally figured the relationship of fact to
hypothetical conception, superior to inferior, master to servant, man
to woman. For the Spanish conquistadores, their language provided
an important element in the history of conquest, and their legacy to
Latin America includes, in many countries, a retention of linguistic
hierarchies signaled not only in the overt forms of courteous address
but, more important, in the various *academias de la lengua* seeded
throughout the continent. And in at least one country, Colombia, the
linguistic hierarchy has found its mirror in a political one: Miguel
Antonio Cano, the founder of that country's *academia de la lengua,*
would also become one of the presidents of the nation. In the metaphorical grammar of narrative, rebellion against the entrenched hierarchy can take a number of forms. Thus, for example, one of the
political-linguistic moves of Carlos Fuentes's playfully bilingual/bicul-
tural text, *Cristóbal Nonato (Christopher Unborn)* is to misuse the subjunctive mood in his complex sentences. Denise Chávez's use of the
grammatical subjunctive in her occasional Spanish constructions—
generally dialogue—is loose and inconsistent, as the hybrid spoken
Spanglish of her characters dictates, whereas her English-dominant
passages are haunted and highlighted by her conditional conceptions
of the possible, the contingent, the desired, the doubtful, the necessary impossible. Both writers throw the unquestioned traditional hierarchy into disequilibrium, disturb the historical prominence of subject
(agent or "ideal proper noun" in Tzvetan Todorov's conception) and
verb (adjectival or verbal predicate) by the "secondary" category of
mood. Book and body no longer maintain their authorized continuity,

their traditional and unopposed machinations of subject-predicate, noun-verb relationships. The book-self coterminality is likewise disrupted. Book-body-self is mediated by the in-significant and indecipherable gesture of the scribble's graceful but nonhieroglyphic arabesque. Narration becomes, in turn, childlike and crippled: autistic. Says Rocío Esquibel in "Space Is a Solid," "I danced around Eulalia's bed. I hugged the screen door, my breasts indented in the meshed wire" (Chávez 15). The dance and the embrace are, syntactically, followed by the reimpression of boundaries, the indenting (like a paragraph) of breasts in the screen. Yet this grammatically subordinate meshing of thresholds and the physical marking of geometrically exact boundaries are also part of the dance, are, in fact, the very essence of the dance without which it would have no meaning: the print of the breasts on the screen, the screening of the breasts in the meeting of flat surface and curve, the mapping of the curve onto the graph-paper squares of the screen door and vice versa.

Writing in the subjunctive mood is an insubordinate's response to subordination. It also provides a response to Derrida's query, informed by his reading of Hegelian dialectics: "And if the *relève* of alienation is not a *calculable* certitude [that is, in Denise Chávez's terms, $X = 6$, but in some circumstances $6 = 9 = $ History of a Friendship], can one still speak of alienation and still produce statements in the system of speculative dialectics? . . . What might be a 'negative' that could not be *relevé?*" (*Margins* 107, my italics). For Derrida, one response might be the machine defined in terms of its functioning rather than its product. Kingston and Chávez, I would argue, present examples of machines that *work,* and work without calculable certitude and without *relève.*

It would perhaps help to clarify my point to have recourse to a related example from another field. One of the instructive controversies following the publication of Isaac Newton's *Principia* in 1686 had to do with his consistent use of the key word *attract* when speaking of gravitational force. Robert Boyle and Christian Huygens, among others, objected that this metaphor signaled a retrogression of science to the medieval concept of sympathy. We, in this historical moment, feel less disturbed by the use of this word, it is said, because of the erasure of sensory value from a commonly used—or "dead"—metaphor (see Derrida, *Margins* 211). J. M. Coetzee argues, however, that the case is more complex:

If what disturbed Huygens and Leibniz about the theory, and what no longer disturbs us, is no more than that the animistic metaphorical content of *attract* was alive for them but has been forgotten by us, and has therefore died or died out or died away, how else can we describe the growth to acceptance of gravitational theory between the time of Huygens and Leibniz and our own time but as, in Koyré's phrase, a "becoming reconciled to the ununderstandable"? Can we really assert that the truth of the theory has emerged out of the attrition of animistic terms like *attraction* in which Newton expressed it? If we do so, we are embracing the most radical idealism: we are asserting that there exists a pure concept of attraction towards which the mind gropes via the sideways processes of metaphorical thinking, and which it attains as the impurities of secondary meanings are shed and language becomes transparent, i.e., becomes thought. ("Newton" 11)

One of the attractions of this passage for me is that Coetzee's bracketing of "attraction" forces us to recognize and delight in the similarly (and surely intentionally) metaphorical gestures of his critique— "died," "growth," "grope," "sideways," "attain," "impurities," "shed," "transparent"—all terms notably animistic in their connotations. There is, I think, something similar to the mode of operation of both Kingston and Chávez in Coetzee's implicit recognition of the scene that remains alive and stirring, if unrecognized or subjected to a Nietzschean active forgetting, beneath the veneer of science or philosophy or literature. Like Kingston and Chávez, Coetzee realizes that the abysses of metaphor are artificial cultural products with temporal and spatial limitations, that the radical idealism Coetzee speaks of is so widespread as to constitute itself a condition not merely of scientific language but of *language* (unmodified). For Chávez and Kingston, the two American writers, however, the underlying scene is compacted and complicated by the need to represent, in addition to the temporal and spatial disjunctions, those imposed by a living awareness of multiple cultures, multiple languages, multiple time frames, and by identification with an undervalued gender, disjunctions that impose their own rules and offer their own separate opportunities for distanciation and irony. To steal an elegant formulation from the fiction of another bicultural writer, Abdelkebir Khatibi, "even in her own language, her body's native land, she made herself unclassifiable" (108).

At the end of Denise Chávez's "Space Is a Solid," nine-year-old Kari Lee Wembley puzzles over the question of how to begin writing the story of her friendship with Rocío Esquibel, her drama appreciation teacher. She looks across the room at her teacher, notes the young woman's blindly intense concentration on her work, writes out the title of her story:

HISTORY OF A FRIENDSHIP
By Kari Lee Wembley
Theatre Appreciation III Class
KARI LEE WEMBLEY = 6
ROCIO ESQUIBEL = 6

and thinks to herself, "If Space is a Solid, then what is the Shape of Darkness?" (136). "*IF* Space is a Solid," the closing sentence of the story, represents a hypothetical construction that contrasts markedly with the rather more straightforward statement of the story's title. "*IF* Space is a Solid" (but is it?) what then, asks the little girl, is the Shape of Darkness? And, I might add, does this "Shape" have a name, as the capitals imply? Denise Chávez's story ends on this question that frames the opening of Kari Lee Wembley's story, and the question remains open in the entire sequence of Chávez's short stories—never addressed, painfully elided when it touches too close to home. Indeed, I might argue that what unifies the stories of *The Last of the Menu Girls* is very much the urge to create (retell or invent) a possible history in order to hold at bay the threatening darkness. And this history is consciously constructed in the face of an implicit recognition that both history and friendship are congruent concepts at one pole of, and always in danger of slipping into, the shapeless amorphousness of darkness she fears and returns to again and again.

Darkness is, then, a particularly potent leitmotif in the collection, a counterpart and companion to the half-visible shapes given by imagination and historical memory. Thus, Regino, the "compadre" of the story of that name, the inept handyman who "was the only one who ever emerged from the darkness to fill my father's place" (149), has only this to offer as advice to his own son in a difficult time: "Let him get low and then come crawling back into himself through the darkness within him like I did. Then maybe he'll be able to love" (182). Rocío's mother, Nieves, the Mexican-American Snow Queen of impervious brightness, is unable to follow this advice, because she is unable to perceive the darkness within her and, for this reason, unable to go within and through that darkness. She closes herself off from others, literally and metaphorically, so that the new door to the house "was the door to a fortress now, where inside Nieves locked herself in, afraid of strangers, herself a stranger. Afraid." Afraid within the boundaries of herself and afraid of herself, praying in this house-fortress for *fortaleza* (189).

The unrelenting claustrophobia is particularly acute in another story, "The Closet." In this story, which immediately precedes "Space Is a Solid," Rocío provides an inventory of the closets in her family home: her mother's closet, the bathroom closet, her own closet, the TV room closet, the living room closet, and most important of all, though least particularized, the real-imaginary Grey Room and Blue Room, Rocío's private space, created by crawling, as Regino has advised, through her own interior darkness to the rooms within herself. Each closet has its own personality; each holds some facet of Rocío's family life. Thus, the living room closet holds the hope of rain, the TV room closet holds "time and fantasy and dreams—and it was Regino's—ill made" (89), her own closet embodies "a me I always wanted to be, was" (88), and the bathroom closet contains memories of summer and a snake.

The most notable of these various family closets, however, is the closet that symbolically engenders the others: the mother's closet. It is the forbidden closet where Rocío and Mercy play, crouching down among her mother's boxes in order to "feel darker" (91). The mother's closet is, curiously, at the same time the space of her unviolated hopes and her present hopelessness. It is the place of the poisoned first husband, the missing second husband, the nameless grandfather. It is the place of concealment and revelation, the dark, private space that yet provides no protection from the infiltration of foreign eyes, the closet where the children hide to view the skeleton of the glow-in-the-dark Jesus, a substitute paternal image, and to contemplate the possibilities of a Christ-like self.

In this story, the closet is where the body, alternately dressed and undressed, glows in the light of phosphorescent empty eyes, where body and text are interchanged and indissolubly linked. Gradually, as Rocío reveals the secrets of her family's closets, the whole of the house becomes imbued with her literary presence. The mother's closet represents for Rocío what the bathroom signifies for Octavio Paz: "For us, the bathroom and the room where we write are absolutely private spaces, into which we enter alone, within which we perform acts alternatively infamous and sublime. . . . Detritus or desires [desechos o deseos]: which is the basic resource of the writer?" (*Signo* 140). For Rocío, the *desechos* are the dusty photographs, the mementos packed away in sad cardboard boxes, the testimony to her own unrecovered history. In searching through the closets, in trying to intuit the shape of this dark history, Rocío enacts a quest for an absolute and absent cause, enacting her first self-inscription in the closed space of the closet which defines both her struggle for self-definition against the darkness and her recognition that it is the darkness itself that most adequately defines her. In that telling of her truths there is little enlightenment, only more of the crouching in the darkness that is already almost lying. The closet, as Lispector reminds us, "looks penetrable because it has a door. Upon opening it, you realize that its penetration has been deferred. . . . Its function: to keep transvestites in the dark. Its nature: the inviolability of things. Relation to people: people always see themselves reflected in its mirror in an awkward light because the wardrobe is never in the right place" (*Legion* 123–24). The closet, one objective correlative of the Shape of Darkness, only *seems* to provide a rich deposit of accrued signification; instead, the empty eyes of the glow-in-the-dark Jesus reveal an evaporation of meaning in the skeletal husks of a life irreducible to a single history. And for this reason, Rocío must escape from the crowded closets and must crawl through the dark passageways of the mind to her encounter with the windswept emptiness of the twilight Grey Room, the dry-ice chill of the Blue Room, the vast emptiness of the celestial No Room.

No Room, No Father, No Place: these are the figures for Rocío's desire and her inability to come to terms with the objects in the closets, the meanings she cannot decipher, the name she cannot quite speak. Each mystery remits the reader to another, increasingly interiorized: from the hospital of "The Last of the Menu Girls," to the "marking-off tree" in "Willow Game," to the "white walls of my father's old study" in "Shooting Stars," to the midnight-blue perfume bottle in "Evening in Paris," to closets imaginary and real in "The Closet," and culminating, finally, in "Space Is a Solid," where the narrative point of view is split between a young-adult Rocío and Kari Lee Wembley, the child she never was. And yet, it is Kari Lee who asks the crucial question— "then what is the Shape of Darkness?"—while graphically representing the question in the interrogative shape of her personal line, the turkey shape that is also a question mark and an inverted "6": cut off, killed, and discarded:

A turkey—
the top of the turkey head

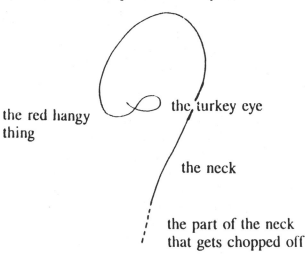

the red hangy thing   the turkey eye

the neck

the part of the neck that gets chopped off

The turkey line, as a generator of the curve of the plot, suggests the expansion of traditional literary concerns into realms bordering on alphabet design, on geometry, on mathematics. Curiously, Kari Lee's line, which begins as a scribble, a doodle, takes on increasing importance as a conditional interrogative for Rocío's history as well as her own. Kari Lee's pitiless curve is a line both arbitrary and meaningful, a scribble that also responds to a careful, if unconventional, calligraphy. It is a line with its own history, its own genealogy, at one extreme bordering on philosophy, at the other, on nonsense. I am reminded of Ramón López Velarde's quatrain—

> Voluptuosa melancolía:
> en su talle mórbido enrosca
> el Placer su caligrafía
> y la Muerte su garabato. (quoted by Paz, *Signo* 203)

> Voluptuous melancholy:
> around its morbid waste coils
> Pleasure its calligraphy
> and Death its scrawl.

—except that the clear slice of Kari Lee's line would obviate the highly erotic undertones of López Velarde's poem. Still, in both the sweeping gesture of the scribble signals an indescribable history. In his commentary on the quatrain, Paz makes a similar point: "The writing of pleasure *coils* like a snake or a vine—like a question mark. . . . And the answer to this question, if death, effectively, is a response, is a *scrawl:* a sign that is not only undeciphered, but indecipherable and, hence *insignificant"* (*Signo* 203). The scribble cannot be read; yet, paradoxically, the critic's effort is exhausted in uncovering its system of unmeaning, the visible image that is perceived in a flash and then made to correspond to its subsequent historicization. Insignificant and unsignifying, a lack and a refusal: these are the undeciphered poles of Kari Lee's two questions, the voiced and unvoiced variations, the Shape of Darkness and the interrogative curve.

Kari Lee's line is also Kari Lee's life, the arbitrary made meaningful through selective interpretation, encoding in this manner the very essence of the historicobiographical undertaking, that which refuses the scribble's recalcitrant in-signification for the delights of an ordered, teleological plot. Furthermore, Kari Lee's line has a history of its own in quite another, more literary sense, in that it harks back to and speaks within and against a venerable tradition of squiggles consecrated in canonical masterpieces of the Western world. Playfully or seriously, such works as Laurence Sterne's *Tristram Shandy,* Carlos Fuentes's *Christopher Unborn* and to a lesser degree, Antoine de Saint-Exupéry's *Little Prince* and Honoré de Balzac's *Magic Skin* all reject the action-oriented narrative for the looping plots of endless self-exploration and self-interpretation. In each of these works, as in Chávez's story, the in-significant squiggle intervenes to undercut the directional force of the story, at the same time alienating the reader within and outside the text, mocking our ritualistic desires for order, as well as our desire to draw symmetrical pictures of their structures. And very beautiful orders we critics have, indeed, to account for literary plots. Take this relatively straightforward plotting, for example, from Jacques Ehrmann's reading of *Cinna* (224):

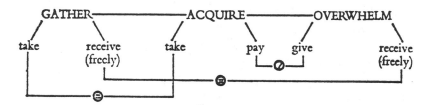

Or this more elegantly curvaceous schematic design of a Mallarmé sonnet by Octavio Paz (*Signo* 74):

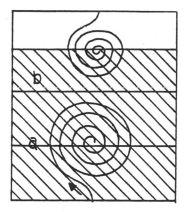

Sterne's mid-eighteenth-century novel anticipates and gently mocks all such efforts, and at this point my own argument will, in Shandyian hobbyhorsical fashion, take a brief detour through these looping arabesques with a view to uncovering the prehistory of these conditional affinities—or disconnections—between history and shape, friendship and darkness, pleasure (or plot or writing) and death (or counterplot or doodle). First, inevitably, the tangled plot of this digression, the hypothetical genealogy of the line:

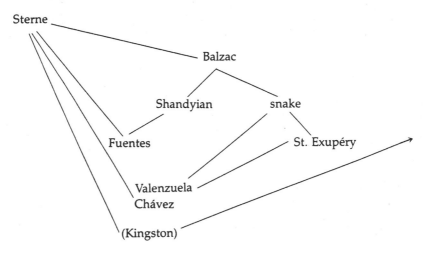

Malcolm Bradbury describes the plot of Laurence Sterne's novel as "literary *coitus interruptus*." It begins "*In flagrante delicto*," and proceeds as "an incomplete conception—a botched performance mismanaged because progression and digression, physiology and chronology, intersect" (37). From the very beginning, then, artistic creativity is related not to the conventional image of sexual energies chaneled into art but rather to the concept of sexual impotence as the backdrop and spur for artistic creation. For Tristram, the directional force of hobbyhorsical thinking is the only thing that keeps the plot moving forward at all, and his own depictions of the plots of the first few books of the novel are riddled by the bumps and curves and arabesques of an interrupted love affair with plots:

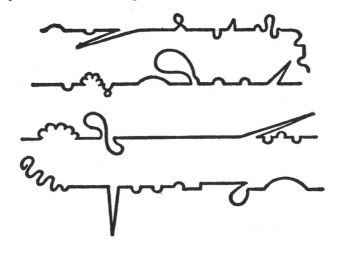

These were the four lines I moved in through my first, second, third, and fourth volumes.————In the fifth volume I have been very good;————the precise line I have described in it being this:

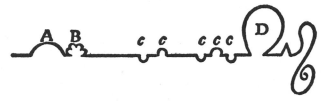

Tristram Shandy's fanciful topologies of plot of course spoof the conventional straight-line plots of his predecessors in the art of writing novels ("This *right line*. . . . The emblem of moral rectitude. . . . The *best line!*" [386]); they also anticipate, and critique, the complex drawings of contemporary literary theorists. Our designs, no less than his, reflect the hobbyhorsical nature of our own overriding concerns, the yearning for pattern and order and sense. Tristram's digressive, if still teleological, plot lines have inspired contemporary nonlinear novelists to new convolutions of digressive arabesque, but it is Corporal Trim's airy twirling of his walking stick that has proved the most perdurable of evanescent gestures, spawning generations of like squiggles. The occasion of the immortal gesture is a conversation between Corporal Trim and his master, the impotent ex-soldier Uncle Toby, whose groin wound sustained in the battle of Namur makes impossible the fulfillment of his platonically (alas!) requited love for the luscious and lascivious widow Wadman. Trim speaks feelingly of the imprisonments of marriage; Toby looks longingly at the widow's house. Trim eulogizes liberty; Toby longs for the freedom of choice. Trim utters his immortal phrase, completed with the swish of his cane: "Whilst a man is free—"

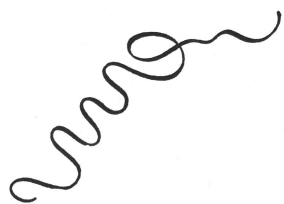

And Tristram adds the comment: "A thousand of my father's most subtle syllogisms could not have said more for celibacy" (491). The bachelor is free, says Trim; free to practice celibacy, says Tristram. And Toby, in whom celibacy is enforced, is not consoled. Thus, the gesture does not, as Peter Brooks writes, "represent the free, unfixed life of the bachelor—desire free and unchanneled" (59); it is, rather, the ironic/comic commentary on the conventional image of the single man: Toby is unwillingly free because the channels of desire have been damned up. "Whilst a man is free," says Trim, and then, in true Shandyian fashion, the discourse is cut off by an ambiguous curve and a bawdy digression on a Jew's widow who keeps a sausage shop.

Trim's gesture is reproduced as an epigraph to Balzac's 1831 novel *La peau de chagrin (The Magic Skin),* as the untrammeled and ironic counterpart to the rigid geometry of the magical talisman's mysterious inscription. Unlike Trim's squiggle, the writing on the talisman is disposed with the regularity of a poem in the original Arabic and compressed into the strikingly regular inverted pyramid in the French translation (both provided by Balzac in the text), a pyramid that ends with the imperative "Soit!" isolated at the point. "Soit," of course, echoes the biblical "Let there be . . ."; it is also the word used by francophone mathematicians to set up the conditions for a proof (Let X = 6, Denise Chávez might say). In later editions of the novel, the talisman retains its regularity, but Trim's line undergoes a strange proliferation of arabesques, from minor transmogrifications of the Shandyian mold, to transformations shading into the serpentine; for example in this simple line

TRISTRAM SHANDY, CHAP. CCXXXIII.

from an 1887 edition of *La peau de chagrin*, where Trim's arabesque drawn in the air is reproduced, tipped on its side, and transformed into a hybrid of Trim's aerial gesture and Tristram's carefully inked plot lines, intimating the drawing's protoserpentine allure. Or this drawing,

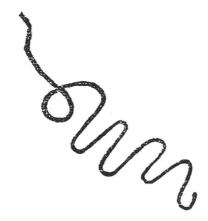

STERNE—Tristram Shandy, ch. cccxxii.

in a 1901 British translation, angling down from the left rather than the right. Or this

La Peau de chagrin

STERNE (*Tristram Shandy*, ch. cccxxii [1])

from the 1974 annotated Gallimard edition, reproducing the design from the original 1831 version; or these two inverted mirror images following. The first serpentine shape comes from an 1891 (?) Calmann-Lévy edition—the margin of the copy in the library at Cornell University bears the penciled annotation, "la serpente est un symbole de l'éternité":

A MONSIEUR SAVARY

MEMBRE DE L'ACADÉMIE DES SCIENCES

STERNE. *Tristram Shandy*, ch. CCCXXII.

And, finally, this last selected image,

the 1976 Pléïade snake. Balzac certainly contributed to the confusion, for stating in 1831 that his novel represents a "drame qui serpente, ondule, tournoie et au courant duquel il faut s'abandonner comme le dit la très spirituelle épigraphe du livre" (Gallimard edition 418). 'It's a serpentine, undulating, meandering drama and one must throw oneself into its current as the very spiritual epigraph of the book suggests.' Equally true is the tendency to seek meaning, spiritual or not, in the chance curves of Sterne's humor, to endow an arbitrary line with significance.

For Balzac's readers, the "syllogism" of Trim's gesture toward freedom—even the freedom from sexual pressures implied in Toby's impotence—takes on the sinister or spiritual overtones of a life both alluringly serpentine and poisonously attractive in the implicit conjunction of predetermination and phallic potency. For in Raphaël de Valentin's case, unlike Toby's, the problem lies not in the pairing of sexual desire and inability to act on that desire. As Peter Brooks reminds us, Raphaël's difficulty lies in the need to reject desire itself, even to the impossible renunciation of the desire not to desire: "The only possible preservation of this self whose most profound desires can be realized by the talisman is in the renunciation of desiring. . . . He has . . . chosen to live . . . by 'castrating his imagination,' arranging his existence so that he may avoid ever pronouncing an imperative or even an optative" (51). Whole vocabularies and grammatical constructions must be sloughed—like an outgrown snake skin?—so as to prevent the magic skin from tightening and cutting off his life. His life, we might say, like his narrative, must trace the predetermined curves of the snake's fatal curves, feeling his skin grow more and more tight as he exercises the desire to tell his story, albeit to an inattentive, intermittently sleeping, reader. The readers, in turn, awaken and seek to retrace the evanescent arabesque, but always trace instead the shape of their own desires, their own inattentiveness in the shifting freedom of the plot outlined by the epigraph. Likewise Chávez's readers add the burden of our own readings, concrete or abstract, over Kari Lee's much walked and variously interpreted line, the disembodied turkey head that is no less a figure for her life than the animal-shaped shrinking skin is for Balzac's Raphaël de Valentin.

Saint-Exupéry picks up the snake motif, reminding us that the associations in his drawings are not intelligible to "grown-ups," who see value only in things like geography and grammar and have lost a child's love of imaginative play. Grown-ups universally take his first drawing of a boa constrictor that has just swallowed an elephant

for an awkwardly drawn hat; his second, more graphically particular cross section

is rejected as a sign of the artist's lack of talent (3, 4). Drawing number one, then, of the boa that takes six months to digest its meal, is misunderstood, totally indigestible. The supposedly more digestible drawing number two is equally misunderstood. Between these two drawings of the two snakes, however, Saint-Exupéry sketches as well the plot of a life: the hidden elephant of the closed boa, discernible to anyone with the imagination to find it, the revealed elephant of the open boa, a happy creature on the verge of its six-month digestion. The child's two drawings, with their slightly distorted bell curve, shape a conscious endgame in which, reading the drawings from left to right, the beginning (the tale/tail of the snake) foreshadows the end (the mouth, the snake's beginning), and the mouth represents the end of the tale—the elephant's, at least. Playfully, the narrator slips into his text, from the beginning, a suggestion of the slow dissolution that will terminate in a flat snake, Sterne's straight, flat, plot line, the end of one tale, the beginning of another. Chávez, of course, is less playful, more straightforward in her reminder that the endgame is shaped not by the slow digestion of a willing volunteer but by the violent death of the holiday turkey; her plot, however, the curving plot of a turkey's head, is equally indigestible.

Sterne and particularly Balzac are acknowledged influences on Carlos Fuentes, and in *Christopher Unborn,* what we might call the last month of the first trimester of the novel, a chapter titled "It's a Wonderful Life" (the Spanish original calls the same section "Una vida padre") contains a delicate and specific homage to Fuentes's forerunners in his Shandyian placement of prologue and epigraph at page 132, and his adornment of that passage with a graphic representation of the sperm/serpent, Shandyian in basic shape, which also, with ironic wink, reminds the reader, should she choose to be reminded, of the snakes inherited by Balzac through fortune and typesetters' creativity, and of the bloated snakes waiting on the first pages of *Le petit prince:*

Prologue: I Am Created

I am a person no one knows. . . . I am a new being surrounded by a hundred million spermatozoa like this one:

imagination engendered me first, first language: it created the black, chromosomic, heraldic snake of ink and words that conceives everything. (132)

Fuentes's scribble offers homage to both his great masters and to the literary tradition they have spawned and to which this work is the latest contribution. Trim's idle gesture, Sterne's burlesque version of the plot of a free man's life, has been overlaid with the ominous overtones, inherited from Balzac, of the deadly and eternal heraldic serpent, and in Fuentes's text reminders of impotence (the enwombed child) are always paired with images of sexual potency—the millions of rushing sperm. As in Sterne's novel, and more consistently so, the narration of the work is in a first-person voice, given to a narrator who, by tradition, should be an eyewitness to the events described, but who, in both books, is clearly in no condition to witness anything at all. In Sterne's novel, Tristram requires the whole of the first half of the work to describe the circumstances of his birth, and he despairs of ever getting ahead: "I am this month one whole year older than I was this time twelvemonth; and having got, as you perceive, almost into the middle of my fourth volume—and no farther than to my first day's life—'tis demonstrative that . . . instead of advancing, as a common writer, in my work with what I have been doing at it—on the contrary, I am just thrown so many volumes back" (230–31).

In Fuentes's novel, even more radically, Christopher spends the entire 531 pages of the novel in his mother's womb; in both works, the time of writing takes over the text, in both, the material presence of words on paper is a crucial referent. Yet, in Fuentes's far more conventionally than in Sterne's, artistic conception is paired with an act of physical conception: the novel begins as Christopher's future parents conceive him in an ecstatic union on an Acapulco beach and ends, congruently, with his birth. Christopher, then, is both the (paternal) snake entering his mother's fruitful Garden of Eden and the helpless but cheerful elephant bloating the center of his mother's snake body, the digestion/gestation of which takes nine rather than a boa's six months. Furthermore, as he and we (the freely chosen *electores*) proceed through these nine months, his story could easily be geometrically plotted as a version of one of Tristram's digressive plots, where the curves and jags of his fits and starts trace a similarly tortured path to the necessary and preordained moment of birth.

The shape of Fuentes's tale, however, as befits the man Suzanne Ruta has called "our leading North American political satirist" (30), is more solid, darker, and more socially committed than that of his eighteenth-century predecessor, more closely aligned with Fuentes's stated aims to create a Latin American counterpart to Balzac's massive *Comédie humaine* than with the antic satires of Sterne. Paradoxically, then, this volume of "the life and opinions of Christopher (unborn) Palomar-to-be" ends with the beginning of life, for this voluble fetus will, like all other newborns, be excluded from language at the moment of birth, his book the impossible book of an inaccessible place and time. And Chávez's story, which also follows the forbidden shape of a man's privates or the whiplashing of a fetus, intimates an unspoken connection to Christopher, the linguistically crippled infant, whose polylinguistic punning facilities are lost at birth and must be painfully relearned.

Luisa Valenzuela reads the more ominous overtones implicit in texts like Fuentes's. She tells an interviewer, "la cola de lagartija [in her novel of that title] es un látigo, no una lagartija" 'The lizard's tale is a whip, not a lizard' (Ordóñez 514). In her work the arabesque snake curve takes on another signification: grammatically bigeneric, physically transsexual. Its political referents are likewise double and ambiguous: the symbol of the master's authority or the torturer's tool and, at the same time, the liberating arabesque of graffiti on oppression's pristine wall. One reading of Chávez's turkey neck would align her with the lash of Valenzuela's whip, another with the helplessness of the whipped child; one with the violent beheader of turkeys, another with the discarded head; one with the potent snake, another with the undigested, indigestible meal.

But here the loop must be cut off, for Kari Lee's line is much less intellectualized than these other lines, and in this sense the turkey shape offers a sharp comment on and refusal of the literary tradition of even such shapely forms as these. The shape of her particular darkness is yet to be discerned and explored, her question yet to be considered.

One response, a sort-of answer, to Kari Lee's question comes to me from another source, from Maxine Hong Kingston's *China Men*. In that volume, the narrator, a young Chinese-American woman, recalls her introduction to the mysteries surrounding the grandfathers:

[Say Goong] pointed into the dark, which dark seemed solid and alive, heavy, moving, breathing. There were waves of dark skin over a hot and massive something that was snorting and stomping—the living night. In the day, here was where the night lived. Say Goong pointed up at a wide brown eye as high as the roof. I was ready to be terrified but for his delight. "Horse," he said. "Horse." He contained the thing in a word—

horse, magical and earthly sound. A horse was a black creature so im-
mense I could not see the outlines. Grasping Say Goong's finger, I dared
to walk past the horse, and then he pointed again, "Horse." There was a
partition, and on the other side of it—another horse. There were two
such enormities in the world. Again and again I looked inside the stalls to
solve the mystery of what a horse was. On the outside of the shed was
horse shit, on the inside, the source of horse shit. . . .

   When I heard hooves clippity-clopping down our street, I ran to the
upstairs window and saw two grandfathers and two horses, which were
contained between the prongs. They had blinders cupping their eyes. I
had discovered the daily shape of horses. (165–66)

"They"—masculine plural, grandfathers or horses or both—"had
blinders," are blinded, trapped in a definition describing "living
night" even in the daytime, even on the outside of the shed, the place
of horse shit rather than the Source, the origin. "I"—feminine singular—"had discovered the *daily* shape of horses," abstracting from the
grandfather's night vision, tracing a singularly conceived continuity
between the shape of darkness and the quotidian sight.

   These two young women, Kari Lee and her Chinese-American
counterpart, are farther apart than the geographical distance between
West Texas and Stockton, California, may seem to suggest, and it
would be a mistake too easily to conflate their perceptions on friendship and kinship, on the weight of a significant curve, on the solidity
and shape of darkness. The young Chinese-American woman's quintessential horse is, after all, very different from the intellectually deprived white child's "line," her tracing through the shape of darkness
in the ambiguously shifting figure of the turkey ("My line reminds me
of: All I can think are turkey thoughts, dang it" [111]). Yet, there is an
underlying congruence in this unintended call and response between
two very different texts, a congruence that rejects the first, naïve
Conradian reading of the heart shape of darkness and calls for another
theoretical aperture into that space: *topos* and *tropos* of the ethnic
minority woman as potential writer in a dominantly white, still dominantly male, society.

   I want to come back to Chávez and to Kingston, to the question of
darkness and what shapes issue forth, to the implicit gender/genre
considerations involved, through a more careful analysis of the use of

emblematic figures in the texts: Kingston's horse, the sound shape that evokes an ideogrammatic presence, and Chavez's turkey, the dramatic dance turned mock glyph, evoking the rejected head of the Thanksgiving turkey, as well as, alternatively and concurrently, an ameba, a fetus, a man's genitals, a piece of wet wax (109–10), a gesture of friendship. The use of language is clearly at issue here, since for both characters there exists an apparently perfect conjunction of signifier and signified, light and darkness, the solid and the insubstantial which can be evoked by the narrators of the texts, but only, as it were, under erasure, as the language of the book or story. Kingston writes in English, the language of the ghosts; and Chávez's dialogic encounter of two denatured versions of mutually unintelligible cultures can capture only the tainted shadows between light and dark.

"History of a Friendship," writes Kari Lee Wembley, and thinks, "What is the Shape of Darkness?" How can she think intelligibly of history, of temporalization, in the absence of a clarification of the meaning of "time" or in the awareness of a bifurcated definition of historical memory, both meanings of which are foreign to the young girl's experience? How can she deal with spatialization of an abstract concept like friendship without the bases to clarify the nature of "shape"? How can she abstract from the truncated dance of her turkey line the curve of a human relationship? What is the semantic continuity that allows her to invert her turkey head–man's privates–ameba–fetus (roughly shaped like the number 9) into the symbolic equivalence expressed in the girl's simple poetry: "KARI LEE WEMBLEY = 6 / ROCIO ESQUIBEL = 6"? How can we mark the cryptotype of her system of unpower?

Let me once again defer the questions to more concrete grounds: Say Goong contains the "thing," the horse, in a word: "*horse*, magical and earthly sound," a sound that cannot be replicated in the very different phonics of the ghost language of *China Men*. Furthermore, as the narrator warns us in the opening of the novel, "outside the family, things have other names" (7). Other names, and other realities. The narrator, older, experiments with the poetry and artistry of gambling, "the many combinations with *horse, cloud, bird*. The lines and loops connecting the words, which were in squares, a word to a square, made designs too" (240). There are, enclosed in these lines, the simple delineation, could we but grasp it, of the ample reasons why the narrator's mother could make no sense of English; the words had no poetry, the pictures, no artistry: "The words had no crags, windows, or hooks to grasp. No pictures. The same *a, b, c*'s for everything. She couldn't make out ducks, cats, and mice in American cartoons either" (246). *Horse* is the deceptively foregrounded cryptonym, the shape of darkness identified, but with its identity veiled from the reader of Maxine Hong Kingston's book. Nothing is given; "horse" contains another magic for us; the "earthly sound" is inaudible to our ears. Perception fails, and we have no hooks to grasp. "Horse," he says/she says, a cryptic utterance, a "hieroglyph."

Kari Lee's question, on these grounds, could be phrased as follows: Can we make out the horse in a Chinese cartoon? The turkey in Kari Lee's "line," like the shapes of Chinese writing, like the sound-shape of "horse," preserves a "hook" for us to grasp with a more than metaphorical grasping at the concept, something to hang on to amid the less intelligible scribbles of *a, b, c* and their attendant abstractions. The typical gesture of Chávez and Kingston, then, would point less to *writing* and more toward the ghost of a culturally coded graphism, displaced or encrypted amid the proliferation of signals, a graphism that is, for both writers, full and empty, energized and repressed. We are led to suspect, not unnaturally, that such graphisms encode as well the possibility of a constellation of meaning, at least dual, probably mutually exclusive: both/and as well as either/or and, indeed, potentially pointing silently toward yet a third term of understanding, or perhaps none at all. Reed Way Dasenbrock agrees. "The meaningfulness of multicultural works," he says, "is in large measure a function of their unintelligibility" (12).

"Meaningfulness," "unintelligibility"—these terms, too, are culturally coded, the latter propped on the former in a manner less cryptic than inevitable, ineluctable. And a third term, also evoked by Dasenbrock, "undecidability," represents the gap over which we critics seek to construct the word-bridges of analysis, adding meaning through this favored metaphor as we illustrate process. Implicitly and correctly, Dasenbrock critiques the old, old dream of a common language by emphasizing the exclusionary function of bicultural usages in which figural assumptions and abstract relations are metaphorized differently from what the language of the text would lead us to expect. Confronted with these texts, it seems that critics (myself included) tend to define our projects as variations on international border hopping. Note the boundary words in three brief examples from Kingston criticism (Chávez, alas, has not yet been so fortunate in academic circles) (my italics): (1) According to the thesis paragraph of the aptly titled "Fiction and Autobiography: *Spatial* Form in *The Golden Cangue* and *The Woman Warrior*": "The nature of their attractiveness has more to do with the fact that they both belong to a *borderline* of genre" (Miller and Chang 75). (2) Leslie Rabine's very perceptive article argues: "Kingston seems to emphasize gender *boundaries between* the two books all the better to reorganize and play with these *boundaries within* each book. . . . *China Men*, about men who have been *forced to cross over* into the feminine gender, is written by a woman, who, in the act of writing, has also, like the woman warrior, *crossed over*, albeit voluntarily, into the masculine gender" (475, 480). (3) Amy Ling argues that the occasion for autobiography informing Kingston's works derives from "the need to *bridge* a psychic split between private and public self" (155).

I cite these critics not to disagree with their interpretations but to point to a rhetorical tradition in which the imagination and reality are discrete spaces, susceptible to metaphorical bridging, whether it be theoretically construed by the upflinging of the Hegelian *Aufhebung,* the minimal slippages of the Derridian *différance,* or the bar between signifier and signified. I could also cite Maxine Hong Kingston herself in this context: "Words are insignificant, insubstantial, not things. So we can use them to arrive at insignificant, insubstantial memories. As I paint part of a vision, the next part becomes clear. It's as if *I am building the underpinnings of a bridge, and then I can cross it,* and see more and more clearly" (Rabinowitz 178–79; my emphasis). The bridge in this formulation, then, images the outflung sweep of metaphors, gives form to the concrete underpinnings between two ghosts—insubstantial memoir, insubstantial word—and is constructed or painted out of the double haunting of experience and language. Or so I could argue, taking into account at least one version of this story, the one written "In the American Grain" (see the Rabinowitz interview for Kingston's discussion of her relation to William Carlos Williams, along with Nathaniel Hawthorne and Gertrude Stein [182]).

For Denise Chávez, the gap exists only for willful denial of bridges. Kari Lee and Rocío speak alternately in the text, occasionally *about* but never *to* each other; theirs are the dominant voices in the twelve discrete sections of the story "Space Is a Solid." Kari Lee's attempt to write a history of friendship in response to the teacher's demand represents, perhaps, the only potential for a bridge text in this world of discontinuities, of cuts that describe real and metaphorical disfigurements: "Arlin was cutting up and Miss E. said, 'Cut it out, just cut it. . . .' Anyway Arlin was cutting up. Now that's pretty crazy 'cause he doesn't have any arms" (97). Cutting up, cutting out, cutting, cutting it off. Cutting and disfigurement are permanent obsessions. Kari Lee meditates, "If space is a solid, then you can cut through it" (100). Or tellingly, we witness her mother's xenophobia, her narrow-minded disenfranchisement of any ethnic minority group from citizenship, her refusal to bridge differences: "If you're American, marry an American. If you're colored, marry a colored. If you're a Chinese, marry a Chinese. . . . None of this other stuff now, no Wembley has ever married anyone but they was from good old West Texas stock. That's the reason we ain't had no disfigurements in this family" (101) The irony here, of course, is that Mrs. Wembley has undergone a radical mastectomy and is hypersensitive about her own hidden disfigurement, a kind of sin against or blot on the Wembley name.

Or most tellingly of all, we observe the abrupt cutting off of Kari Lee's line, which responds so neatly to her mother's prejudices. Kari Lee's line is a turkey line, a quintessential image of "Americanness" and the bridging of cultures. Her line, however, is not the roasted turkey, the trussed and stuffed and headless body, but the turkey head, the piece that is cut off and discarded, the violence that precedes and is the other face of the bridging. Kari Lee's turkey, inverted, is outcast as Rocío Esquibel ("=6") an ostracism that Kari Lee intuitively shares with her favorite teacher, torn internally between her mother's line and her own developing sense of a self apart from her mother's stories. We would all be dissatisfied, however, and rightly so, with an explanation that sees in this inverse reflection of one line in another (the "9" in the intuited "6") merely a cultural bridge.

Let us try, briefly, to imagine another space, in which the dense complicity between thought and language, evident in our reaction to the bicultural text, in our incomplete satisfaction with the rhetoric of cut and bridge, is more immediately apparent because culturally or psychologically distanced:

The Hopi word-thought has no imaginary space. The corollary to this is that it may not locate thought dealing with real space anywhere but in real space, nor insulate any real space from the effects of thought. . . . A

Hopi would naturally suppose that his thought (or he himself) traffics with the actual . . . corn plant that he is thinking about. The thought then should leave some trace of itself with the plant in the field. (Whorf 150)

I want to defer the implicit romanticism of Whorf's discussion for another occasion, noting here only his delineation of the trace of the thought in the thing, a conception related to, but the inverse of, the contemporary recognition of the sedimentation of sensory images in abstract concepts. In the case of the Wolf Man, the inversion of the inversion responds to a pathological condition:

The Wolf Man's Magic Word shows how a sign, having become arbitrary, can remotivate itself. And into what labyrinth, what multiplicity of heterogeneous places, one must enter in order to track down the cryptic motivation. . . . For example, when *Turok* . . . says (?), means (?), translates (?), points out (?), represents (?), or *in any case* also imitates, induces the word-thing *tieret*. (Derrida, *"Fors"* xlvii)

Again, I want to remove the taint of psychosis from this discussion and directly infer a relation with the bicultural writer. At issue in this induction of the word-thing is not the duplication of reality in an analogous world, over which the writer must throw—or refuse to throw—the bridge of metaphor; rather, it is something more like the discovery of an unexpected space—not, as Abraham and Torok remind us, housed in the unconscious—and the recovery of a force other than repression (lxxi) to decrypt the delicate and expressive traces of the word-thing: the corn-thought, the magical horse, the turkey dance.

"He also let me play with the hole puncher. . . . I played gambler punching words to win—'cloudswallow,' 'riverswallow,' 'river forking,' 'swallow forking.' I also punched perfect round holes in the corners so I could hang the papers like diamonds and like pigeons" (*China Men*, 240–41). There is an essence haunting Kingston's work which cannot be captured in the forms of the ghost writing she practices, an essence that the formal abstractions of English are not capable of handling. For the narrator, this Chinese essence in the English text can be grasped at only through the metaphor of a phonic representation—"horse," he said—or, alternatively, through the "ideophonographic" (Henri Cordier's word)[3] reassembly of the living word in the

[3]Longxi writes: "As Chinese scripts are nonphonetic signs, Chinese writing is truly ontological in the sense of being detached from the spoken word. But contrary to

interstices of the gambling slips, in the interplay between hole and paper, a double work of art, both for the poetry of the punched word—"cloudswallow," "riverfire"—substantial and insubstantial at the same time, and for the beauty of the paper itself—pigeondiamond.

The narrator's gambler-father is coterminous with the teacher-father in China and certainly more successful in transmitting his love of learning and the power of poetry. "Take a guess," begs the Chinese father of his students. "Taking a guess is the same as making up a story" (32). The students, dull, unimaginative, understand neither the concept of "guessing" nor the idea of the "story." For the Californian gamblers, however, the lure of the pigeon papers involves both the joy of sharing their poetry and the stories of win and loss. The narrator, too, shares the excitement in this "best of the father places" (238), and indeed, the whole of her narration could be construed as a gambler's bet, tossing the bright words in a drum—"BaBa let me crank the drum that spun words. It . . . looked like the cradle that the Forty-Niner ancestors used to sift for gold" (240), pulling out the combinations dictated by chance or necessity, a public act, but carried out in a secret setting, a semiprivate setting, on the fringes of legality. And the nameless narrator, like her father, has the gift and power of naming, of choosing by chance the correct name to fit the situation, of *creating* the situation through the guesswork of imagination and the power of story, no longer, as in *The Woman Warrior*, the talk-story but the written story, paralyzed and set free in the space of the machine, the paper. The silence of this writing, and the sharing of the poetry, are contrary impulses, which, when superimposed in the gamblers' space, interrupt the movement of the Hegelian *Aufhebung*, disrupt the bridge-space. Derrida asks, in the context of an analysis of "what talking means": "What might be a 'negative' that could not be *relevé*? . . . but would work, then, as pure loss?" And he answers his own question:

A machine defined in its pure functioning, and not in its final utility, its meaning, its result, its work. . . . what Hegel, the *relevant* interpreter of the entire history of philosophy, *could never think* is a machine that would work. That would work without, to this extent, being governed by an

popular misconceptions, Chinese writing is not pictographic. . . . [Henri Cordier] remarked with good reason that 'as the graphic system is not hieroglyphic, or symbolic, or syllabic, or alphabetic, or lexigraphic, but ideophonographic, we shall, in order to avoid misconception and for the sake of brevity, call its characters *sinograms*.'" The key word, as Longxi notes, is the neologism *ideophonographic* (126).

order of reappropriation. . . . Doubtless philosophy would see in this a nonfunctioning, a nonwork; and thereby philosophy would miss that which, in a such a machine, works. By itself. Outside. (*Margins* 107)

Kingston's machine works, in this sense, in the way that other word-machines (for example, Jonathan Swift's combinatory matrix in *Gulliver's Travels* or Borges's hallucinatory library of Babel) do not. The word-machine/gold-cradle figures, in all its strangeness and familiarity, the limitations and the combinatory freedoms of what Abraham and Torok have called the "crypt." Poetry is tossed in; chance dictates the poetry that comes out, always as alike and as different as the various fathers, the multiple grandfathers: a perfect conjunction of form and spirit, beauty and simplicity. Outside the reader, however, and quite, quite outside the mechanism that is English, is a machine that nostalgically recalls but does not reproduce the cryptic utterance, the semantic chain.

The poetry hidden in the belly of the machine—for example, the simple and breathtaking revelation of the essential "horse"—persists in a crippled form outside the strict boundaries of the machine in the broken poetry of such bicultural, bilingual manifestations as the pidgin (pigeondiamond?) English of the "modern aunt," who refers with pride to her "hus-u-bun," and who feeds her guests cake and pie in the exotic flavors of "chuck-who-luck" and "le-mun" (204). It survives in the menace of the "Hit-lah" moths, the "plain, no-color butterflies," killed, as the narrator tells us, with "a hit on the first syllable . . . every summer of the War." The name of the moths, time-bound, spatially limited ("outside the family, things have other names" [7]), imbued with violence, still manages access to that lucky gambler's conjunction of thought and word and action that suggests the dazzling isomorphism of image with process typical of Kingston's poetry.

Fully outside the poetry machine are "terrible words" like "*if, old, but*," which signal "gapping, gaping spaces" with none of beauty's intimate compression, or the stark, rather than poetic, simplicity of the brother-teacher's letters, sent from a Vietnam-era aircraft carrier, perpetually en route to Asia:

"Dear Mom: How are you? I am fine." (Words from the Navy textbook, copied by illiterate soldiers shape by shape in illusion of communication with family members at home.)

"How are you? I am fine." (The educated brother's unelegant Chinese letters to his parents, handicapped by a small Chinese vocabulary.)

"How are you? I am fine." (The same brother's English letters to his sisters; vague, because he didn't want them to worry.) (290–91)

These pedestrian phrases resonate with pathos, with a too-careful attention to detail, not torn from but carefully masking the heart. They stand in strict contrast to the elegance of "rivercloud," "river-fire," "cloudswallow," "riverswallow," to the black humor of "hit-lah" and "chuck-who-luck": combinations dictated by chance and beauty, plucked from the crypt, the machine, the heart.

Denise Chávez tears a beauty out of violation itself, creating a tale out of bitterness, out of "the angular cut of a shattered word" (Derrida, "*Fors*" xlviii) upon the tongue. Indeed, if we can say that Kingston's method involves throwing things and words together in a linguistic gambler's drum, Chávez's method, arguably, involves the exact opposite: tearing apart and privileging the cut, until that cut itself becomes the locus of the cryptic message, revealed through a series of fragmented narratives: distorted, disfigured, animalized, aborted. Cut off. Rocío's work in this story brings her into daily contact with the disjunctions between personal history and the intensely different histories of the people and community in which she now lives, stranded, cut off from family and friends. In this very extremity of disjunction, however, resides the unwanted, unrecognized link, the common thread between her experience and that of the physically or emotionally mutilated beings among which she now finds herself, giving birth, grotesquely, to monstrosity. "I tried on a strait-jacket," Rocío notes, as if it were a wedding gown, "my first fitting." She recalls as she does so, her boyfriend, Loudon, limping still from a leg broken the week before he was to leave for Vietnam, limping, she says, "in memory of his departed brothers, all of them blown up, blown away," recalling as well, with detachment, her detachment from her own hands, first noted on an elevator: "Who hasn't imagined death in an elevator, crushed between floors, bodies piled up in broken heaps, strangers no longer"? (103) Rocío gives voice, gives birth, to all that is left so carefully unwritten in the contentless letters of *China Men:* to the featureless death, the broken bodies, no longer even human, the helpless binding of hands and arms unable to assist.

Arlin, the Thalidomide baby, is the figure for all these crippled

souls. Arlin Threadgill has no arms, only "stumps which stick out like
the gills of a fish" (97) or like pathetic, flightless "chicken wings" (98),
disfigured and for that reason cut off metaphorically and literally from
society, such as it is. As Mrs. Wembley complains, "I don't know
what's wrong with Mrs. Threadgill, showing off Arlin all over town
like he was normal. No, Kari Lee, it ain't decent" (99). Mrs. Wembley,
of course, objects strenuously only to *public* disfigurement. Her own is
private. Therefore, she believes, in the eyes of the town, if not quite in
her own eyes, she is "decent." She too, however, confesses to Rocío:

> "Miss Esquinel [sic, her typical, many times corrected, mutilation of
> Rocío's last name], I don't have no breasts. . . ."
> "I'm...."
> "Oh no, no, no, no.... Don't you be sorry. Sorry ain't enough. After all
> these years, sorry ain't enough. Now to look at me, anyone would see a
> normal woman. Do you know what it's like to have your female flesh cut
> away from you?" (115)

For her daughter Kari Lee, the reflex of cutting off, cutting out, cutting
up a chain of association is unsurprisingly natural: "Your arm is like a
knife, and your body is a knife, too, and when you walk . . . you're
cutting through space" (100). Or in her notebook jottings: "This is my
line. I've walked it so many dang times I'm getting dizzy. . . . I gotta
speed up coming around the top part . . . and then go bumpity hop
hop hop hopping with a SUDDEN STOP" (108). Or later: "My line has a
sound, a high-pitched cry—revving up and then dying out. Ploom,
Ploom. Hard crash. The turkey neck falls to the ground" (111). Kari
Lee's turkey has its exact, if unrecognized, replica in the dead black-
bird Rocío finds on the porch and wraps for burial in white notebook
paper (118), her not-quite-abstract knifing through space with Rocío's
dinner knife, used to break into her house, cutting her lip in the
process (119), her aborted turkey cry with the shrieking of Joe's voice
heard through the walls as the cat Oriene, frightened, gives birth in
Rocío's lap (121). Kari Lee, again: "My line reminds me of: A turkey. . . . A man's privates. . . . My line reminds me of: Thanksgiving.
If you turn it upside down, it looks like an amoeba, kind of, or a fetus
that's whiplashing around, or a piece of wet wax that's drying up"
(109–10). Chávez' text is, in the double sense of the phrase, an illegitimate conception.

In this "History of a Friendship," then, relationships of kinship and friendship are inevitably undermined by the reliance on a disfigured "line," a bastard language. The grotesques that people this story only further underline the absence of the "natural," the "whole" or "wholesome," abandoning the unsafe attractions of friend and family in favor of a conflictual demarcation of territory, a metaphorical abyss with no other side to bridge to, a chimeric monster produced in a violation of linguistic integrity. Implicitly, the "wholeness" or "wholesomeness" of language is likewise denied; there is no linguistic unity in English or, implicitly, in Spanish. Denied, as well, is the traditional basis of rhetorical, theoretical, literary, linguistic legitimation, a primary disfigurement prefacing and auguring the distorted articulations of narration. "To labor" (another word that must be taken in its double sense) to open the crypt, the womb, and give birth to this text-child is not, as the Spanish would have it, to give a child to the light (*dar luz*) but rather to suggest a continuity of darkness, cut, as the umbilical cord is cut, with the inevitable pain of separation. Rocío, in "The Closet," in some sense explains her attraction to these dark, closed places by remembering-inventing the circumstances of her own birth, as a wobbly table comes crashing down and mother and daughter shoot "into a closet full of old clothes, old shoes" (84), the Ur-closet that will later be fractured into all the other closets of the house and into the inaccessible space of the Grey Room ("Birth and Death" [85]). Birth is hidden in the confines of the closet, the child slipping from dark to dark, in anticipation of another slippage into the darkness of death. Kari Lee, finally, like Arlin, like Rocío, is also a crippled child, who takes charge of positing an organization—one truncated in the story proper—for the events recounted, temporalizing them, naming them "history of a friendship," producing a protective shield, a line and a limit, a crypt to contain the cut, the wound, the disfigured abortion-distortion beneath. Thus Kingston's immensely productive game of continually metamorphosing repetitions shifts to its darker side in Chávez's story, into a mocking surface of sterile reproductions, emptied out, thrust prematurely into the world, and cut off.

Kingston and Chávez nevertheless represent, I would argue, two versions of a parallel discourse, a fantastic cryptonymy now light, now dark, here beautiful, there grotesque. Both authors allow us to see the force of dark and light, creating in this necessary juxtaposition neither a heliocentric metaphysics nor recourse to the dark continent of the so-called primitive metaphorical linking of word and thing. These deli-cate distinctions and subtle displacements cipher a particular reper-toire of linguistic practice which responds and corresponds to the need of the bicultural-bilingual writer to encode, in a more than trivial, more than superficial manner, her shifting set of mutually exclusive, equally valid alternate roles. It is a life, I would say, taking my example from Spanish grammar, lived in the subjunctive mood, attentive to nuance and capable of taking a cue from context without losing its autonomy: "a metonymy of words," as Abraham and Torok would have it, repre-senting the slippage as well as the continuity between the roles, an impassioned relationship to syntactical relations which reveals, as Whorf reminds us, the covert markings of a cryptotype, a function without a concrete form.

It is here, finally, where I rejoin my opening remarks and take up again the issue, so long held in abeyance, of gender, another term traditionally, if metaphorically, written in the subjunctive. Rabine has already said it very well at the end of her excellent *Signs* article on Kingston: "Such is our present sociosymbolic order that feminine difference has to be expressed in a way acceptable to these institutions in order to even be recognized as feminine difference" (492). It is a chilling reminder in the context of gender studies as a whole, and, unfortunately, an absolutely correct one. There is a degree of sanc-tioned illegitimacy, of licit license, in which the conflictual violence of difference and the same are resolved and reconciled in the mocking surface of reflection, a game of continually changing positional refer-ences, of changes that end up always and only as the same thing. It is not the least of their accomplishments that both Kingston and Chávez struggle with these cautionary rituals, attempt to bypass these old myths of the *Same* and the *Other*, risk loss (of readers, of self), and forcefully suggest new kinds of feminine difference, intuiting the shape of darkness and naming it their own, discovering the curve of a turkey's neck or the daily shape of horses.

Conclusion: Sweeping Up

This book began in the kitchen, and moved from there to the attic, before passing on to other, less concrete spaces: silence and superficiality and the subjunctive, appropriation and negation and marginality. Other key words and phrases, essentially untranslatable, have appeared again and again throughout this text, perhaps less systematically but equally important, as keys to help unlock the doors to these metaphorical rooms: *el lector enemigo, el/la lector(a) hembra, la palabra azotada, pudor* (which echoes so strangely with *poder*), *propiedad, loca,* and one vexed term that *is* translatable: *authenticity.* In exploring these spaces, I have tried not only to make works by women the subject of my text—a passive role at best—but also to demonstrate the more assertive potentialities of the Latin American woman as a subject speaking the text. She is, therefore, at the same time both subject and object of this work, the quester and the goal of this quest through the attic/Attic, with side tours into Viramontes's no-place, Valenzuela's apartment-cell, Ferré's brothel, Campos's sewing room, Lispector's maid's room, Castellanos's ark of memory, Puga's hotel room, Chávez's closet, and Kingston's stable, among other places.

The voices heard here echo through rooms that may seem to have been strangely emptied, and they speak against voices whose presence is unmeasured, whose significance is never weighed. Yet those voices and that emptied structure have shaped and tempered writing women's voices and defined their place. There are some voices that never speak, at least in writing, or do so only in mediated forms: the muted voice of the mother, the *ama de casa*, the idealized *santa*, la

293

abnegada, as well as the Indian woman, the underworld prostitute, and all the other abject, illiterate, marginal, unseen, and unheard mothers of Latin America. Their more vocal representatives, only marginally evoked here, include "madwomen" like the *locas* of the Plaza de Mayo in Argentina, the Comadres in El Salvador, the women who danced *la cueca* partnerless in Chile, the members of the Housewives' Committee in Bolivia; women like Rigoberta Menchú in the Guatemalan high-lands and Domitila Barrios de Chungara in the Bolivian mining towns.

There is another voice, too, which this book has repressed and which has been grudgingly admitted only in the inevitable interstices of a female discourse. That voice, is, of course, the father's voice, and that place, the public forum. (This is to leave aside, of course, such minimally sketched, problematic father figures as Jacques Derrida, who is read in this text as I read him reading through his image of the distanced, ultimately unknowable feminine.) In politics the father's voice belongs to the military dictator; his place is the presidential palace. In literature, that voice is the canonical writers'; that place, consecrated literary history. These two sets of voices—those of the father, which tradition officially recognizes and publicly values; those of the mother, which the same tradition brutally rejects and publicly scorns—murmur indistinctly behind and beside this text, shaping it, defining its conditions of possibility.

But I want to speak here about the critic's place and will do so beginning from an unlikely place, a place where woman is given neither space nor voice, with Roberto González Echevarría's all-too aptly titled book *The Voice of the Masters: Writing and Authority in Modern Latin American Literature.* I choose González Echevarría because I see his powerful book as one of the most important Latin American critical works to come into my hands in recent years. Nevertheless, I find it lacking in significant ways. Thus, I want to read through his discourse toward an alternative, feminist discourse, to look at the texts of the master(s) in order to describe a way of thinking and writing not caught up in the suppression of women, to engage with his voice and find my own.

A quick review of the index of *The Voice of the Masters* reveals one Latin American woman writer: Lydia Cabrera. She is given two sen-tences in the body of González Echevarría's text acknowledging her book *El monte* as an antecedent for Miguel Barnet's *Biografía de un cimarrón.* This observation is, of course, not surprising given that

Le mujer no es maestra todavía de la literatura

González Echevarría's stated topic is the voice of the "masters" and not that of the subordinates, and in this book neither women writers nor female characters achieve a masterly role. Yet, González Echevarría wants to make a distinction between the voice of the masters and his own voice; he wants to write about "writing and authority" without either taking an authoritarian stance or assuming an authoritarian voice. For whereas "authority and authoritarianism" are the first words of his book, and the author tells us that "the dictators and the language in which their image is cast start simultaneously" (1), González Echevarría's intent is to expose this factitious complicity between language and authoritarianism, to deconstruct their unsalutary propping up of each other, leaning upon each other. He intends to achieve this object in two ways: in the texts he studies and in the way he studies those texts. First, he says, such representatives of modern Latin American literature as Fuentes, Cortázar, and Cabrera Infante dismantle the link between authority and rhetoric through the operations of their critical-literary works. Second, his own critical style, unlike the "authoritarian" criticism he deplores, is intentionally disconnected: "To have written a sustained, expository book . . . would have led me to make the same kind of critical error that I attribute to most criticism of Latin American literature. In so doing, I would have naïvely assumed an authoritative voice while attempting a critique of precisely that critical gesture" (6). Such authoritarian voices, he would argue, falsify what they attempt to explain. Therefore, he proposes, the examination of literary as well as political institutions should begin with a careful critique of the language used to support them.

Yet, curiously, González Echevarría's warning about the danger of an authoritarian discourse sharpens his readers' awareness of his perhaps unintended displacement of authoritarianism into other forms. In the studies collected in this book, if González Echevarría manages to avoid sounding dogmatic and authoritarian, he is, at least, (as many reviews of the book agree) magisterial, and this compliment to the quality of his work reflects a point of entry for its critique. In ostensibly rejecting the authoritarian master, González Echevarría creates a fiction of alterity, a doubled aporia in his book, which is signally revealed when he opens it with a study of José Enrique Rodó's "magisterial rhetoric"—presumably in *différance* with his own—and closes with the brilliantly inconclusive "Meta-End" translation and commentary. Yet the critical aporia is only apparently held open, for the unexplored nature of this abstract and fragmentary alterity is never carefully questioned. In his bilingual study,[1] I posit, the counterpoint to the dictator/author/official language (the master) is the figure of the *maestro*, the teacher, whose impact in exploring the nature of Latin American identity and in constructing and verifying that cultural identity extends beyond the classroom into the realms of the political. Or so it seems in Latin America at least, and González Echevarría himself points to the examples of Octavio Paz, Roberto Fernández Retamar, Alfonso Reyes, Domingo Faustino Sarmiento as critics (essayists) and political figures of some import: they are both masters and *maestros*. In the United States, of course, the ties between politics and the academy are less apparent; the *maestros*, as *maestros*, rarely have the opportunity to exhibit mastery in the political sense, and though they may talk about power, they sublimate their own will to power in the form of lectures that impart discrete and measurable quantities of knowledge to their students. The question returns then, bilingually, biculturally: does González Echevarría, the discreet and masterly *maestro*, the highly visible chaired professor in one of the most elite schools in the United States, enact a will to power or a will to knowledge?

For George Yúdice, González Echevarría's book represents yet another mode for the disingenuous displacement of an authoritarian discourse onto a national romance that Doris Sommer has so acutely dissected in her *One Master for Another: Populism as Patriarchal Rhetoric in Dominican Novels* (49–52). In the bilingual slippage between master and *maestro*, Yúdice finds, González Echevarría embarks on a clandestine reassertion of a denied authoritarianism, transcribing a translation that repeats, as it replaces, an approach that his entire strategy of observation otherwise undermines. In *The Voice of the Masters*, as Yúdice comments, "Sólo se oye la voz de los maestros, de la autoridad. . . . el hueco y el 'otro implícito' a que se refiere González Echevarría no son más que abstracciones" (52). 'The only voices heard are those of the masters, of authority. . . . the hole and the "implicit other" referred to by González Echevarría are nothing more than abstractions.' Yúdice's comment about the politics of literary judgment is well taken and is applicable to both sides of the bilingual divide;

---

[1]González Echevarría says, "I take my chief contribution as a reader of Latin American texts in a North American context to be a bilingual reader, as it were, whose critical activity consists precisely in transferring a text from one code to another to sift out in that process what holds it together" (15).

neither master nor *maestro* nor González Echevarría endows that abstractly posited "other" with any significant particulars of race, sex, class, or age. Furthermore, both the master and the *maestro* exercise their authoritarian force in the same form: by imposition of their ideas on that highly generalized imagined other. And because the other—whether envisioned in Latin or in North American terms—is so abstractly imagined, even in such scenes of seduction as González Echevarría's account of *Ariel*'s persistence as a Latin American dream, there is something lacking; masterly desire is launched into a field with no concrete object to seduce or conquer.

Let me demonstrate with one particular example. Consider this scene, drawn from González Echevarría's translation of Cabrera Infante's "Meta-Final," a work González Echevarría sees as "one of the most important texts written in Latin America," which "ought to figure in all anthologies of Latin American literature. It is more important than a great deal of Borges, Carpentier, and Neruda" (*Voice* 138–39). "Meta-Final" takes off from a particular episode in one of Cabrera Infante's earlier works, his novel *Tres tristes tigres (Three Trapped Tigers)*, and describes the strange death in Mexico of the enormously fat black nightclub singer Estrella and the even stranger peregrinations of her cadaver as it journeys back toward Cuba for burial. Like the novel, this episode is narrated by a member of the loose group of prerevolutionary Cuban friends, all male, for consideration by that group. The woman, the ostensible subject of the narrative, is converted into a vaguely phallic object, a wordless, silent singer given value and importance through her insertion into this system of male dialogue and exchange.

The episode begins with the comment that "there are no inauthentic lives, but all deaths are authentic" (145) and follows with the narrator's retelling of the sequence of errors that resulted from the secretary's attempt to have Estrella's body shipped back to Cuba from Mexico. The embalming of her elephantine body is botched, and even though it is polyurethaned and encased in a thick shell of solid plastic, the body begins to decompose. After tolerating the decaying corpse for a few hours aboard a Havana-bound vessel, the ship's crew decides to throw the odiferous casket overboard, but it refuses to sink and refuses to distance itself from the boat:

> They were already catching up to it when a wave and then a change of
> wind, the ship's own wake, the current, the Tropic of Cancer, chance (or

everything together) made the casket beat about abruptly, turn around windward and charge the boat, opening a regular size hole in it before anyone could avoid the collision and much less hit the coffin with a saving axe, good at least to paralyze the aggressor, and it was instead the boat that made water, listed and began to sink in the midst of the sea and the sailors' silence. A silence that didn't last very long because a second charge of the casket scraped the bow with a triumphant shriek and the boat sank at the same time that the two Mexicans swam furiously toward the ship and the Liberian splashed around, swallowed water, seemed to drown and finally swims to the ship anxiously. The other sailors could do nothing more than pick them off the sea with ropes and life preservers as Captain Acá ordered, Call me Ishmael, the ship's doctor before seeing Estrella fade away in her floating tomb, which for him was an enviable destiny: the unsinkable, perfect ship, the anti-Titanic. Or perhaps a myth: a María Celeste of flesh, bones and wood, a Flying Dutchman. He looked at her with the naked eye of a sea wolf, later with mariner's eyes, later with eyes dirtied by tears, later with binoculars, later with cataracts and saw how the boat turned to naught, to nothing, to nothingness. First it was a whale of wood and grease, later a funereal fish, then blackcap on a black wave, then fly in the horizon until distance swallowed her up and she was lost in the sea, in our eternity, Silvestre, sailing, traveling, floating on the Gulf Stream at 13 knots per hour in a North by North West direction. (*Voice* 155, 157)

González Echevarría comments that he sees Estrella "as a kind of Orphic voice issuing from the earth." Lost overboard, "she does not return to earth, but floats forever on the sea, a floating island, a Floating Signifier, unmoored by referentiality and all cultural codes" (163). Estrella is at the same time larger than life and less meaningful; even her name, "Estrella," serves as no more than an abstract sign pointing to her role in life: she is superstardom incarnate. As the tightly interwoven structure of narrator and commentator and author suggest, instead of representing any single individual, she is meaningful solely as a "floating signifier," an unanchored, abstract object of interest only insofar as a male gaze (sailor/narrator/audience/author/critic) endows her with meaning. As González Echevarría notes of Estrella, and other similar female figures in modern Latin American narrative, "There is an obvious contradiction in their being at the same time female and authoritative. . . . By being deformed and outsized, however, they point to the supplemental character of their authority, built, as it were, on an absence, a lack or fissure" (164–65). To remind my readers that this "absence, lack, or fissure" refers to a physical as well as a linguistic condition is perhaps unnecessary; we need to note, however, that in González Echevarría's work such "absences" are "supplemented" by an authority derived directly from the masculine. In this respect his imagery is quite straightforward. Dead and with her song forever silenced, Estrella's "monstrous maternal self becomes a ramming projectile, an aggressive phallus" (141), a defeminized female stand-in for Moby Dick, the classic floating signifier of idealized masculinity. Estrella in this manner joins those few other female figures mentioned in González Echevarría's book: the authoritarian woman deformed by power (doña Bárbara), the huge and hyperbolic Mamá Grande in Gabriel García Márquez's story, who, because of her exaggerated proportions, is therefore "devoid of meaning" (58), and Severo Sarduy's ambiguous Cobra/Cadillac, the one castrated, the other endowed with a penis to cover her/his original lack. Like the rammed ship, Cabrera Infante's highly masculine-oriented text, feminized in its confrontation with the authoritarian critic, first resists and then is punctured by the driving force of that criticism, giving way to the little phallic thrusts of González Echevarría's endnotes beyond the meta-end.

All this may be very well for the male reader, the *lector cómplice*, but a *lectora hembra* can be pardoned for finding herself deeply concerned. Like the originally female transsexual Cadillac, in reading this story, and in meditating on González Echevarría's interpretation of it, we are asked to take on an imaginary phallus to cover our own signifying lack. A *lector cómplice* reading the Estrella passage would be expected to identify with its projected universality, suggested through the allusion to Melville's *Moby Dick*, among other literary and cultural allusions, to feel his difference from the dead woman and to acknowledge the threat she poses to all systems of meaning, including that established between the narrator and his audience, the critic and his readers. Woman readers are traditionally taught to seek supplements for their fissured selves, to take on the imaginary phalluses and insert themselves into this discourse as pseudomen, in a process Judith Fetterley called "immasculation" in her book on American fiction, *The Resisting Reader*. The immasculated woman allows the text to draw her in, agrees to identify with the *maestro* and accept his authority, to become complicitous in this denigration of female difference to a bloated, vacuous floating signifier, a slash or wound of absence and lack covered over with an artificial, symbolic phallic rigidity and resistance.

The resisting female reader can, on the one hand, simply refuse to read the patriarchal text. She can refuse to participate in the embalming of femininity, refuse to allow the *maestros* to pour molten plastic down her throat, refuse to be converted into a maternal phallus. But the solution of outright refusal is both impractical and essentially impossible, given the dominance of such texts in the literary and critical canons, and the feminist reader will only and necessarily become so after a long process of immasculation and rejection of immasculation. On the other hand, the resisting reader can teach herself to read otherwise, rejecting the model of the critic who rams/punctures the feminized text, realizing that the woman's relation to authority, textuality, desire is based on a historical relation to identity different from her male counterpart's. His fantasy of wholeness is not necessarily hers. His image of phallic potency and feminine lack does not always speak to her own sense of her condition.

To enact such a reading is not to convert oneself into that strident, humorless feminist caricature invented by misogynists; it is, rather, to explore the ways in which a theory of modern literature must take into account a poetics of gender, to blend a healthy respect for the master's voice with an unwillingness to be seduced by the *maestro*, to refuse to allow the master/*maestro* to inhibit the careful, patient, critical reading of masterworks. Such a reader is not a dutiful wife but a rebellious student, "a prodigal daughter," in Jerry Aline Flieger's words. For Flieger, the prodigal daughter "goes beyond the fold of restrictive paternal law, only to return. But unlike the prodigal son of legend, who returns repentant, she returns enriched—for she is 'prodigal' in the second sense of the term as well: she is lush, exceptional, extravagant, and affirmative" (59–60). Flieger's discussion may itself sound a bit extravagant and utopian; it does however, suggest a critical practice that resists the "voice of the masters" and challenges readers to rethink the category of the woman as discursive subject/object outside the essentialist frame into which she has so traditionally been cast. It counterposes a practice of heterogeneity to false assumptions of universality and forces us to return to a question relative to the field at large, that of the struggle with and against the power of words—as they are used to liberate women or to hold women back or as they are deployed structurally in the canonical texts that provide our common resources and common language.

But we have left Estrella—or the mediated image of the poor, black, monumental, mythic, (now silenced) Cuban singer—floating away in her smelly phallic coffin on the currents of the Gulf Stream, which will sooner or later fetch her up against the coasts of Europe, plastic sarcophagus and all. In some sense there is, within the confines allowed us by Cabrera Infante and González Echevarría, little we can say about Estrella. For if, as González Echevarría has so ably demonstrated, the masters and their voice pose a significant problematic that needs to be dissected, the same cannot be said about the black woman. In Cabrera Infante's text, as in González Echevarría's, Estrella is the narrative subject, which is to say, the object, of the story. The dominant voices of the narrators, of the critics—those who exercise the will to knowledge and who define what is and what ought to be known—are complex and richly nuanced. Estrella, in that respect, represents no problem. Or rather, let us say that the only problem she holds is in relation to the resources necessary to satisfy her reader that he has constituted an adequate approximation to her as an object of knowledge. She is not problematic in and of herself, merely insufficiently known, and what little is known of her is highly susceptible to incorporation under the rubric of the masterly voice (her silenced song) and bodily presence (in life, the fatty supplement of her elephantine body; in death, her maternal phallicity).

Let us propose, hypothetically, that Estrella has another side. The "Meta-Final" is supposedly hers, after all, as well as the narrative's. Let us imagine that she is just floating, with no end at all in sight, that she does not represent a floating signifier or a maternal phallus but merely *is*, and is a woman's body, buried at sea. Suppose we refuse to identify reality with the production of signs. Immediately, the abstraction slips away and another side of the subject/object is revealed, one that is caught in another narration, as corpse and as literary corpus, with another textured history of social or ideological production. We could say with Masiello (who is actually referring to something quite different, but I refuse to let context deny me a good quotation) that this other Estrella describes "a body that resists the tactics of naturalization and eludes the careful and predictable anticipatory level that always accompanies repressive discourses" ("Discurso" 56). The tactics of naturalization employed by González Echevarría in assimilating Estrella to a patriarchal (phallic) or literary-canonical (Melville) discourse are clear; they involve an undeconstructed essentialism that fails to take sufficient account of the position from which he speaks as the subject of his own discourse. Despite the surface fragmentation of texts he includes in *The Voice of the Masters*, such tactics implicate him in that unitary, hegemonic, masterly voice, writing "truth" across the woman's body. And one of those master's truths is that Estrella has no place in the institutionalized canon and no voice in the deliberations of the masters except as mediated in the anticipatory intervals of monstrosity, abstract alterity, or masculinized recuperation.

The strategy of the feminist critic at this stage is to challenge the ideological implications in this characterization, as well as to work through the consequences of her immasculation. Even if we agree with González Echevarría that all writers, men and women, need to reexamine and understand their relationships to the many textual authorities that make up the (unitary) voice of the masters, the network of communication—invisible lines of genealogy and of empowerment—function differently for a man describing his affiliation with the masters and for a woman writing against the deafening reach of their voice. If we go one step farther and suggest, with Jean-François Lyotard, that this particular moment in time can be characterized by the loss of the master text, then the voice of the masters, too, begins to fragment and split into cacophony. The significance of woman-centered interpretative strategies, among other interpretative modes formerly stifled by the authoritarian voice, begins to be understood; women's voices begin to be heard, and the gossamer lines of communication among men and women who challenge the ideology of repression lengthen and grow stronger.

Clearly, the loss of the master text does not mean a parallel loss of the speaking subject: quite the contrary. As Ruth Salvaggio writes, "In a game where the object is to subvert mastery, everyone wants to be the woman. Yet the space that she occupies seems to differ according to the peculiar womanly processes effected by different writers" (157). The prodigal daughter of the masterful father insists upon the ideological loading of even the well-meaning father's authoritarian stance, and she also assumes responsibility for her own imbrication in societal and cultural processes. Thus, whereas it is important to take into account the struggle with a language that, while her own, still seems stiff and foreign to her, it is also important to remember that more is at stake than the struggle with language. This double task of linguistic/literary and political reform is both necessary and, discouragingly, impossible. Why impossible? The problem is epistemological as well as political. Politically speaking, we have to make others recognize as significant that which has traditionally been ignored but which we are incapable of ignoring. Epistemologically, the concern can be described in the lack of unequivocal knowledge that makes the effacement of certain preestablished limits the condition of possibility for a feminist analysis. Within those boundaries, something demands interpretation, but the interpretation can only take place outside the rules of the game. Maybe, as Salvaggio affirms, everyone wants to be the woman, but only on his or her own terms and within the rules of the game. And many, many people have no interest in playing with the subject-effects of a woman's voice at all. Certainly, in the Cabrera Infante selection we have been exploring, the breaking up of the master-text through the strategic deployment of Estrella as an indecipherable woman-effect deprives the voice of the master(s) of none of its strength. And for the feminist critic to speak against the master's voice is to come up against the barrier of an unfulfillable lack in Estrella's fictional nature.

Estrella, though central to the text of "Meta-Final," is at the same time envisioned at one remove from that text. The exotic outsider to the great narrative taking place between men, she is read and recuperated for their text and for their narrative in a familiar metaphor of male bonding against the unknown.[2] The Nietzschean figure of woman as truth returns in new guise, narrative form is consolidated rather than fragmented, institutional processes allow for a smooth interpellation of Estrella's difference into the canonical metanarrative, and the issues of who is reading Estrella and how she is conscripted into this system of meaning are left unaddressed.

But just as there is no end for Estrella, neither is there any clear end for feminist practice, not when one of the dangers we hold most present is the concern that in deconstructing the image of woman-as-truth in the service of a masculinist theoretical enterprise we continually run the danger of endorsing other truth claims derived from a feminist reading of women as Woman. In this respect, one of our main concerns has to be an exploration of how a feminist practice can avoid constructing a hegemonic woman in opposition to a hegemonic man. In responding to the structures and strategies we decry, a feminist theory needs to prevent implication in those familiar processes, just as it must avoid replication in and recuperation by those perspectives.

[2]Powerful female figures like Estrella are, paradoxically, particularly difficult to study from a feminist point of view. I am reminded here of Showalter's pointed question, "If women are the silenced and repressed Other of Western discourse, how can a feminist theorist speak *as* a woman about women or anything else?" ("Criticism" 365).

Campos might say that in just floating Estrella undertakes a heroic enterprise, and a more nuanced study of the nature of that silent resistance (or lack of resistance) to wind and waves, that dark unreadability that poses a speechless affront to the male-gendered hegemonic voice, could no doubt be imagined and undertaken. But I hesitate to draw my final metaphor for a female-oriented practice from the interstices and gaps in an authoritarian "meta-end" or to define how I am talking back to the voice of the masters based on a hypothetical reading of a woman who once moved a nation with her voice but is now voiceless. So let me come back to my house, or room, of fiction, not to the madwoman in the attic or to the Attic madwoman or the *ama de casa* but rather to that other woman, the one who inhabits the *cuarto de azotea,* that room built on the roof of flat-topped Latin American houses. She is the woman who shares that cramped space next to the clotheslines and laundry sinks with the mops and brooms and unneeded items stored there so they won't take up space in the main house. Each morning, she gets up and prepares to take on the daily ritual of cooking, scrubbing, and sweeping, of picking up and putting away, of dusting, polishing, washing, and watching over children, so that the house is transformed and she recedes to the background. Housework, as she well knows, is never done, or is always to do over again, and again. Although she may never read in her *cuarto de azotea* or may only read photonovels and comic books written for the marginally literate, the *palabra azotada,* the *espalda azotada* are intimately, by a concrete tracing of genealogies, hers.

That woman who keeps house for the *ama de casa* is not, however, invisible nor silent, though her network of communication and relationships may run outside those licensed by the masters and mistresses. Among the episodes Rigoberta Menchú chooses to depict from her life in Guatemala is a chapter on her experience as a servant in the city. Lucía Rodríguez's testimonial, as captured by Leonor Cortina, is a picaresque chronicle of the multiplicity of relationships among her acquaintances and of her strategies to deal with the masters, male and female, which have served to ensure her survival, in life and in print, and which continue to serve her in dealing with those more fortunate.[3] Furthermore, to some degree domestic inscription all

---

[3]In her prologue, Cortina writes, apparently without consciousness of her manipulation by the servant woman, that Lucía proposed the book: "Tú que tienes facilidad para

and always belongs to this woman. Although her official territory is strictly demarcated and severely reduced, it is in some sense the mistress who lives on the periphery of the house, and as in Clarice Lispector's startling and powerful portrait in absentia of the maid's rage in *The Passion according to G. H.*, it is that woman, and not her upper-class white employer, who repositions herself from margin to center with her searingly potent inscription on the wall.

You see where I am going. I said at the opening of this book that my strategy was to give you this piece of writing like the first step in an exchange, like a recipe for use and modification, as the continuation of a dialogue opened in the first taste of a food we both savor. I add now that the practice undertaken in this book is like the housework done by that woman from the *azotea;* it is not always done patiently, not always good-humoredly, and sometimes certain rooms are given short shrift, and sometimes things are shoved under beds or into corners. But it is done persistently. And this housework/bookwork is undertaken in the knowledge that once it is done, everything is still to be done, that in the doing I undermine the possibility of its ever being, once and forever, done. There is still and always the cleaning of the house of fiction to be done, the polishing of the prose, the finding of the lost object. And other tasks. And while the subject and object of this task might be continuous, the practice and the instrumentality are always in process.

What I have not done, or spoken of at length in all this talk of strategy and practice, is theory. This is not to say that I shy away from theory, or from the theories I have employed in my project. I recognize that describing a feminist practice as housework or as a recipe also enjoins a theoretical positioning that proposes that what we say involves not only taking back (ourselves) but talking back (to the masterly voice, to each other) and that the job is never finished because, like housework, it is by definition interminable. Thus, I cannot adhere unconditionally to any polished theory, because such theories tend to

---

eso de los libros, ¿por qué no escribes mi vida? yo te regalo mi historia, verás que es como una novela." 'Since you're so good at book writing, why don't you write my story? I'll give it to you, free; you'll see it's like a novel.' Cortina adds, "La idea me entusiasmó y Lucía me entregó una serie de notas que había escrito" (5) 'I was enthusiastic about the idea and Lucía provided me with a series of notes she had written.' Lucía begins by flattering the upper-class woman, who has access to publishing circles, then proposes an economic exchange: her story for rights of authorship. Cortina agrees.

create a norm for practice in unforeseeable, sometimes unacceptable ways and because long practice has shown me that—in theoretical positions as in furniture—polish seems to attract dust. Yet this practice, too, insofar as it represents an ideological project and a particular mental orientation, involves an implicit theoretical positioning, though perhaps neither so dusty nor yet so polished as those theories and those practices I fragment and deploy throughout this work. By privileging practice over theory (defined as a universalizing tendency), I am, of course, making another sort of generalization, another kind of truth claim, but it is one that jettisons a hypothetical theoretical purity and an unalterable conviction of rightness.

Housekeeping is, after all, a pragmatic enterprise. It entails sweeping up and putting in order. It promises a house where the visitor will not be constantly tripping over other people's belongings. Accordingly, I find it necessary to make certain clarifications as I finish my tidying up and putting away. One needed clarification is suggested to me by Hernán Vidal. In his introduction to *Cultural and Historical Grounding for Hispanic and Luso-Brazilian Feminist Literary Criticism*, he writes: "En particular se me surgió que esta introducción debía dedicar cierto espacio a la discusión ocurrida en torno al término castellano 'género' en la crítica literaria feminista hispánica como traducción de la palabra inglesa 'gender', que hace una diferenciación social con respecto a la categoría biológica 'sex.' La participante que promovió la discusión manifestó incomodidad con el término castellano que, al contrario del inglés, su enorme variedad de significados lo hace ambigüo" (13). 'In particular, it came to me that this introduction ought to dedicate a certain amount of space to the discussion that occurred around the Spanish term *género* in Hispanic feminist literary criticism as the translation of the English word *gender*, which makes a social differentiation with respect to the biological category "sex." The participant who began the discussion was uncomfortable with the Spanish term, which, unlike its English counterpart, demonstrates an enormous variety of meanings that make it ambiguous.' Vidal's remarks are echoed in almost the same terms in Elena Sánchez-Mora's recapitulation and closing remarks (583) and elsewhere throughout the volume in various contributions. These repeated explorations of possibility indicate a general longing for a way of talking about "gender" in the Latin American context, for gender studies seem to open up the field of inquiry beyond women-centered readings of texts to an exploration of how all reading and writing and talking is to some degree affected and marked by that social category, gender, thus eliminating entirely the category of male-universal, female-other from our literary-historical vocabularies. Showalter adds that "talking about gender, moreover, is a constant reminder of other categories of difference, such as race and class, that structure our lives and our texts, just as theorizing gender emphasizes the parallels between feminist criticism and other forms of minority discourse" (*Speaking* 2–3). It strikes me that the frustration surrounding the untranslatability of the crucial term *gender* for Latin Americanists is one of those paradigmatic problems the urgency of which everyone recognizes, but no one can get beyond the initial shock of recognition. The question is, of course, why is the term perceived as both crucial and unresolvable?

The problem is partly that Spanish includes a nuanced concept of grammatical gender missing in English but more that Spanish conflates the ideas of gender, genre, and generic in phrase *sistema genérico*, which could as easily be translated by "generic system" or "genre system" as by "gender system." But there is more: the problem with "gender" also involves cultural loadings of the term, already suggested in Showalter's weighting of race and class issues alongside questions of feminist and minority discourse on the same side of the scale, whereas in Latin America the distribution would have to be somewhat different. And still further, there seems to me to be an unstated wariness among Latin Americanists deriving from a sense of critical and theoretical belatedness on the international feminist theoretical scene. Hispanist critics are uneasily aware that gender theory began to develop in Anglo-European circles in the 1980s only after a considerable evolution of diverse and complex feminist theorization. In the absence of such a generally recognized and developed body of criticism, gender studies in the Latin American context may seem both premature and politically disabling, as well as culturally and linguistically disjunctive. Thus, they may look both radical and irrelevant to those who are only beginning to examine literature from a woman-centered point of view and who lack confidence about their ability to generate a theory of their own. Gabriela Mora's essay "Un diálogo entre feministas hispanoamericanas," which takes the form of a dialogic encounter among various Hispanic feminists identified only by initials, raises several of these issues succinctly and discretely, if indirectly:

A. No puedes negar que el igualador del sistema genérico/sexual, borra
   las diferencias de etnias o clases. Ese igualador nos ha relegado a
   todas, desde tiempos inmemoriales, a las labores domésticas y a la
   crianza de niños. Por muchas criadas que la rica tenga, la responsabilidad de estas áreas cae sobre ella, no sobre el hombre. . . .
D. . . . aún si tuvieras razón en eso del igualador genérico, habría que
   preguntarse qué de común tiene una sirvienta india, analfabeta, con
   una escritora como Victoria Ocampo, pongamos por caso. ¿No crees
   que esa india se igualaría mejor con su hombre que con su seme-
   jante/mujer?
A. . . . D habló de "género," supongo para aludir a lo que en inglés las
   feministas llaman "gender system." A mí no me parece que la simple
   traducción funciona en el español, por las multiples conotaciones de
   la palabra "género," por eso prefiero decir "sistema genérico/sexual,"
   pero tampoco estoy satisfecha. (54–55)

A. You can't deny that the equalizer of the sex/gender system erases
   ethnic and class differences. That equalizer has relegated all of us,
   from time immemorial, to domestic work and bringing up children.
   No matter how many maids a rich woman has, responsibility in these
   areas falls on her, not on her husband. . . .
D. . . . even if you're right about this gender equalizer, we still have to
   ask what an illiterate Indian servant has in common with, for example, a writer like Victoria Ocampo. Don't you believe that Indian
   woman would "equalize" better with her male counterpart than with
   her fellow woman?
A. . . . D spoke about "gender," I suppose in order to allude to what in
   English the feminists call the "gender system." I don't think that the
   simple translation works in Spanish, because of the multiple connotations of the word *género;* for that reason I prefer to say "sex/gender
   system," but I'm not satisfied with that either.

The debate is a curious one: at one level merely linguistic, at another reflecting a poor cultural fit between Latin American and U.S.-
European variants of feminism, at still another pointing to what, from
a Eurocentric point of view, looks like a theory vacuum in Hispanic
thought. Moreover, Mora's version of the debate demonstrates how
such concerns can be deployed as a question-begging side issue to
sweep more crucial social and political problems under the rug. Problems of this sort, posed by Latin American or Latin Americanist critics
who live in this theoretical climate, almost inevitably seem to locate

themselves between the two spaces depicted by Mora in her exchange between A and D, between two alternative generating forces for a Hispanic feminist practice: the upper-class, white, purely theoretical Anglo-European woman, and the lower-class, nonwhite, purely practical, autochthonous Hispanic woman. These two spaces, as I have been showing, overlap incompletely with and at times are conceptually neutralized by other, historically validated positions relating to representations of the Latin American voice of authority. These voices I can very schematically represent as (1) a vexed affiliation with/rejection of the Anglo-Eurocentric-oriented father figure, who can alternately represent either Ariel or Caliban in contradistinction to the Anglo-European Prospero (my typical example has been Roberto González Echevarría), and (2) a longing for/disdain of the abject, purely domestic, and above all *mute* mother figure, recently entering public life as *la loca* of the Plaza de Mayo or the mediated "I" of increasingly popular testimonials—Rigoberta Menchú, Domitila Barrios de Chungara, and others—where the figure of the politically active, illiterate or marginally literate Indian woman consolidates the newly emerging hegemonic figure of the counterhegemonic Woman as Truth.

In all this, so many things are getting swept under the rug that we are beginning to accumulate quite a hump, so let me sweep it back out again and pick it up. In so doing, I am reminded of something Silvina Bullrich said in her book, *La mujer postergada* (Postponed woman): "Pero es tan ardua la tarea de ser una mujer moderna que una se pregunta si las feministas no se equivocaron al pedir que tuviéramos los mismos derechos que los hombres porque a la postre salimos teniendo los mismos deberes y la tercera parte de los derechos o aún menos, según los países. Pero conquistamos algo inapreciable: nuestra identidad" (45) 'The labor of being a modern woman is so arduous that one wonders if the feminists were not mistaken in asking that we have the same rights as men, because it seems that when dessert comes around we end up with the same duties and about a third of the rights, or even less, depending on the country. But we did conquer something priceless: our identity.' Sweep up the material and we find, however confused, our gendered identity.

Sweep. Out with the first-order readings of texts, which seem merely to reverse poles with a hegemonic masculinist critique and to substitute a valorized figure of woman for the formerly valorized figure of man. Such a procedure, as I have noted, seems suspiciously universalizing in that it reinstitutes one essentialist and ahistorical figure of woman for another, reaffirming the hegemony and inaugurating its own recuperation by the patriarchal forms it intends to rebut.

Sweep. Out with appeals to experience as the only indisputable ground of knowledge. For whereas the basic fact of experience can both authorize and empower a speaker/writer, I have too often seen experience deployed as a tactic to close off discussion, to control the audience, and to foment guilt. As Diana Fuss writes, "It is certainly true that there is no such thing as 'the Black experience' or 'the Jewish experience.' . . . And it seems likely that simply *being* a woman, or a Black, or a Jew [we can add, or a Hispanic] (as if 'being' were ever simple) is not enough to qualify one as an official spokesperson for an entire community" (117). Unexamined appeals to experience function as another undeconstructed form of essentialism which has not yet explored its own ideological basis.

Sweep. Out (painfully now) with a playful, tolerant, nonthreatening pluralism as a strategy for negotiating among the competing demands of the masters, or their opponents. A playful pluralism can tend to reject commitments of all sorts, and in refusing to judge among competing theories, it conceals the only implicit commitment it does make: to preserving the status quo. Moreover, a preference for dialogue and pluralist stances means that feminist discussions in general have made no great progress toward a unified theory, or even, their harshest critics might claim, to theoretical clarity. Indeed, the unresolved (unresolvable?) problem of the unified theory harks back to a nostalgia for an imagined universal (already swept out). Maintenance of a dialogue and a refusal to endorse exclusionary practices are hard and vigilant labor and, like housework, always to be done again. We need to be attentive to the instrumental value of a certain preferred constellation of theories, at least pragmatically, as tools to open up texts and ideologies—and to be aware of the degree to which we pretend our (diverse) pluralistic stances have self-evident, hence unexplored, identities.

Sweep. Out with inbred inferiority complexes. If this book has shown nothing else, I hope that at least it has demonstrated the strength and lucidity of Latin American women's own theorizing about their condition. They, like me, have learned from their European and North American counterparts, but the studies of Luisa Valenzuela, Clarice Lispector, Rosario Castellanos, and other Latin American women, as well as the expansion of their practical, theoretical insights in their works of fiction, are no mere wholesale (mis)appropriations.

Sweep. Out with other ethnocentric statements that set up too-neat binarisms for analysis. For example, this, from Sharon Magnarelli's *Lost Rib:* "Apparently the Hispanic, because of his culture and religion, tends to view women in more neatly polarized terms than many other national or ethnic groups" (187). Such binaries set the stage for inevitable over- and underreadings, for elements that cannot be integrated into this Manichean framework are bracketed and ignored.

Sweep one last time, painfully again. Out with what Spivak calls the structure of "translation-as-violation," which operates from an aseptic distance that mutilates and neutralizes works. Spivak says, "For example, our own mania for 'Third World Literature' anthologies, when the teacher or critic often has no sense of the original languages or of the subject-constitution of the social and gendered agents in question (and therefore the student cannot sense this as a loss), participates more in the logic of translation-as-violation than in the ideal of translation as freedom-in-troping" ("Imperialism" 331). In such cases, reading involves an intent *not* to read that author in his/her particularity but rather to annex the unfamiliar as a complementary authority in a familiar system.

The same structure of translation-as-violation holds for theoretical writings as well. Theoretical appropriations should not operate to the exclusion of indigenous cultural factors or as indicators of a specific, privileged, prestigious professional status. It is hard sometimes to remember to use only what is useful, to apply only what is applicable, and to employ the chosen fragments as a retranslated freedom-in-troping that both recalls and transforms the cultural heritage of the selected theoretical text.

In all this industrious sweeping up and sweeping out, at least one thing has uncovered itself. It is far, far easier to describe undesirable stances than to propose a positive program. It is far less wearing to imagine that my own critical identity is self-evident and needs no elaboration than to recognize that this elusive identity is at least partly so because, by its enunciation, I am opening myself to a dialogue that will, almost certainly, involve a catalogue of my own shortcomings. Justification and consolation are not lacking; as Donna Haraway writes, "It has become difficult to name one's feminism by a single adjective—or even to insist in every circumstance upon the noun"

(179). Fortunately, Spanish grammar, which is of no assistance in sorting out the problem of a translation for "gender" that neither violates nor appropriates Latin cultural experience, comes to my rescue at this point, reasserting Haraway's statement in a particularly Latin American context, helping me to name a functional juncture of my critical practice. In *la palabra asesino*, or *la palabra azotada*, or *cambio de armas*, Spanish permits an ambiguity that English cannot always capture, hinging on the difficulty of signaling the verb, naming the adjective, or identifying the noun. It is this fluid boundary between these multiply hinged and weighted words that recalls the shifting valences of a Latin American literary practice, in which the woman is at the same time the speaking subject, the violator of the authority's language, and the object of a literal and linguistic violation. It is this ambivalent hinge between violence and violation, between subject and object, between noun and verb, or noun and noun, or noun and adjective that reminds us of how each word in the clause props itself on the other, implicating that other term in a relationship that threatens to explode the more closely it is held to that imbricated and antagonistic adjacency. The subject hinges upon and unhinges the object, and vice versa. Thus, not the least of the contributions of Latin American feminist practice to international feminism is its method for dislocating the hinge between linguistic and extralinguistic binaries such as the one that has exercised us over the last few pages: father/authority/*maestro*/voice : mother/subordinate/student/mute. All of us who shuttle between housekeeping and bookmaking know at least one variation of this hinged/unhinged existence, one that is translatable by a freedom-in-troping, even if we do not all have the precise multilingual vocabularies to express it.

As a critic on one side of the hinge, talking about and to women who mostly live, conceptually at least, on the other side, I am constantly aware of my own precarious position as I stage-manage the dialogue among their texts, between those texts and my own, between my own two voices as they speak to and against each other here, and implicitly at least, between this book and you. This dialogue is not a dialectic, at least not in the ordinary senses of the word; it is, if you permit me one last borrowing, something more like a "diatactics."[4] It involves a multi-

---

[4] I borrow this term from Hwa Yol Jung' book *The Question of Rationality*. He describes *diatactics* as a heterocentric literary practice marked by its privileging of the senses, that is, *diatactics* for this author refers specifically to the realm of the tactile (14–17).

ply centered literary-critical practice that wants to engage both the concretely sensual (tactile) and the more abstractly strategic (tactics). It aspires to make sense and hint at a stimulation of the senses; it wants to confront the voice of the masters with a chorus of voices, to speak of product and process in the same breath.

With my last note in this text, let me cycle back to my very first reference and call to mind once again my mother-in-law. From dialogue with her I learned much about the women who do not speak in this book, and that part of the unspoken dialogue that does not appear in this text, although it helps to shape the form I have given it, is hers. She will not read this book though, her eloquence does not extend to a knowledge of English. Her name is not Estrella, but Estela, and she is a housekeeper, a superlative cook, a student of cosmetology, and a performing artist who, under the stage name of La Calandria Tapatía, *sings*.

Reprise: Uñas y Huesos

Las quejas de los problemas de uñas son variadas y constantes.

Que si no crecen, que si se rompen, que se descarapelan, que se abren de la punta, en fin, quejas de todas.

Bueno, mi primer consejo para el cuidado de las uñas es el siguiente:

Todas las mañanas se deben tomar una gelatina con el desayuno y otra gelatina en la noche con la cena o antes de dormirse, de preferencia sin sabor. Esto es infalible si lo hace con constancia.

Además, también para fortalecerlas por fuera, deben seguir este otro consejo. Se parte un diente de ajo a la mitad y se lo unta a sus uñas bien limpias, las deja ventilar aproximadamente una hora con el fin de que el ajo penetre. Después de ese tiempo, se aplica su barniz de uñas ya sea natural o con color, y listo. . . .

También es muy importante la manera como usted se lima las uñas. Debe tener mucho cuidado al hacerlo para evitar que las uñas se abran o se partan. Tiene que limarse parejo siguiendo el contorno de la uña, sin dejar asperezas.

Si sus uñas son escamosas o ásperas de naturaleza, les recomiendo que las remojan unos 10 minutos en aceite de almendras o de olivo calientito. Luego de este tiempo, saca usted sus uñas y les da un masaje con un algodón, así las escamas se irán saliendo y las uñas se suavizarán.

Ese mismo aceite tibio se lo puede poner después en sus manos, frotándolas con cuidado para que también aproveche y se haga un tratamiento de aceite.

Mientras espera que el aceite penetre en sus manos, usted puede tomar un pedazo de franela seca o una lija suave de papel y pulirse las uñas.

Cuando termine, se enjuaga las manos con agua fría para quitarse el aceite y al mismo tiempo para que las uñas se endurezcan, y al final, se da otro enjuague con té de manzanilla frío en las manos y en las uñas.

Si sigue usted mis consejos, lucirá unas manos preciosas y unas uñas envidiables.

Recuerde que la belleza cuesta, pero los resultados valen la pena.

Alfredo Palacios

por eso en las más grandes páginas de su vida ahí esta:
su cuerpo, su alma, sus huesos, músculos, nervios, lunares,
pezones, dedos, piel;
sus uñas y dientes y caprichos y celos

Agustín Monsreal

Onde reinventar o gesto e a palavra? Tudo está invadido pelos significados antigos, e nós próprios, e nós mulheres que pretendemos revolucionar, até aos ossos, até à medula.

Maria Isabel Barreno,
Maria Teresa Horta,
Maria Velho da Costa

Y si es superficie pulámosla para que no oponga ninguna aspereza al tacto, ningún sobresalto a la mirada.

Rosario Castellanos

Mi padre murió una lenta y amarilla tarde de noviembre. . . . Antes de morir fue intensamente frotado por mi madre y las mujeres de la casa, por lo cual puede decirse que murió en pleno brillo. Al morir, su estado de limpieza era perfecto, pues mi madre había acomodado escrupulosamente sus huesos sobre la mesita, separándolos bien de la porción de carne que aún tenía, procurando que las tibias, los parietales y las apéndices xifoideas no chocaran entre sí, asustándolo, aunque, a pesar de su esfuerzo, hay que confesarlo, el ruido de los huesos fue oído por toda la casa, como el sonido que producen las maderas, al ser frotadas, cuando se hace música o se hace fuego.

Cristina Peri Rossi

Ella inventa canciones laborales
se afila las uñas para el salto
encaramada en su existencia
propia se viste
va de dientes al colmado
a refrescarse la melena con cerveza.

Mayra Santos-Febres

Bella la sólida, enterita en apariencias, en su casa esperando sin saber muy bien qué, quizá algún viejo y olvidado retorno, algún afecto perdido en el camino, quizá. Bella la actriz representando su propio papel de espera. Limándose las uñas.

Limándose las uñas cuando sonó el timbre....

—Nada de afilarme nada. O al menos por fuera. Yo me afilo por dentro, me relamo, me esponjo las plumas interiores (a veces). Por fuera sólo soy la que soy con ligeras variantes y con las menores asperezas posibles. No tengo por qué afilarme de manera alguna. He dicho.

Luisa Valenzuela

Tantos años de rabia atarascada en la garganta como un taco mal clavado, Ambrosio, tantos años de pintarme las uñas todas las mañanas acercándome a la ventana para ver mejor, de pintármelas siempre con Cherries Jubilee, porque era la pintura más roja que había entonces, siempre con Cherries Jubilee mientras pensaba en ella, Ambrosio, en Isabel la Negra, o a lo mejor ya había empezado a pensar en mí. . . . Siguiendo una a una el contorno de las lunas blancas en la base de mis uñas, pasando cuidadosamente los pelitos del pincel por la orillita de mis uñas limadas en almendra, por la orillita de la cutícula que siempre me ardía un poco al contacto con la pintura porque al recortármelo siempre se me iba la mano, porque al ver el pellejito indefenso y blando apretado entre las puntas de la tijera me daba siempre un poco de rabia y no podía evitar pensar en ella.

Rosario Ferré

—¿Las ven… ? Como uña y mugre…

Devolveré mis manos a la tierra. Mis ojos al calor de los abismos, de las aguas azules, del viento entre los mangos, no quiero renunciar al llanto ni a las rondas de amor, al caramelo y los corozos, mis caballos;

al color que yo vi en ciertas auroras. Mi entrada en el letargo conducirá mi corazón hasta la roca del silencio, y allí se quedará, envuelto en vidrio.

Albalucía Angel

Carvão e unha se juntando, carvão e unha, tranqüila e compacta raiva daquela mulher que era a representante de um silêncio como se representasse um país estrangeiro, a rainha africana.

Clarice Lispector

limándose las uñas . . .
puliendo los huesos . . .

Appendix:

Translations: Recetario and Reprise

Recetario: Home, Cooking

But, Madam, what is there for us women to know, if not bits of kitchen philosophy?

Sor Juana Inés de la Cruz

The important thing is to apply that fundamental lesson taught to us by our mothers, who were the first to show us how to summon the spirit of the cookstove. The secret of writing, like the secret of good cooking, has nothing to do with gender. It has to do with the skill with which we mix the ingredients over the fire.

Rosario Ferré

What would you suggest for today's meal, experienced homemaker, inspiration of mothers both absent and present, voice of tradition, secret whisperings in supermarkets? I open a cookbook at random and read: "Don Quijote's Supper." Very literary but very unsatisfactory. Because Don Quijote was known as an absent-minded dreamer, not a gourmet. Although a more careful analysis of the text reveals that— etc., etc., etc. "Fowl Face Up." Esoteric. What kind of face? . . . "Veal à

la Rumanian." Who on earth do you think you're talking to? If I knew
what tarragon and scallions were, I wouldn't have to consult this book
because I would be all-knowing.

Rosario Castellanos

Eagerly, she gave herself the task of reading the list of ingredients for
succulent sauces, and it was like fishing in a river swarming with thousands of words of all sizes and colors: exotic spices that slipped away
like eels in the coming and going of her eager fingers, fragrant herbs
that reminded her, she didn't know why, of strange costal botanies,
sensual condiments whose name alone awoke sleepy caliphs and ma-
harajahs. And in front of that luxurious overflow of names—tarragon-
foliatedsalsifysaffronparsley—that struggled bravely to attach themselves to her memory, she felt inhibited, with the terrible sensation of
ineffectiveness that she felt so many times before throughout her
thirty-six years.

Carmen Lugo Filippi

Pedro's gaze had allowed her to recuperate her confidence in the love
he professed. She had spent months poisoned with the idea that either
Pedro had lied to her on his wedding day when he declared his love,
with the sole purpose of making her suffer, or that as time passed
Pedro really had fallen in love with Rosaura. This insecurity was born
when, inexplicably, he stopped praising her dishes. Tita anxiously
outdid herself in cooking better every day. Desperately, at night, obviously after knitting a good chunk of her comforter, she invented a
new recipe with the intention of recuperating the relationship that had
developed between herself and Pedro over her food. From this period
of suffering were born her best recipes.

    And exactly as a poet plays with words, so she played whimsically
with ingredients and amounts, obtaining phenomenal results.

Laura Esquivel

This is the way I pictured it:

> His wife in the kitchen wearing a freshly ironed apron, stirring a pot of soup, whistling a whistle-while-you-work tune, and preparing frosting for some cupcakes so that when he drove home from work, tired and sweaty, he would enter his castle to find his cherub baby in a pink day suit with newly starched ribbons crawling to him and his wife looking at him with pleasing eyes and offering him a cupcake.

It was a good image I wanted him to have and everyday I almost expected him to stop, put down his lunch pail and cry at the whole scene. If it wasn't for the burnt cupcakes, my damn varicose veins, and Marge blubbering all over her daysuit, it would have made a perfect snapshot.

Helena Maria Viramontes

They left a bread on the table,
half burned, half white,

. . . . .

It smells like my mother's milk,
it smells like the three valleys I have passed through:
Aconcagua, Pátzcuaro, Elqui,
and like my inmost recesses when I sing.

Gabriela Mistral

Preparing them was a complicated task and took time. First she would put them in a box lined with grass, and give them a certain rare herb that they would eat—seemingly with pleasure—and which acted as a purgative. There they would spend the first day. On the following morning she would bathe them carefully so as not to harm them, she would dry them, and she would place them in the pot full of cold water, spices, aromatic herbs, salt, and vinegar.

When the water began to heat they would start shrieking, shrieking, shrieking . . . They would shriek like newborn babies, like squashed mice, like bats, like strangled kittens, like hysterical women.

Amparo Dávila

No one can eat a woman whole.

Juan José Arreola

Here. Take this gingerbread lady
and put her in your oven.

. . . . .

we must all eat sacrifices.
We must all eat beautiful women.

Anne Sexton

The son ate stews of heart with potatoes, that his mother cooked for
him with her heart pierced by four wounds . . . : four open wounds
from four swords bathed in oil from the Garden of Olives and lemons
from the hot and tragic south to dress a bitter salad—mother and son
in the Golgotha of the most livid sadness—bathed with drops of
vinegar also, drops that were tears, that were blood.

Carmen Gómez Ojea

Let us say that when we cut onions, we cry; but when we peel the
artifically superimposed layers from our identity as Latin American
women, we find a center. So, let's go; pick up the skillet by the handle
and let's cook.

Patricia Elena González

Furtively, you verify your own continued existence in the mirror, and
you return to your cooking. . . . With your milk, mother, I swallowed
ice.

Luce Irigaray

Reprise: Nails and Bones

Complaints about problems of the nails are frequent and various.

That they don't grow, that they break, that they peel, that they chip—all sorts of problems.

Well, my first piece of advice on the care of the nails is the following:

Every morning one ought to have gelatin with breakfast, and another gelatin in the evening, with dinner or before bed, preferably unflavored. This is infallible if done consistently.

Besides that, to strengthen them outside, one should follow this other piece of advice. Cut a clove of garlic in half and rub it into well-cleaned nails, let them air for about an hour so the garlic can penetrate. After that time, clear or colored nail polish can be applied, and ready, set go. . . .

How you file your nails is also very important. You must be careful while doing it so that the nails don't crack or chip. You have to file evenly, following the curve of the nail, without leaving rough spots.

If your nails are naturally scaly or rough, I recommend that you soak them for ten minutes or so in nice warm almond or olive oil. After that, take the nails out and give them a massage with a piece of cotton and the scales will come off and the nails will soften up.

You can use this same warm oil to put on your hands, rubbing carefully so that your hands can also take advantage of an oil treatment.

While you're waiting for the oil to soak into your hands, you can take a piece of dry flannel or a strip of soft paper and polish your nails.

When you've finished, rinse your hands with cold water to remove the oil and to harden your nails, and, finally, give your hands and nails another rinse in cold camomile tea.

If you follow my advice, you will be able to show off your lovely hands and enviable nails.

Remember, beauty costs but the results are worth the price.

Alfredo Palacios

for this reason in her life's greatest pages there are:
her body, her soul, her bones, muscles, nerves, moles, nipples,
fingers, skin;
her nails and teeth and caprices and jealousy.

Agustín Monsreal

Where to reinvent the gesture and the word, if everything is invaded
by outworn significations, and our very selves, down to the bones,
down to the innermost marrow?

Maria Isabel Barreno
Maria Teresa Horta
Maria Velho da Costa

And if it is surface, let us polish it, so that it leaves no roughness to the
touch, no shock to the gaze.

Rosario Castellanos

My father died on a slow and yellow November afternoon. . . . Before
he died, he was rubbed intensely by my mother and by the other
women of the household, and for this reason it can be said that he died
at his most brilliant. When he died, his state of cleanliness was perfect,
since my mother had arranged his bones scrupulously on the bedside
table, separating out the bits of meat that still clung to them, trying to
make sure that the tibias, the parietals, and the xiphoid appendixes
did not bang together, scaring him, although, despite her efforts, it
must be confessed, the bones' noise was heard throughout the house,
like the noise that pieces of wood make when they are rubbed together
to make music or to make a fire.

Cristina Peri Rossi

She invents workers' songs
she files her nails for the leap
reaching up in her own
existence she dresses
going from the teeth to the brim
to refresh her streaming hair with beer.

Mayra Santos-Febres

Solid Bella, so composed it seems, waiting at home, not knowing exactly what for, possibly for something old and forgotten to return, some affection lost along the way, perhaps. Bella, the actress, playing her own waiting role. Filing her nails.

Filing her nails when the doorbell rang....

"I'm not filing anything. Anyway, I don't sharpen the outside. I sharpen the inside. I lick myself clean, I puff up my innermost feathers (sometimes). On the outside I'm just what I am, with slight variations and with the least possible roughness. I've no reason to sharpen anything. And that's that.

Luisa Valenzuela

So many years of hatred stuck in the throat like a badly driven plug, Ambrosio, so many years of polishing my nails every morning near the window so I could see better, of always polishing them with Cherries Jubilee, because it was the deepest red nail polish there was in those days, always with Cherries Jubilee while I thought about her, Ambrosio, about Isabel the Black, or perhaps she had already begun to think about me. . . . Following one by one the contours of the white half-moons at the base of my fingernails, carefully brushing the little hairs of the nail polish brush along the edge of my nails filed into an almond shape, along the edge of the cuticle that always burnt a bit when it came in contact with the polish, because when I cut them back I always cut too much, because just seeing that little scrap of soft and defenseless white hide pressed between the points of the scissors always made me a little furious and I couldn't prevent myself from thinking about her.

Rosario Ferré

"Do you see them...? Like a nail and its dirt..."

I will return my hands to the earth. My eyes to the heat of the abyss, of the blue water, of the wind in the mangos. I do not want to renounce weeping nor the rounds of love, the sweetness and the palms, my horses, the color I saw in certain dawns. My entrance into lethargy will drive my heart to the rock of silence, and there it will rest, covered with glass.

Albalucía Angel

Charcoal and fingernails join, charcoal and fingernails, calm, compact
fury of that woman who was the representative of a silence as if she
represented a foreign country, the African queen.

Clarice Lispector

        filing nails . . .
        polishing bones . . .

Works Cited

Abbott, H. Porter. "Autobiography, Autography, Fiction: Groundwork for a Taxonomy of Textual Categories." *New Literary History* 19 (1988): 597–615.

Abraham, Nicolas, and Maria Torok, *The Wolf Man's Magic Word: "A Cryptonymy."* Trans. Nicholas Rand. Minneapolis: University of Minnesota Press, 1986.

Acebey, David, ed. *¿Aquí también, Domitila!* Mexico: Siglo XXI, 1985.

Ahern, Maureen, ed. and intro. *A Rosario Castellanos Reader: An Anthology of Her Poetry, Short Fiction, Essays, and Drama.* Austin: University of Texas Press, 1988.

Altieri, Charles. "Judgment and Justice under Postmodern Conditions; or, How Lyotard Helps us Read Rawls as a Postmodern Thinker." In Dasenbrock: 61–91.

Appiah, Kwame Anthony. "Out of Africa: Topologies of Nativism." *Yale Journal of Criticism* 2 (1988): 153–78.

Armstrong, Nancy, and Leonard Tennenhouse, eds. *The Ideology of Conduct: Essays in Literature and the History of Sexuality.* New York: Methuen, 1987.

Balmori, Clemente Hernando. "Habla mujeril." *Filología* 8 (1962): 123–38.

Balzac, Honoré de. *La peau de chagrin.* Ed. S. de Sacy. Paris: Gallimard, 1974.

Barthes, Roland. *Camera Lucida.* Trans. Richard Howard. New York: Hill and Wang, 1981.

Baudrillard, Jean. *Seduction.* Trans. Brian Singer. New York: St. Martin's Press, 1990.

Belli, Gioconda. *La mujer habitada.* Managua, Nicaragua: Vanguardia, 1988.

Benedetti, Mario. "Rosario Castellanos y la incomunicación racial." In *Letras del continente mestizo.* Montevideo: Arca, 1969: 165–70.

Benjamin, Jessica. *The Bonds of Love: Psychoanalysis, Feminism, and the Problem of Domination.* New York: Pantheon, 1988.

Bhabha, Homi K. "Of Mimicry and Man: The Ambivalence of Colonial Discourse." *October* 28 (1984) 125–33.

——. "Signs Taken for Wonders: Questions of Ambivalence and Authority under a Tree outside Delhi, May 1817." In Gates 12.1: 144–65.

Birus, Hendrik. "Adorno's 'Negative Aesthetics'?" In Budick and Iser: 140–64.

Blanco, José Joaquín. *Cuando todas las chamacas se pusieron medias nylon.* Mexico: Enjambre, 1988.

Bradbury, Malcolm. *Possibilities: Essays on the State of the Novel.* London: Oxford University Press, 1973.

Brodzki, Bella, and Celeste Schenck. *Life/Lines: Theorizing Women's Autobiography.* Ithaca: Cornell University Press, 1988.

Brooks, Peter. *Reading for the Plot: Design and Intention in Narrative.* New York: Vintage, 1984.

Bruns, Gerald L. "Disappeared: Heidegger and the Emancipation of Language." In Budick and Iser: 117–139.

Budick, Sanford, and Wolfgang Iser, eds. *The Play of Negativity in Literature and Literary Theory.* New York: Columbia University Press, 1989.

Bullrich, Silvina. *La mujer postergada.* Buenos Aires: Sudamericana, 1982.

Bush, Andrew. " 'Señalar las discrepancias': Rosario Ferré y Antonio Skármeta hablan de Cortázar." *Revista de estudios hispánicos* 21 (1987): 73–87.

Campos, Julieta. "La ciudad." In *Celina o los gatos.* Mexico: Siglo XXI, 1968.

——. *Función de la novela.* Mexico: Joaquín Mortiz, 1973.

——. *La imagen en el espejo.* Mexico: UNAM, 1965.

——. "Mi vocación literaria." *Revista iberoamericana* 51 (1985): 467–70.

——. *Muerte por agua.* 1965. Mexico: Fondo de cultura económica, 1985.

——. *Tiene los cabellos rojizos y se llama Sabina.* Mexico: Joaquín Mortiz, 1974.

Candido, Antonio. "No raiar de Clarice Lispector." In *Vários escritos.* São Paulo: Livraria duas ciclades, 1977.

Carpentier, Alejo. *Tientos y diferencias.* Buenos Aires: Calicanto, 1967.

Carrol, John B. Introduction to *Language, Thought, and Reality: Selected Writings of Benjamin Lee Whorf.* New York: Wiley, 1956.

Castellanos, Rosario. *Another Way to Be: Selected Works of Rosario Castellanos.* Ed. and trans. Myralyn F. Allgood. Athens: University of Georgia Press, 1990.

——. *Balún-Canán.* 1957; Mexico: Fondo de cultura económica, 1984. Translated by Irene Nicholson as *The Nine Guardians.* London: Faber and Faber, 1959.

——. *El eterno femenino: Farsa.* Mexico: Fondo de cultura económica, 1975. Translated in Ahern.

——. *Jucios sumarios.* 1966; Mexico: Fondo de cultura económica, 1984.

——. *Meditación en el umbral.* Mexico: Fondo de cultura económica, 1985. Translated by Julian Palley as *Meditation on the Threshold.* Tempe, Ariz.: Bilingual Review Press, 1989.

——. *Mujer que sabe latín. . . .* 1973; Mexico: Fondo de cultura económica, 1984.

——. *Oficio de tinieblas.* 1962; Mexico: Joaquín Mortiz, 1972.

——. *Salomé y Judith: Poemas dramáticos.* Mexico: Editorial Jus, 1959.

——. *El uso de la palabra.* Ed. José Emilio Pacheco. Mexico: Excélsior, 1974.

Castro-Klarén, Sara. "La crítica literaria femenista y la escritora en América latina." In González and Ortega: 27–46.

——. "The Novelness of a Possible Poetics for Women." In Vidal: 95–106.

Cavell, Stanley. "Naughty Orators: Negation of Voice in *Gaslight*." In Budick and Iser: 340–77.

——. "Postscript (1989): To Whom It May Concern." *Critical Inquiry* 16 (1990): 248–89.

Chávez, Denise. *The Last of the Menu Girls*. Houston: Arte Público, 1986.

Chevigny, Bell Gale, and Gari Laguardia, eds. *Reinventing the Americas: Comparative Studies of Literature of the United States and Spanish America*. London: Cambridge University Press, 1986.

Cixous, Hélène. "L'approche de Clarice Lispector." *Poétique* 40 (1979): 408–19.

——. Foreword to Clarice Lispector, *Stream of Life (Água viva)*. Trans. Verena Conley. Minneapolis: University of Minnesota Press, 1989.

Coetzee, J. M. "Alex La Guma and the Responsibilities of the South African Writer." In *New African Literature and the Arts*. Ed. Joseph Okpaku. New York: Third Press, 1973: 116–124.

——. "The First Sentence of Yvonne Burgess's *The Strike*." *English in Africa* 3 (1976): 47–48.

——. "Newton and the Ideal of a Transparent Scientific Language." *Journal of Literary Semantics* 11 (1982): 3–13.

——. "A Note on Writing." In Daymond, Jacobs, and Lenta: 11–13.

Cohen, Ralph, ed. *The Future of Literary Theory*. New York: Routledge, 1989.

Cohn, Jan. *Romance and the Erotics of Property*. Durham: Duke University Press, 1988.

Cortázar, Julio. *Rayuela*. Buenos Aires: Sudamericana, 1963. Translated by Gregory Rabassa as *Hopscotch*. New York: Avon, 1966.

Cortina, Leonor. *Lucía*. Mexico: Libros de México, 1988.

Cresta de Leguizamón, María Luisa. "En recuerdo de Rosario Castellanos." *La palabra y el hombre* 19 (1976): 3–18.

Cypess, Sandra Messinger. "*Balún-Canán*: A Model Demonstration of Discourse as Power." *Revista de estudios hispánicos* 19 (1985): 1–15.

Dasenbrock, Reed Way. "Intelligibility and Meaningfulness in Multicultural Literature in English." *PMLA* 102 (1987): 10–19.

——, ed. *Redrawing the Lines: Analytic Philosophy, Deconstruction, and Literary Theory*, Minneapolis: University of Minnesota Press, 1989.

Davis, Lennard J. *Resisting Novels: Ideology and Fiction*. New York: Methuen, 1987.

Daymond, M. J., J. U. Jacobs, and Margaret Lenta, eds. *Momentum: On Recent South African Writing*. Pietermaritzburg, South Africa: University of Natal Press, 1984.

de Certeau, Michel. *Heterologies: Discourse on the Other*. Trans. Brian Massumi. Minneapolis: University of Minnesota Press, 1986.

Derrida, Jacques. "But, beyond . . . (Open Letter to Anne McClintock and Rob Nixon)." In Gates 13.1: 155–70.

——. *Dissemination*. Trans. Barbara Johnson. Chicago: University of Chicago Press, 1981.

——. "*Fors:* The Anglish Words of Nicolas Abraham and Maria Torok." Trans. Barbara Johnson. In Abraham and Torok: xi–xlviii.

——. "How to Avoid Speaking: Denials." Trans. Ken Frieden. In Budick and Iser: 3–70.

——. *Margins of Philosophy.* Trans. Alan Bass. Chicago: University of Chicago Press, 1982.

——. *Of Grammatology.* Trans. Gayatri Chakravorty Spivak. Baltimore: Johns Hopkins University Press, 1976.

——. *Positions.* Trans. Alan Bass. Chicago: University of Chicago Press, 1981.

——. "The Question of Style." Trans. Ruben Berezdivin. In *The New Nietzsche: Contemporary Styles of Interpretation.* Ed. David B. Allison. New York: Dell, 1977: 176–89.

——. "Racism's Last Word." In Gates 12.1: 290–99.

Devi, Mahasveta. "Drapaudi." Trans. and foreword Gayatri Chakravorty Spivak. *Critical Inquiry* 8 (1981): 381–402.

Ehrmann, Jacques. "Structures of Exchange in *Cinna.*" In *Introduction to Structuralism.* Ed. Michael Lane. New York: Basic Books, 1970.

Espinosa Rugarcia, Amparo, Marcela Ruiz de Velasco, and Gloria M. Prado Garduño. *Palabras de mujer.* Mexico: Diana, 1989.

Esquivel, Laura. *Como agua para chocolate: Novela de entregas mensuales con recetas, amores y remedios caseros.* Mexico: Planeta, 1989.

Feal, Rosemary Geisdorfer. "Spanish American Ethnobiography and the Slave Narrative Tradition: *Biografía de un cimarrón* and *Me llamo Rigoberta Menchú.*" *Modern Language Studies* 20 (1990): 100–111.

Feldstein, Richard, and Henry Sussman, eds. *Psychoanalysis and. . . .* New York: Routledge, Chapman, and Hall, 1990.

Fernández Olmos, Margarite. "From a Woman's Perspective: The Short Stories of Rosario Ferré and Ana Lydia Vega." In Meyer and Fernández Olmos, *Introductory Essays:* 78–90.

——. "Luis Rafael Sánchez and Rosario Ferré: Sexual Politics and Contemporary Puerto Rican Narrative." *Hispania* 70 (1987): 40–46.

Ferré, Rosario. *El árbol y sus sombras.* Mexico: Fondo de cultura económica, 1989.

——. *Maldito amor.* Mexico: Joaquín Mortiz, 1986. Translated by Ferré as *Sweet Diamond Dust.* New York: Ballantine, 1988.

——. *Papeles de Pandora.* Mexico: Joaquín Mortiz, 1979. "La muñeca menor" ("The Youngest Doll") and "La bella durmiente" ("Sleeping Beauty") have been translated by Diana Vélez and Rosario Ferré in *Reclaiming Medusa: Short Stories by Contemporary Puerto Rican Women.* Ed. Diana Vélez. San Francisco: Spinsters/Aunt Lute, 1988: 27–63. The English stories are more properly versions than translations, as they differ considerably from the Spanish. "Cuando las mujeres quieren a los hombres" ("When Women Love Men") has been translated by Cynthia Ventura in Meyer and Fernández Olmos, *New Translations:* 176–85.

——. *Sitio a Eros.* Mexico: Joaquín Mortiz, 1980. The essay "La cocina de la escritura" has been translated by Diana L. Vélez as "The Writer's Kitchen." *Feminist Studies* 12 (1986): 227–42.

Fetterley, Judith. *The Resisting Reader: A Feminist Approach to American Fiction.* Bloomington: Indiana University Press, 1978.

Fineman, Joel. " 'The Pas de Calais': Freud, the Transference, and the Sense of Woman's Humor." *Yale Journal of Criticism* 1 (1988): 129–43.

Fiscal, María Rosa. "La mujer en la narrativa de Rosario Castellanos." *Texto crítico* 5 (1979): 133–53.

Fitz, Earl E. *Clarice Lispector.* Boston: Twayne, 1985.

Flax, Jane. *Thinking Fragments: Psychoanalysis, Feminism, and Postmodernism in the Contemporary West.* Berkeley: University of California Press, 1989.

Flieger, Jerry Aline. "The Female Subject: (What) Does Woman Want?" In Feldstein and Sussman: 54–63.

Fraden, Rena. "Response to Professor Carolyn Porter." *New Literary History* 21 (1990): 273–78.

Franco, Jean. "Apuntes sobre la crítica feminista y la literatura hispanoamericana." *Hispamérica* 15.45 (1986): 31–43.

——. "Beyond Ethnocentrism: Gender, Power, and the Third-World Intelligentsia." In *Marxism and the Interpretation of Culture.* Ed. Cary Nelson and Lawrence Grossberg. Urbana: University of Illinois Press, 1988: 503–15.

——. *An Introduction to Spanish American Literature.* Cambridge: Cambridge University Press, 1969.

——. "The Nation as Imagined Community." In *The New Historicism.* Ed. H. Aram Veeser. New York: Routledge, 1989: 204–12.

——. *Plotting Women: Gender and Representation in Mexico.* New York: Columbia University Press, 1989.

Frischmann, Donald H. "El sistema patriarcal y las relaciones heterosexuales en *Balún-Canán* de Rosario Castellanos." *Revista iberoamericana* 51.132–33 (1985): 665–78.

Fuentes, Carlos. *Cristóbal Nonato.* Mexico: Fondo de cultura económica, 1987. Translated by Alfred J. MacAdam and the author as *Christopher Unborn.* New York: Farrar, Straus and Giroux, 1989.

——. *La nueva novela latinoamericana.* Mexico: Joaquín Mortiz, 1972. "La palabra enemiga" has been translated by Suzanne Jill Levine as "The Enemy: Words" in White and Newman: 111–22.

Fuss, Diana. *Essentially Speaking: Feminism, Nature, and Difference.* New York: Routledge, 1989.

Gámbaro, Griselda. "Feminism or Femininity?" *Américas* 30.1 (1978): 18–19.

García Pinto, Magdalena. *Historias íntimas: Conversaciones con diez escritoras latinoamericanas.* Hanover, N.H.: Ediciones del norte, 1988.

Garro, Elena. "La culpa es de los Tlaxcaltecas." In *La semana de colores.* Mexico: Grijalbo, 1987. Translated by Alberto Manguel as "It's the Fault of the Tlaxcaltecas" in his *Other Fires: Short Fiction by Latin American Women.* New York: Clarkson N. Potter, 1986: 159–78.

Gates, Henry Louis, Jr. *Figures in Black: Words, Signs, and the "Racial" Self.* New York: Oxford University Press, 1987.

——, ed. *"Race," Writing, and Difference.* Special issues of *Critical Inquiry* 12.1 (1985) and 13.1 (1986).

332   Works Cited

Glantz, Margo. *De la amorosa inclinación a enredarse en cabellos*. Mexico: Océano, 1984.
——. *La lengua en la mano*. Mexico: Premiá, 1983.
Godzich, Wlad. "Emergent Literature and the Field of Comparative Literature." In Koelb and Noakes: 18–36.
Gomes, Renato Cordeiro, and Amariles Guimarães Hill, eds. *Selecta de Clarice Lispector*. Rio de Janeiro: José Olympio, 1975.
Gomringer, Eugen. "Silencio." In *Worte sind Schatten die Konstellationen, 1951–1968*. Ed. Helmut Heissenbüttel. Hamburg: Rowohlt, 1969.
González, Patricia Elena, and Eliana Ortega, eds. *La sartén por el mango*. Río Piedras, P.R.: Huracán, 1985.
González Echevarría, Roberto. *The Voice of the Masters: Writing and Authority in Modern American Literature*. Austin: University of Texas Press, 1985.
Gould, Stephen Jay. "Animals and Us." *New York Review of Books* 34 (1987): 20–25.
Guerra-Cunningham, Lucía. "Algunas reflexiones teóricas sobre la novela feminina." *Hispamérica* 10 (1981): 29–39.
——. "Las sombras de la escritura: Hacia una teoría de la producción literaria de la mujer latinoamericana." In Vidal: 129–64.
——. "Tensiones paradójicas de la femineidad en la narrativa de Rosario Ferré." *Chasqui* 13 (1984): 13–25.
Guillaumin, Colette. "Practique du pouvoir et idée de nature." *Questions féministes* 2 (1978): 5–29.
Gutiérrez, Ana, ed. *Se necesita muchacha*. Mexico: Fondo de cultura económica, 1983.
Haraway, Donna. "A Manifesto for Cyborgs: Science, Technology, and Socialist Feminism in the 1980s." In *Coming to Terms: Feminism, Theory, Politics*. Ed. Elizabeth Weed. New York: Routledge, 1989: 173–204.
Hayman, David. *Re-forming the Narrative: Toward a Mechanics of Modernist Fiction*. Ithaca: Cornell University Press, 1987.
Heath, Stephen. "Male Feminism." In *Men in Feminism*. Ed. Alice Jardine and Paul Smith. London: Methuen, 1987: 1–32.
——. *The Nouveau Roman: A Study in the Practice of Writing*. Philadelphia: Temple University Press, 1972.
Heilbrun, Carolyn G. "Non-autobiographies of 'Privileged' Women: England and America." In Brodzki and Schenck: 62–76.
Hollier, Denis. *The Politics of Prose*. Trans. Jeffrey Mehlman. Minneapolis: University of Minnesota Press, 1986.
Hwa Yol Jung. *The Question of Rationality*. Tokyo: International University of Japan Press, 1989.
Irigaray, Luce. *Speculum of the Other Woman*. Trans. Gillian C. Gill. Ithaca: Cornell University Press, 1985.
Jacobus, Mary. *Reading Woman: Essays in Feminist Criticism*. New York: Columbia University Press, 1986.
JanMohamed, Abdul R. "The Economy of Manichean Allegory: The Function of Racial Difference in Colonialist Literature." In Gates 12.1: 59–87.

Jardine, Alice. *Gynesis: Configurations of Women and Modernity.* Ithaca: Cornell University Press, 1985.

Johnson, Barbara. "Thresholds of Difference: Structures of Address in Zora Neale Hurston." In Gates 12.1: 278–89.

Jozef, Bella. "Clarice Lispector: La recuperación de la palabra poética." *Revista iberoamericana* 50 (1984): 239–57.

Sor Juana Inés de la Cruz (Juana de Asbaje). *A Sor Juana Anthology.* Trans. Alan S. Trueblood. Cambridge, Mass: Harvard University Press, 1988.

——. *Obras completas.* 4 volumes. Ed. Alfonso Méndez Plancarte. Mexico: Fondo de cultura económica, 1952.

Kaminsky, Amy. "Lesbian Cartographies: Body, Text, and Geography." In Vidal: 223–56.

Khatibi, Abdelkebir. *Love in Two Languages.* Trans. Richard Howard. Minnesota: University of Minnesota Press, 1990.

Kingston, Maxine Hong. *China Men.* New York: Ballantine, 1977.

——. *The Woman Warrior: Memoirs of a Girlhood among Ghosts.* New York: Vintage, 1975.

Kirkpatrick, Susan. *Las Románticas: Women Writers and Subjectivity in Spain, 1835–1850.* Berkeley: University of California Press, 1989.

Koelb, Clayton, and Virgil Lokke, eds. *The Current in Criticism.* West Lafayette, Ind.: Purdue University Press, 1987.

Koelb, Clayton, and Susan Noakes, eds. *The Comparative Perspective on Literature: Approaches to Theory and Practice.* Ithaca: Cornell University Press, 1988.

Kojève, Alexandre. *Introduction to the Reading of Hegel.* Trans. James H. Nichols, Jr. Ithaca: Cornell University Press, 1969.

Kristeva, Julia. *Powers of Horror: An Essay on Abjection.* Trans. Leon S. Roudiez. New York: Columbia University Press, 1982.

——. *Tales of Love.* Trans. Leon S. Roudiez. New York: Columbia University Press, 1987.

Lagos-Pope, María Inés. "Mujer y política en *Cambio de armas* de Luisa Valenzuela." *Hispamérica* 16. 4607 (1987): 71–83.

Lakoff, Robin. "Language and Woman's Place." *Language in Society* 2 (1973): 45–80.

Lejeune, Philippe. *On Autobiography.* Trans. Katherine Leary. Minneapolis: University of Minnesota Press, 1989.

Leonardi, Susan J. "Recipes for Reading: Summer Pasta, Lobster à la Riseholme, and Key Lime Pie." *PMLA* 104 (1989): 340–47.

Levine, Linda Gould, and Gloria Waldman. *Feminismo ante el franquismo: Entrevistas con feministas de España.* Miami: Universal, 1980.

Lévi-Strauss, Claude. *The Elementary Structures of Kinship.* Boston: Beacon Press, 1969.

Lewis, Philip. "The Post-Structuralist Condition." *Diacritics* 12.1 (1982): 2–24.

Lichtenstein, Jacqueline. "Making up Representation: The Risks of Femininity." In *Misogyny, Misandry, and Misanthropy.* Ed. R. Howard Bloch and Frances Ferguson. Berkeley: University of California Press, 1989.

Lindstrom, Naomi. "Articulating Woman's Experience." *Chasqui* 8 (1978): 43–52.

——. "A Feminist Discourse Analysis of Clarice Lispector's 'Daydreams of a Drunken Housewife.'" *Latin American Literary Review* 9.19 (1981): 7–17.

Ling, Amy. "Thematic Threads in Maxine Hong Kingston's *The Woman Warrior*." *Tamkang Review* 14 (1983–84): 155–64.

Lionnet, Françoise. *Autobiographical Voices: Race, Gender, Self-Portraiture.* Ithaca: Cornell University Press, 1989.

Lippard, Lucy R. *From the Center: Feminist Essays on Women's Art.* New York: Dutton, 1976.

Lispector, Clarice. *Água viva.* Rio de Janeiro: Editôra artenova, 1974. Translated by Elizabeth Lowe as *The Stream of Life.* Minneapolis: University of Minnesota Press, 1989.

——. *Laços de família.* 1960; Rio de Janeiro: José Olympio, 1974. Translated by Giovanni Pontiero as *Family Ties.* Austin: University of Texas Press, 1972.

——. *A Legião estrangeira.* Rio de Janeiro: Editôra do autor, 1964. Translated by Giovanni Pontiero as *The Foreign Legion.* Manchester, Eng.: Carcanet Press, 1986.

——. *A paixão segundo G. H.* Rio de Janeiro: Editôra do autor, 1964. Translated by Ronald W. Sousa as *The Passion according to G. H.* Minneapolis: University of Minnesota Press, 1988.

Loaeza, Guadalupe. *Las niñas bien.* 1987; Mexico: Aguilar, León y Cal, 1990.

——. *Las reinas de Polanco.* Mexico: Cal y Arena, 1988.

Longxi, Zhang. "The Myth of the Other: China in the Eyes of the West." *Critical Inquiry* 15 (1988): 108–31.

Lowe, Elizabeth. "The Passion according to C. L." (interview). *Review* 24 (1979): 34–37.

Ludmer, Josefina. "Tretas del débil." In González and Ortega: 47–54.

Lyotard, Jean-François. "A Success of Sartre's." Foreword to Hollier.

MacCannell, Dean, and Juliet Flower MacCannell. "The Beauty System." In Armstrong and Tennenhouse: 206–38.

MacDonald, Regina Harrison. "Rosario Castellanos: On Language." In *Homenaje a Rosario Castellanos.* Ed. Maureen Ahern and Mary Seale Vásquez. Valencia: Albatros, 1980: 41–64.

McLeod, Anne. "Gender Difference Relativity in GDR-Writing; or, How to Oppose without Really Trying." *Oxford Literary Review* 7 (1985): 41–61.

Magnarelli, Sharon. *The Lost Rib: Female Characters in the Spanish-American Novel.* Lewisburg, Pa.: Bucknell University Press, 1985.

——. "Luisa Valenzuela's *Cambio de armas*: Subversion and Narrative Weaponry." *Romance Quarterly* 34 (1987): 85–94.

Maier, Carol, and Noël Valis, eds. *In the Feminine Mode.* Lewisburg, Pa.: Bucknell University Press, 1989.

Masiello, Francine. "Between Civilization and Barbarism: Women, Family, and Literary Culture in Mid-Nineteenth-Century Argentina." In Vidal: 517–66.

——. "Discurso de mujeres, lenguaje de poder: Reflexiones sobre la crítica feminista a mediados de la década del 80." *Hispamérica* 15.45 (1986): 53–60.

Meyer, Doris, ed. and intro. *Lives on the Line: The Testimony of Contemporary Latin American Authors.* Berkeley: University of California Press, 1988.

Meyer, Doris, and Margarite Fernández Olmos, eds. *Contemporary Women Authors of Latin America.* 2 vols.: *Introductory Essays* and *New Translations.* New York: Brooklyn College Press, 1983.

Michaels, Walter Benn. "The Contracted Heart." *New Literary History* 21 (1990): 495–531.

Michie, Helena. *The Flesh Made Word: Female Figures and Women's Bodies.* New York: Oxford University Press, 1987.

Miller, Beth, ed. *Women in Hispanic Literature: Icons and Fallen Idols.* Berkeley: University of California Press, 1983.

Miller, Beth, and Alfonso González. *26 autoras del México actual.* Mexico: B. Costa-Amic, 1978.

Miller, Lucien, and Hui-chuan Chang. "Fiction and Autobiography: Spatial Form in *The Golden Cangue* and *The Woman Warrior.*" *Tamkang Review* 15 (1984–85): 75–96.

Modleski, Tania. *Loving with a Vengeance: Mass-Produced Fantasies for Women.* New York: Methuen, 1982.

Mohanty, Satya P. "Us and Them: On the Philosophical Bases of Political Criticism." *Yale Journal of Criticism* 2 (1989): 1–31.

Monsreal, Agustín. "Prólogo." In Espinosa Rugarcia, Ruiz de Velasco, and Prado Garduno: 9–14.

Mora, Gabriela. "Un diálogo entre feministas hispanoamericanas." In Vidal: 53–78.

Mull, Dorothy S. "Ritual Transformation in Luisa Valenzuela's 'Rituals of Rejection.'" *Review of Contemporary Fiction* 6.3 (1986): 88–95.

Ngũgĩ wa Thiong'o. *Decolonising the Mind: The Politics of Language in African Literature.* London: James Currey, 1986.

——. *Writers in Politics.* London: Heinemann, 1981.

Nietzsche, Friedrich. *The Gay Science.* Trans. Walter Kaufmann. New York: Random House (Vintage), 1974.

Nkosi, Lewis. "Fiction by Black South Africans." In *Introduction to African Literature.* Ed. Ulli Beier. Evanston, Ill.: Northwestern University Press, 1967.

——. *Home and Exile and Other Selections.* New York: Longman, 1965.

——. *Tasks and Masks: Themes and Styles of African Literature.* New York: Longman, 1981.

Noakes, Susan. "On the Superficiality of Women." In Koelb and Noakes: 339–55.

Nunca Más: The Report of the Argentine National Commission on the Disappeared. Intro. Ronald Dworkin. New York: Farrar Straus Giroux, 1986.

Nunes, Maria Luisa. "Clarice Lispector: Artista andrógina ou escritora?" *Revista iberoamericana* 50 (1984): 281–89.

Ocampo, Aurora M. "Debe haber otro modo de ser humano y libre: Rosario Castellanos." *Cuadernos americanos* 250.5 (1983): 199–212.

Ocampo, Victoria. *Testimonios.* 10 vols. Buenos Aires: Sur, 1935–77.

Ordóñez, Monserrat. "Máscara de espejos, un juego especular: Entrevistaasociaciones con la escritora argentina Luisa Valenzuela." *Revista iberoameri-cana* 51 (1985): 511–17.

Partnoy, Alicia. *The Little School: Tales of Disappearance and Survival in Argentina.* Trans. Alicia Partnoy with Lois Athey and Sandra Braunstein. Pittsburgh: Cleis, 1986.

Paz, Octavio. Foreword to Jacques Lafaye, *Quetzalcóatl and Guadalupe: The Formation of Mexican National Consciousness, 1531–1813.* Trans. Benjamin Keen. Chicago: University of Chicago Press, 1974.

—— *El laberinto de la soledad.* 1959; Mexico: Fondo de Cultura Económica, 1980. Translated by Lysander Kemp as *The Labyrinth of Solitude.* New York: Grove, 1961.

——. *El signo y el garabato.* Mexico: Joaquín Mortiz, 1973.

Peixoto, Marta. "*Family Ties:* Female Development." In *The Voyage In: Fictions of Female Development.* Ed. Elizabeth Abel and Marianne Hirsch. Hanover, N.H.: University Press of New England, 1983: 287–303.

Peri Rossi, Cristina. *El museo de los esfuerzos inútiles.* Barcelona: Seix Barral, 1983.

——. *Los museos abandonados.* Barcelona: Lumen, 1974.

Pezzoni, Enrique. "Victoria Ocampo, escritora." *Sur* 348 (1981): 143–50.

Poniatowska, Elena. *Hasta no verte, Jesús mío.* Mexico: Era, 1975.

——. "La literatura de las mujeres es parte de la literatura de los oprimidos." *Fem* 6.21 (1982): 23–27.

——. *¡Ay vida, no me mereces!* Mexico: Joaquín Mortiz, 1985.

Potter, Alicia Rivero. "La creación literaria en Julieta Campos: *Tiene los cabellos rojizos y se llama Sabina.*" *Revista iberoamericana* 51 (1985): 899–907.

Puga, María Luisa. *Las posibilidades del odio.* Mexico: Siglo XXI, 1978.

Puga, María Luisa, and Mónica Mánsour. *Itinerario de palabras.* Mexico: Folios ediciones, 1987.

Rabine, Leslie W. "No Lost Paradise: Social Gender and Symbolic Gender in the Writings of Maxine Hong Kingston." *Signs* 12 (1987): 471–92.

Rabinowitz, Paula. "Eccentric Memories: A Conversation with Maxine Hong Kingston." *Michigan Quarterly Review* 26 (1987): 177–87.

Ramos Otero, Manuel. *El cuento de la mujer del mar.* Río Piedras: Huracán, 1979.

Reichel, D., Elizabeth de Von Hildebrand, and Jorge Arias de Greiff, eds. *Etnoastronomías americanas.* Bogotá: Ediciones Universidad Nacional de Colombia, 1987.

Robles, Martha. *Escritoras en la cultura nacional.* 2 vols. 1985; Mexico: Diana, 1989.

Rodríguez Monegal, Emir. "Clarice Lispector en sus libros y en mi recuerdo." *Revista iberoamericana* 50 (1984): 231–38.

Ruddick, Sara. *Maternal Thinking: Toward a Politics of Peace.* Boston: Beacon Press, 1989.

Ruta, Suzanne. "Nine Months That Shook the World." *New York Times Book Review* Aug. 20, 1989: 1, 30.

Sá, Olga de. "Clarice Lispector: Processos criativos." *Revista iberoamericana* 50 (1984): 259–80.

Saint-Exupéry, Antoine de. *Le petit prince*. New York: Harcourt, Brace, and World, 1943.

Saint-Jacques, Bernard. "Sex, Dependency, and Language." *Linguistique* 9 (1973): 89–96.

Salvaggio, Ruth. "Psychoanalysis and Deconstruction and Woman." In Feldstein and Sussman: 151–60.

Sammons, Jeffrey. "Squaring the Circle: Observations on Core Curriculum and the Plight of the Humanities." *Profession 86:* 14–21.

Sánchez-Mora, Elena. "Reacciones generales y comentarios." In Vidal: 581–86.

Scarry, Elaine. *The Body in Pain: The Making and Unmaking of the World*. Oxford: Oxford University Press, 1985.

Schutte, Ofelia. "Philosophy and Feminism in Latin America: Perspectives on Gender Identity and Culture." *The Philosophical Forum* 20 (1988–89): 62–84.

Schweickart, Patrocinio. "Engendering Critical Discourse." In Koelb and Lokke: 295–317.

Sedgwick, Eve Kosofsky. "The Beast in the Closet: James and the Writing of Homosexual Panic." In Showalter, *Speaking:* 243–68.

Sefchovich, Sara. *Mujeres en espejo*. 2 vols. Mexico: Folios, 1983.

Showalter, Elaine. "A Criticism of Our Own." In Cohen, pp. 347–69.

——. "Feminist Criticism in the Wilderness." *Critical Inquiry* 8 (1981): 179–205.

——, ed. *Speaking of Gender*. New York: Routledge, Chapman, and Hall, 1989.

Sommer, Doris. " 'Not Just a Personal Story': Women's *Testimonios* and the Plural Self. In Brodzki and Schenck: 107–30.

——. *One Master for Another: Populism as Patriarchal Rhetoric in Dominican Novels*. Lanham, Md.: University Press of America, 1983.

Sommers, Joseph. *After the Storm*. Albuquerque: University of New Mexico Press, 1968.

Soyinka, Wole. "This Past Must Address Its Present." *PMLA* 102 (1987) 762–71.

Spivak, Gayatri Chakravorty. "Displacement and the Discourse of Woman." In *Displacement: Derrida and After*. Ed. Mark Krupnick. Bloomington: Indiana University Press, 1983: 169–95.

——. Foreword to Mahasveta Devi, "Drapaudi." *Critical Inquiry* 8 (1981): 381–402.

——. "Imperialism and Sexual Difference." In Koelb and Lokke: 319–37.

——. "Three Women's Texts and a Critique of Imperialism." In Gates, 12.1:243–61.

Steele, Cynthia. "The Other Within: Class and Ethnicity as Difference in Mexican Women's Literature." In Vidal: 297–328.

Sterne, Laurence. *The Life and Opinions of Tristram Shandy, Gentleman*. New York: New American Library, 1960.

Stimpson, Catharine R. "Woolf's Room, Our Project: The Building of Feminist Criticism." In Cohen: 129–43.

Taylor, Mark C. *Altarity*. Chicago: University of Chicago Press, 1987.

Timerman, Jacobo. *Chile: Death in the South*. Trans. Robert Cox. New York: Knopf, 1987.

Traba, Marta. "Hipótesis sobre una escritura diferente." In González and Ortega: 21–26.

Trilling, Lionel. *Sincerity and Authenticity.* Cambridge: Harvard University Press, 1971.

Trinh T. Minh-ha. "Not You/Like You: Post-Colonial Women and the Interlocking Questions of Identity and Difference." *Inscriptions* 3/4 (1988): 71–77.

——. *Woman, Native, Other: Writing, Postcoloniality, and Feminism.* Bloomington: Indiana University Press, 1989.

Umpierre, Luz María. "Un manifiesto literario: *Papeles de Pandora* de Rosario Ferré." *Bilingual Review/Revista Bilingüe* 9 (1982): 120–22.

Updike, John. "Michel Tournier." *New Yorker,* July 10, 1989: 92–6.

Valencia, Tita. *Minotauromaquia: Crónica de un desencuentro.* Mexico: Joaquín Mortiz, 1976.

Valenzuela, Luisa. *Cambio de armas.* Hanover, N.H.: Ediciones del norte, 1982. Translated by Deborah Bonner as *Other Weapons.* Hanover, N.H.: Ediciones del norte, 1985.

——. "La mala palabra." *Revista iberoamericana* 51 (1985): 489–91.

——. "The Other Face of the Phallus." In Chevigny and Laguardia: 242–48.

——. "Pequeño manifiesto." *Hispamérica* 15 (1986): 81–85.

——. "Los porteños y sus literaturas." In *Literature and Popular Culture in the Hispanic World.* Ed. Rose S. Minc. Gaithersburg, Md.: Hispamérica, 1981: 25–29.

——. "The Word, That Milk Cow." In Meyer and Fernández Olmos, *Introductory Essays:* 96–97.

Vega, Ana Lydia. "De bípeda desplumada a escritora puertorriqueña con E y P machúsculas: Testimonios autocensurados." *La torre del viejo* 1.2 (1984): 44–48.

——, ed. *El tramo ancla.* Río Piedras: University of Puerto Rico Press, 1988.

Vidal, Hernán, ed. *Cultural and Historical Grounding for Hispanic and Luso-Brazilian Feminist Literary Criticism.* Minneapolis: Institute for the Study of Ideologies and Literature, 1989.

Viezzer, Moema. *"Si me permiten hablar . . .": Testimonio de Domitila, una mujer de las minas de Bolivia.* 2d ed. Mexico: Siglo XXI, 1978.

Viramontes, Helena Maria. *The Moths and Other Stories.* Houston: Arte Público, 1985.

White, George Abbott, and Charles Newman, eds. *Literature in Revolution.* New York: Holt Rinehart Winston, 1972.

Whorf, Benjamin Lee. *Language, Thought, and Reality: Selected Writings of Benjamin Lee Whorf.* New York: Wiley, 1956.

Woolf, Virginia. *A Room of One's Own.* 1929; New York: Harcourt Brace Jovanovich, 1957.

Yúdice, George. "El asalto a la marginalidad." *Hispamérica* 15.45 (1986): 45–52.

Zapata, Luis. *En jirones.* Mexico: Posada, 1985.

Index

Abraham, Nicolas, 260–62, 286, 288, 292
Academics: and feminism, 22–23, 30–31; and lesbianism, 23
Adorno, Theodor, 190–91
Água viva (Lispector), 101–2, 193–203, 215
Alegría, Claribel: *No me agarran viva: La mujer salvadoreña en la lucha (They'll Never Take Me Alive)*, 28
Allende, Isabel, 23, 31
Angel, Albalucía: *Misía señora (Mrs. ma'am)*, 104, 316–17
Appropriation: as strategy, 43–47, 52; in Valenzuela, 99–100, 111, 129, 137, 132
Arreola, Juan José, xi
Atico, 6–8; definition of, 7–8; relation to Woolf's room, 7, 24–25, 67–70, 304
Austen, Jane, xv–xviii
Authenticity, 230, 293; definition of, 34; in Lispector, 188, 190; and public voice, 38; as strategy, 33–34
Authority: in Castellanos, 8, 9; and discourse, 295; male, 8–10; and women, 296–302
Autobiography, 221, 230; in Castellanos, 223–31, 241–43. See also Testimonials

Balmori, Clemente Hernando, 96–98, 111–12
Balún-Canán (Castellanos), 40, 223–47
Balzac, Honoré de: *The Magic Skin (La peau de chagrin)*, 270, 274–80
Barreno, Maria Isabel, 315; *New Portuguese Letters*, 105
Barrios de Chungara, Domitila, xvii–xviii, 224n, 309; on racism and class, 13–14; *Si me permiten hablar . . . Testimonio de Domitila, una mujer de las minas de Bolivia (Let me speak! Testimony of Domitila, a Woman of the Bolivian Mines)*, 28
Barthes, Roland, 4, 119, 186
Baudrillard, Jean: on makeup, 150–51; on surface, 171; on women, 139
Belli, Gioconda: *La mujer habitada (The inhabited woman)*, 15, 163, 241n; on makeup, 149
Bombal, María Luisa, 50–51; *La amortajada (Shrouded woman)*, 105
Bourgeoisie, and writing, 13–15
Brontë, Charlotte: *Jane Eyre*, xv–xviii, 7, 24, 96. See also Madwoman
Bullrich, Silvina: *Bodas de cristal (Crystal wedding)*, 104–5; *La mujer postergada (Postponed woman)*, 309; on women's work, xiv–xv

Cabrera, Lydia: *El monte*, 294
Cabrera Infante, Guillermo, 295; "Meta-Final," 297–303; *Tres tristes tigres (Three Trapped Tigers)*, 172, 297
Cambio de armas (Other Weapons) (Valenzuela), 103–4
"Cambio de armas" ("Other Weapons") (Valenzuela), 104, 107–32, 260
Campos, Julieta, 304; "La ciudad," 173–74; and feminist theory, 174–75; *Función de la novela*, 173; and guilt, 170–71; *El miedo de perder a Eurídice*, 175; *Muerte por agua*, 170–84; plurality of characters, 153–54n; and surfaces, 169; *Tiene los cabellos rojizos y se llama Sabina*, 152–75

339

Reading
WOMEN
Writing

A SERIES EDITED BY SHARI BENSTOCK
AND CELESTE SCHENCK

Library of Congress Cataloging-in-Publication Data

Castillo, Debra A.
   Talking back : toward a Latin American feminist literary criticism /
Debra A. Castillo.
      p.   cm. — (Reading women writing)
   Includes bibliographical references and index.
   ISBN 0-8014-2608-1 (alk. paper). — ISBN 0-8014-9912-7 (pbk. : alk.
paper)
      1. Feminist literary criticism.   2. Feminist literary criticism—Latin
America.   3. Latin American literature—20th century—History and
criticism.   4. Latin American literature—Women authors—History and
criticism.   I. Series.
PN98.W64C37 1922
860.9'9282—dc20   91-27789